STUDY GUIDE

for

PRINCIPLES OF ACCOUNTING
Third Edition

STUDY GUIDE

for

PRINCIPLES OF ACCOUNTING
Third Edition

A. Douglas Hillman
Drake University

THE DRYDEN PRESS
Chicago New York Philadelphia
San Francisco Montreal Toronto
London Sydney Tokyo Mexico City
Rio de Janeiro Madrid

Production typing by Sandra Lopez

Address orders to:
383 Madison Avenue
New York, New York 10017

Address editorial correspondence to:
One Salt Creek Lane
Hinsdale, Illinois 60521

ISBN 0-03-063321-4
Printed in the United States of America
456-016-987654321

CBS College Publishing
The Dryden Press
Holt, Rinehart and Winston
Saunders College Publishing

Table
of
Contents

■■■

Introduction

■■

This *Study Guide* has been designed especially for use with *Principles of Accounting,* third edition by Reynolds, Sanders, and Hillman. Chapter titles are the same as those in *Principles of Accounting,* third edition, and all references herein are to figures and illustrations in that textbook.

Each chapter in the *Study Guide* has four sections, entitled:

        1. EXPLANATION OF MAJOR CONCEPTS
        2. GUIDED STUDY OF THIS CHAPTER
        3. SELF TEST OF LEARNING GOAL ACHIEVEMENT
        4. ANSWERS TO LEARNING GOAL ACHIEVEMENT TEST

Section 1 contains a short summary (and some simple illustrations) of important concepts covered in the corresponding textbook chapter. Section 2 uses a progressive question and answer format to help the student understand the principles behind some of the accounting methods described in the corresponding textbook chapter. Keyed directly to specific textbook illustrations, the questions in the *Study Guide* constitute a step-by-step explanation of textbook concepts. It is important that the student feel comfortable with each of the beginning-of-chapter learning goals when he or she has completed the study of a chapter. To help in self-evaluation of competence in each of the learning goal concepts, Sections 3 and 4 provide a set of short achievement tests with solutions. If they are taken on a "closed-book" basis, they will confirm the student's competence in learning goal achievement or point to specific topical areas where more study is needed.

Students find a *Study Guide* of this type useful in various ways. Most students report that they get the greatest benefits from the following procedure:

1. Study the entire textbook chapter before attempting to work with the *Study Guide* material.
2. Then read Section 1 of the *Study Guide* chapter, referring to the textbook as necessary.
3. After you have studied the textbook chapter and Section 1 of the *Study Guide,* go to Section 2 of the *Study Guide.* Use it in this manner:
   a. The right-hand side of each page has questions with spaces to write in the answers. The left-hand side of each page has answers to the questions; each answer is positioned one frame lower on the page than the question. Place a sheet of paper over the page so that you can see all of the first question, but cannot see the answer.
   b. Write in the answer to the question. (You may need to refer to the textbook.)

    c. Now move the paper covering the page down one frame and compare the answer with the one you've written. If you are correct, go to the next question. If not, restudy that bit of textbook material to learn why your answer did not agree with the *Study Guide,* then move ahead.

    d. In most cases, you will be able to determine why your answer differs. If you cannot, mark that frame for discussion with your instructor.

4. After you have completed study of the chapter and done the assigned exercises and problems, administer the self test of learning goal achievement. Take the complete test without any reference to the textbook or notes. Then use Section 4 to check your answers.

In addition to the above method of using the *Study Guide,* some students find it helpful to go back for a quick review prior to quizzes and tests. There is no one best method of study that applies to all students. However, the author has noted over several years of experience with a study guide of this type that the most successful students are those who have a definite study plan and follow it strictly. You are urged to adopt and follow carefully a self-study plan in order to obtain the greatest possible level of competence in *Principles of Accounting,* third edition.

A. Douglas Hillman
Drake University
Des Moines, Iowa
December 1983

Chapter 1
The Environment and Basic Structure of Accounting

■■

EXPLANATION OF MAJOR CONCEPTS

What is Accounting?

To understand the function of accounting, the student must look beyond the tasks that accountants perform and see the results of accounting work. Accounting provides reports that describe the financial health of organizations. Financial reports are important because they are the basis for decisions made about organizations by people at all levels. Some decision makers are *inside* the organizations--for example, managers. Other decision makers are *outside* the organizations--for example, investors. Taken together, all the decisions based upon accounting reports have an effect on how the world's economic wealth will be distributed and used.

Thus, accounting can be defined as the procedures by which financial and economic data are collected, processed, and summarized into reports which are useful in making decisions.

Accounting is not a new discipline. It has been used by people engaged in commercial ventures for thousands of years. Because of the increased complexity and number of commercial, government, and not-for-profit organizations, accountants perform a large variety of tasks. However, all accounting jobs require an understanding of certain basic accounting concepts. These basic concepts are explained and illustrated in the textbook. An understanding of the entity concept and the accounting equation are basic to your study of accounting.

The Entity Concept

Each set of accounting records focuses on a specific organization. Transactions are recorded from the viewpoint of that specific unit only. Each unit or organization for which accounting records are maintained is a separate accounting entity. A bank is an accounting entity. A pizza parlor that has borrowed money from that bank is another accounting entity. The loan from the bank to the pizza parlor is recorded in the accounts of both entities, but from differing points of view. To the bank the loan is a *receivable;* to the pizza parlor it is a *payable*. It is even possible that the bank and pizza parlor could be owned by the same persons, but for accounting purposes they are separate entities and have separate sets of accounting records.

1

The Accounting Equation

Every accounting entity has three basic elements: assets, liabilities, and owner's equity. *Assets* are things of value found in the organization--for example, money, supplies, tools, land, buildings, or equipment. Each asset has a monetary valuation (usually its cost), so that assets can be added together and the dollar amount of total assets in an entity determined. Assets have two types of claims against them. They are either *owed* to someone (creditor claims) or they are *owned* by someone (ownership claims). Creditor claims are known as *liabilities*. Ownership claims are known as *owner's equity*.

The fact that all assets are subject to these two types of claims makes the basic accounting equation true: Assets = Liabilities + Owner's Equity. Suppose you buy a new car for $9,500 and make a $1,500 down payment. This leaves you owing $8,000 to the bank or other financing institution. If you are an accounting entity and the car is your only asset, the accounting equation is:

Assets	=	Liabilities	+	Owner's equity
$9,500	=	$8,000	+	$1,500
The car	=	Finance company's claims	+	Your claims

Although the mix of claims against the assets changes, the basic equation continues to hold true. This is not an artificial accounting device but a fact. In every entity, total assets are subject to some mixture of these two types of claims (although either may sometimes be zero). Accordingly, all accounting techniques are built on this basic equation:

$$A = L + OE.$$

The Balance Sheet

Entities have more than one asset and usually have more than one type of creditor claim and ownership claim. The *balance sheet* is a financial statement that shows details of each of the three elements of the accounting equation. It is a snapshot of the financial status of an entity at a moment in time. The balance sheet in Figure 1-2 (repeated in slightly different form in Figure 1-3) is simply a statement of the accounting equation (A = L + OE) in detail for an accounting entity, the Modern Clothing Store.

Classification of Equation Elements

Information of any type is more useful when it is organized into meaningful categories. Because the three basic elements of the accounting equation are each made up of many individual items, it is useful to group the individual items into similar classes. One classification used for both assets and liabilities is *current*. An asset is a *current asset* if it is cash or is expected to be consumed or converted into cash within the year. A liability is a *current liability* if it will be liquidated (or paid off) with current assets. This is usually the same as saying that a liability is current if it must be paid in one year. Note that there is a more specific definition of *current* in Footnote 7, but you may safely use the one-year rule to determine when an asset is current at this time.

Noncurrent assets have several classifications. The most common is *property, plant, and equipment*. A property, plant, and equipment asset is a *long-lived* asset (not to be converted to cash in a year) that is used in operations of the entity. There are also long-lived liabilities called *long-term liabilities*. Some of these are debts that are due to be paid over periods as long as twenty or thirty years.

Owner's equity in a *single proprietorship* (a business owned by one person) has only one classification. In Figures 1-2 and 1-3, the owner's equity is simply called "Lucy Genova, capital." Because of the basic accounting equation, we know that Lucy Genova has claims against \$20,570 of the total assets. If A = L + OE, then A - L = OE. For this reason, another name sometimes given to owner's equity is net assets. The owner's equity is the residual interest in the assets of the business.

Overview of Financial Reports

The interrelationship between three financial statements (balance sheet, income statement, and statement of owner's equity) was illustrated in the chapter. You should understand how these statements are interrelated. Basically, the income statement and statement of owner's equity tie together the balance sheets at the beginning and end of a period. The owner's equity off of the balance sheet at the beginning of the period plus the profit off of the income statement minus the owner's withdrawals gives the owner's equity to be used on the balance sheet at the end of the period. This is diagrammed in Figure 1-5.

Accounting Transactions

We illustrated the basic accounting equation earlier by assuming that you purchased a car. Each economic event that changes elements in the accounting equation is called a *transaction*. Businesses have hundreds of transactions each month that change elements of A = L + OE. To keep up to date with the changes, a business needs an accounting system in which to record each transaction.

The Global Realty Company illustration shows how certain types of transactions change elements of A = L + OE. Note that before *Transaction 1*, the equation had to be:

$$\$0 = \$0 + \$0.$$

Immediately after *Transaction 1*, the equation became:

$$\$50,000 = \$0 + \$50,000.$$

In studying the six transactions and Figure 1-6, you should note that individual elements *increase* or *decrease* with each transaction. However, at the end of each transaction, the basic equation (A = L + OE) *is still valid. It must always be valid or there has been an error in recording.* For example, after the July 11 transaction, the left side totals $58,000 and the right side totals $58,000.

Accumulation of Data

To keep up to date on the status of elements of A = L + OE, an accounting system has an *account* for each subelement of the equation. As the dollar amounts of subelements (cash, accounts receivable, accounts payable, and so on) increase or decrease due to transactions (purchases, sales, payments, collections, and so on), the changes are recorded in the accounts. The balance in the Cash account on a specific date tells us how much cash is held at that date. You should study Figure 1-8 carefully. It is very important at this point that you know how each of the amounts in the figure were derived and why they are placed in the account where they are.

Debits and Credits

Every transaction causes increases or decreases to *two or more* subelements of A = L + OE. The words *debit* and *credit* are used to transfer a record of these increases and decreases from the business documents on which they are originally recorded to the accounting records. *In terms of any account,* a debit goes on the left-hand side, and a credit goes on the right-hand side. Using a T account to illustrate, then:

Any type of Account	
The debit side	The credit side

Remembering that every transaction involves increases and decreases in sub-elements of A = L + OE, we then must have a set of arbitrary rules to know when to debit and when to credit. Actually, you need to memorize only one rule--*an increase in an asset is a debit*. All other rules can be derived from this basic rule and the position of the subelement in the equation.

It is not normal for a subelement of the equation to have a negative balance. You might overdraw your bank account and have a temporary negative balance in cash, but can you imagine having a negative balance in a furniture account? You could have a zero balance (no furniture) but never less than zero. The positive side of an account is its *increase* side. *The increase side of an account is determined by its position in the equation, A = L + OE.* Therefore, the following system falls into place:

ASSETS		=	LIABILITIES	+	OWNER'S EQUITY	
Asset Accounts		=	Liability Accounts	+	Owner's Equity Accounts	
Increase side				Increase side		Increase side

If an account is on the left side of the equation when it has a positive sign (as are Cash, Land, Furniture, and all other asset accounts), its increase side is the left or debit side of the account. If on the other hand, the account is on the right side of the equation when it has a positive sign (as are Accounts Payable, and Lucy Genova, Capital), its increase side is the right or credit side. Decreases would be just the opposite. If an account is increased by a debit, it is logical that it would be decreased with a credit and vice versa. Keep this in mind as you decide whether to debit or credit specific accounts to record increases or decreases in subelements. *Remember debit does not always mean increase.* It is necessary to know what type of account you are dealing with to know whether debit means increase or decrease.

As you analyze transactions, you should train yourself to go through a step-by-step process as follows:

1. Determine which items from the accounting equation or accounts are changed by the transaction.
2. Decide how each account has been changed, an increase or decrease.
3. Decide which category of the accounting equation that each account falls in-- asset, liability, or owner's equity.
4. Translate this information into a debit or credit.

GUIDED STUDY OF THIS CHAPTER

A. *This first group of questions is aimed at helping you understand what accounting is all about. Use the textbook to help find the answers to them.*

1. What is the basic unit of measurement in accounting?

_____

_____

A1.   Money. In the United States and Canada, it is dollars.

2. How could accounting reports be useful to the manager of a bowling alley? _____

_____

_____

_____

A2. Setting prices, keeping costs down, or deciding to use more advertising are only a few of many ways.

A3. All of them.

A4. Yes. They may be considering an investment in or a loan to the company.

A5. Yes. They need to keep costs under control and to show that money they received was used properly.

A6. To decide whether to continue, increase, or stop their contributions.

A7. No answer required.

3. How many of the foregoing reasons involve decision making by the bowling alley manager?

_____

4. Would people who do not work for Exxon Corporation be interested in accounting reports of that company? _____ Explain. _____

_____

_____

5. Do organizations other than businesses operated for a profit need to perform accounting? _____ Explain. _____

_____

_____

_____

6. Why do contributors to charities have a reason to be interested in accounting reports of the groups to which they contribute?

_____

_____

_____

7. Note that in all the foregoing questions some type of decision about economic resources was involved, and in each, accounting information was helpful in making the decision.

8. In your own words, define accounting.

_____

_____

_____

_____

_____

_____

A8. It is the set of rules and methods by which information on economic events is collected and made into reports that are useful in making decisions.

A9. A budget is a financial plan for a future period.

A10. Accounting provides information on cost to acquire a good. Selling prices must be set at least as high as cost.

A11. In business, governmental, and not-for-profit organizations.

A12. Business.

A13. Certificate in Management Accounting, Certified Public Accountant.

A14. CPAs.

A15. Yes. Hundreds of thousands of people work as accountants in all types of organizations.

9. An important part of the planning function of management is budgeting. Define a budget.
_____
_____

10. What is the relation between accounting and the selling prices of goods? _____
_____
_____
_____

11. In what types of organizations do accountants work? _____
_____

12. Which of the three foregoing types of organizations employs the most accountants? _____
_____

13. What is the meaning of CMA? CPA? _____
_____
_____

14. Which of these certificate holders review the work of other accountants? _____

15. Do many people other than these certificate holders work directly in the field of accounting? _____ Explain. _____
_____
_____

B. Accounting Concepts. This next series of questions will help you understand basic accounting terms.

1. In the textbook illustration involving Lucy Genova, is she the accounting entity because she is the owner of several businesses? _____

_____

_____

B1. No, she is not the accounting entity, each unit she owns is an entity.

2. How many entities are shown in the example? _____ Name them. _____

_____

_____

_____

B2. Six. The clothing store, the wholesale company, the trucking company, the repair shop, the realty company, and her personal items.

3. Could the accounting records of Genova's stores and companies be made more efficient by recording all wage costs in a single sum? _____ Explain. _____

_____

_____

_____

B3. No. She needs to be able to make decisions about each entity and needs separate information about them.

4. In your own words, define an accounting entity. _____

_____

_____

B4. An organization for which separate accounting data are gathered and processed.

5. What is the name given to something of value owned by an accounting entity? _____

B5. An asset.

6. Which of the following are assets: cash, snow on the sidewalk in front of a store, a delivery truck, a candy display case, serving trays in a cafeteria? _____

_____

B6. All of them except the snow, which has no value.

7. What are the two types of claims against total assets of a business? _____

_____

B 7. Creditor claims and ownership claims.

8. What is the name for creditor claims?

_____

B 8. Liabilities.

9. What is the name for ownership claims?

_____

B 9. Owner's equity.

10. Write out the basic accounting equation.

_____

B 10. Assets = Liabilities + Owner's Equity.

11. What is the term for an economic event recorded by the accountant? _____
Give two or three examples of such events.

_____

_____

B 11. A transaction. Lending of money by banks, investment in a business, sale of electric power.

12. If assets of Lucy Genova's Good Times Wheels Repair Shop were $10,000 and liabilities were $2,000, what would be the amount of her equity in that store? $_____

B 12. 8,000.

13. Assume the same information as in B 12; what is the amount of net assets of Genova's repair shop? $_____

B 13. 8,000.

14. Is net assets another term for owner's equity?

_____

B 14. Yes.

15. Suppose Genova paid the liabilities. Would this destroy the basic accounting equation?
_____ Explain. _____

_____

_____

B 15. No. She would reduce cash by $2,000 and also reduce liabilities by $2,000.

16. In dollars, what would be the basic accounting equation for Genova's repair shop after she paid the liabilities? _____

B 16. $8,000 = $0 + $8,000.

C. *The following questions are to improve under-standing of the balance sheet and the elements of the balance sheet.*

1. Do Figures 1-2 and 1-3 illustrate two different reports? _____ Explain._____

_____

_____

C1. No. They are alternate forms of the same report, both of which are acceptable for use.

2. Let's concentrate on Figure 1-2. Using total dollar amounts, give the basic accounting equation. _____

C2. $49,660 = $29,090 + $20,570.

3. Does this balance sheet cover a period of time or present a picture as of a certain date? What date? _____

_____

C3. It presents a picture as of December 31, 1985.

4. What is the amount of Modern Clothing Store's assets that are cash or are expected to be converted into cash (or consumed) within a year? $_____

C4. 30,910.

5. Give the name for that class of assets._____

_____

C5. Current assets.

6. Modern Clothing Store does not own a computer. If it were to purchase one, into which balance sheet classification would it fall?

_____

C6. Property, plant, and equipment.

7. Is the $10,000 mortgage payable due before December 31, 1986? _____ How do you know? _____

_____

C7. No. It is not included in current liabilities.

8. What is the total dollar value of debts Modern Clothing Store expects to pay before December 31, 1986? $_____

C8. 15,090.

9. Compute the amount of net assets._____

_____

C9. $49,660 - $29,090 = $20,570.

C10.   Yes.

C11.   Current asset, Prepaid rent.

C12.   It is expected to be consumed in operations during the next year.

C13.   Choose any five from Figure 1-2 or 1-3.

C14.   Cash or any asset that will be consumed or converted into cash within one year.

C15.   18,750.

C16.   Land. Because it is listed first in the property, plant, and equipment section.

C17.   Building.

C18.   Yes.

10.   Suppose next month's rent were paid in advance. Would it be shown on the balance sheet? _____

11.   Under what classification and label would it be shown? _____

12.   Why is prepaid insurance listed as a current asset? _____ _____

13.   List at least five current assets. _____ _____ _____ _____

14.   In your own words, what is a current asset? _____ _____ _____

15.   What is the total dollar value of property, plant, and equipment owned by the Modern Clothing Store? $_____

16.   Which item of property, plant, and equipment do you consider to be the most permanent? _____ Why? _____ _____

17.   Which is the next most permanent item? _____

18.   Do the property, plant, and equipment items appear to be listed on the balance sheet in order of permanence? _____

19.   In contrast, what appears to be the rule for listing current assets? _____ _____

C 19.   They are listed in
order of liquidity.

20.   Record the dollar amount of creditors' equity
that must be satisfied from current assets.

$_____

C 20.   15,090.

21.   Are accounts receivable owed to the Modern
Clothing Store or owed by the Modern Clothing
Store? _____

C 21.   Owed to the store
by customers.

22.   Are accounts payable also owed to the store
by customers? _____ Explain. _____

_____

C 22.   No. They are owed
by the store to
suppliers.

23.   Are notes payable (or receivable) also
normally due in thirty days? _____
Explain. _____

_____

C 23.   No. Each has a
special period of
time payment.

24.   What are some differences between notes and
open accounts? _____

_____

_____

_____

C 24.   Notes are formal
written promises by
the entity. Also,
notes very often
require the payment
of interest. Accounts
do not require the
payment of interest.

25.   What is the meaning of the word *accrue?*

_____

_____

C 25.   To increase or grow
in a uniform manner.

26.   Modern Clothing Store has a caption, "Accrued
wages payable." How does this differ (as a
caption) from "Wages payable"? _____

_____

_____

_____

C 26.   Accrued wages
payable describes
wages that have
accumulated, but
are not yet due.
Wages payable are
due to be paid.

27.   How many forms of long-term debt are found
on the balance sheet of Modern Clothing
Store? _____ Name them. _____

_____

C27. Two. Bank loan payable and mortgage payable.

28. Another long-term liability is bonds payable. No such caption is found on the balance sheet because Modern Clothing Store is a single proprietorship. Single proprietorships do not issue bonds.

C28. No answer required.

29. What is a single proprietorship? _____

_____

C29. A business owned by one person.

30. Who owns the Modern Clothing Store? _____

_____

C30. Lucy Genova.

31. Without looking back in your textbook, write out the basic accounting equation. _____

_____

C31. Assets = Liabilities + Owner's Equity.

32. Using Figure 1-5, what time period is covered by the statements shown? _____

_____

C32. Typically a month, quarter, or year.

33. The owner's equity from the balance sheet at the beginning of the period is used on what statement? _____

C33. Owner's equity statement.

34. The income statement calculates what number?

_____

C34. Profit.

35. Profit is used again on what statement? _____

_____

C35. Owner's equity statement.

36. The statement of owner's equity is used to calculate what figure? _____

C36. Ending owner's equity.

37. Ending owner's equity is carried to what statement? _____

_____

C37. Balance sheet at end of each period.

38. Therefore, the income statement and owner's equity statement are used to explain the change in owner's equity.

C38. No answer required.

D. *Let's begin study of the recording of changes in elements by following the Global Realty Company illustration.*

1. In the July 1 transaction, items from two elements of the accounting equation changed. Cash increased from zero to $50,000. Also, owner's equity increased from zero to $50,000.

D1.   No answer required.

2. In the July 5 transaction, what items from elements of the accounting equation changed?

_____

D2.   Cash, land, and building.

3. Which items increased and by how much?

_____

D3.   Land by $5,000 and building by $25,000.

4. Classify the items that increased as assets, liabilities, or owner's equity._____

_____

D4.   Both are assets.

5. What item(s) decreased and by how much?

_____

D5.   Cash, by $30,000.

6. Classify the item that decreased as to asset, liability, or owner's equity. _____

_____

D6.   Cash is an asset.

7. If you were applying the rules of debit and credit at this point, would the increases be debits? _____

Would they be credits? _____

D7.   Yes, increases in assets are debits. No, they would not be credits.

8. Would the decrease in cash be a debit or a credit? _____

D8.   A credit (because cash is also an asset).

9. In this exchange of cash for land and a building, do the total debits equal total credits? _____

D9.   Yes.

10. Therefore, we have a complete transaction with total debits equal to $_____ and total credits equal to $_____.

D10. 30,000, 30,000

11. Look at the July 11 transaction and analyze what has actually happened. The asset entitled _____ has increased by $_____. The liability entitled _____ has increased by $_____.

D11. Furniture, 8,000; Accounts Payable, 8,000.

12. Is the $8,000 increase in an asset a debit or a credit? _____

D12. A debit.

13. Is the $8,000 increase in the liability a debit or is it a credit? _____

D13. A credit.

14. If total debits equal total credits, we have completed the analysis of this transaction. Is this the case here? _____

D14. Yes.

15. A pattern is beginning to unfold. Increases in assets are always debits, so decreases in assets must be _____.

D15. credits

16. Increases in liabilities are _____, and decreases in liabilities are _____.

D16. credits, debits

17. To be sure that you can analyze a transaction, move to the July 20 transaction. First, what elements changed and what are their classifications? _____

_____

D17. Cash, an asset, decreased and accounts payable, a liability, decreased.

18. Translate these changes into debits and credits. _____

_____

E. *Accounts.*

D18. A decrease in cash is a credit. A decrease in accounts payable is a debit.

1. Looking again at the accounting equation, A = L + OE, we expect normal account balances to be as follows:

If account is   *Balance should be*

a. An asset   _____
b. A liability   _____
c. Owner's equity   _____

E1.   (a) A debit; (b) A credit; (c) A credit. Note in each case that the normal balance is on the same side as an increase.

2.   Find Global's footed Cash account in the general ledger in Figure 1-8. The total of debit entries is $_____.

E2.   51,000

3.   The total of credit entries is $_____.

E3.   35,000

4.   Global had Cash account increases of $51,000 and decreases of $35,000. Since the company started with no cash on July 1, 1985, the amount of cash on hand now is $_____.

E4.   16,000

5.   The amount of cash now on hand, $16,000, is called the account _____.

E5.   balance

6.   Each account in Global's general ledger has a balance. Some are debits and some are credits. Do you expect the total of all debit balances to equal the total of all credit balances? _____

E6.   Yes.

7.   Why? _____

_____

_____

_____

E7.   Total debits and credits in each journal entry posted to the ledger were equal. This overall equality must be true in the ledger.

8.   In Global's trial balance (Figure 1-9), how many accounts have debit balances? _____ Credit balances? _____ The total of each column is $_____.

E8.   Five, Two, 53,000

9.   Since Global's total debit and credit balances both equal $53,000, does this prove that journalizing and posting have been done correctly? _____ Explain. _____

_____

_____

_____

_____

E9. No. However, it offers evidence strong enough that we will assume there is no error. (We may find an error later, however.)

E10. Yes.

E11.

GLOBAL REALTY COMPANY
Trial Balance
July 31, 1985

10. Does a trial balance have dollar signs?_____

11. Without looking at your textbook, try to write the heading for Global's trial balance.

_____

_____

_____

Note: You have completed a chapter of guided study in this *Study Guide*. Are you using it exactly as suggested in the introduction by forcing yourself to make a commitment *in writing* before checking the answer? If not, you are depriving yourself of full benefit of the guided study of the textbook.

SELF TEST OF LEARNING GOAL ACHIEVEMENT

1. Indicate whether each of the following statements is true or false:

____ a. Accounting has many purposes, but the primary purpose is to provide information that is useful to people in decision making.

____ b. The only people who would give careful study to financial reports of General Motors Corporation are its board of directors, officers, managers, and employees.

____ c. Even though you are not responsible for operations of the American Cancer Society, you could use its accounting reports to form an opinion of how much of its contribution receipts actually get through to persons intended to receive help under its charitable relief programs.

____ d. Federal and state governments have a legitimate reason to be interested in financial reports of businesses.

____ e. Accounting began in the United States when the first income tax laws were passed requiring individuals and corporations to report their incomes and pay income tax.

____ f. There is a natural relationship between the study of accounting and the study of management because all managers use accounting information in some way.

____ g. Only a certified public accountant is allowed to head the accounting department of a large company.

____ h.   A person who holds either a CMA or a CPA certificate is licensed by the state to attest to the fairness of presentation of information in a company's financial statements.

____ i.   Many accountants work for federal, state, or local governments.

____ j.   As a student, it is unlikely that you are using actual accounting information today.

2.   Of the following listed organizations, circle those that are accounting entities:

   a.   A grocery store owned by Mollie Newton.
   b.   A dry cleaning shop owned by Mollie Newton.
   c.   Feinberg's, a large department store.
   d.   The Applicances Department of Feinberg's.
   e.   The Newton Reporter, a business forecasting service owned and operated by Mollie Newton.
   f.   The Loan Department of the First National Bank.

3.   Write out in words the basic accounting equation. _____

   _____

4.   Opposite each item listed below show by coding it with a numeral whether it is:

   1.   A current asset.
   2.   A property, plant, and equipment asset.
   3.   A current liability.
   4.   A long-term liability.
   5.   An owner's (or owners') equity item.

   ___ a.   Eric Amash, capital.   ___ h.   Mortgage payable (due in 20 years).
   ___ b.   Accounts payable.   ___ i.   Notes payable (due in 60 days).
   ___ c.   Cash.   ___ j.   Office supplies.
   ___ d.   Accounts receivable.   ___ k.   Accrued wages payable.
   ___ e.   Notes payable (due in 1992).   ___ l.   Prepaid insurance.
   ___ f.   Buildings.
   ___ g.   Temporary investments.

5. Fill in the blanks opposite each account title below.

Account Title	Would a decrease be recorded as a debit or a credit?	Is its normal balance a debit or a credit?
Accounts Payable		
Accounts Receivable		
Buildings		
Furniture		
George Amati, Capital		
Land		
Mortgage Payable		
Notes Payable		
Notes Receivable		
Repair Supplies		
Temporary Investments		

6. Following in alphabetical order are the account balances from the Valley Roller Rink on March 31, 1985:

Account Title	Balance
Accounts Receivable	$20
Accounts Payable	5
Buildings	40
Cash	10
Clara Franzini, Capital	30
Land	10
Long-Term Bank Loan Payable	20
Mortgage Payable	30
Notes Payable	10
Temporary Investments	15

The notes payable are all due in 1986; the mortgage and long-term bank loan are both due in 1990.

Required: Prepare a trial balance.

ANSWERS TO LEARNING GOAL ACHIEVEMENT TEST

1. a. T   f. T
    b. F   g. F
    c. T   h. F
    d. T   i. T
    e. F   J. F

2. a, b, c, and e.

3. Assets = Liabilities + Owner's Equity.

4. a. 5   g. 1
    b. 3   h. 4
    c. 1   i. 3
    d. 1   j. 1
    e. 4   k. 3
    f. 2   l. 1

5.

Account Title	Would a decrease be recorded as a debit or a credit?	Is its normal balance a debit or a credit?
Accounts Payable	Debit	Credit
Accounts Receivable	Credit	Debit
Buildings	Credit	Debit
Furniture	Credit	Debit
George Amati, Capital	Debit	Credit
Land	Credit	Debit
Mortgage Payable	Debit	Credit
Notes Payable	Debit	Credit
Notes Receivable	Credit	Debit
Repair Supplies	Credit	Debit
Temporary Investments	Credit	Debit

6.

VALLEY ROLLER RINK
Trial Balance
March 31, 1985

Account Title	Debits	Credits
Cash	$10	
Temporary Investments	15	
Accounts Receivable	20	
Buildings	40	
Land	10	
Accounts Payable		$ 5
Notes Payable		10
Mortgage Payable		30
Long-Term Bank Loan Payable		20
Clara Franzini, Capital		30
Totals	$95	$95

Chapter 2
Income Statement Accounts:
Fundamentals and Journalizing

■■■

EXPLANATION OF MAJOR CONCEPTS

Overview of the Accounting System

Thus far a simple accounting system has been developed. This begins with the existence of objective evidence of a transaction, usually in the form of a business document. From the document, a record of the effect of the transaction is first made in the journal or book of original entry. Next, the data in the journal is transferred or posted to the ledger. Periodically a test of the accounting system is made with a trial balance, which checks on the equality of debits and credits in the ledger. After this has been completed, the financial statements are prepared.

Recording

Time spent now learning the exact details of how to make journal entries and postings to the ledger accounts will save you hours of searching for errors in your homework in the next few chapters. The July 1 transaction is illustrated in Chapter 2 in Figure 2-2. The numbered explanations that accompany that journal entry tell you exactly how to record any journal entry. Figure 2-3 explains exactly how to post that journal entry. After studying those two illustrations, it is a good idea to go immediately to the total illustration of the Global Realty Company's transactions and observe how the rules are applied.

The relationship of a journal to a *ledger* (the entire group of accounts) is shown in the following diagram:

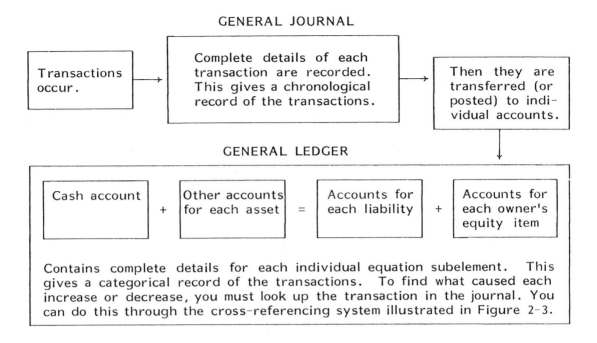

GENERAL JOURNAL

| Transactions occur. | → | Complete details of each transaction are recorded. This gives a chronological record of the transactions. | → | Then they are transferred (or posted) to individual accounts. |

GENERAL LEDGER

| Cash account | + | Other accounts for each asset | = | Accounts for each liability | + | Accounts for each owner's equity item |

Contains complete details for each individual equation subelement. This gives a categorical record of the transactions. To find what caused each increase or decrease, you must look up the transaction in the journal. You can do this through the cross-referencing system illustrated in Figure 2-3.

Changes in Owner's Equity

Owner's equity is the dollar amount of ownership rights in or claims against total assets. In Chapter 1, Lucy Genova obtained owner's equity in the Global Realty Company by investing her personal cash in the business. Each time an owner invests cash (or other assets) in a business, the amount of owner's equity will increase.

Chapter 2 begins the explanation of accounting for another way to increase owner's equity. This second means--*making a profit from business operations*-- is the thing that keeps businesses in operation. Not all business transactions have a direct effect on making a profit, but most of them do. If an accountant were to record transactions which affect profit directly in the owner's equity account, it would make the computation of profit difficult if not impossible. It is possible, however, to accumulate changes in owner's equity related to profits in separate revenue and expense accounts and to use these accumulations at the end of an accounting period to determine the change in owner's equity resulting from operations. If total revenues are greater than total expenses, the business has operated at a profit for the period and owner's equity has increased. On the other hand, if expenses are greater than revenues, the business has operated at a loss and owner's equity has decreased.

The name given to the increase in owner's equity caused by profitable operations is *net income*. It follows that

Total Revenues - Total Expenses = Net Income.

Just as the *balance sheet* shows the status of the basic accounting equation (A = L + OE) in detail, the *income statement* shows details of revenues and expenses. The concepts of revenue and expense are presented in Chapter 2. The income statement is explained and illustrated in Chapter 3.

Revenue and Expense Accounts

To accumulate information about changes in owner's equity, we use three types of accounts that have not been introduced to you before. Two of these are *revenue accounts* and *expense accounts*. There are many types of revenues and expenses; each is accumulated in an account bearing a title that describes that particular revenue or expense.

Revenues are earned by a company when it performs a service or delivers a product. The amount of the revenue earned is equal to the value of the asset received in exchange for the goods or services (typically cash or accounts receivable). Expenses are incurred when the economic benefits embodied in an asset are consumed by the company. The amount of the expense is measured by the cost of the asset which was used up or which the company promised to give up in the future (accounts payable). You must bear in mind as you study this chapter that:

▶ Revenues cause an asset to *increase* and therefore cause owner's equity to *increase,* and

▶ Expenses cause an asset to *decrease* and therefore cause owner's equity to *decrease*.

Because of the two foregoing statements, we would conclude that:

▶ Revenues, being increases in owner's equity, have the *same* rules for debit and credit as an owner's equity account. You should credit to show an increase in a revenue account and debit to show a decrease.

▶ Expenses, being decreases in owner's equity, have debit and credit rules that are the *opposite* of rules for owner's equity. You should debit to show an increase in an expense and credit to show a decrease.

Withdrawals

The third type of account introduced in Chapter 2 is the owner's drawing account. Just as an investment of assets increases owner's equity, a reduction of investment by withdrawing assets from the business causes a decrease in owner's equity. When an owner makes periodic withdrawals (usually of cash) to meet living expenses, we could *debit* that owner's capital account to show the reduction. In practice, however, we need to keep a separate record of periodic withdrawals. To do this, a new account with the title *Drawing* is used. It is *debited* as the withdrawals are made because increases in the drawing are working to decrease the owner's equity. (If a major reduction in an owner's investment is made by withdrawing assets, the capital account would be debited.)

The Chart of Accounts

Each business is somewhat different. Most businesses have some similar accounts, such as Cash, Accounts Receivable, Accounts Payable, and so on, but there are usually some accounts that are suitable only for a specific entity. For example, can you imagine a law firm needing an asset account with the title Repair Supplies? Or would a repair shop need a revenue account with the title Legal Fees Earned? Because these differences exist, each entity must prepare its own chart of accounts. A chart of accounts is a listing of the accounts to be used by that particular business. The list is in account number order and shows the account number and the title of the account. Figure 2-12 shows the chart of accounts for the Good Times Wheels Repair Shop. These are the only account titles that are contained in the company's general ledger. In recording transactions in the general ledger, *every debit and credit entry must be made to one of the accounts in the chart of accounts.* This point is crucial. One of the most common errors made by students at this point is to record debits and credits in the journal to words such as "Paid Cash," "Purchase of Supplies," "Payment of Electric Bill," and so on. These are *not* account titles; they are part of the journal entry explanation.

Some exercises and problems in Chapter 2 and later chapters provide a chart of accounts. If they do, these are the *only* account titles that you are allowed to use. Some exercises and problems do not provide a chart of accounts; in these cases, you must prepare one. Usually you can do this as you work the problem, but be careful not to use two different accounts for the same thing.

The Accounting Equation Expanded

In Chapter 2, the accounting equation has been expanded to include three new account types. The equation now is:

Assets = Liabilities + Owner's Equity + Revenues - Expenses - Drawing.

Owner's Equity as it appears in the equation includes the beginning amount plus any investments made by the owner during the period. The changes in owner's equity during the period resulting from operating events and owner's withdrawals have been recorded in their respective categories.

This expanded equation can be restated as:

Assets + Expenses + Drawing = Liabilities + Owner's Equity + Revenues,

or in symbols:

$$A + Exp + Dwg = L + OE + Rev.$$

You can use this expanded equation to derive the rules for debit and credit. As noted in Chapter 1 of the *Study Guide,* accounts in classifications which are on the left side of the equation when positive have normal left-hand (or *debit*) balances. Accounts which are on the right side of the equation when positive have a normal right-hand (or *credit*) balance. Remember, that it is not normal for any account to have a negative balance. Therefore, you should follow this pattern on how to increase an account:

Debit to increase:	*Credit to increase:*
▸ Assets	▸ Liabilities
▸ Expenses	▸ Owner's Equity
▸ Drawing	▸ Revenues

Decreases in accounts would be just the opposite.

Subsidiary Ledgers

Many companies find that, as the number of customers increases, the general ledger would become unwieldy as they opened an accounts receivable account for each customer. This problem can be avoided by removing the individual customer accounts receivable from the general ledger and placing them in what is called a *subsidiary ledger*. In order to keep the general ledger in balance, these individual accounts are replaced in the general ledger by a controlling account entitled *Accounts Receivable*. When the journal entry for a sale on account is posted, the debit to accounts receivable would be posted at least twice, once to the controlling account in the general ledger and once to each specific customer's account in the Accounts Receivable Subsidiary Ledger. Thus, the general ledger is kept in balance by the debit to accounts receivable and credit to revenue, and the detail necessary to send out monthly statements and manage receivables is kept in the subsidiary ledger.

At the end of any accounting period the accuracy of the general ledger is substantiated by using the *trial balance*. The accuracy of the subsidiary ledger is supported by making a listing of the individual subsidiary account balances. Since we have posted only one-half of each transaction to the subsidiary ledger and the accounts usually all have debit balances, we don't have the self-balancing feature (debits equal credits). But the total of the accounts in the subsidiary ledger must be equal to the balance in the controlling account in the general ledger.

Subsidiary ledgers can be created for any general ledger account for which management desires the additional detail. We normally find them for Accounts Receivable and Accounts Payable. But, equipment would also be a possibility.

Let's now move to some specific study of concepts in Chapter 2.

GUIDED STUDY OF THIS CHAPTER

A. *Journalizing and posting. Refer to Figures 2-2 and 2-3.*

1. In recording a transaction in journal form, what is the first step? _____

_____

A1. The first step is to enter the year on the first line of the date column. Note that it is not repeated for each transaction.

A2. Enter the month of the first transaction.

A3. The date of the transaction is entered.

A4. Write the debit account title at the left margin of the explanation column.

A5. All of the debit accounts are listed at this point in the journal entry.

A6. The debit dollar amounts are entered into the debit amount column. No dollar signs are used.

A7. The credit account titles are listed with an indentation from the left margin.

A8. The credit dollar amounts are entered into the credit amount column.

2. What is the second step in journalizing? _____
    _____
    _____

3. What is the third step? _____
    _____

4. What is the fourth step in journalizing trans-
    actions? _____
    _____

5. If more than one account is to be debited, how many are listed at this point? _____
    _____

6. What is the next step to journalize? _____
    _____
    _____

7. What is the sixth step? _____
    _____
    _____

8. What is the seventh step? _____
    _____
    _____

9. What is the last step? _____
    _____
    _____
    _____
    _____

A9.   An explanation of the
transaction is written
in below the credit
account titles. A
phrase which gives
the essence of the
transaction is all
that is necessary.

10.   The journal entry shows a $50,000 debit to
Cash. Does this mean that Cash increased
or that it decreased? _____

A10.   Cash increased.

11.   It also shows a $50,000 credit to Lucy Genova,
Capital. Into what classification does this
account fall? _____

A11.   Owner's equity.

12.   Is the $50,000 credit an increase or a decrease
to this owner's equity account? _____

A12.   Increase.

13.   What is the name of the process by which
items entered in the journal are transferred
to a ledger account? _____

A13.   Posting.

14.   Global Realty Company's general ledger is
made up of a set of accounts. What account
number is given to Cash? _____ To Lucy
Genova, Capital? _____

A14.   101; 301.

15.   What is the first step in posting this transaction? _____
_____
_____
_____
_____

A15.   The date, journal
page number, and
amount of the debit
are entered in
appropriate columns
on the debit (left-
hand) side of the
Cash account.

16.   What is the second step in posting this transaction? _____
_____
_____
_____
_____

A16.   The number 101 (for
the Cash account) is
immediately entered
in the folio column of
the *journal* opposite
the Cash account.

17.   This is one of the most important steps of the
process. Why? _____
_____
_____
_____

A 17. Its presence in the journal means that this item has been posted. To enter it *now (not earlier or later)* helps prevent double posting or failure to post an item.

18. What is the third posting step?_____

_____

_____

_____

_____

A 18. The date, journal page number, and amount of the credit are entered on the credit (right-hand) side of the account, Lucy Genova, Capital.

19. The fourth step follows immediately. What is it?_____

_____

_____

A 19. The number 301 (for Lucy Genova, Capital) is entered in the folio column of the journal.

20. If you look in the ledger at the Cash account only, can you identify the source of the $50,000 increase? _____ What can you know about it?_____

_____

_____

A20. No. That it occurred on July 1, 1985, and was posted from page 1 of the journal.

21. If you look at the Lucy Genova, Capital account only, can you determine what caused the $50,000 increase? _____ What can you know about it?_____

_____

_____

A21. No. That it occurred on July 1, 1985, and was posted from page 1 of the journal.

22. However, if you look at the entry on journal page 1, what additional facts can you discover?

_____

_____

_____

A22. That Lucy Genova invested $50,000 to start a business to be called Global Realty Co.

23. The major function of the journal, then, is to capture the total data of each transaction in enough detail to describe each economic event. The major function of the ledger accounts is to bring together in one place all the changes that affect each subelement of the accounting equation.

A23.　No answer required.

A24.　No. (Every posting in a ledger must come from a journal.)

A25.　No. We usually wait and post several journal entries at one time.

A26.　compound

A27.　Yes.

A28.　Nothing except that more than two accounts must receive postings.

B1.　increase

B2.　credited

24.　Is it acceptable to record some items directly into the ledger accounts without journalizing them first? _____

25.　Should we post to the ledger immediately after making each journal entry? _____ Explain.

_____

_____

26.　A journal entry with more than one debit or with more than one credit is called a _____ entry.

27.　In a compound journal entry, do total debits equal total credits? _____

28.　What is different about posting a compound entry? _____

_____

B.　*Revenue and Expense Accounts. Let's begin with a study of the nature and use of revenue and expense accounts.*

1.　A revenue describes the source of an inflow of assets (or reduction of liabilities). It is the result of providing goods or services to someone outside the business. Revenues tend to _____ (increase/decrease) owner's equity.

2.　Therefore, each time a transaction generates revenue, a revenue account should be _____ (debited/credited).

3.　From the following transactions, choose those that are revenue transactions (show only the letter representing them).
a.　Borrowed $1,000 from the bank. ____
b.　Billed customers for services rendered to them. ____
c.　Sold an item of merchandise for cash. ____
d.　Sold an item of merchandise but did not collect the cash for it at the time of sale. ____
e.　Received the cash from customers for services billed in b. ____
f.　An owner invested additional funds in her business. ____

B3.   b, c, d.

4. From the foregoing, we see that borrowing is *not* revenue. Why?_____

_____

_____

B4. Although borrowing is an inflow of assets, it increases liabilities instead of owner's equity.

5. Why is revenue generated when customers are billed for services rendered but no cash has been received?_____

_____

_____

B5. There is an inflow of assets (accounts receivable) and an increase in owner's equity.

6. When these bills are collected later, we do not have a revenue transaction. Explain._____

_____

_____

_____

B6. There is an inflow of assets (cash), but it is in exchange for another asset (accounts receivable). There is no change in owner's equity.

7. An owner's investments represent an inflow of assets and an increase in owner's equity. Therefore, is investment by an owner a revenue? _____

B7. No.

8. Why not? _____

_____

_____

B8. It is not the result of providing goods or services to someone outside the business.

9. Indicate by letter which of the following are revenue account titles.
   a.   Rent Earned.____
   b.   Interest Earned.____
   c.   Accounts Receivable.____
   d.   Sales.____
   e.   Cash.____
   f.   Service Fees.____

B9.   a, b, d, f.

10.   In your own words, describe an expense.

_____

_____

_____

_____

_____

_____

B10.   It is an outflow of assets (or increase in liabilities) from business transactions that decrease owner's equity. It results when a business consumes the economic benefits of an asset in the process of generating revenues.

11.   Would the expired costs of consumption of office supplies be an expense? _____

B11.   Yes.

12.   Wages and salaries of employees are expenses. What expired cost is being consumed by the business?_____

_____

B12.   The employee's services are consumed or used-up and cash is given up.

13.   Is the payment of an account payable an expense? _____ Explain._____

_____

B13.   No. It is simply an exchange of an asset for a liability.

14.   For each of the following transactions, suggest an appropriate expense account title:
a.   A one-year insurance policy runs out (expires) which had previously been paid for. _____

b.   Postage is paid to mail a package of merchandise to a customer. _____

c.   Interest is paid on money borrowed from the bank._____

d.   A bill is received from a carpenter for repairing an office desk._____

_____

B 14. a. Insurance Expense.
     b. Postage Expense
       or Delivery
       Expense.
     c. Interest Expense.
     d. Repairs Expense.

15. In each foregoing case, would the expense account be debited or credited? _____
Why? _____
_____

B 15. Debited. Each is an increase in expense.

16. To complete the recording of each of these four transactions, show the title of the account to be credited.
   a. _____
   b. _____
   c. _____
   d. _____

B 16. a. Prepaid Insurance.
     b. Cash.
     c. Cash.
     d. Accounts Payable.

17. Let's review the rules for debit and credit and expand them to revenue and expense accounts. Complete the following table:

Type of Account	Increase	Decrease
Asset	Debit	
Liability		
Owner's equity		
Revenue		
Expense		

B 17.
Debit	Credit
Credit	Debit
Credit	Debit
Credit	Debit
Debit	Credit

18. Another action that changes owner's equity is withdrawal of assets by an owner. In the textbook example, when Lucy Genova withdrew $500 on September 2, the account debited was _____.

B 18. Lucy Genova, Drawing

19. The withdrawal decreased an asset, Cash. What was the effect of the change on the drawing account (increase/decrease)?
_____

B 19. Increase.

20. Therefore, to record an increase in drawing, we _____ (debit/credit) the drawing account.

B20.   debit

21.   Why was the drawing account increased with a debit? _____

_____

_____

_____

_____

_____

21.   A withdrawal of assets by the owner has the ultimate effect of decreasing owner's equity which is accomplished by debits. Thus, the more withdrawals the owner makes, the less owner's equity they have, and debits decrease owner's equity.

C.   General ledger and Subsidiary Ledgers

1.   What is the name given to the collection of accounts that produce information for the balance sheet or the income statement?

_____

C1.   General ledger.

2.   By what process does an amount get recorded in the general ledger? _____

_____

C2.   It must be posted or transferred from a journal.

3.   When a general ledger account represents the total of many different individual items, we keep a record of each of these individual items in a *subsidiary ledger*. Give an example of a subsidiary ledger._____

_____

C3.   The accounts receivable ledger or accounts payable ledger.

4.   If we establish an accounts receivable ledger (a subsidiary ledger), it would contain a separate account for each _____.

C4.   customer

5.   In the general ledger, Accounts Receivable would be known as a _____ account.

C5.   controlling

6.   Refer to Figure 2-11 in the textbook. In the general journal, what account was debited with $900 on August 3, 1985?_____

_____

C6.   Accounts Receivable.

7.   How many customer bills are represented by this $900 debit?_____

C7.   Three.

8.   In the general ledger, is Accounts Receivable posted with three amounts or with only one amount? _____

C8.   Only one ($900).

9.   How do you know by looking only at the journal that this $900 amount has been posted to Accounts Receivable in the general ledger?

_____

_____

C9.   The presence of the account number in the folio column.

10.   *Special note to the student:* Never enter account numbers in the folio column of the journal until you have actually posted the item. Failure to follow this rule will cost hours in wasted time searching for duplicate postings or items not posted.

C10.   No answer required.

11.   In the general ledger, can you determine how much of the $900 debit balance of Accounts Receivable is due from Jay Jones? _____

C11.   No.

12.   To find out how much Jones owes Ace Small Business Services, we must go to his account in the _____ ledger.

C12.   accounts receivable subsidiary

13.   In the accounts receivable subsidiary ledger, we find that Jay Jones's balance is $_____.

C13.   550

14.   The receivable side of this transaction was posted twice--once to Accounts Receivable in the _____ ledger and once to Jay Jones' account in the _____

_____ ledger.

C14.   general, accounts receivable subsidiary

15.   How do we indicate in the journal that $550 has been posted to Jay Jones' account?

_____

_____

C15.   Place a check (√) by his name in the explanation.

16.   Is Jay Jones' $550 balance in the subsidiary ledger a debit or a credit? _____

C16. Debit.

17. Why is it a debit?_____

_____

C17. It is a normal balance of an asset.

18. What is the total of all the debit balances in the accounts receivable ledger? $_____

C18. 900.

19. Is this the same amount as the single debit in Accounts Receivable in the general ledger?

_____

C19. Yes.

20. If it were not the same amount, what would we assume?_____

C20. That an error exists.

21. If instead of Accounts Receivable Figure 2-11 had been illustrating an Accounts Payable Subsidiary Ledger, what general ledger account would be the controlling account?

_____

C21. Accounts Payable.

22. Would the balance of Accounts Payable normally be a debit or a credit? _____

C22. Credit.

23. What would be the normal balance of each account in the accounts payable ledger (debit or credit)? _____

C23. Credit.

24. Would the sum of the individual accounts payable ledger account balances be expected to equal the balance in the controlling account, Accounts Payable?_____

_____

C24. Yes, provided all posting is up to date.

D. *Let's begin the study of the Good Times Wheels Repair Shop illustration.*

1. What is the name given to the listing of all the accounts used in the shop's general ledger?_____

D1. Chart of accounts.

2. Are each of the customer accounts listed separately in the chart of accounts?_____

Explain._____

_____

_____

_____

D2. No. The specific subsidiary ledger accounts are not included. Only the controlling account is included in the general ledger.

D3. No. The account numbering system should be one that is appropriate for the individual business.

D4. Any unused number between 121 and 149.

D5. a. Neither.
b. Expense.
c. Expense.
d. Neither.
e. Neither.
f. Revenue.

D6. No answer required.

D7. The items have not yet been posted to the ledger.

3. Is it required that a three-digit system of account numbers be used?_____ Explain.

_____
_____
_____

4. If the shop needed to use an Office Supplies asset account, what number would you assign to it?_____

5. Using the Good Times Wheels Repair Shop journal (Figure 2-13), classify each of the following selected transactions as (1) a revenue transaction, (2) an expense transaction, or (3) neither:
a. The transaction of January 3. _____
b. The transaction of January 4. _____
c. The *first* transaction of January 5.
_____
d. The *second* transaction of January 5.
_____
e. The transaction of January 10. _____
f. The transaction of January 12. _____

6. If you had difficulty with question 5, review carefully the analysis of transactions that precedes the journal illustration in the text-book. Ask your instructor to explain any that you do not understand clearly.

7. Why aren't the account numbers shown in the folio column of the journal?_____

_____

SELF TEST OF LEARNING GOAL ACHIEVEMENT

1. Record the following transactions in the general journal provided, and post them to the general ledger accounts:

1985
Aug.   8   Purchased dental supplies to be used during the next four months for $800, paying for them with check number 362.

       11   Sold one-half of the dental supplies for $400 cash to another dentist in the same building who had a temporary shortage of supplies.

GENERAL JOURNAL   Page 27

Date	Account Titles and Explanation	F	Debit	Credit

GENERAL LEDGER

Cash   Acct. No. 101

Date	Explanation	F	Debit	Date	Explanation	F	Credit

Dental Supplies   Acct. No. 123

Date	Explanation	F	Debit	Date	Explanation	F	Credit

2. Post the following journal entries into the three-amount-column form of accounts provided. Show all cross-references.

GENERAL JOURNAL   Page 10

Date		Account Titles and Explanation	F	Debit	Credit
1985					
Mar.	1	Cash		800	
		Fees Earned			800
		Collection of March fees.			
	3	Repair Supplies		350	
		Cash			350
		Purchase of supplies.			

GENERAL LEDGER

Cash   Acct. No. 101

Date		Explanation	F	Debit	Credit	Balance

Repair Supplies   Acct. No. 133

Date		Explanation	F	Debit	Credit	Balance

Fees Earned   Acct. No. 703

Date		Explanation	F	Debit	Credit	Balance

3. Choose the word *increase* or *decrease* to fill in each blank space that follows:

   a. If expenses of an accounting period are greater than revenues, the owner's equity will _____.
   b. If revenues are greater than expenses, the owner's equity will _____.
   c. A debit to an expense account is recording a(n) _____.
   d. A debit to the drawing account is recording a(n) _____.
   e. A credit to a revenue account is recording a(n) _____.
   f. A credit to an expense account is recording a(n) _____.
   g. A debit to a revenue account is recording a(n) _____.
   h. Revenues _____ owner's equity.
   i. Expenses _____ owner's equity.
   j. Drawings _____ owner's equity.

4. Campus Dry Cleaners performed cleaning work for 80 customers today. All work was done for credit, and the accountant is preparing to record today's business in the accounting records. The total amount of the revenues for the 80 customers is $543.80.

   a. How many general journal entries will the accountant make? _____
   b. What account in the general ledger should be recorded as the debit account? _____
   c. What general ledger account will be recorded as the credit account? _____
   d. How many postings will be made to the subsidiary ledger? _____
   e. Are they debits, credits, or both in the subsidiary ledger? _____
   f. What is the total of the amounts posted to the subsidiary ledger? $_____
   g. If the entries to the general ledger are posted today, how much will be posted to Accounts Receivable? $_____
   h. In the general ledger, Accounts Receivable is called a _____ account.

5. Vicki Roupe owns a jewelry repair shop. She collects for some work in cash at the time it is done; other customers are billed monthly. Operating in a rented building, she owns the repair equipment that she uses. She carries a stock of parts and supplies to be used in making repairs and also a small stock of office supplies. Roupe started her business last month by investing some of her own money and borrowing an additional amount from the bank on a one-year note. She pays cash for some repair parts and supplies and buys others on credit. She allows herself to withdraw $1,000 per month for living expenses.

   Required: Prepare a chart of accounts for this business showing account numbers and titles.

6. Reliable Tax Service uses the following chart of accounts:

Account Number	Account Title
101	Cash
121	Accounts Receivable
131	Office Supplies
160	Office Equipment
201	Accounts Payable
202	Notes Payable
301	Sid Bean, Capital
302	Sid Bean, Drawing
401	Tax Service Revenue
501	Rent Expense
502	Wages Expense
503	Office Supplies Expense

The following transactions occurred in February 1985:

Feb. 1   Sid Bean invested $10,000 by making a transfer from his personal bank account to the business bank account to establish the Reliable Tax Service.

2   Purchased forms and various other office supplies on credit for $500.

3   Received cash of $800 for preparing ten tax returns.

4   Since there was more work than one person could perform, hired an assistant at $350 per week to begin work on Monday, February 7.

11   Sent bills to thirty persons for whom tax work had been done this week; total amount was $2,500.

6. continued

   Feb. 11   Recorded collections of cash for tax work this week of $2,000. This work had not been previously billed.

   11   Paid the assistant his weekly salary of $350.

   15   Received checks in payment of some of the bills sent out on February 11; the total collections were $900.

   18   Paid for all supplies purchased on February 2; total was $500.

   18   Withdrew cash in anticipation of income, $500.

   18   Paid the assistant his weekly salary, $350.

   18   Counted office supplies on hand. Since $350 of office supplies remained on hand, determined that $150 must have been used. Made the journal entry to record this usage.

   Required: Prepare general journal entries as appropriate for the above transactions. Show explanations.

GENERAL JOURNAL   Page 1

Date	Account Titles and Explanation	F	Debit	Credit

GENERAL JOURNAL

Page 2

Date		Account Titles and Explanation	F	Debit	Credit

GENERAL JOURNAL   Page 3

Date		Account Titles and Explanation	F	Debit	Credit

ANSWERS TO LEARNING GOAL ACHIEVEMENT TEST

1.

GENERAL JOURNAL   Page 27

Date		Account Titles and Explanation	F	Debit	Credit
1985					
Aug.	8	Dental Supplies	123	800	
		Cash	101		800
		Purchase of supplies			
		with check number 362.			
	11	Cash	101	400	
		Dental Supplies	123		400
		Sale of one-half the supplies			
		to another dentist.			

GENERAL LEDGER

Cash   Acct. No. 101

Date		Explanation	F	Debit	Date		Explanation	F	Credit
1985					1985				
Aug.	11		27	400	Aug.	8		27	800

Dental Supplies   Acct. No. 123

Date		Explanation	F	Debit	Date		Explanation	F	Credit
1985					1985				
Aug.	8		27	800	Aug.	11		27	400

2.

GENERAL JOURNAL   Page 10

Date		Account Titles and Explanation	F	Debit	Credit
1985					
Mar.	1	Cash	101	800	
		Fees Earned	703		800
		Collection of March fees.			
	3	Repair Supplies	133	350	
		Cash	101		350
		Purchase of supplies.			

GENERAL LEDGER

Cash   Acct. No. 101

Date		Explanation	F	Debit	Credit	Balance
1985						
Mar.	1		10	800		800
	3		10		350	450

Repair Supplies   Acct. No. 133

Date		Explanation	F	Debit	Credit	Balance
1985						
Mar.	3		10	350		350

Fees Earned   Acct. No. 703

Date		Explanation	F	Debit	Credit	Balance
1985						
Mar.	1		10		800	800

3.
   a. decrease   f. decrease
   b. increase   g. decrease
   c. increase   h. increase
   d. increase   i. decrease
   e. increase   j. decrease

4.
   a. One.   e. Debits.
   b. Accounts Receivable.   f. 543.80.
   c. Cleaning Revenue.   g. 543.80.
   d. 80.   h. controlling

5.   Account Number[a]   Account Title[a]

    101 . . . . Cash
    121 . . . . Accounts Receivable
    131 . . . . Office Supplies
    132 . . . . Repair Parts and Supplies
    151 . . . . Repair Equipment
    201 . . . . Accounts Payable
    202 . . . . Notes Payable
    301 . . . . Vicki Roupe, Capital
    302 . . . . Vicki Roupe, Drawing
    401 . . . . Repair Service Revenue
    501 . . . . Rent Expense
    502 . . . . Office Supplies Expense
    503 . . . . Repair Parts and Supplies Expense

a.   *Note to Student:* The above account numbers and titles are suggested for this business. You would not be incorrect if you used different ones, as long as the numbering system is logical and the account titles adequately describe the subelement they represent. For example, it would be equally correct to have separate accounts for Repair Parts and Repair Supplies. If you separated these two current assets, it would be a good idea to separate the related expense accounts.

6.

GENERAL JOURNAL   Page 1

Date		Account Titles and Explanation	F	Debit	Credit
1985					
Feb.	1	Cash		10,000	
		Sid Bean, Capital			10,000
		Investment to start the			
		Reliable Tax Service.			
	2	Office Supplies		500	
		Accounts Payable			500
		Purchase of forms and supplies.			
	3	Cash		800	
		Tax Service Revenue			800
		Cash collections for			
		preparing tax returns.			
	4	*Note to Student:* There is no entry			
		for this event since no change			
		occurred in any subelements of the			
		accounting equation.			

GENERAL JOURNAL   Page 2

Date		Account Titles and Explanation	F	Debit	Credit
1985					
Feb.	11	Accounts Receivable		2,500	
		Tax Service Revenue			2,500
		Billing for work done on			
		credit this week.			
	11	Cash		2,000	
		Tax Service Revenue			2,000
		Cash collections for tax work			
		not previously billed.			
	11	Wages Expense		350	
		Cash			350
		Paid weekly salary.			
	15	Cash		900	
		Accounts Receivable			900
		Collections on account.			
	18	Accounts Payable		500	
		Cash			500
		Payment on account.			
	18	Sid Bean, Drawing		500	
		Cash			500
		Withdrawal by owner.			
	18	Wages Expense		350	
		Cash			350
		Paid weekly salary.			
	18	Office Supplies Expense		150	
		Office Supplies			150
		To record supplies used.			

Notes to Student: **These are some points to check:**

▶ Skip one line after each transaction.
▶ Record debits and credits to account titles only.
▶ Record debit accounts and amounts first, then indent and record credits.
▶ Do not enter account numbers; these entries are not yet posted.
▶ Other adequate explanations are acceptable.
▶ Your page numbers are not likely to be the same as those in this solution.

Chapter 3
Income Statement Accounts and Completion of the Basic Accounting Sequence

■■

EXPLANATION OF MAJOR CONCEPTS

Journalizing and Posting

Chapter 3 continues with the Good Times Wheels Repair Shop illustration. Chapter 2 showed the journalizing of the transactions. In Chapter 3, the general ledger is shown. The transactions which were journalized in Chapter 2 are now posted to the ledger. Notice that each of the postings in the general ledger has a number in the folio column. This is the page number in the general journal where the entry can be found, and it's insertion in the ledger indicates that the posting process has been completed. At the same time the account number would be placed in the folio column of the general journal.

It is strongly suggested that you learn and use the correct journalizing and posting procedures. To summarize the steps in sequence:

▶ *First*, enter the transactions in the journal, being careful to debit and credit the account titles only, those names which appear in the chart of accounts. (Students often confuse account titles with explanations and make the debit or credit entries to phrases such as "Paid Cash Today" or "Purchased Stores Supplies on Account.")

▶ *Second*, post from the journal to ledger accounts. Enter (in sequence) the date, the journal page number and the amount in the proper ledger account for each item debited or credited in the journal. (Watch debits and credits; a common error is to post a debit as a credit or a credit as a debit.)

▶ *Third*, immediately after posting each item--*and at no other time*--go back to the journal and enter the account number in the folio column. As problems become more complex, students who save ten minutes by using a short-cut procedure end up spending hours trying to find why their trial balance debit and credit totals are not equal. When posting to a ledger account, say Cash, there is no objection to posting all entries to that account before going to another account if you go back to the journal and *enter the account number after posting each entry*.

Take the time at this point to trace the above steps to the journal entries in Chapter 2 and the postings in Chapter 3. Make sure you understand each journal entry and can trace the step-by-step posting that has taken place.

The three-amount-column form of account that is shown in Chapter 3 is used in the general ledger and the subsidiary ledgers. The three money columns always represent Debit, Credit, and Balance, in that order, regardless of the classification of the account. The balance is considered normal unless it is indicated to be negative or abnormal by placing a circle around the number. Thus, when the normal account balance is a debit (assets, expenses, and drawings), the account balance is debit unless it is circled. And when the normal account balance is a credit (liabilities, owner's equities, and revenues), the account balance is credit unless it is circled. In the accounts for the Good Times Wheels Repair Shop, a label in a box tells you whether the balance is a debit or a credit. This is done in the illustration only to help you learn the normal balances; it is not done in an accounting system, and you should *not do it when working problems.*

Preparing a Trial Balance

Upon completion of journalizing and posting all of the transactions for a period, a trial balance is prepared to test the equality of debits and credits in the general ledger. This is done by listing all of the accounts in the general ledger and their respective balances. The debit and credit columns are then totaled to check their equality. At the same time a *schedule of accounts receivable* and a *schedule of accounts payable* are prepared to test the accuracy of the subsidiary ledgers. Each schedule should total to the balance in the respective control account.

Financial Statements

Two new financial statements illustrated are the *income statement* and the *statement of owner's equity.* You need to learn the form of these statements. Note first that both cover a period of time and that the date in the heading must let the reader know what that period of time is.

The income statement sets forth in detail the equation: Revenue - Expenses = Net Income. The form is simply:

COMPANY NAME
Income Statement
For the *period* Ended *date*

Revenue (by title)		$XXX
Expenses (each listed by title with	$XX	
a subtotal placed in the same	XX	
column as the revenue amount)	XX	XXX
Net income		$XXX

The form of the statement of owner's equity is easy to learn if you will picture the captions as meaning the following:

COMPANY NAME
Statement of Owner's Equity
For the *period* Ended *date*

Amounts at beginning of period	$XXX
Amounts that were added	XXX
Subtotal	$XXX
Deduct amounts withdrawn	XXX
Amount you have at end of period	$XXX

The form of the balance sheet was introduced in Chapter 1 and is reviewed again in the following outline:

COMPANY NAME
Balance Sheet
date

Assets

Current assets:
(each account is listed by title) . . . . $XXX
. . . . XXX
. . . . XXX
    Total current assets . . . . $XXX
Property, plant, and equipment:
(each account is listed by title) . . . . $XXX
. . . . XXX
. . . . XXX
    Total property, plant, and equipment XXX
Total assets . . . . $XXX

Liabilities and Owner's Equity

Current liabilities:
(each account is listed by title) . . . . $XXX
. . . . XXX
. . . . XXX
    Total current liabilities . . . . $XXX
Long-term liabilities:
(each account is listed by title) . . . . $XXX
. . . . XXX
    Total long-term liabilities XXX
    Total Liabilities . . . . $XXX
Owner's equity:
Owner name, capital XXX
Total liabilities and owner's equity . . . . $XXX

The financial statements are a major reason for accounting, and you need to understand what purpose each serves. They tell this story:

▸ The *income statement* provides information on results of business operations over a period. How well did the company perform in terms of earning a profit?

▸ The *statement of owner's equity* shows changes in owner's equity over a period. It tells us the things that increased and that decreased the owner's interest in the business.

▸ The *balance sheet* gives an expanded picture of the accounting equation. A person reading a balance sheet can tell what assets the business holds and how much the business owes creditors. Because the balance sheet is classified, you can compare current assets with current liabilities to get some idea of the short-term ability of the firm to pay its debts. It is a financial picture of the company at a point in time.

The Closing Process

Most firms go through the closing process only once each year. However, for internal management use, financial statements are needed much more frequently. In this textbook--especially in the earlier chapters--some illustrations and problems assume that the closing process takes place at the end of each month. This allows you to study the process with much less complex data.

Note to *close* a revenue account, we simply record a debit to the account for its balance. And to *close* an expense, we simply record a credit to the account for its balance. The opposite debit or credit is recorded against an account called Income Summary. After this has been done, all expense and revenue accounts have equal debits and credits (their balances are all zero). The debits and credits that were accumulated in expense and revenue accounts during the month have been moved into a single account, Income Summary. If that account has a credit balance, the company's total revenues were greater than expenses, and it had a profit for the month. A debit balance would mean that expenses closed into Income Summary were greater than credits. This indicates a loss for the month.

The Income Summary is closed into the owner's capital account. If a profit, the owner's equity increase shows up as an increase in capital. Finally, the owner's drawing account is also closed into the capital account. Since the withdrawals recorded in drawing are the opposite of investment, this entry records a reduction in owner's equity. Note that any additional investments made by the owner would have been recorded directly to the capital account. Thus, there would be no account for investments to be closed.

In summarized form, the closing entries would appear as follows:

Revenue Accounts (each listed separately)		XXX	
. . . .		XXX	
Income Summary			XXX
To close revenue accounts.			
Income Summary		XXX	
Expense Accounts (each listed separately)			XXX
. . . .			XXX
. . . .			XXX
To close expense accounts.			
Income Summary		XXX	
Owner's Capital			XXX
To close Income Summary.			
Note, this would be opposite			
for a loss.			
Owner's Capital		XXX	
Owner's Drawing			XXX
To close drawing account.			

GUIDED STUDY OF THIS CHAPTER

A. *Journalizing and Posting. This section of the Study Guide will use the journal entries from Chapter 2 and the general ledger from Chapter 3 for the Good Times Wheels Repair Shop.*

1. What heading is given to the folio column of the general journal (Figure 2-13)?_____

A1.   F.

2. When is the number of the account placed in the folio column of the journal?_____

_____

A2.   Only after the item has been posted to the ledger account.

3. In the second January 5 journal entry, there is a $400 amount in the explanation. In which subsidiary ledger will this be posted? _____

_____

A3.   The accounts payable ledger.

4. Is it posted as a debit or as a credit?_____

_____

A4.   As a credit.

5. Since this transaction is posted to Southern Supply Company's account in the accounts payable ledger, is it also necessary to post it to the general ledger? _____

A5.   Yes.

6.   Isn't this a double posting that will destroy the equality of debits and credits?_____

Explain._____

_____

_____

A6.   No. The equality of debits and credits is in the general ledger only.

7.   Stop at this point and locate the $400 credit posting in the general ledger. In what account number did you find it?_____

A7.   201.

8.   What was the balance in that account after this posting? $_____

A8.   400.

9.   Look in account number 201 at the next posting. What is its date, and where did it come from?_____

A9.   January 29, from journal page 2.

10.   It is also a credit. The amount is $250. What is the new balance in account number 201? $_____

A10.   650.

11.   Locate the original entry on journal page 2 from which this posting was made. What event caused this $250 increase in Accounts Payable?

_____

A11.   A purchase of parts from Delco Supply House.

12.   The next journal entry on page 2 also involves Accounts Payable. Describe the second transaction that was journalized on January 29.

_____

_____

A12.   A $300 payment was made to Southern Supply Company.

13.   Why is Accounts Payable debited instead of being credited?_____

_____

A13.   The payment of cash decreases the liability.

14.   What is the new balance in general ledger account number 201? $_____ In the subsidiary ledger account with Southern Supply Company? $_____

A 14.   350, 100.

15.   From a study of Southern Supply's subsidiary ledger account, what does it appear
has happened during the month of January?

_____

_____

_____

A 15.   We have apparently
made a $400 purchase
on account and then
paid off $300 of that
amount. This leaves
a balance of $100
still owed.

B.   *Trial Balance and Financial Statements*

1.   The January 31, 1985, trial balance of Good
Times Wheels Repair Shop follows the ledgers
in the textbook illustration. What is the
source of the $23,450 debit labeled "Cash"?

_____

_____

B 1.   It is the latest
balance in the Cash
account in the
general ledger.

2.   If the account illustration were not labeled
"Balance is a debit," how would you know
that it belongs in the Debit column of the
trial balance?_____

_____

B 2.   The normal balance
of an asset is debit.

3.   The first item in the Credit column is $350.
Where did it come from?_____

_____

B 3.   It is the balance in
Accounts Payable in
the general ledger.

4.   Is the $100 balance due Southern Supply
Company listed in this trial balance?_____
Explain._____

_____

_____

B 4.   No. It is not listed
separately, but it is
a part of the $350
Accounts Payable
balance.

5.   What accounts appear in the trial balance?

_____

_____

B 5.   Every general ledger
account that has a
balance.

6.   Does this include revenue and expense
accounts? _____

B6. Yes. (Every account that has a balance must be included.)

7. Is $41,370 equal to total assets at this point? _____ Explain. _____ _____

B7. No. $41,370 is simply the total of all debit balances in the ledger.

8. Why do we expect total debits to equal total credits in the trial balance? _____ _____ _____ _____

B8. Because each journal entry from which these balances came had equal debit and credit amounts.

9. By using the Schedule of Accounts Receivable for Good Times, what condition lends support to the fact that the individual customer account balances are accurate? _____ _____ _____ _____ _____

B9. This is supported by the fact that the $210 total of the schedule is equal to the balance in Accounts Receivable account in the general ledger.

10. Where does the amount $5,020 in Figure 3-2 come from? _____ _____ _____ _____

B10. It is the balance of the Motorcycle Repair Revenue account in the trial balance and in the general ledger.

11. Where does the amount $1,700 in Figure 3-2 come from? _____ _____ _____

B11. It is the balance in the Salaries Expense account in the trial balance and the general ledger.

12. Where does the amount $2,435 in Figure 3-2 come from? _____ _____ _____

B12. It is the sum of all the expense accounts.

13. How do we determine that net income (Figure 3-2) is $2,585? _____ _____

B13. By subtracting total expenses from total revenue = ($5,020 – $2,435).

14. Would you say that the Good Times Wheels Repair Shop had a successful month in January? _____ Explain._____

_____

_____

B14. Yes. Net income was greater than 50 percent of total revenue (a very high rate of profit).

15. In what other financial statement will the amount $2,585 be used? _____

_____

B15. In the statement of owner's equity (Figure 3-3).

16. How is it used there? _____

_____

B16. As an increase to owner's equity.

17. What is the title of the owner's equity caption?

_____

B17. Lucy Genova, capital.

18. Does the original investment plus net income equal the new January 31 capital balance?

_____ Explain. _____

_____

B18. No. Lucy Genova withdrew $300 from the business.

19. Therefore, the owner's equity in the balance sheet (Figure 3-4) amounts to $32,285. It is a combination of what amounts?_____

_____

_____

B19. Original investment of $30,000 + net income of $2,585 – withdrawal of $300.

20. In Figure 3-4, what is the sum of the assets that represent cash or are expected to be consumed or turned into cash in one year? $_____

B20. 24,635.

21. The assets in this total are called _____

_____.

B21. current assets

22. Why are the remaining assets grouped under the caption Property, plant, and equipment?

_____

_____

_____

_____

B22. They are assets that will not be converted into cash or used in place of cash within the year. And, they will be used in the operation of the business.

B23. 6,350.

B24. None. (Financial statements do not have debits and credits. Debits and credits are used only in the journal, ledgers, and trial balance.)

B25. Yes.

B26. No.

B27. No. All that we can say is that creditors have claims of $6,350 and Lucy has a claim of $32,285 against total assets.

B28. Yes. Total cash held by the business is much greater than its debts.

B29. Revenue and expense (or temporary) accounts.

23. What is the amount of liabilities expected to be paid by using current assets? $_____

24. What are the total debits in the balance sheet (Figure 3-4)? $_____

25. Then, is it correct to say that there is no debit column and no credit column in an income statement? _____

26. Can Lucy Genova's equity in amount $32,285 be related to any specific assets? _____

27. Is there any way to know how much of the land is claimed by Lucy and how much by the creditors? _____ Explain. _____

_____

_____

28. Does the Good Times Wheels Repair Shop have the ability to pay all debts tomorrow?_____

Explain._____

_____

_____

29. Let's review the basic function of accounts. Which classes of accounts were used to prepare the income statement? _____

_____

30. Which classes of accounts were used to prepare the balance sheet? _____

_____

B30. Asset, liability, and owner's equity (or real) accounts.

C.   *The Closing Process*

1.   What is the purpose of the Income Summary account? _____

_____

_____

C1. It is a device to bring together all revenues and expenses into a single account to determine net income.

2.   In Figure 3-6, how did the accountant know that the amount to debit Motorcycle Repair Revenue was $5,020?_____

_____

_____

C2. Its credit balance was $5,020. A debit of equal amount was needed to bring the balance to zero.

3.   Then, is it true that "closing an account" is the act of bringing its balance to zero? _____

C3. Yes.

4.   When a debit of $5,020 was journalized to close Motorcycle Repair Revenue, what account was credited? _____

C4. Income Summary.

5.   This closing entry appears to transfer a credit balance in a revenue account to a credit balance in the Income Summary account. In fact, that is what happens. At this point, the balance in Income Summary is equal to the total revenue.

C5. No answer required.

6.   The second entry in Figure 3-6 has one debit and several credits. What is the name given to a journal entry with more than one debit or credit? _____

C6. A compound entry.

7.   Would you expect that most entries closing expense accounts would be compound entries?

_____ Explain. _____

_____

C7. Yes. A business usually has several expenses.

8.   The debit to Income Summary of $2,435 (second entry in Figure 3-6) is a familiar dollar amount. Where have we seen it before?

_____

_____

C8. As the total of expenses in the income statement.

9. Then, could we say that this second closing entry has the effect of transferring all the debit balances in expense accounts to a single debit in Income Summary? _____

C9. Yes.

10. This second entry also has the effect of doing what to each of the expense accounts?_____
_____
_____

C10. It will leave a zero balance in each of the expense accounts.

11. Look at the Income Summary account in Figure 3-7. What is the balance after the *first two* closing entries are posted? $_____

C11. 2,585.

12. Again, this is a familiar amount. What does it represent? _____

C12. Net income.

13. Two more entries are to be made in the Good Times closing procedure. They are (1)_____
_____, and

(2)_____
_____.

C13. (1) close the Income Summary balance to Capital, and (2) close the Lucy Genova's Drawing balance to Capital.

14. When all closing entries are posted, the nominal (or temporary) accounts have zero balances. Why doesn't Lucy Genova, Capital (shown in Figure 3-8) have a zero balance?
_____
_____

C14. It is not a temporary account. It is a real (or permanent) account.

15. When the accountant for Good Times Wheels Repair Shop begins to journalize transactions in February, is it necessary to start a new journal page, or can he or she begin where the closing entries ended on journal page 4?
_____
_____

C15. Simply skip one line and begin on page 4 where closing entries ended.

16. Must new ledger account pages be opened for February, or can the accountant continue to post in the same accounts?_____
_____

C16. Continue to post in the same accounts.

17. What is the purpose of making a postclosing trial balance? _____
_____
_____

C17. To prove that total debits equal total credits in the ledger after all closing entries are posted.

18. Does it prove that all account balances are correct? _____
_____

C18. No, but it is good evidence that they probably are.

19. Why are there no revenue or expense accounts in the postclosing trial balance?
_____

C19. Because their balances are all zero.

20. Is this why the account Lucy Genova, Drawing also does not appear in Figure 3-9? _____

C20. Yes. (It also has a zero balance.)

D. *Interrelationship of Financial Statements. This part is based on Figure 3-12.*

1. The statement of owner's equity begins with the figure $32,285. Where did it come from?
_____

D1. Balance sheet, January 31, 1985.

2. The second number on the statement of owner's equity is $5,000. Where was this number taken from? _____
_____
It represents what? _____

D2. Income statement for the month ended February 28, 1985. Net income for the month.

3. The $1,000 figure for withdrawals was taken from where? _____

D3. General ledger.

4. The final number on the statement of owner's equity represents what? _____
_____
It is used also on what statement? _____
_____

D4. Lucy Genova capital on February 28, 1985. February 28, 1985, balance sheet.

SELF TEST OF LEARNING GOAL ACHIEVEMENT

1. Following is the year-end trial balance of Lieberman Consultants on June 30, 1985:

Account Title	Debits	Credits
Cash	$ 5	
Accounts Receivable	20	
Office Supplies	10	
Office Equipment	30	
Accounts Payable		$ 10
Notes Payable (due in 90 days)		15
S. Lieberman, Capital		35
S. Lieberman, Drawing	15	
Consulting Revenue		150
Wages Expense	60	
Rent Expense	50	
Supplies Expense	20	
Totals	$210	$210

Required: Using the data above, prepare the following in the spaces provided (complete headings as necessary): (a) an income statement, (b) a statement of owner's equity, (c) a balance sheet, (d) closing entries, and (e) a postclosing trial balance. Be precise in attention to details.

a.   Exhibit A

Income Statement

b.

Exhibit B

Statement of Owner's Equity

c.

Exhibit C

Balance Sheet

d.

	GENERAL JOURNAL			Page 9
Date	Account Titles and Explanation	F	Debit	Credit
1985	Closing Entries			

e.

Postclosing Trial Balance

2. Following are the Withdrawals and Income Summary accounts after closing of the Creekbend Company. The company's only revenue source was Professional Fees. It has only two expense accounts: Marketing Expense, with a balance of $38,000 for the year, and General Expense, with a balance of $12,000.

GENERAL LEDGER

J. Creekbend, Drawing   Acct. No. 311

Date		Explanation	F	Debit	Credit	Balance
1985						
Nov.	10		16	10,000		10,000
Dec.	31		28		10,000	0

Income Summary   Acct. No. 600

Date		Explanation	F	Debit	Credit	Balance
1985						
Dec.	31		28		87,000	87,000
	31		28	50,000		37,000
	31		28	37,000		0

Required: Reconstruct the closing entries in the following general journal form:

GENERAL JOURNAL   Page 28

Date		Account Titles and Explanation	F	Debit	Credit
1985		Closing Entries			

ANSWERS TO LEARNING GOAL ACHIEVEMENT TESTS

1. a.   LIEBERMAN CONSULTANTS   Exhibit A
                                Income Statement
                          For the Year Ended June 30, 1985

Revenue:
  Consulting revenue $150
Expenses:
  Wages expense $60
  Rent expense   50
  Supplies expense   20
    Total expenses   130
Net income . . . . $ 20

    b.   LIEBERMAN CONSULTANTS   Exhibit B
                            Statement of Owner's Equity
                          For the Year Ended June 30, 1985

S. Lieberman, capital, July 1, 1984 . . . . $35
  Add: Net income for 1985   20
    Subtotal $55
  Deduct: Withdrawals   15
S. Lieberman, capital, June 30, 1985 . . . . $40

    c.   LIEBERMAN CONSULTANTS   Exhibit C
                                  Balance Sheet
                                  June 30, 1985

                                     Assets
Current assets:
  Cash . . . . $ 5
  Accounts receivable   20
  Office supplies 10 $35
Property, plant, and equipment:
  Office equipment   30
Total assets $65

                        Liabilities and Owner's Equity
Current Liabilities:
  Accounts payable $10
  Notes payable   15
    Total liabilities $25
Owner's equity:
  S. Lieberman, capital   40
Total liabilities and owner's equity $65

d.

GENERAL JOURNAL   Page 9

Date		Account Titles and Explanation	F	Debit	Credit
1985		Closing Entries			
Jun.	30	Consulting Revenue		150	
		Income Summary			150
		To close revenue account.			
	30	Income Summary		130	
		Wages Expense			60
		Rent Expense			50
		Supplies Expense			20
		To close expense accounts.			
	30	Income Summary		20	
		S. Lieberman, Capital			20
		To close net income to capital.			
	30	S. Lieberman, Capital		15	
		S. Lieberman, Drawing			15
		To close drawing account.			

e.

LIEBERMAN CONSULTANTS
Postclosing Trial Balance
June 30, 1985

Account Title	Debits	Credits
Cash	$ 5	
Accounts Receivable	20	
Office Supplies	10	
Office Equipment	30	
Accounts Payable		$10
Notes Payable		15
S. Lieberman, Capital		40
Totals	$65	$65

2.

GENERAL JOURNAL   Page 28

Date		Account Titles and Explanation	F	Debit	Credit
1985		Closing Entries			
Dec.	31	Professional Fees		87,000	
		Income Summary			87,000
		To close revenue accounts.			
	31	Income Summary		50,000	
		Marketing Expense			38,000
		General Expense			12,000
		To close expense accounts.			
	31	Income Summary		37,000	
		J. Creekbend, Capital			37,000
		To close net income.			
	31	J. Creekbend, Capital		10,000	
		J. Creekbend, Drawing			10,000
		To close the drawing account.			

Chapter 4
End-of-Period Adjusting Entries

■■■

EXPLANATION OF MAJOR CONCEPTS

Cash versus Accrual Basis

To *accrue* means to increase by regular growth. In a business, some revenues
and expenses build up gradually day by day. Although payday may not occur
until the end of the month, wages expense is actually building up every day that
employees work. To prepare an income statement on a date between paydays and
fail to include the wages expense that has accrued since last payday--but not yet
been paid--would be incorrect. We would be ignoring an important expense that
has been incurred; this would cause the statement to show a net income greater
than the actual net income. Many other expenses accrue in similar fashion.

Revenues also accrue, but probably not in as great a variety as expenses.
The telephone company is a good example of a business whose revenues accrue.
Telephone service, provided to thousands of customers every day, is not billed
until the end of the month. If a telephone company were to prepare an income
statement in the middle of the month and not recognize the accrued revenues
earned (but not collected) up to that date, the statement would be completely
inaccurate. It might even show a net loss, when the company is making an
appropriate profit. You can see that such an erroneous income statement would
cause management personnel to make the wrong decisions about future operations.

Recording expenses and revenues only when they are paid for--that is, when
the cash actually flows in or out of a business--is the *cash basis* of accounting.
The cash basis may be acceptable in some very small businesses that do not have
many expenses or revenues to accrue, but not very often. Most organizations,
including government agencies and not-for-profit groups, have many types of
expenses that accrue and several types of revenues. Therefore, the *accrual
basis of accounting* is usually the only system that will provide useful information to managers at all levels.

Adjusting Entries

If the accrual basis is to be used, it is necessary to make special accounting
entries at the end of each accounting period. These entries are known as
adjusting entries. Adjusting entries bring the revenues and expenses up to
date on an accrual basis. Thus, an income statement will properly contain the

actual amounts of each and will accurately reflect net income. There are several types of adjusting entries, but they all have one purpose: to bring expenses and revenues *to their actual amount on an accrual basis*. Therefore, the adjusting process will be much easier for you if you think through each adjustment, keeping in mind the basic purpose. In each case, ask yourself the following questions:

▶ What has happened to make the current account balances outdated? Has an expense been incurred or has a revenue been earned?

▶ What should the actual expense or revenue be?

▶ What income statement account is involved, and what is the related balance sheet account?

▶ What must be done to the accounts to give them the accurate balances?

In making adjustments, the following hints may be helpful:

▶ Every adjustment *must* involve either an *expense* or a *revenue* account.

▶ The way an original transaction entry was recorded determines the form and amount of adjustment. Not all adjustments debit expense accounts; sometimes a credit to an expense is required. (This point will be illustrated in the guided study of this chapter.)

▶ Adjusting entries *never* involve the Cash account. If you find yourself debiting or crediting Cash in an adjusting entry, something is wrong. Stop and analyze the situation again.

▶ Every adjusting entry has two parts: *determination* of the accounts to be debited and credited, and *computation of the amount*. Separate them in your mind. Then determine each before you make the entry.

Accruals and Deferrals

Throughout Chapter 4, the terms *accruals* and *deferrals* are used. The accrual concept is relatively easy to understand. It is simply an item that has grown or accumulated with the passage of time but that has not been recognized on the books. Interest on your passbook savings account at the bank is an example; it accrues daily, but the bank only records it once per month. It isn't necessary to record it more often, and it would be very expensive to do so.

The term *deferral* really means a deferred or delayed recognition of expense or revenue. Deferrals refer to items that are already recorded on the books. After they have been recorded, their status begins to change. However, as in the case of accruals, it is just not feasible or practical to recognize the continuous change. An insurance policy is an asset the moment it is purchased, but as time passes, you are using insurance protection, and the asset is slowly changing to expense. We defer (or delay) the recognition of that change until it is time to close the books. To make our financial statements more accurate, we must adjust to update the deferred recognition of expense. The adjustment, like that for accruals, may involve either a revenue or an expense.

A summary of accruals and deferrals appears in Figure 4-3 of the text. It would be a good idea to review the figure at this point.

Reversing Entries (Appendix)

A *reversing entry* is an entry which is made at the beginning of an accounting period and which is the opposite of one of the adjusting entries made at the end of the prior period. It is made to ease the subsequent recording of transactions. For example, if a company has a weekly payroll of $500 ($100 per day), they normally record payroll by a debit to Wages Expense and a credit to Cash for $500. If on December 31, 1985, it is necessary to accrue two days wages, they would debit Wages Expense and credit Accrued Wages Payable for $200. On the next payday, January 3, 1986, the $500 payment would be paying off $200 in accrued liability and $300 in 1986 wages expense. If no reversing entry were made, this would require that the person making the payroll entry understand the adjusting entry made on December 31, 1985, and take it into consideration when recording the January 3 payroll. This trouble can be eliminated by reversing the adjusting entry on January 1, 1986.

If the adjusting entry had been reversed on January 1, 1986, the accrued liability account would have been zeroed out, and the wages expense would have had a credit (negative) $200 balance. Then the normal payroll entry on January 3, 1986, could have been made similarly to every other payday entry. Wages Expense would have been debited and Cash credited for $500. The $500 debit to Wages Expense would have made the balance $300, the proper amount of expense for 1986. The entries, as they would affect the Wages Expense and Accrued Wages Payable accounts, are summarized in T accounts below.

Wages Expense				Accrued Wages Payable			
12/31	200^a	12/31	200^b			12/31	200^a
Bal	0					Bal	200
1/3	500^d	1/1	200^c	1/1	200^c		
Bal	300					Bal	0

a. December 31, 1985, adjusting entry.
b. December 31, 1985, closing entry.
c. January 1, 1986, reversing entry.
d. January 3, 1986, regular payroll entry.

GUIDED STUDY OF THIS CHAPTER

A.   The Accounting Basis

1.   Under the cash basis of accounting, when is revenue recognized? _____

_____

A1.   When the cash is received.

2.   Under the cash basis of accounting, when are expenses recognized? _____

_____

A2.   When the cash is paid out.

3.   Although cash basis is a simple method of accounting, what major problem does it cause?

_____

_____

A3.   The mismatching of revenue and expense.

4.   Under accrual accounting, when are revenues recognized? _____

_____

A4.   When the services are performed or the goods are delivered.

5.   Under accrual accounting, when are expenses recognized? _____

_____

_____

A5.   When the benefits are consumed in the production of revenue.

6.   What is the central goal of accrual accounting?

_____

_____

A6.   To better match revenue and expense.

7.   How will adjusting entries correct the potential mismatching of revenue and expense?

_____

_____

_____

_____

_____

A7. They will record the revenue in the period it was earned and the expense in the period it was incurred, regardless of when the cash changed hands.

8. Name the two basic types of adjusting entries.

_____

A8. Deferral and accrual.

9. Why are the cost and revenue apportionment adjustments called deferrals?_____

_____

_____

_____

_____

A9. Because the recognition of expense or revenue has been postponed until a future period even though the cash has changed hands.

10. How do the accrual adjustments get their name?_____

_____

_____

_____

A10. Revenues or expenses have accumulated but have not been recorded, and the term accrued simply means accumulated.

11. Name the three types of deferrals. _____

_____

_____

_____

A11. Short-term cost apportionments, short-term revenue apportionments, and long-term cost apportionments.

12. Name the two types of accruals. _____

_____

A12. Accrued revenues and accrued expenses.

13. All adjustments involve a(n) _____ _____ account and a(n) _____ account.

A13. balance sheet, income statement

14. Would the account Cash ever be involved in an adjusting entry? _____

A14. No.

B. *Cash versus Accrual Basis. The Carolyn Elfland Company provides an example of the way that income can be incorrectly reported by the cash basis.*

1. In what month did the Carolyn Elfland Company perform the landscaping work?_____

B1.   August.

2. Was any landscaping work done in September? _____

B2.   No.

3. How much was the total revenue *earned* for this work? $_____

B3.   1,000.

4. On the cash basis, how much of the revenue was reported in the August income statement? $_____

B4.   600.

5. Why was the remaining $400 *not* reported in the August income statement on a cash basis?
   _____

B5.   It had not been collected.

6. On the accrual basis, how much revenue was reported in the August income statement? $_____

B6.   1,000.

7. Since all the work was performed in August, is it more accurate to report all the revenue in that month?_____

B7.   Yes.

8. Expenses of $550 were paid in August. What is the amount of unpaid expenses on August 31? $_____

B8.   None.

9. Since there were no unpaid expenses to accrue on August 31, should there be any difference in the cash basis and accrual basis expenses? _____

B9.   No.

10. Was any work performed in September to earn revenue?_____

B10.   No.

11. Therefore, there was really no income produced in September. Which accounting basis correctly shows no income for September?
    _____

B11.   The accrual basis.

12.   The idea expressed in the Carolyn Elfland Company illustration is the basis for adjusting entries. Revenues and expenses should be matched against each other in the period *in which they actually occurred* to determine net income accurately.

B12.   No answer required.

C.   *Adjusting Entries. To study adjustments, let's move directly to a study of the Genova Trucking Company.*

1.   In Figure 4-1, how many different revenue items have already been recognized in the accounts? _____

C1.   One. (Trucking Revenue.)

2.   How many different expense items appear in this trial balance? _____ Give the total amount of expenses in this trial balance. $_____

C2.   Five. 2,235. (Did you make the mistake of including the drawing account as an expense?)

3.   What is the total value of revenue in the trial balance in Figure 4-1? $_____

C3.   7,465.

4.   Then it appears that net income for June (total revenues minus total expense) is $_____ .

C4.   5,230.

5.   But Lucy Genova (the owner) could make some poor decisions if she assumed this to be the net income. Let's now study the adjustments needed to change that amount to the correct income.

C5.   No answer required.

6.   The first adjustment involves rent expense. How much rent expense is shown in the trial balance in Figure 4-1? $_____

C6.   None.

7.   When rent for three months (June, July, and August) was paid on June 1, an asset account, Prepaid Rent, was debited for $1,500. Is the account a true asset account on June 30?

_____ Explain. _____

_____

C7.   No. Part of the
asset has expired.

8.   How much of the Prepaid Rent account is
actually rent that is *prepaid* as of June 30?
$_____

C8.   1,000.

9.   Then the adjustment must reduce the asset
account by $_____.

C9.   500

10.   The reduction to the asset is equal to the
value of the June rent (that has been used
or has expired). What account should be
debited to show consumption of June rent?

_____

C10.   Rent Expense.

11.   This adds a new expense account to the trial
balance. What account should be credited?

_____ Why? _____

_____

C11.   Prepaid Rent. To
show the reduction
in the asset value.

12.   Genova's accountant did not do so, but assume
that the account, Rent Expense, had been
debited for $1,500 when the original rent pay-
ment was made. What account would be over-
stated on June 30? _____
By how much? $_____

C12.   Rent Expense, 1,000.

13.   If Rent Expense was debited originally for
$1,500 and is now overstated by $1,000,
record the adjusting entry needed on June 30.

Account Title	Dr.	Cr.

C13.
Prepaid Rent   1,000
  Rent Expense   1,000

14.   You should see from the foregoing that an
adjusting entry (both form and amount)
depends on how the original transaction was
recorded. If the original transaction debited
an asset, the asset was decreased in the adjustment by the amount that had expired and
become an expense. If the original transaction debited an expense, the expense was
decreased in the adjustment by the amount
that was to be deferred to a future period.
Deferred revenues would be similar except
the original entry would have involved credits
to either a liability or a revenue.

C14. No answer required.

15. In the next adjustment, Prepaid Insurance is credited (decreased). The original payment for three years (thirty-six months) was $_____.

C15. 2,160

16. What fraction of the total coverage expired (was used up) in June? _____

C16. 1/36.

17. Since 1/36 of the three-year policy was used up in June, the original asset of $2,160 should be reduced by $_____. This would leave a balance in Prepaid Insurance of $_____, which is the portion of the original amount that is applicable to future periods--an asset.

C17. 60, 2,100

18. The debit recognizes another expense that had not yet been recognized in June. In what account is this new expense recorded?_____

_____

C18. Insurance Expense.

19. On June 30, after the adjustment is posted, Prepaid Insurance has a balance of $2,100. Is this account now a mixture of asset and expense, or is it a pure asset? _____

C19. Pure asset.

20. By July 31, 1985, would Prepaid Insurance again be a mixed account?_____

C20. Yes.

21. Compute the amount of the expense element that would be contained in Prepaid Insurance on July 31. $_____

C21. 60. (It expires at the rate of $60 per month.)

22. In these first two adjustments, the accumulation of rent expense and insurance expense was simply caused by the passage of time. This is not true of the next adjustment. What is the factor that determines the amount of office supplies expense? _____

_____

C22. The actual consumption of supplies.

23. Since no records were kept at Genova Trucking Company to show how much of the office supplies were used, how do we determine that amount? _____

_____

_____

_____

C23. Count the quantity left on hand June 30 and subtract from the total amount purchased.

24. The amount purchased was $_____ and the physical count on June 30 showed $_____ of unused supplies left on hand. Therefore, Genova must have used supplies amounting to $_____.

C24. 230, 60, 170

25. Since the amount on hand on June 30 was $60, would it be correct to credit the Office Supplies account with $60 to make the adjustment? _____ Explain. _____

_____

_____

_____

_____

C25. No. Office Supplies must be credited with an amount that will reduce the asset account to its new balance, $60.

26. Again, a new expense account, Office Supplies Expense, has been added. Why is the process for these adjustments called cost apportionment? _____

_____

_____

C26. In each case, a previously recorded amount is being divided (apportioned) into asset and expense elements.

27. The fourth adjustment also illustrates an apportionment. This time a revenue is being allocated to June and the five following months. How much is actual June revenue? $_____

C27. 100.

28. How much is the Unearned Rent at the end of June? $_____

C28. 500.

29. What adjusting entry would be made to apportion the amounts as you have answered in questions 27 and 28?

Account Title	Dr.	Cr.

C29.
Unearned Rent   100
  Rent Earned   100

30. Jane Anderson, to whom Genova rented the truck, paid six months rent in advance on June 1. When she paid the $600 on June 1, Jane would credit cash and debit _____ _____.

C30. Prepaid Rent

31. As of June 30, how much of the Prepaid Rent would have expired or been used? $_____ What would Jane Anderson's adjusting entry on June 30 be?

Account Title	Dr.	Cr.

C31. 100.
Rent Expense   100
  Prepaid Rent   100

32. Note the relationship between the two parties to this transaction. Genova's revenue has increased by $100, while Anderson's expense has increased by $_____. And, Genova's liability has a balance of $_____, while Anderson's _____ has a balance of $500.

C32. 100, 500, asset

33. The fifth adjustment introduces a new concept, depreciation. *Depreciation* is the process of periodically allocating original cost of a long-lived asset to periods in which it is used. When this piece of office equipment (purchased for $1,400) is disposed of, how much does Wheelo expect to sell it for as used equipment? $_____

C33. 200.

34. The net cost to Genova to use this office equipment for ten years, then, is $_____.

C34. 1,200 = ($1,400 − $200).

35. Since ten years is the same as 120 months, it would be appropriate to assign 1/120 of $1,200 to each month as expense. The June expense, therefore, should be $_____.

C35. 10

36. Instead of reducing the value in the long-lived asset account with each adjustment, we use a contra account. Since a *contra asset account* reduces the asset valuation, we expect its balance to be a _____ (debit/credit).

C36. credit

37. Each time we allocate an amount to Depreciation Expense--Office Equipment on Genova's
books, we add to the balance in the account

_____.

C37. Accumulated Depre-
ciation--Office
Equipment

38. An asset and its related contra asset account
work together to determine the *book value* or
carrying value of the asset. After five of the
ten useful life years have passed, the accounts
look like this:

Office Equipment

1985			F	Dr.	Cr.	Bal.
Jun.	1		2	1,400		1,400

Accumulated Depreciation--Office Equipment

1985			F	Dr.	Cr.	Bal.
Jun.	30		4		10	10
1990						
Jun.	30		104		10	600

What is the carrying value now? $_____

C38. 800 = ($1,400 - $600).

39. After the last credit to Accumulated Depreciation has been recorded at the end of ten
years, the book value or carrying value will
be $_____.

C39. 200 (Note: This is
equal to the expected
salvage value.)

40. Has a similar accumulation been building up
in Depreciation Expense--Office Equipment
over the past ten years? _____ Explain.

_____

_____

C40. No. Each year the
expense account has
been closed to Income
Summary.

41. Over the ten years of useful life, how much
of the cost of this equipment has appeared as
expense in income statements? $_____

C41. 1,200.

42. The Trucks adjustment is also a long-term
cost apportionment. Each period, $_____
of the total cost of two trucks will be converted into expense over a total period of
_____ years.

C42. 400, 5

43. At the end of their useful life of five years, *each* truck will have a carrying value of $_____.

C43. 1,000

44. Accruals are items of expense or revenue that have increased *but are not yet recorded* on the books. Note that unlike apportionments, there are no balances in ledger accounts that have become a mixed account. The amount to be adjusted does not appear in any ledger account before adjustment. The adjustment for wages is an accrued _____ (expense/revenue).

C44. expense

45. The adjustment for interest liability is an accrued _____ (revenue/expense).

C45. expense

46. The adjustment for interest earned is an accrued _____ (revenue/expense).

C46. revenue

47. In making adjustments for accruals, there is a relationship that is helpful to understand:
a. Accrued expenses bring on liabilities.
b. Accrued revenues bring on assets.
Therefore, the debit to Wages Expense in the adjustment was accompanied by a credit to

_____.

C47. Accrued Wages Payable

48. The interest in the adjustment for $12 is owed _____ (to/by) Genova. Therefore, it is a debit to a(n) _____ and a credit to a(n) _____.

C48. to, asset, revenue

49. The interest in the adjustment for $64 is owed _____ (to/by) Genova. It is, therefore, a debit to a(n) _____ and a credit to a(n) _____.

C49. by, expense, liability

50. Take time to record here the effect of all the adjustments made by Genova Trucking Company, using the following format:

Adjustment	Increased Expense	Increased Revenue
(a) Prepaid Rent	$_____	$_____
(b) Prepaid Insurance	_____	_____
(c) Office Supplies	_____	_____
(d) Unearned Rent	_____	_____
(e) Office Equipment	_____	_____

	Adjustment	Increased Expense	Increased Revenue
(f)	Trucks	$_____	$_____
(g)	Interest Receivable		
(h)	Wages		
(i)	Interest Payable		

C50.

Adj.	Inc. Exp.	Inc. Rev.
(a)	$500	
(b)	60	
(c)	170	
(d)		$100
(e)	10	
(f)	400	
(g)		12
(h)	150	
(i)	64	

C51. 1,354, 112, 1,242

C52. 5,230, 3,988

C53. No answer required.

D1. The first day of the new accounting period.

D2. opposite

51. Total expenses were increased by $_____, and total revenues were increased by $_____. This is a net increase in expenses in excess of revenues of $_____.

52. Therefore, the net income we computed as $_____ in question 4 is actually going to be $_____.

53. If Genova Trucking Company had not made the adjusting entries in June 1983, the net income for that month would have been in error by about 25 percent. The adjustment process is obviously necessary to get a correct matching of expense and revenue in a period.

D. *Reversing Entries (Appendix)*

1. The reversing entry is made on what date?

_____

2. The reversing entry involves the same accounts as the adjusting entry, but the entry is the _____.

3. In the chapter illustration, the December 31 entry _____ (increases/decreases) expense and _____ (increases/decreases) the liability.

D3. increases, increases

4. The reversing entry on January 1 reduces the liability to a balance of $_____ and creates a balance in the expense account of $_____, _____ (negative/positive).

D4. zero, 1,500, negative

5. The regular payroll entry on January 2 _____ (debits/credits) the expense for $_____. This produces a balance in the expense account of $_____. The proper amount of wages and salaries expense for year 2 would be $_____.

D5. debits, 2,500, 1,000, 1,000

6. The payroll entry on January 2 would be the _____ as every other payroll entry during the year.

D6. same

SELF TEST OF LEARNING GOAL ACHIEVEMENT

1. In one week, Sampson Company had the following transactions:

    a. Purchased $5,000 of fuel for trucks using credit cards.
    b. Hauled twenty contract loads of freight, collecting $9,500 for nine of them and billing customers a total of $13,500 for the other eleven loads.
    c. Paid last month's credit card bills for fuel for a total of $6,000.
    d. Paid no wages, but drivers earned $8,000 that will be paid next week.

    Required: Assuming that there were no other transactions, compute net income on (1) the cash basis and (2) the accrual basis. Explain which basis more accurately reflects the true income and why.

2. Plate Airlines needs financial statements each month for management purposes. Plate owns a fleet of aircraft that are partly paid for and pledged as security for long-term debt on the balance due. Employees are paid on the fifth and twentieth day of each month. Many passengers purchase and pay for tickets in advance.

    Required: List four adjustments that should be made at the end of a typical month, classify them by type, and show their effect on net income. Use the form that follows:

Description of the Adjustment	Accrual or Deferral?	Effect on Income	
		Increase	Decrease

3. Prepare the end-of-period adjusting entries for each of the following situations that exist in Beloit Company on December 31, 1985. At the end of each explanation, show in parentheses whether the entry is an accrual or a deferral.

    a. The company borrowed $10,000 on a note payable at 15 percent interest on December 1, 1985.
    b. A one-year fire insurance policy was purchased on December 1 at a cost of $1,200 and debited to Prepaid Insurance.
    c. The company's $76,000 building was estimated to have a forty-year life and a net salvage value of $4,000. Depreciation is recorded monthly.
    d. The company rents a piece of land it owns to a parking lot operator. Rent is paid in advance quarterly at the rate of $12,000 per year. The last payment was received on December 1, 1985.
    e. Supplies costing $2,800 were purchased on December 15 and debited to Supplies On Hand. A physical count shows that $1,900 of supplies is still on hand.

GENERAL JOURNAL   Page 32

Date		Account Titles and Explanation	F	Debit	Credit

4.   (Appendix)
     Valley Company has accrued interest expense on a loan on December 31, 1985, of $120. If they follow the practice of reversing, record the reversing entry and the payment of $180 in interest on January 21, 1986.

GENERAL JOURNAL   Page 42

Date	Account Titles and Explanation	F	Debit	Credit

ANSWERS TO LEARNING GOAL ACHIEVEMENT TEST

1.

	(1) Cash Basis		(2) Accrual Basis
Revenue:			
Trucking revenue		$9,500	$23,000
Expenses:			
Fuel expense	$6,000		$5,000
Wages expense	0		8,000
Total expenses		6,000	13,000
Net income		$3,500	$10,000

The accrual basis more accurately reflects income because it matches expenses of this week with revenues actually earned this week. Both revenues and expenses exist at the time of incurrence, not when they are collected or paid.

2.

Description of the Adjustment	Accrual or Deferral?	Effect on Income	
		Increase	Decrease
Depreciation of aircraft	Deferral		X
Interest on long-term debt	Accrual		X
Earned but unpaid wages	Accrual		X
Prepaid tickets that have not been used	Deferral	X	

3.

GENERAL JOURNAL   Page 32

Date		Account Titles and Explanation	F	Debit	Credit
1985					
Dec.	31	Interest Expense		125	
		Accrued Interest Payable			125
		December interest on $10,000,			
		15% note (accrual).			
	31	Insurance Expense		100	
		Prepaid Insurance			100
		One month's expiration of $1,200,			
		one-year policy (deferral).			
	31	Depreciation Expense--Building		150	
		Accumulated Depreciation--Building			150
		One month's depreciation on			
		building with a forty-year life			
		(deferral).			
	31	Unearned Rent		1,000	
		Rent Earned			1,000
		One month's rent due on			
		land (accrual).			
	31	Supplies Expense		900	
		Supplies On Hand			900
		Amount of unused supplies			
		on hand (deferral).			

4.

GENERAL JOURNAL   Page 42

Date		Account Titles and Explanation	F	Debit	Credit
1986					
Jan.	1	Accrued Interest Payable		120	
		Interest Expense			120
		To reverse adjustment.			
	21	Interest Expense		180	
		Cash			180
		To record payment of interest.			

Chapter 5
Completion of the Accounting Cycle

■■

EXPLANATION OF MAJOR CONCEPTS

The Work Sheet

Accountants use work sheets to simplify the adjusting and closing process and to organize the information for financial statement preparation. They also use work sheets for other purposes, so it is important that you understand them well now. As you prepare a work sheet, *follow the four steps* discussed in the text. These four steps are:

1. Enter the heading at the top and the unadjusted trial balance in the first set of columns. This step completes the trial balance process and a separate statement is unnecessary.

2. Work out the adjustments and enter them in the second set of columns. An identification key is used to identify the corresponding debits and credits.

3. Combine the amounts in the first set of columns with those in the second set to arrive at the adjusted trial balance in the third set of columns. Remember to keep debits and credits straight as you do this.

4. Extend each amount in the adjusted trial balance columns to one other set of columns, either the income statement columns or the balance sheet columns. Remember to preserve the debit/credit nature of the amount. Total these two sets of columns to determine the net income and balancing of the balance sheet.

As you work through these four steps, the following suggestions should make your work more accurate.

▶ Take each of the steps one at a time. Don't try to use short-cut methods such as moving figures across the work sheet before you reach step 4.

▶ Stop at the end of steps 1, 2, and 3 to total amounts and be sure that you have kept total debits equal to total credits.

▶ *Never* introduce a new figure—for example, an adjustment amount—into the work sheet only once. Every new amount entered into the work sheet *must be entered both as a credit and a debit.*

▶ In step 4, *every amount* in the Adjusted Trial Balance column is moved into one, *and only one,* of the four "working" columns. This means the following:

> *Assets, liabilities,* and *owner's equity* (including drawing) account figures are moved into one of the two Balance Sheet columns. The reason: These figures go on the balance sheet.

> *Revenue* and *expense* figures are moved into one of the two Income Statement columns. The reason: These figures go on the income statement.

▶ Use the work sheet to prepare the financial statements, adjusting entries, and closing entries. *Every dollar amount that you need to perform these tasks is on your work sheet.*

The Financial Statements

The statements in Chapter 5 are excellent models. If you find that you still must look back at a sample to prepare financial statements, take the time now to study the format of the statements in Chapter 5. Make sure that you understand what each section contains. It is important to understand the concept of the statements and not just memorize the format. It will save you a lot of time as the course progresses.

There is a definite sequence for preparation of the financial statements. It follows, with a brief comment on each statement:

1. Prepare the *income statement*. It is just an expansion of the equation, Revenues - Expenses = Net Income. You should first get the individual *revenues* from the Income Statement Credit column of the work sheet. The total revenues on the income statement will be the subtotal of Income Statement Credit column on the work sheet. Next, you should get the individual *expenses* from the Income Statement Debit column. The total of expenses on the income statement would then be the subtotal of the Income Statement Debit column off the work sheet. Subtracting total expenses from total revenues should give you the net income amount that you already have on the work sheet.

2. Prepare the *statement of owner's equity*. Here, you need to select from two sets of columns, as follows:
   a. Take the *beginning* owner's capital figure from the Balance Sheet Credit column.
   b. Add to it the *net income* figure from the income statement or from the work sheet. (You will get a subtotal here.)
   c. Subtract the *drawings* amount that you obtain from the Balance Sheet Debit column.
   d. The result is the ending amount of owner's capital.

3. Prepare the *balance sheet*. Take all the figures except owner's drawing and owner's capital (you've already used them) from the Balance Sheet columns of the work sheet. Follow these simple steps:

   a. The debits are assets. Current assets are listed first; stop at the end of them and compute a subtotal.

   b. Property, plant, and equipment assets are listed next. Be sure to *deduct each contra asset account* from the asset to which it applies. (A common error is to add contra asset accounts to liabilities.)

   c. The credits other than contra assets are liabilities and owner's equity items. List the current liabilities first and subtotal them. Then list long-term liabilities (with a subtotal *if more than one*).

   d. The owner's capital amount in the Balance Sheet Credit column is the beginning figure that you've already used in the statement of owner's equity. For the current balance sheet, obtain the new owner's capital amount from the statement of owner's equity that you have just prepared.

Adjusting and Closing Entries

You are not yet finished with the work sheet. All of the *adjusting entries* and *closing entries* can be journalized directly from the work sheet. The adjusting entries are made first; then, the closing entries are journalized.

For the adjusting entries, go to the Adjustments columns. Starting with adjustment (a), enter the debit(s) and credit(s) and provide an explanation. Then go to adjustments (b), (c), and so on, *until a journal entry has been made for each adjustment*. These entries are then posted to the ledger.

Next, the closing entries are taken from the Income Statement columns. The accounts in the Credit column should be debited for their individual balances, and the subtotal of the credit column on the work sheet is the amount of the credit to Income Summary. Then, each account in the Debit column is credited for its individual balance, and the subtotal of the Debit column on the work sheet is the amount of the debit to Income Summary. This should make the balance in the Income Summary account equal to the amount which was entered as the balancing number in the Income Statement columns. Two final closing entries are needed:

1. Close the Income Summary balance (it is equal to the net income) into the owner's capital account.

2. Close the owner's drawing into the owner's capital account.

These closing entries are then posted to the general ledger. After the posting, the net income and withdrawals have been transferred to the capital account. The owner's capital account balance is now equal to the amount which appeared on the balance sheet. Also, the temporary owner's equity accounts (revenue, expense, and drawing) all have a zero balance. And, the real accounts (asset, liability, and capital) are the only one's with a balance. Take the time at this point to review the accounts in Chapter 5 to see that these summary statements are true.

GUIDED STUDY OF THIS CHAPTER

A. *The Work Sheet.* *Go back to Figure 4-1 and compare the items and dollar amounts in Genova Trucking Company's trial balance with the items and amounts in the Trial Balance columns of the work sheet in Figure 5-3.*

1. Are they the same? _____

A1. Yes.

2. What is the source of the titles and amounts in the trial balance in Figure 4-1?_____

_____

A2. The general ledger accounts.

3. Then it is obvious that the trial balance account titles and amounts on the work sheet could be taken directly from the ledger. Is it necessary to prepare a trial balance as a formal statement before entering it onto the work sheet? _____

A3. No. (It was done in Chapter 4 because the work sheet had not been introduced to you.)

4. Compare the adjustments in Chapter 4 with adjustments (a) through (i) entered on the work sheet in Figure 5-4. Are they the same? _____

A4. Yes.

5. In practice, which comes first--adjustments on the work sheet or the adjusting entries in the journal? _____

A5. Adjustments on the work sheet. (They were introduced in journal form in Chapter 4 because the work sheet had not been explained.)

6. Note that each adjustment in Figure 5-4 is keyed with a letter. Adjustment (a) is in the debit column opposite Rent Expense in amount $_____.

A6. 500

7. Since total debits equal total credits in the work sheet, there must be one or more credits for adjustment (a). Where and in what amount(s)? _____

A7. Opposite Prepaid Rent, $500.

8. Adjustment (c) shows a credit to the asset Office Supplies. Is this credit of $_____ increasing the asset or reducing it? _____

_____

A8.   170, Reducing it.

9.   Where is the debit for adjustment (c)?

_____

A9.   Opposite Office
       Supplies Expense.

10.   Is this debit increasing or reducing Office
       Supplies Expense? _____

A10.   Increasing it.

11.   Go back to Chapter 4 and read the explanation
       of adjustment (c). How much was the asset
       Office Supplies before the end-of-month
       inventory count was taken? $_____ .
       Can this number be found anywhere on the
       work sheet? _____ Where? _____

       _____

A11.   230, Yes, The trial
       balance columns for
       Office Supplies.

12.   The end-of-month count (inventory) shows
       only $_____ of supplies left on hand,
       so usage of office supplies in June must have
       been $_____ .

A12.   60, 170

13.   Therefore, the adjustment on the work sheet
       will show a reduction to the asset by a
       _____ (debit/credit) of $170 and
       an increase in the expense account by a
       _____ (debit/credit) of $170.

A13.   credit, debit

14.   In adjustment (c), a short-term _____
       (cost/revenue) is being apportioned.

A14.   cost

15.   Adjustment (d) shows a $100 debit to
       Unearned Rent. What is the account classi-
       fication for Unearned Rent? _____

A15.   A liability.

16.   Entering a debit to a liability account
       _____ (increases/decreases) it.

A16.   decreases

17.   To what account is the credit for adjustment
       (d) made? _____

A17.   Rent Earned.

18.   The account Rent Earned is a(n) _____
       (expense/revenue) account. A credit of $100
       _____ (increases/decreases) it.

A18.   revenue, increases

19.   So adjustment (d) is a short-term revenue
       apportionment. An original amount of $600
       is being apportioned--$_____ to liability
       and $_____ to revenue.

A19. 500, 100

20. Are the debit and credit totals to the Adjustments columns equal? _____ What is their amount? $_____

A20. Yes, 1,466.

21. Why should total debits always equal total credits in the Adjustments columns?_____

_____

_____

A21. Because each individual adjustment had equal debits and credits.

22. Moving now to Figure 5-5, let's examine the Adjusted Trial Balance columns of the work sheet. Each entry in these columns is the net sum of the Trial Balance and the Adjustments. For example, the $525 debit in Cash is the sum of the Trial Balance debit of $_____ plus $_____ .

A22. 525, zero.

23. In adding the Trial Balance to Adjustments, we must pay attention to debits and credits. In Office Supplies, a debit of $230 added to a credit of $170 equals a debit of $60. In Prepaid Rent a _____ of $_____ added to a _____ of $_____ equals a _____ of $_____ .

A23. debit, 1,500, credit, 500, debit, 1,000

24. In Wages Expense, a _____ of $_____ added to a _____ of $_____ equals a _____ of $_____ .

A24. debit, 1,200, debit, 150, debit, 1,350.

25. The *new accounts* added during the adjustment process must also be brought across to the Adjusted Trial Balance columns. In Accrued Wages Payable, for example, the amount in the Trial Balance columns is $_____ .

A25. zero

26. However, zero added to $150 brings $_____ into the Adjusted Trial Balance Credit column.

A26. 150

27. In the same manner, $_____ of Interest Expense Is brought over to the Adjusted Trial Balance _____ column.

A27. 64, debit

28. The debit and credit totals of the Adjusted Trial Balance columns should be equal. In the Genova example, the totals are both $_____ .

A28. 41,901

29. Once a balanced Adjusted Trial Balance is achieved, *each figure in that column must be moved to one of the columns on the right.* The general rule is to follow the financial statement in which that figure is used. Therefore, you would expect assets to go into the _____ columns.

A29. Balance Sheet

30. Referring to Figure 5-6, trace a few assets. For example, Cash, Accounts Receivable, and Trucks are all moved into the Balance Sheet columns as _____ (debits/credits).

A30. debits

31. Contra asset accounts and liability accounts also help make up the balance sheet. Note that Accumulated Depreciation--Trucks, Accounts Payable, Notes Payable, and Un-earned Rent are all moved into the Balance Sheet columns as _____.

A31. credits

32. Revenues and expenses make up the income statement. It would seem appropriate for those accounts to be moved into the _____ _____ columns.

A32. Income Statement

33. Three revenues are moved into Genova's Income Statement columns as _____ (debits/credits). These three are _____ _____, _____, and _____.

A33. credits, Trucking Revenue, Rent Earned, Interest Earned

34. Expenses are brought to the debit side of the Income Statement columns. Genova's total expenses so transferred were $_____.

A34. 3,589

35. Also on the Totals line, the total revenues were $_____.

A35. 7,577

36. The difference, $_____, is net income. It is entered on the side with the smaller total and labeled "Net Income."

A36. 3,988

37. The same difference is added to the Balance Sheet columns. Since it was inserted into the Income Statement Debit column, it must be carried over to the Balance Sheet _____ column in order to keep debits and credits equal.

A37. Credit

A38. increase

A39. credit

A40. loss

A41. debit, reduces

B1. 3,988

B2. 7,465, 12, 100

B3. 7,577

B4. 3,589

38. It is logical that the net income be entered as a credit in the Balance Sheet columns, because it is going to _____ (increase/decrease) Lucy Genova, Capital, which has a normal credit balance.

39. If expenses had been greater than revenues, the difference would have been added in the Income Statement columns as a _____ to balance.

40. If a credit is needed to balance these columns, there must be a net _____ instead of net income.

41. This would mean a _____ in the Balance Sheet columns because a loss _____ (increases/reduces) owner's equity.

B. *Financial Statements. Let's study the preparation of financial statements. Here is where the usefulness of the work sheet really shows.*

1. We already know that there is a net income and that its amount is $_____.

2. The revenues are taken directly from the work sheet. We can simply list the three revenue accounts and their amounts: $_____, $_____, and $_____.

3. We don't need to add to get their total. The work sheet tells us that it is $_____.

4. We can also list the eleven expense items from the debit column. Again, we don't need to add; the work sheet gives us their total as $_____.

5. We already know net income, but we can subtract total expenses from total revenues on the Income Statement to have an accuracy check. $_____ minus $_____ equals $_____.

B5.   7,577, 3,589, 3,988

6.   The statement of owner's equity can also be taken directly from the work sheet. In Figure 5-8, the $25,000 figure came from the Balance Sheet Credit column. The net income of $_____ is added to it, and drawings of $_____ are subtracted. Both these amounts are in the work sheet.

B6.   3,988, 500

7.   In the same manner, the balance sheet data come from the work sheet. Assets come directly from the debit column; if an asset has a contra account, the contra balance is _____ (added to/ subtracted from) the asset.

B7.   subtracted from

8.   Liabilities come from the Balance Sheet Credit column. We must be careful to *look for current liabilities added to the bottom of the work sheet*. For the Genova Trucking Company, these are _____

and _____.

B8.   Accrued Wages Payable, Accrued Interest Payable

9.   The subtotals, for example, for current assets and current liabilities, are not shown in the work sheet. We must compute them. Also not shown in the work sheet is the new value of the owner's capital account. We get that amount from the statement of _____ _____ just completed.

B9.   owner's equity

10.   Do the totals of the Balance Sheet columns on the work sheet equal total assets and total liabilities and owner's equity on the balance sheet? _____

B10.   No.

11.   Why don't they? _____

_____

_____

_____

B11.   Because the contra accounts are deducted in the balance sheet and the owner's drawing is deducted from the new capital account.

C.   *Adjusting and Closing Entries. Another reason that the work sheet is so useful is that adjusting and closing entries are taken directly from it. Adjustment (a) in the work sheet is the first entry in Figure 5-10, adjustment (b) is the next adjusting entry, and so on.*

C1.   nine

C2.   June 30

C3.   the adjusting entries
       have been posted to
       those accounts

C4.   Income Statement
       Credit

C5.   an offsetting debit
       will make their
       balance zero

C6.   3,589, Income
       Statement columns

C7.   debits

C8.   7,577, 3,589

C9.   zero, reduces

1.   There are nine adjustments on the work sheet
      and _____ adjusting entries.

2.   Each adjusting entry in Figure 5-10 is dated

      _____.

3.   By way of review, the fact that account num-
      bers are entered in the Folio column of
      Figure 5-10 indicates that _____

      _____.

4.   Compare Figures 5-6 and 5-11. The debits
      for the revenue closing entry came directly
      from the _____
      column of the work sheet.

5.   Amounts that are credits in the work sheet
      are debited in the closing entry because

      _____

      _____.

6.   The debit to Income Summary in the second
      closing entry in Figure 5-11 is $_____.
      That amount came from the work sheet as the
      total of _____
      debits.

7.   The expense accounts in closing entry 2 are
      credited because their balances are now
      _____ and we wish to bring the
      balances to zero.

8.   The third and fourth closing entries in Figure
      5-11 also come from the work sheet. The
      Income Summary balance, equal to credits of
      $_____ minus debits of $_____,
      is closed into Lucy Genova, Capital.

9.   Lucy Genova, Drawing, is also a temporary
      account. The last closing entry changes its
      balance to $_____ and _____
      (increases/reduces) Lucy Genova, Capital.

10.   In the general ledger, which accounts do *not*
      now have zero balances? _____

      _____

C10. The real or perma-
nent (asset, liability,
and owner's equity)
accounts.

11. Can you find any revenue or expense account
with a balance? _____ Does the Drawing
account have a balance? _____

C11. No, No.

12. In this entire end-of-period process, the
work sheet has been the key. It is an in-
formal document, but one of the accountants
most important tools. In the Genova illustration, there were only nine adjustments, three
revenues, and eleven expense accounts to
deal with. Can you imagine a company with
a hundred adjustments and as many as two
or three hundred expense accounts to close?
Think of the usefulness of an organized work
sheet in such a situation.

C12. No answer required.

SELF TEST OF LEARNING GOAL ACHIEVEMENT

1. Chapter 5 gave ten steps in the accounting cycle. List them in proper
sequence.

1. _____
2. _____
3. _____
4. _____
5. _____
6. _____
7. _____
8. _____
9. _____
10. _____

2. The following is a trial balance on December 31, 1985, for the Fernandez
Company:

Cash	$ 5
Equipment	30
Accounts Payable	2
Notes Payable	6
Maria Fernandez, Capital	20
Maria Fernandez, Drawing	1
Service Revenue	30
Materials Expense	22

Required:

(1) Enter the trial balance on the following work sheet and complete the work sheet using the following supplementary data:
   a. Depreciation for the year is $3.
   b. Accrued interest on notes payable is $1 on December 31.
   c. Materials inventory, December 31, is $4.

(2) Prepare an income statement, a statement of owner's equity, and a balance sheet.

(3) Prepare the adjusting and closing entries from the work sheet.

(4) Prepare a postclosing trial balance.

(1)

Work Sheet											
Account Title	**Trial Balance**		**Adjustments**		**Adjusted Trial Balance**		**Income Statement**		**Balance Sheet**		
	Dr.	Cr.	Dr.	Cr.	Dr.	Cr.	Dr.	Cr.	Dr.	Cr.	

(2)

Income Statement

Statement of Owner's Equity

Balance Sheet

(3)

GENERAL JOURNAL   Page 4

Date		Account Titles and Explanation	F	Debits	Credits
		Adjusting Entries			

GENERAL JOURNAL   Page 5

Date		Account Titles and Explanation	F	Debit	Credit
		Closing Entries			

(4)

Postclosing Trial Balance

3. Statewide Company recorded the following adjustment on January 31, 1985.

1985					
Jan.	31	Wages Expense		450	
		Accrued Wages Payable			450
		To accrue pay earned on			
		Monday, January 31, but not			
		due until Friday, February 4.			

Payday for the week was Friday, February 4, when employees were paid a total of $1,850.

Required: Record the payment of this payroll, assuming no reversing.

GENERAL JOURNAL   Page 40

Date		Account Titles and Explanation	F	Debit	Credit

ANSWERS TO LEARNING GOAL ACHIEVEMENT TEST

1.
1. Collecting information on business documents.
2. Journalizing.
3. Posting.
4. Preparing the trial balance.
5. Preparing the work sheet.
6. Preparing schedules of accounts receivable or payable.
7. Preparing financial statements.
8. Journalizing and posting adjusting entries.
9. Journalizing and posting closing entries.
10. Preparing the postclosing trial balance.

2.

(1)

FERNANDEZ COMPANY **Work Sheet** **For the Year Ended December 31, 1985**											
Account Title	Trial Balance		Adjustments		Adjusted Trial Balance		Income Statement		Balance Sheet	
	Dr.	Cr.	Dr.	Cr.	Dr.	Cr.	Dr.	Cr.	Dr.	Cr.
Cash	5				5				5	
Equipment	30				30				30	
Accounts Payable		2				2				2
Notes Payable		6				6				6
M. Fernandez, Capital		20				20				20
M. Fernandez, Drawing	1				1				1	
Service Revenue		30				30		30		
Materials Expense	22			(c) 4	18		18			
Totals	58	58								
Depr. Expense--Equipment			(a) 3		3		3			
Accum. Depr.--Equipment				(a) 3		3				3
Interest Expense			(b) 1		1		1			
Accrued Interest Payable				(b) 1		1				1
Materials On Hand			(c) 4		4				4	
Totals			8	8	62	62	22	30	40	32
Net Income							8			8
Totals							30	30	40	40

(2)   FERNANDEZ COMPANY   Exhibit A
                                   Income Statement
                          For the Year Ended December 31, 1985

Revenue:
  Service revenue $30
Expenses:
  Materials expense $18
  Depreciation expense--equipment   3
  Interest expense   1
    Total expenses   22
Net income . . . . $ 8

                                 FERNANDEZ COMPANY   Exhibit B
                              Statement of Owner's Equity
                          For the Year Ended December 31, 1985

Maria Fernandez, capital, January 1, 1985 . . . . $20
  Add: Net income for 1985   8
    Subtotal $28
  Deduct: Withdrawals   1
Maria Fernandez, capital, December 31, 1985 . . . . $27

                                 FERNANDEZ COMPANY   Exhibit C
                                    Balance Sheet
                                  December 31, 1985

                                        Assets

Current assets:
  Cash . . . . $ 5
  Materials on hand   4
    Total current assets . . . . $ 9
Property, plant, and equipment:
  Equipment $30
  Deduct: Accumulated depreciation--Equipment.   3   27
Total assets $36

                           Liabilities and Owner's Equity

Current liabilities:
  Accounts payable . . . . $ 2
  Notes payable   6
  Accrued interest payable   1
    Total liabilities . . . . $ 9
Owner's equity:
  Maria Fernandez, capital   27
Total liabilities and owner's equity $36

(3)

GENERAL JOURNAL   Page 4

Date		Account Titles and Explanation	F	Debit	Credit
1985		Adjusting Entries			
Dec.	31	Depreciation Expense--Equipment		3	
		Accumulated Depreciation--Equipment			3
		To record depreciation for 1985.			
	31	Interest Expense		1	
		Accrued Interest Payable			1
		To record accrued interest			
		on notes payable.			
	31	Materials On Hand		4	
		Materials Expense			4
		To recognize materials			
		unused at end of year.			

GENERAL JOURNAL   Page 5

Date		Account Titles and Explanation	F	Debit	Credit
1985		Closing Entries			
Dec.	31	Service Revenue		30	
		Income Summary			30
		To close revenue account.			
	31	Income Summary		22	
		Materials Expense			18
		Depreciation Expense			3
		Interest Expense			1
		To close expense accounts			
	31	Income Summary		8	
		Maria Fernandez, Capital			8
		To close net income.			
	31	Maria Fernandez, Capital		1	
		Maria Fernandez, Drawing			1
		To close drawing account.			

(4)

FERNANDEZ COMPANY
Postclosing Trial Balance
December 31, 1985

Account Title	Debits	Credits
Cash	$ 5	
Materials On Hand	4	
Equipment	30	
Accumulated Depreciation--Equipment		$ 3
Accounts Payable		2
Notes Payable		6
Accrued Interest Payable		1
Maria Fernandez, Capital		27
Totals	$39	$39

3.

GENERAL JOURNAL   Page 40

Date		Account Titles and Explanation	F	Debit	Credit
1985					
Feb.	4	Accrued Wages Payable		450	
		Wages Expense		1,400	
		Cash			1,850
		Payment of payroll for week.			

Chapter 6
Accounting for a Merchandising Firm

■■

EXPLANATION OF MAJOR CONCEPTS

Merchandising Accounts

Up to this point, you have studied accounting only for firms that earned revenue by providing services. In Chapter 6, you will be dealing with accounting procedures for businesses that earn revenue by selling products or goods. These are called *merchandising firms*. They do not manufacture the goods they sell; they buy goods at wholesale (or cost) price and resell these goods at retail (or sales) price. To record purchase and resale transactions, we need to add a new group of accounts--the merchandising accounts--to the general ledger.

It will be helpful to review the merchandising accounts and their use. The Sales account is a revenue account and is used to record the revenues received from the sale of goods. *Like other revenue accounts*, it is credited to record increases. Accordingly, it has a *normal credit balance*. Rather than directly reduce the Sales account when goods are returned by buyers or a price concession is granted to a buyer after they have taken delivery of the goods, a contra sales account is used. Two common contra sales accounts are Sales Returns and Allowances and Sales Discounts. Since they reduce sales, these accounts have *normal debit balances* and are *increased with debits*.

The other merchandising accounts relate to the purchase of merchandise for resale. Purchases is an account used to record the invoice price of merchandise purchased. While it is not an expense account in the sense that Salaries and Wages Expense is, it has the same effect on owner's equity. It is debited to record increases when merchandise is purchased and its *normal balance is debit*. Contra purchases accounts also exist to record transactions which decrease total purchases but for which the separate information is necessary for management. Purchases Returns and Allowances is used to record the cost of merchandise returns or price concessions granted to keep the merchandise. It is increased with a debit and has a normal balance of debit. Purchases Discounts is used to record reductions in the amounts which must be paid because of early payment. It also is increased with debits and has a normal balance of debit.

Accounting with the merchandise accounts is summarized in the table on the following page.

Account	Increase	Decrease	Normal Balance
Revenue accounts:			
Sales	CR	DR	CR
Contra revenues:			
Sales Returns and Allowances	DR	CR	DR
Sales Discounts	DR	CR	DR
Cost of goods sold accounts:			
Purchases	DR	CR	DR
Transportation In	DR	CR	DR
Contra purchases:			
Purchases Returns and Allowances	CR	DR	CR
Purchases Discounts	CR	DR	CR
Current asset account:			
Merchandise Inventory	DR	CR	DR

A further review of the uses of these accounts can be found in the section of the chapter entitled *Functions of the Merchandise Accounts*. As you study the accounts in this chapter, be sure to note that entries to other than the normal side are not made except to close the account. If, for example, you find yourself crediting Sales Discounts and you are not closing the account, something must be wrong.

Merchandise Inventory

The method of handling Merchandise Inventory on the work sheet is diagrammed in Figure 6-3. Note that the amount which appears in the Trial Balance Debit column is the beginning inventory balance. This amount is carried across to the Income Statement Debit column. No adjustments are entered for this account, even though the ending amount is usually given to you in problems with the adjustment data. The ending (new) inventory amount is entered in the Income Statement Credit column and also the Balance Sheet Debit column. By entering this new amount in both a Debit and a Credit column, we preserve the equality of debits and credits on the work sheet.

Discounts

Cash discounts are used in business to encourage people to pay their bills early. Two accounting methods are described: the gross method and the net method. *Learn the gross method first.* After you understand it, the net method of recording discounts will be easier for you to understand.

Do not confuse cash discounts with trade discounts. Trade discounts are simply devices to determine the invoice price or cost. Trade discounts are not shown in the accounting records; we record items at the price determined after deduction of the trade discount.

Sales Taxes Payable

In most states, a retail business must collect sales taxes on sales to the consumer. Since the business is simply acting as a collecting agent for the state government, the receipt of the sales tax from the customer represents a liability to the state. Thus, when a sale is made, the seller credits the Sales account for the retail price of the merchandise and Sales Taxes Payable for the amount of the sales tax.

Work Sheet and Financial Statements

There is really no basic difference between the work sheet and financial statements for a service business and those for a merchandising business. In the work sheet, you must handle the merchandising accounts carefully. Remember the discussion of merchandising accounts in the first part of this explanation; watch for obvious errors in making debits and credits.

The merchandise accounts are used in the income statement to determine and show the gross margin which a firm earns on sales. You must learn how to set up this section of the income statement. Start your amounts in the right-hand column, moving to the left to develop subtotals. A summary of the top portion of the income statement for a merchandising firm is shown below. Notice the details of the computation of net sales revenue, cost of goods sold, and gross margin.

FIRM NAME
Partial Income Statement
For the *period* Ended *date*

Gross sales revenue			$ X
Deduct: Sales returns and allowances		$ X	
Sales discounts		X	X
Net sales revenue			$ X
Cost of goods sold:			
Merchandise inventory, beginning		$ X	
Purchases	$ X		
Transportation In	X		
Gross delivered cost of purchases	$ X		
Deduct: Purchases returns and			
allowances	$ X		
Purchases discounts	X	X	
Net cost of purchases		X	
Cost of merchandise available for sale		$ X	
Deduct: Merchandise inventory, ending . . .		X	
Cost of goods sold			X
Gross margin on sales			$ X

Note that the income statement in Figure 6-2 shows only the primary revenue, Sales, at the top. Secondary revenues, such as Interest earned and Rent earned, are shown as "other revenues" in a special section at the bottom of the statement. In like manner, only the operating expenses are shown in the expense section;

nonoperating expenses are shown as "other expenses" at the bottom of the statement. You should use this form of income statement from now on.

The balance sheet for a merchandising business is very little different from that of a service business studied in the first five chapters. Since Merchandise Inventory is a new current asset account, it will appear in the balance sheet. Note in Figure 6-7 that Merchandise Inventory is included in the current assets section between Accounts Receivable and the prepaid expenses.

GUIDED STUDY OF THIS CHAPTER

A. Merchandising Accounts. Let's try to gain a thorough understanding of these accounts at the beginning.

1. Sales is a *revenue* account. Each time a sale is recorded, we are representing _____ (a decrease/an increase) in revenue.

A1.   an increase

2. Since an increase in a revenue is a _____ (debit/credit), we should journalize a _____ (debit/credit) to the Sales account when goods are sold.

A2.   credit, credit

3. Do we wait until sales are paid for before recording them as revenue? _____

A3.   No.

4. When we journalize a sale that we make on account (for credit), what account is debited?

_____

A4.   Accounts Receivable

5. It is, of course, normal that some sales are made for cash. In that case, we debit the _____ account while crediting Sales.

A5.   Cash

6. In any business, customers may return merchandise because it is the wrong size or for many other reasons. Accepting such returns and giving the customer credit for them _____ (increases/decreases) total revenue from sales.

A6.   decreases

7. A decrease in a revenue is a debit, but if we debit Sales for such returns, there is no easy way for a manager to know how frequently this sort of thing is happening. Therefore, we debit a contra account called _____

_____.

A7.   Sales Returns and
       Allowances

8.   When Sales Returns and Allowances is debited,
     the account usually credited is _____

     _____ .

A8.   Accounts Receivable

9.   Cash discounts on sales are offered to en-
     courage customers to pay earlier. Discounts
     on sales would _____ (increase/
     decrease) revenue.

A9.   decrease

10.   Accordingly, we would debit another contra
      account when customers take advantage of
      cash discounts that we offer. It is called

      _____ .

A10.   Sales Discounts

11.   How would you determine *net sales revenue*
      for any accounting period? _____

      _____

      _____

A11.   Subtract both sales
        returns and allow-
        ances and sales
        discounts from sales.

12.   Purchases is a merchandising account that is
      debited only with the cost of _____

      _____ .

A12.   goods acquired to
        be resold

13.   Therefore, would Purchases be debited with
      the cost of paper clips bought to be used in
      the accounting department? _____

A13.   No.

14.   What account would be debited for the paper
      clips? _____

A14.   Office Supplies or
        Office Expense.

15.   Is the actual inventory of goods for resale
      being increased each time we purchase mer-
      chandise for stock? _____

A15.   Yes.

16.   And, isn't the actual inventory of goods
      being decreased each time we make a sale?

      _____

A16.   Yes.

17.   Then why don't we make continuing debits
      and credits to the Merchandise Inventory
      account for these transactions? _____

      _____

      _____

      _____

      _____

A 17. We are using a *periodic inventory system* in which changes to the Merchandise Inventory account are determined by physical count at the end of each period.

18. How do we maintain a record of cost of new goods purchased for resale during a period?

_____

_____

_____

_____

A 18. By debiting the Purchases account each time so that total gross purchases accumulate therein.

19. How do we keep a record of cost of the merchandise that we sell in daily operations?

_____

_____

_____

A 19. We don't. The *cost of goods sold* must be computed after we take a physical count.

20. As in the case of sales, it is helpful to management to separate the gross cost of purchases. The amount of returns or allowances for defective merchandise are shown in a contra Purchases account called _____

_____.

A 20. Purchases Returns and Allowances

21. Since the Purchases account has a normal _____ (debit/credit) balance, any account contra to it should have a normal _____ (debit/credit) balance.

A 21. debit, credit

22. The _____ account is used to record the cash discount allowed for early payments on merchandise.

A 22. Purchases Discounts

23. The Purchases Discounts account is increased with a _____ (debit/credit).

A 23. credit

24. Purchases (net) means purchases minus _____ and

_____.

A 24. purchases discounts, purchases returns and allowances

25. Show, in summary, a computation to determine the cost of goods sold in a period.

_____

_____

_____

_____

A25. Beginning inventory + purchases (net) = total available – ending inventory = cost of goods sold.

26. The difference between net sales and cost of goods sold is called _____ _____.

A26. gross margin on sales

27. Go to Figure 6-2 in the textbook. The net sales revenue of $_____ resulted from deductions of $2,400 and $_____ from gross sales revenue.

A27. 120,000, 1,800

28. The Sales account of Tarrant Wholesale Company had a _____ (debit/credit) balance of $_____ on December 31, 1985.

A28. credit, 124,200

29. Sales Discounts had a _____ (debit/credit) balance of $1,800 on the same date, and Sales Returns and Allowances had a _____ (debit/credit) balance of $2,400.

A29. debit, debit

30. The beginning inventory for 1985 was $_____; it was a _____ (debit/credit) balance in the Merchandise Inventory account.

A30. 15,400, debit

31. The Purchases account had a _____ (debit/credit) balance of $_____ on December 31, 1985. Also, Transportation In had a _____ (debit/credit) balance of $_____.

A31. debit, 63,580, debit, 4,800

32. Therefore, transportation in appears to be an addition to the cost of goods sold and not an operating expense. Is this correct?_____

A32. Yes.

33. Is transportation in a part of net purchases? _____

A33. Yes.

34. What other items are considered to be a part of net purchases?_____

A34. Purchases returns and allowances and purchases discounts.

35. What was the total cost of merchandise available for sale by the Tarrant Wholesale Company in the year 1985? $_____

A35. 78,680.

36. How much of this remained unsold on December 31, 1985? $_____

A36. 11,480.

37. This, of course, is the ending inventory. How is it determined? _____

_____

A37. By physical count.

38. Deducting the ending inventory from total goods available indicates that goods costing $_____ were sold in 1985.

A38. 67,200

39. Subtracting this amount from net sales shows a gross margin on sales of $_____ .

A39. 52,800

40. Gross margin on sales is sometimes called *gross profit*. It is equal to net sales minus

_____.

A40. cost of goods sold

B.   *Merchandise Inventory Account*

1. Tarrant Wholesale Company had a merchandise inventory of $_____ on January 1, 1985.

B1. 15,400

2. This is the account balance in Merchandise Inventory on December 31, 1984. It was determined by _____.

B2. physical count

3. Since cost of goods sold by Tarrant in 1985 was $67,200, it is obvious that additional merchandise was purchased. It was not debited to the Merchandise Inventory account, but to the _____ account.

B3. Purchases

4. In Figure 6-3, what is shown as being done to the beginning balance in Merchandise Inventory? _____

_____

B4. It is extended to the Income Statement Debit column of the work sheet.

5. Let's move to Figure 6-4. To what column is the Purchases amount extended? _____

_____

B5. Income Statement Debit

6. So, these two amounts, along with others, are reflecting _____ (an increase/a decrease) in cost of goods sold.

B6.   an increase

7.   Going back to Figure 6-3, what is the amount of the ending inventory? $_____
We see that this amount is inserted in the work sheet as a debit in the Balance Sheet column and a credit in the _____ _____ column.

B7.   11,480, Income Statement

8.   The credit in the Income Statement columns will reflect _____ (an increase/ a decrease) in cost of goods sold.

B8.   a decrease

9.   It makes sense that ending inventory should be a decrease in cost of goods sold because this is the portion of total goods available for sale that is left _____.

B9.   on hand or unsold

10.   In the balance sheet, it should be classified as a _____.

B10.   current asset

11.   In Figure 6-7, the amount of inventory shown in the current assets is $_____.

B11.   11,480

12.   This is, of course, the new December 31, 198__, amount determined by physical count.

B12.   5

13.   Remember not to make an adjustment for the new inventory; instead insert it in the work sheet in the _____ Debit column and the _____ Credit column.

B13.   Balance Sheet, Income Statement

14.   The inventory amount _____ (will/ will not) be part of the *adjusting* entries.

B14.   will not

C.   *Closing Entries*

1.   The closing entries are taken directly from the work sheet after the statements are prepared and after the _____ are journalized and posted.

C1.   adjusting entries.

2.   Figure 6-8 illustrates the closing entries. The new inventory amount is entered by a _____ (debit/credit) to Merchandise Inventory and a credit to _____ _____.

C2.   debit, Income
      Summary

3.   The old (beginning) inventory amount is
     closed out by a _____ to Merchan-
     dise Inventory and a debit to _____
     _____.

C3.   credit, Income
      Summary

4.   How many of the other merchandising
     accounts are closed to Income Summary?

     _____

C4.   All of them.

5.   Does the cost of goods sold show as a separate
     amount in Income Summary? _____
     Explain. _____
     _____

C5.   No. The expense
      and revenue accounts
      are in the same entry.

6.   So, is it correct that we must compute cost of
     goods sold by using selected amounts from
     the work sheet? _____

C6.   Yes. (They are
      shown in boldface
      type in Figure 6-8.)

7.   Are entries to close Income Summary and the
     Drawing accounts different in a merchandising
     firm from such entries for a service firm?

     _____

C7.   No.

8.   When the closing entries shown in Figure 6-8
     are posted, which of those accounts (if any)
     do *not* have a zero balance? _____
     _____

C8.   Merchandise Inven-
      tory and Lucy
      Genova, Capital.

D.   *Discounts. The Tarrant Wholesale Company
     granted sales discounts to customers in 1985
     amounting to $1,800, discussed in the "Sales
     Revenue Accounts" section of the chapter.*

1.   On December 6, 1985, Tarrant made a credit
     sale of $200 to John Roundtree. The *cash
     discount* terms were 2/10, n/30, as shown in
     Figure 6-1. This means that Roundtree may
     deduct _____ percent from the invoice price
     if he pays within _____ days.

D1.   2, ten

2.   On December 9, 1985, Roundtree returned
     $_____ of defective goods, leaving him owing
     a balance of $_____ to Tarrant Wholesale.

D2.   10, 190

3.   John Roundtree paid the balance due on
     December 16, 1985. This _____ (is/is
     not) within the discount period of ten days.

D3. is

D4. 3.80

D5. 186.20, 190

D6. Sales Discounts

D7. No.

D8. 196
        196

4. So Roundtree is entitled to deduct 2 percent, or $_____, from the balance due.

5. Roundtree actually paid only $_____; however, Accounts Receivable is credited with the full $_____ remaining due.

6. The discount taken, $3.80, is debited to the account _____.

7. The foregoing is an illustration of the gross price method. Accounts Receivable is debited with the full amount of the sale. If the customer pays within the discount period, Accounts Receivable is credited with the full amount due. Cash, however, will be less. The remainder shows as a debit to Sales Discounts. Under this procedure, we know the total amount of discounts taken by customers; do we also know the amount of discounts not taken (or lost)? _____

8. Using the net method, we would know the amount of discounts lost (not taken) but would not know the amount of discounts taken. If Tarrant Wholesale Company used this method, the sale to Roundtree would be recorded *net of discount* as follows:

Date		Account Titles	F	Debit	Credit
1985					
Dec.	6	Accounts Receivable			
		Sales			
		Sold merchandise			
		on account.			

9. And the return of December 9 would be credited to Accounts Receivable in the amount of $_____, leaving a balance due of $_____.

D9.   9.80, 186.20

10.   The payment entry of December 16 would be recorded as:

1985					
Dec.	14	Cash			
		Accounts Receivable			

D10.   186.20

           186.20

11.   Would there be any indication of the discount taken in this case? _____

D11.   No.

12.   But if Roundtree did not pay until December 24 (and lost the discount), the collection entry would be:

1985					
Dec.	24	Cash	190.00		
		Sales Discounts			
		Not Taken			?
		Accounts Receivable			186.20

D12.   3.80 (credit).

13.   The Sales Discounts Not Taken account accumulates the amount of discounts that customers failed to take. This may be less important to the seller than it is to the buyer.

D13.   No answer required.

14.   Study the example of recording of purchases discounts by the net method that follows the closing entries. If recorded by the gross method, the $5,000 purchase from Ace Company would appear as follows:

1985					
Jul.	5	Purchases	5,000		
		Accounts Payable			5,000

D14. No answer required.

15. If not paid until July 30, the payment entry would be:

1985					
Jul.	30	Accounts Payable			
		Cash			

D15. 5,000

          5,000

16. Would management be aware that a $100 purchase discount had been lost? _____

D16. No.

17. But if recorded by the net method as illustrated in the textbook, a payment on July 30 would require a $100 debit in the account

_____.

D17. Purchases Discounts Lost

18. Purchases Discounts Lost is an expense account and would show as an expense in the _____ statement.

D18. income

19. Thus, management _____ (would/would not) know amounts of cash discounts taken.

D19. would not

20. But the amount of lost discounts _____ (would/would not) be known.

D20. would

E. *Other Topics*

1. Many states require that a retailer collect sales tax from the customer. Is this a revenue to the retailer? _____

E1. No.

2. If it is not a revenue and the retailer has received cash or an account receivable, what is the credit recorded to? _____

E2. A liability.

3. Why is it recorded to a liability? _____

_____

_____

_____

E3.   Because the retailer is simply collecting it for the state and owes it to the government.

4.   If merchandise with a list price of $500.00 had been purchased with a trade discount of 10 percent, 20 percent, and 5 percent, Purchases would have been debited for the invoice price of $_____ .

E4.   342.00   If you got this wrong, follow the illustration in the book using the percentages given here.

SELF TEST OF LEARNING GOAL ACHIEVEMENT

1.   Indicate whether each of the following is true or false (based on a periodic inventory system):

_____a.   Recurring purchases and sales of merchandise during a year are *not* recorded as continuous increases or decreases to the Merchandise Inventory account.

_____b.   The net cost of goods purchased during an accounting period can be determined by examining the entries to the Purchases account.

_____c.   Purchases Discounts is an account that reflects reductions in amounts paid for purchases.

_____d.   Sales Discounts is an account that reflects reductions in amounts collected for sales.

_____e.   Both the Purchases Discounts and Sales Discounts accounts are increased by debits.

_____f.   The beginning inventory of 1985 is the same as the ending inventory of 1984.

_____g.   The balance of Transportation In must be added to the Purchases balance to determine the gross delivered cost of purchases.

_____h.   The ending inventory valuation *must* be determined by a computation using data from the other merchandising accounts.

_____i.   The term 2/10, n/30 means that a 2 percent discount may be taken if the bill is paid in thirty days.

_____j.   A purchase of $3,000 of merchandise with terms of 2/10, n/30 recorded using the *purchases discounts lost method* would be debited to Purchases at $2,940.

2. Compute the missing figures in each of the following cases:

	Case A	Case B	Case C
Beginning inventory	$200	$ 100	$?
Purchases	800	1,000	500
Transportation in	50	50	10
Purchases discounts	20	30	5
Purchases returns and allowances	?	60	15
Total goods available for sale	990	?	540
Ending inventory	?	80	?
Cost of goods sold	840	?	510

3. The following is a partial work sheet for the Wappacoma Company:

Account Title	Trial Balance		Adjustments		Adjusted Trial Balance		Income Statement		Balance Sheet	
	Dr.	Cr.	Dr.	Cr.	Dr.	Cr.	Dr.	Cr.	Dr.	Cr.
Merchandise Inven.										

The beginning inventory is $400; the ending inventory is $450.

Required: Enter the inventory amounts in all columns in which they would normally appear when the work sheet is completed.

4. Following are some of the December 31, 1985, account balances from Your Computer Retailer Company:

Account Title	Debits	Credits
Merchandise Inventory	$ 1,200	
Suzie Ling, Capital		$12,270
Suzie Ling, Drawing	8,000	
Sales		90,000
Sales Discounts	300	
Sales Returns and Allowances	800	
Purchases	50,000	
Purchases Discounts		1,000
Purchases Returns and Allowances		400
Transportation In	900	
Selling Expenses	4,000	

The ending inventory is $1,800.

Required:
(1) Record the closing entries.
(2) Compute the cost of goods sold.

(1)

GENERAL JOURNAL   Page 36

Date		Account Titles and Explanation	F	Debit	Credit

(2)

5. Sammual Martin Company sold merchandise to Dale Simons. The list price was
    $10,000 subject to a trade discount of 20, 10, and 5 percent. The invoice is
    further subject to a cash discount of 2/10, n/30.

    Required:
    (1) Compute the amount Simons should pay if the invoice is paid thirty days
         after date.
    (2) Compute the amount Simons should pay if the invoice is paid nine days
         after date.
    (3) Explain how the trade discount should be recorded in the accounting
         records.
    (4) Explain how the cash discount would be shown in the accounting records:
         a. If lost and the *purchases discounts lost procedure* is used.
         b. If taken and the gross price method is used.

    (1)

    (2)

    (3)

    (4a)

    (4b)

ANSWERS TO LEARNING GOAL ACHIEVEMENT TEST

1. a. T
    b. F (must also consider transportation in, discounts, and returns and allowances)
    c. T
    d. T
    e. F (Purchases Discounts is increased by a credit)
    f. T
    g. T
    h. F (it is determined by physical count)
    i. F (must pay in ten days to take discount)
    j. T

2.

	Case A	Case B	Case C
Beginning inventory			$50
Purchases returns and allowances	$ 40		
Total goods available for sale		$1,060	
Ending inventory	150		30
Cost of goods sold		980	

3.

Account Title	Trial Balance		Adjustments		Adjusted Trial Balance		Income Statement		Balance Sheet	
	Dr.	Cr.	Dr.	Cr.	Dr.	Cr.	Dr.	Cr.	Dr.	Cr.
Merchandise Inven.	400				400		400	450	450	

4.

(1)

| | GENERAL JOURNAL | | | Page 36 |

Date		Account Titles and Explanation	F	Debit	Credit
1985		Closing Entries			
Dec.	31	Sales		90,000	
		Purchases Discounts		1,000	
		Purchases Returns and Allowances		400	
		Merchandise Inventory		1,800	
		Income Summary			93,200
		To close the revenue, credit			
		balance merchandising accounts,			
		and enter the ending inventory.			

	31	Income Summary		57,200	
		Merchandise Inventory			1,200
		Sales Discounts			300
		Sales Returns and Allowances			800
		Purchases			50,000
		Transportation In			900
		Selling Expenses			4,000
		To close the beginning inventory, debit balance merchandising accounts and expense account.			
	31	Income Summary		36,000	
		Suzie Ling, Capital			36,000
		To close net income.			
	31	Suzie Ling, Capital		8,000	
		Suzie Ling, Drawing			8,000
		To close the drawing account.			

(2)

Computation of cost of goods sold:

Merchandise inventory, January 1, 1985 . . .			$ 1,200
Purchases	$50,000		
Transportation In	900		
Gross delivered cost of purchases	$50,900		
Deduct: Purchases returns and allowances .	$1,000		
Purchases discounts	400	1,400	
Net cost of purchases			49,500
Cost of merchandise available for sale . . .			$50,700
Deduct: Merchandise inventory, December 31, 1985			1,800
Cost of goods sold			$48,900

5.　(1)　$10,000
　　　　　－ 2,000　(20% of $10,000)
　　　　　$ 8,000
　　　　　－　 800　(10% of $8,000)
　　　　　$ 7,200
　　　　　－　 360　(5% of $7,200)
　　　　　$ 6,840　invoice price　　OR $10,000 x 0.80 x 0.90 x 0.95 = $6,840

　　(2)　$6,840 – (0.02 x $6,840) = $6,703.20.

　　(3)　It is not recorded in the records. It serves to determine the invoice price.

　　(4a)　It would be shown as a debit to Purchases Discounts Lost in the amount of $136.80.

　　(4b)　It would be shown as a credit to Purchases Discounts in the amount of $136.80.

Chapter 7
An Introduction to Accounting Systems: Special Journals

■■■

EXPLANATION OF MAJOR CONCEPTS

An Accounting System

An *accounting system* is the set of forms and business papers, journals and ledgers, and accounting equipment and the rules and procedures that tie all of them together to:

1. Capture information about transactions.
2. Record it in an organized and understandable way.
3. Use it to prepare reports that are useful for making decisions.

There is no one best accounting system. For each entity, the accountant must design a system that suits the unique needs of that organization. Sometimes a simple system with only a general journal and ledger accounts will be adequate. As the entity becomes larger and more complex, the accounting system must contain more journals and equipment.

Systems are divided into 3 parts--input, processing, and output. In an accounting system the input is represented by the source documents which form the basis for the entries into the accounting system. The processing consists of the operations performed to record and classify the input data for use in accounting reports. The output from the accounting system includes the financial statements and management reports. The flow from the source of input to the use of the output should take into consideration the following questions:

Where will the data be found and stored?
Who will use the information?
How will the information be used?
When will the information be used?

Special Journals

Special journals are an addition to--*not a replacement for*--the general journal. An accounting system can operate without special journals, but it must always include a general journal. Because the special journals illustrated in Chapter 7 are clearly illustrated and explained, there is no need to repeat explanations here. These suggestions are offered to help you understand their use.

▶ Regardless of its name or special nature, a *journal* is still a book of original entry. A transaction is first recorded in one *(and only one)* of the journals; from there it is posted to ledger accounts.

▶ Ledger accounts receive postings directly from all of the journals. Postings from special journals are *not* run through the general journal.

▶ So that ledger account entries can be accurately traced back to the journals, it is important to use correctly the symbols, S, P, CR, CP, and J, when posting to accounts in the general ledger *and in the subsidiary ledgers*.

▶ Introducing special journals into the system does not destroy the journal/ledger relationship that you have already learned. Nor does it affect the use of a work sheet. It simply expands and makes the use of the journals more efficient in recording transactions from business papers.

▶ To determine which journal to use for any transaction, a specific decision process is suggested. Ask the questions indicated in the following chart. Whenever the answer is *yes*, you have found the proper journal.

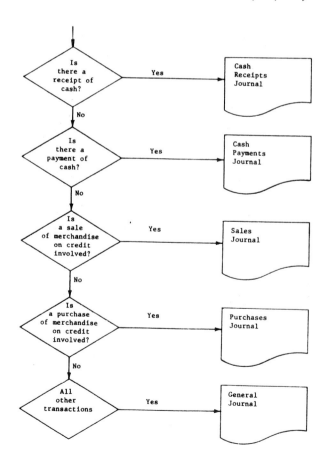

The posting of special journals can be summarized as follows:

Special Journal	Posting
Special columns provided for a single account (with no subsidiary ledger).	Post the total to the appropriate general ledger account. Do not post the individual amounts.
Special columns provided for an account with a subsidiary ledger.	Post the total to the appropriate general ledger account and the individual amounts to the appropriate subsidiary ledger account.
Other accounts columns.	Post the individual amount to the appropriate general ledger account, and do not post the total.

Automated Processing

With the significant decreases in the cost of computer systems, more and more businesses are able to afford computerized accounting systems. Owners of the smallest retail stores are finding that they are able to computerize their accounting with the use of a micro-computer. Thus, computerized accounting systems are today found in business from the very smallest to the very largest. The principles of accounting which you are learning in this text are just as appropriate to these computerized systems as they are to the manual systems which are being illustrated here. Instead of the records being in human readable form as they are in the text, they are recorded magnetically on disk or tape. The computer simplifies the recording process, eliminates all of the mathematics, and speeds up the preparation and dissemination of accounting reports. But, the fundamentals which you are learning still apply. (You may be using one or more of the computerized practice sets which accompany the text to achieve a basic understanding of what the computer can accomplish.)

GUIDED STUDY OF THIS CHAPTER

A. *Special Journals. Let's establish clearly the rules for the type of journal to be used. Refer to the flow chart on page 130 of the Study Guide if necessary.*

1. The cash receipts journal is used to record every transaction that involves _____

_____ .

A1.   a receipt of cash

2.   If the cash receipt is for a sale of merchandise, the entry would be recorded in the _____ journal.

A2.   cash receipts

3.   However, a sale of merchandise for credit would be recorded in the _____ journal.

A3.   sales

4.   If the item being sold for credit were a piece of office equipment, it would be entered in the _____ journal.

A4.   general (It is not a sale of merchandise.)

5.   Collections of accounts receivable follow sales for credit. Such collections are entered in the _____ journal.

A5.   cash receipts

6.   If the collection is only a partial payment (not payment in full) for a sale, it should be entered in the _____ journal.

A6.   cash receipts

7.   A purchase of office supplies on credit should be entered in the _____ journal.

A7.   general

8.   A purchase of merchandise for credit should be entered in the _____ journal.

A8.   purchases

9.   If we pay cash for a purchase of merchandise, we should enter the transaction in the _____ journal.

A9.   cash payments

10.   If we pay cash for office supplies, we should make the entry in the _____ journal.

A10.   cash payments

11.   A return of erroneous merchandise to us from a customer should be entered in the _____ journal.

A11.   general

12.   Payment of rent in advance should be entered in the _____ journal.

A12.   cash payments (The fact that the payment is in advance has no bearing on the journal to use.)

13.   Adjusting entries would be made in the _____ journal.

A13.   general

14.   Closing entries would be made in the _____ journal.

A14. general

A15. cash receipts

A16. general

A17. cash payments

A18. No. (Only credit purchases of merchandise.)

A19. No. (If cash is involved, the entry goes in a cash journal.)

A21. fewer, divided

B3. Yes. They are posted to the customer's account in the accounts receivable ledger and to the general ledger.

---

15. If an owner invests cash in a business, it would be entered in the _____ _____ journal.

16. If an owner invests store equipment in a business, the transaction would be entered in the _____ journal.

17. A $10,000 contribution by a business to a local college would be entered in the _____ _____ journal of the business.

18. Is it true that every credit purchase should be entered in the purchases journal? _____

19. Is there any instance in which a transaction involving payment or receipt of cash would be entered in a journal *other than* the cash journals? _____

20. Special journals will strengthen internal control. The general ledger will be more compact and less likely to contain errors because it will contain _____ entries. Also, because we have separate journals for different categories of transactions, the recording duties can be _____ among employees.

B. *Posting. Let's study Figure 7-4.*

1. Are sales of merchandise posted twice? _____ Explain. _____

_____

_____

2. Are both postings made at the same time? _____ Explain. _____

_____

_____

_____

B2.   No. Individual postings to the accounts receivable ledger are made daily, but postings to the general ledger are made monthly.

3.   Is the same relationship true of collections of accounts receivable? _____ From what journal are such collections posted? _____

_____

B3.   Yes. Cash receipts journal.

4.   To follow through on sales postings, turn to Figure 7-6. When is the $400 sale to Shirley Lloyd posted to her account in the subsidiary ledger? _____

_____

B4.   On June 7, 1985, the date the sale was made.

5.   When is this sale posted to Accounts Receivable in the general ledger? _____

_____

B5.   On June 30, 1985, when the total is posted.

6.   Won't the controlling account and the subsidiary ledger be out of balance during June? _____

B6.   Yes.

7.   When will they be in balance? _____

_____

B7.   On June 30 when all posting is up to date.

8.   To follow Shirley Lloyd's account, move to Figure 7-9. When did she pay for her purchase of June 7? _____

B8.   On June 17.

9.   Since her payment involved a cash receipt to the New Generation Shop, it was entered in the cash receipts journal. Did she pay early enough to qualify for the 2 percent cash discount? _____

B9.   Yes.

10.   In Figure 7-9, seven transactions are entered in the cash receipts journal. Of these, _____ required posting to a subsidiary ledger.

B10.   three

11.   These three transactions were the payments by Frank P. Allen, Shirley Lloyd, and Linda Weavil. Were these three transactions also posted to the general ledger on the dates they occurred? _____ Explain. _____

_____

_____

B11. No. Since special columns involve posting of totals, they are posted on June 30.

B12. Cash, Sales Discounts, Accounts Receivable, and Sales.

B13. June 30, 1985.

B14. Notes Receivable; J. Cox, Capital; and Notes Payable

B15. No. The date of the transaction is shown.

B16. Yes.

B17. 3,300. ($200 + $2,500 + $600)

B18. Six. (Seven entries posted with one total.)

12. From the cash receipts journal in Figure 7-9, which accounts were posted with total amounts? _____

_____

13. In these accounts, what date is used for the posting of totals? _____

14. What accounts were posted individually from the cash receipts journal (Figure 7-9)?

_____

_____

15. These postings are made on June 30. Is June 30 the date shown in the account?_____

Explain. _____

_____

16. Has every dollar amount entered in the cash receipts journal been posted to the general ledger either in total or individually?_____

17. What is the total dollar amount of postings made individually? $_____

18. How many individual postings were eliminated by posting to the Cash account in total?

_____

19. Post from Figures 7-8 and 7-10 to the Cash account for the New Generation Shop.

		Cash			Acct. No. 101	
Date		Explanation	F	Debit	Credit	Balance

B19.

1985					
Jun.	30	CR1	6,130		6,130
	30	CP1		2,424	3,706

20. If the New Generation Shop had only a general journal, how many postings would have been made to the Cash account in June?

_____

B 20. Fourteen.

21. Also, collections on accounts receivable occur daily. Use of a cash receipts journal allows us to make only _____ posting(s) to Cash and _____ posting(s) to Accounts Receivable instead of many postings to each account for June collections.

B 21. one, one

22. The same saving of postings occurs because other special journals are used. Instead of many credits to the Sales account, we make only _____ from the _____ journal for the credit sales in June.

B 22. one, sales

23. And, from the sales journal, only one debit to _____ instead of many postings.

B 23. Accounts Receivable

24. Also, many postings each to the accounts _____ and _____ are saved by using a purchases journal.

B 24. Purchases, Accounts Payable

25. Since a need exists to record unusual current transactions, correcting entries, and adjusting and closing entries, the accounting systems must still have a _____ journal.

B 25. general

26. The accounting system illustrated in Chapter 7 is adequate for many small businesses. It is a model you could actually use; all you would need to do is design the chart of accounts and decide which accounts should have special columns in the cash journals.

B 26. No answer required.

SELF TEST OF LEARNING GOAL ACHIEVEMENT

1. Arrapaho Sales Company deals in household and art objects purchased from area craftsmen or from various national suppliers. Purchases and sales are made on credit; payment for all purchases is made by check in time to take advantage of discounts. All incoming merchandise is inspected to ensure that the quantities conform to the amount ordered and there are no defects. Credit customers are billed monthly; the top half of the bill is returned with the customer's check. The accountant has designed a set of business documents on which various information is recorded. Some of them are described on the following page. For each document, indicate the journal in which the transaction it represents should be recorded. Use the journal symbols that are used in Chapter 7.

	Document	Journal
a.	A receiving report attached to a vendor's invoice for merchandise	_____
b.	A receiving report attached to a supplier's invoice for electrical repairs	_____
c.	A copy of a sales invoice indicating that merchandise has been shipped to a customer who will be billed later	_____
d.	A batch of cash sales tickets with a summary sheet showing total cash sales for the day	_____
e.	The group of returned portions of monthly bills to customers, each showing the amount and stamped "Received" by the cashier	_____
f.	Copies of checks written that day, each attached to a form that describes and shows authorization for the payment	_____
g.	Copies of a form called a credit memorandum that credits a customer's account receivable for returned sales	_____
h.	The end-of-period work sheet showing adjustments and with the Income Statement and Balance Sheet columns completed (for closing entries)	_____
i.	A copy of the payroll listing showing check numbers	_____

2. For each letter appearing in the special journals on the following page, indicate how frequently (M = monthly; D = daily) and to what ledger (G = general; S = subsidiary) an amount appearing at that position would be posted or that it is not posted (NP).

	Frequency	*Ledger*
a.	_____	_____
b.	_____	_____
c.	_____	_____
d.	_____	_____
e.	_____	_____
f.	_____	_____
g.	_____	_____
h.	_____	_____
i.	_____	_____
j.	_____	_____
k.	_____	_____
l.	_____	_____
m.	_____	_____
n.	_____	_____
o.	_____	_____
p.	_____	_____

CASH RECEIPTS JOURNAL

Date	Explanation	Debits					Account Credited	Credits				
				Other Accounts				Accounts Receivable			Other Accounts	
		Cash	Sales Discounts	Title	F	Amt		√	Amt	Sales	F	Amt
		a	b						c			
		d				e						f
		g										h
		i	j			k			l			m

PURCHASES JOURNAL

Date	Account Credited	Terms	F	Amount
				n
				o
				p

3. General Company uses only a general journal. Special Company, in the same line of business, uses a general journal and the four special journals described in Chapter 7. Assume that both companies had identical transactions in March 1985.

   a. Which company will have the greater number of postings to the Cash account? _____

   b. Which company will write the account title, Accounts Receivable, in journals a greater number of times? _____

   c. Which company will have the greater number of postings to the accounts receivable subsidiary ledger? _____

   d. Will the total amount posted to the Cash account be greater for Special Company? _____

   e. Must Special Company total its cash receipts and cash payments journals and record those totals in the general journal before posting? _____

   f. Which company will not total the debits and credits in its journal(s)? _____

   g. Suppose each company began the month with a balance of $10,000 in Cash. Which will have the larger cash amount in the end-of-month trial balance? _____

ANSWERS TO LEARNING GOAL ACHIEVEMENT TEST

1. a. P   d. CR   g. J
   b. J   e. CR   h. J
   c. S   f. CP   i. CP

2.   *Frequency*   *Ledger*

   a.   NP   NP
   b.   NP   NP
   c.   D   S
   d.   NP   NP
   e.   M   G
   f.   M   G
   g.   NP   NP
   h.   M   G
   i.   M   G
   j.   M   G
   k.   NP   NP
   l.   M   G
   m.   NP   NP
   n.   D   S
   o.   D   S
   p.   M   G

3. a. General   e. No
   b. General   f. General
   c. Neither   g. Neither
   d. No

Chapter 8
Payroll System

■■

EXPLANATION OF MAJOR CONCEPTS

Payrolls and Deductions

Employees are paid on a regular basis. In some organizations, the payroll is computed and paid weekly, in others every two weeks, and in some monthly. There are many methods of determining the amount of employees' pay. Two of the most common are an agreed upon salary per month or year or an hourly wage rate. If the first method is used, a person with a salary of $26,000 per year would earn $500 = ($26,000 ÷ 52 weeks) in *gross pay* per week. Under the second method, a person with an hourly rate of $10.50 would earn gross pay of $420 = ($10.50 x 40 hours) in a forty-hour week.

Gross pay is the amount of total pay earned before any deductions. Employees' pay checks are almost always less than gross pay because of deductions required by law and voluntary deductions. Gross pay minus deductions equals *net pay*. Net pay is *take home pay*. Please note that, in the journal entry to record the payroll, *expense* is equal to gross pay. The total amount must be paid to someone. Deductions are not kept by the employer; they are deducted in order to be remitted to a government agency, a union, or to some other entity.

Most employees are covered by the Fair Labor Standards Act (the Federal Wage and Hour Law). It defines all time worked in excess of forty hours per week as overtime for which the employee must be paid at least time and one-half. A typical wage computation is the one for Cynthia Winters in the text. She worked forty-five hours in one week. Winters' wage rate is $12 per hour, and her gross pay computation is:

$$
\begin{array}{rcll}
40 \text{ hours x } \$12 = & \$480 & = & \text{Gross pay.} \\
5 \text{ hours x } 12 = & 60 & = & \text{Overtime pay.} \\
5 \text{ hours x } 6 = & \underline{30} & = & \text{Overtime premium pay.} \\
& \underline{\$570} & = & \text{Total gross pay.}
\end{array}
$$

Note that the (5 hours x $12) + (5 hours x $6) is the same as 5 hours x $18, or time and one-half for the overtime that Winters worked this week.

Payroll Taxes

Two major forms of payroll taxes paid by employees through payroll deductions are income tax and FICA (or social security) tax. Employees are subject to federal income tax deductions in all states and in most states are also subject to state income tax. Income tax is based on earnings for the entire year and is deducted from employee gross pay for each of the fifty-two weeks of the year. FICA tax has an annual ceiling; after a certain amount is earned, the tax ceases until the next year.

Employers do not bear the burden of employee income tax. The company simply withholds it and remits it to the proper government agency. Employers do, however, have to pay two major payroll taxes: a matching amount of FICA and the unemployment compensation tax. These are expenses in *addition* to the expense of gross pay. Their amount is debited to an account called Payroll Tax Expense.

To illustrate payroll deductions, consider the case of James B. Skinner in Figure 8-3. His gross pay appears in the total column. Deductions from that gross pay withheld by the Orbit Company are shown as follows:

Gross pay		$552.00
Deductions		
FICA	$ 38.64	
Federal income tax . . .	117.60	
State income tax	9.29	
Group health	18.75	184.28
Net pay to Skinner . .		$367.72

After Skinner has earned a base amount--assumed to be the first $36,000 per calendar year in this book--the FICA tax withholding is stopped, and he pays no more FICA tax until the next calendar year. Both federal and state income tax continue all year. Total amounts of these three taxes withheld from Skinner's pay are remitted to the appropriate government agencies periodically.

Employers pay payroll taxes in addition to those withheld from the employees' pay. The three most common ones are:

▶ A matching amount of FICA.
▶ State unemployment compensation tax.
▶ Federal unemployment compensation tax.

As in FICA withholding, the employer's tax also stops when a specific employee reaches a base amount in a calendar year. It is important to be able to compute the tax in a cutoff period. Assume that in a week ending in November 1985, James B. Skinner earns gross pay of $400 and has earned year-to-date cumulative pay of $35,750 up through the end of the last pay period. Only the first $250 = ($36,000 - $35,750) of the $400 gross is taxable *both to Skinner and his employer*. No FICA is paid by either for the remainder of 1985.

Unemployment taxes are computed in a manner similar to FICA taxes in that they are charged only on a base amount (in this book, an assumed $10,000). Unlike FICA, however, all unemployment taxes fall on the employer except in some states. When an employee has reached the cumulative year-to-date base, the tax ceases and is not charged again until the next calendar year.

Payroll Entries

There are three basic payroll entries as follows:

▸ Recording the payroll (made in the general journal).
▸ Paying the payroll (made in the cash payments journal if one is used).
▸ Recording the payroll tax expense (made in the general journal).

The typical form for these three journal entries (using the general journal for all for ease of illustration) is:

1	Salaries and Wages Expense	Gross Pay	
	FICA Payable		7 percent
	Federal Income Tax Withholding Payable.		Actual $
	State Income Tax Withholding Payable. .		Actual $
	Other Liabilities for Deductions		Actual $
	Wages and Salaries Payable		Net Pay
	To record payroll for a specified period.		
2	Salaries and Wages Payable.	Net Pay	
	Cash		Net Pay
	To record payment of employees; should be in CP.		
3	Payroll Tax Expense	Total	
	FICA Payable		7 percent
	Federal Unemployment Taxes Payable . .		1 percent
	State Unemployment Taxes Payable . . .		4 percent
	To record employer's payroll taxes.		

Note that entries 1 and 3 involve two different expense items to the employer. Their sum is the total expense of buying people's services.

Payroll Records

Payroll records are needed to ensure that employees receive the proper amount of compensation. They must also provide information required to prepare the tax reports that an entity must make to federal and state governmental agencies. A business must have at least a *payroll register* (illustrated in Figure 8-3) and an *earnings record* for each individual employee. In a small organization, these may be typed or handwritten. In a large organization, they are usually maintained by computer.

Liabilities for Compensated Absences

When a business gives its employees periods of time off with pay, the wages for these periods of absence should be charged to the periods when the employee performs services for the business. Therefore, each week that an employee works, not only should the business record the wages expense and payroll tax expense, but they should also record expense for the anticipated absence. Assuming that the compensated absence is for vacation, each week that the employee works the following entry would be made:

Vacation Pay Expense	X	
Liability for Vacation Pay		X

Then, when the employee takes the vacation, the entry to record the payment would be as follows:

Liability for Vacation Pay	X	
FICA Taxes Payable		X
Federal Income Tax Withholding Pay		X
State Income Tax Withholding Pay		X
Cash		X

Similar accruals would be required for sick pay or other forms of compensated absences.

GUIDED STUDY OF THIS CHAPTER

A. *Computation of Pay. As a starting point in Chapter 8, let's use Figure 8-3.*

1. Figure 8-3 illustrates a _____ _____ which is prepared for each pay period.

A1. payroll register

2. The pay period covered by this payroll register is the _____ ended _____.

A2. week, 5/31/85

3. Three employees, Skinner, Burke, and Howard, work in the _____ Department.

A3. Sales (The code S means sales.)

4. The total number of employees in this company is _____.

A4. five

5. Is James Skinner paid a salary or an hourly rate? _____ How much? $_____

A5.   Hourly rate. 12.

6.   Skinner worked _____ hours this week at a rate of $12, for total regular and overtime earnings of $_____.

A6.   forty-four, 528 = (44 x $12)

7.   Skinner also worked _____ hours overtime. Since overtime premium is one-half the regular hourly rate, Skinner has earned an additional $_____ for overtime premium pay.

A7.   four, 24 = (4 x $6)

8.   Note carefully that $24 is only the premium portion of Skinner's pay for overtime hours. We have already included these four overtime hours in the computation of his regular pay.

A8.   No answer required.

9.   Let's make this point clear: If Skinner had worked only forty hours at $12 per hour, he would have earned $_____.

A9.   480

10.   However, Skinner's total earnings were $_____. This means that in the four hours of overtime, he earned $_____.

A10.   552, 72

11.   The $72 is equal to "time and one-half" for overtime. In other words, four hours at $12 = $_____ of regular pay and the additional one-half for overtime premium = $_____. This is the total of $72.

A11.   48, 24

12.   Let's continue to examine James Skinner's pay. Since this is May, he is not likely to have earned the assumed FICA taxable base of $36,000 in 1985. His FICA deduction is 7 percent of total earnings for this week, 7 percent of $552 = $_____.

A12.   38.64

13.   His federal income tax to be withheld is based on a wage bracket withholding table similar to Figure 8-2. The company has deducted $_____ this week for Skinner's income tax.

A13.   117.60

14.   Skinner has a weekly deduction of $_____ to buy _____.

A14.   18.75, group health

15.   What is the total amount of Skinner's payroll deductions? $_____

A15.   184.28.

16.   Gross pay of $_____ minus deductions of $184.28 equals $_____, which is Skinner's net pay (or take-home pay).

A16.   552.00, 367.72

17.   The same procedure is followed to obtain similar figures for each employee in the company. Total earnings of all employees this week are $_____.

A17.   2,924.50

18.   Total deductions from earnings are $_____, but they must be computed individually for each employee.

A18.   1,034.86

19.   The total deductions are made up of $_____ for FICA, $_____ for federal income tax, $_____ for group health, and $_____ for state income tax.

A19.   204.72, 630.40, 150.00, 49.74

20.   Total net pay for this week is $_____.

A20.   1,889.64

21.   The journal entry to record this payroll should debit expenses with gross pay of $_____. Of this amount, $_____ should be debited to Sales Salaries Expense.

A21.   2,924.50, 1,529.50

22. $_____ should be debited to Executive Salaries Expense, and $_____ should be debited to Office Salaries Expense.

A22.   750, 645

23.   Check to be sure that total debits in this entry are $2,924.50. The FICA deductions of $_____ should be credited to FICA Taxes Payable, the federal income tax deductions of $_____ should be credited to Federal Income Tax Withholding Payable, and the group health deductions of $_____ should be credited to Group Health Insurance Premium Payable.

A23.   204.72, 630.40, 150.00

24.   A deduction of $_____ for _____ _____ is not included in A23 above.

A24.   49.74, state income tax

25.   The total of all deductions is $_____, which, when subtracted from gross pay of $2,924.50, leaves $_____ of net pay to be credited to Salaries and Wages Payable.

A25. 1,034.86, 1,889.64

26. Review the payroll entry for the Orbit Company illustrated in the textbook. Was that entry made up from the foregoing amounts?

_____

A26. Yes.

B. *Employer's Payroll Taxes. The payroll taxes shown on the payroll register in Figure 8-3 will be paid by the Orbit Company but were deducted from earnings. That tax burden, therefore, falls on the employees.*

1. What additional taxes on this payroll must be paid by Orbit Company? _____

_____

_____

B1. A matching FICA amount and the federal and state unemployment tax.

2. Since Orbit Company pays an additional FICA amount equal to employee deductions, it will have $_____ more FICA taxes payable.

B2. 204.72

3. The state in which Orbit Company operates has a merit-rating plan. Orbit has a good record of employment stability and qualifies for a 2 percent rate for state unemployment tax. The liability account State Unemployment Taxes Payable will be credited with $_____ this week.

B3. 58.50

4. At 1 percent, Federal Unemployment Taxes Payable will be credited with $_____.

B4. 29.25 = ($2,924.50 x .01)

5. The total debit to Payroll Tax Expense this week will be $_____.

B5. 292.47

6. Since both the payroll entry and the payroll tax entry record expenses and liabilities (but not payments), they are entered in the _____ journal.

B6. general

7. Both FICA and unemployment compensation tax rates were applied to total gross pay this week because _____

_____

_____

_____.

B7. it is early in the year (May) and no employee has earned the base amount

8. Later in the year, say in October or November, some employees will have accumulated earnings to date equal to or greater than the base amounts. For those persons, FICA deductions and company FICA payroll taxes will cease.

B8. No answer required.

C. *Tax Returns and Tax Forms. Although tax return forms carry specific instructions, there are some things about payroll taxes that you should understand thoroughly at this point.*

1. An individual employee must provide to his or her employer certain information about taxable status on Form _____.

C1. W-4

2. Form W-4 is illustrated in Figure 8-1. On this form, the employee certifies his or her marital status because there are different income tax rates for single and married persons. The employer uses this information to determine

_____

_____.

C2. how much to withhold from gross earnings for income tax

3. May the employee have a lesser amount withheld than provided for in the table? _____
A greater amount? _____

C3. No. Yes.

4. May a single person check the Married block in order to have smaller amounts withheld? _____ Explain. _____

_____

C4. No. The employee certifies to the truth of statements on Form W-4.

5. At the end of each year, each employer must give each employee a wage and tax statement on Form _____.

C5. W-2

6. Form W-2 is illustrated in Figure 8-6. This form is prepared by an employer named

_____.

C6. Orbit Company

7. It shows the 1982 earnings and tax withholdings of an employee named _____

_____.

C7. William S. Ford

8. Why is the figure for Ford's FICA wages in block 13 less than the total wages in block 10?

_____

_____

_____

_____

C8. Because this is an actual form for the year 1982, when the FICA base was less than $32,318; he earned more than the base amount.

9. The assumed FICA rate in this text is 7 percent. Check to see if the amount of FICA tax withheld (block 11) is correct (at 7 percent). _____

C9. 0.07 x $30,000 = $2,100.

10. How much federal income tax did Orbit withhold from William S. Ford's pay? $_____ How much state income tax? $_____

C10. 6,073.60. 580.00.

11. What did Orbit do with these tax amounts withheld? _____

_____

_____

C11. Paid them to the Internal Revenue Service and the State Tax Department.

12. Does William Ford get credit for these withholdings when he files his tax return for 1982? _____

C12. Yes. (He will send in a copy of Form W-2.)

13. Even though the employer has no legal liability to pay or withhold taxes on accrued wages, should a firm make an adjusting entry for accrued payroll at the end of the accounting year? _____ For accrued employer's taxes? _____

C13. Yes. Yes.

14. Suppose that L. Solomon Company had accrued gross wages of $5,000 with deductibles for income tax, FICA, and union dues on December 31, 1985. Is it necessary to show the credits in detail in the adjusting entry? _____ Explain. _____

_____

_____

C14. No. The allocation of $5,000 to 1985 expense is primary in this entry.

15. Show the December 31 adjusting entry.

Date		Account Titles	F	Debit	Credit

C15.

Date	Act.Tles.	Dr.	Cr.
1985			
Dec.31	Salaries and Wages		
	Expense	5,000	
	Accrued Wages		
	Payable		5,000

D. *Liabilities for Compensated Absences*

1. Absences for which employees are paid are called _____.

D1. compensated absences

2. If a worker earns $500 per week and is allowed two weeks paid vacation per year, the company should record the worker's wages of $_____ for the two weeks they will be absent over the _____ weeks they work.

D2. 1,000 = ($5,000 x 2), 50

3. Thus, they will record expense for vacation pay of $_____ each week for the worker.

D3. 20.00 = ($1,000 ÷ 50)

4. When this is journalized, a debit is made to _____ and a credit is made to _____.

D4. Vacation Pay Expense, Liability for Vacation Pay

5. Then when the worker takes their vacation, the journal entry to record the wages for that week would debit _____ and credit the normal withholding accounts and cash.

D5. Liability for Vacation Pay

6. If the liability account ended up with a debit balance, it would be classified as a current asset and called _____.

D6. prepaid vacation pay

SELF TEST OF LEARNING GOAL ACHIEVEMENT

1. Pedro Raul earns $16 per hour. In the week ended February 22, 1985, he worked a total of forty-five hours. Determine the following:

    a. Gross pay earned.

    b. Federal income tax withheld if Raul has three exemptions. Use the table in Figure 8-2.

    c. Amount of FICA tax withheld.

    d. Amount of federal FUTA tax on his employer.

    e. Amount of state FUTA tax on his employer, no merit rating.

2. Ando Company had a gross payroll of $25,000 for the week ended September 27, 1985. Deductions were as follows:

> Federal income tax $5,200
> State income tax   600
> FICA tax (no employee has yet earned
>   the base amount of $36,000) . . . . . .   ?
> Union dues   100

The company pays the regular federal rate under FUTA. Under a merit-rating plan, the state rate is 3 percent.

Required:
(1) Record the payroll for the week ended September 27, 1985.
(2) Record the employer's payroll taxes (total payroll is taxable).

GENERAL JOURNAL

Date		Account Titles and Explanation	F	Debit	Credit

3. Assuming that the unemployment base is $10,000, the federal rate is 1 percent, and the state rate with merit is 2 percent, what would be a company's journal entry to record the employer's payroll tax expense with the following earnings facts for the week ended May 10, 1985.

Employee	Prior Total Earnings	Current Earnings
Sam Jones	$ 8,000.00	$500.00
Dave Anjo	9,900.00	600.00
Andria Answorth	11,000.00	800.00

Computations:

FICA--

State unemployment--

Federal unemployment--

GENERAL JOURNAL

Date	Account Titles and Explanation	F	Debit	Credit

4. Icor Company gives its employees two weeks paid vacation each year. They conform to the practice of recording the cost of compensated absences. Their employees total gross earnings are $25,000 for each of the 50 weeks they work. Journalize the entry to record the liability for compensated absence for the week ended January 25, 1985.

GENERAL JOURNAL

Date	Account Titles and Explanation	F	Debit	Credit

If two employees with a total gross pay of $1,000 per week took the week ending March 15, 1985, for vacation with pay, record the journal entry for their pay, assuming a 7 percent FICA rate, federal income tax withholding of $200, and state income tax withholding of $40.

GENERAL JOURNAL

Date	Account Titles and Explanation	F	Debit	Credit

ANSWERS TO LEARNING GOAL ACHIEVEMENT TEST

1. a.   40 hours x $16 = $640 regular pay.
         5 hours x   16 =   80 overtime pay.
         5 hours x   8 =   40 overtime premium.
                          $760 gross pay.

    b.

	Exemptions			
Wages	0	1	2	3
$760–$770				$152.50

    c. $760 x 0.07 = $53.20.

    d. $760 x 0.01 = $ 7.60.

    e. $760 x 0.04 = $30.40.

    Note: By late February, Mr. Raul cannot have earned a total of either $10,000 or $36,000.

2.

GENERAL JOURNAL

Date		Account Titles and Explanation	F	Debit	Credit
1985		(1)			
Sep.	27	Salaries and Wages Expense		25,000	
		Federal Income Tax Withholding Payable			5,200
		State Income Tax Withholding Payable			600
		FICA Payable			1,750
		Union Dues Payable			100
		Salaries and Wages Payable			17,350
		To record payroll for week ended September 27.			
		(2)			
	27	Payroll Tax Expense		2,750	
		FICA Payable			1,750
		Federal Unemployment Tax Payable			250
		State Unemployment Tax Payable			750
		To record employer's payroll taxes.			

3. Computations:

FICA--$1,900 x .07 = $133.00.

State unemployment--$600 x .02 = $12.00.

Federal unemployment--$600 x .01 = $6.00.

GENERAL JOURNAL

Date		Account Titles and Explanation	F	Debit	Credit
1985					
May	10	Payroll Tax Expense		151	
		FICA Payable			133
		Federal Unemployment Tax Payable			6
		State Unemployment Tax Payable			12
		To record employer's payroll taxes.			

4.

GENERAL JOURNAL

Date		Account Titles and Explanation	F	Debit	Credit
1985					
Jan.	25	Vacation Pay Expense		500	
		Liability for Vacation Pay			500
		Accrual of liability for 1/50			
		of vacation pay.			

GENERAL JOURNAL

Date		Account Titles and Explanation	F	Debit	Credit
1985					
Mar.	15	Liability for Vacation Pay		1,000	
		FICA Taxes Payable			70
		Federal Income Tax Withholding			
		Payable			200
		State Income Tax Withholding			
		Payable			40
		Cash			690
		Payment to two employees			
		for one week's vacation.			

Chapter 9
Internal Control of Cash:
The Voucher System

■■■

EXPLANATION OF MAJOR CONCEPTS

Cash and Internal Control

Although internal control refers to protection of all assets, cash control is of primary importance in most organizations. Among the methods used to strengthen internal control over cash are:

▶ Separation of the duties and responsibilities of persons who handle and record cash.

▶ Use of mechanical devices (such as cash registers) to record cash transactions.

▶ Daily deposits of cash receipts intact, that is the exact cash and checks received are those which are deposited.

▶ Organize the recording of cash so that, whenever possible, the work of one employee is checked by another employee.

▶ Operation of internal controls should be periodically checked on a surprise basis by someone outside the cash area.

▶ Controls should be established over the use of computers.

▶ All payments, except minor amounts, should be made by check.

▶ Minor amounts should be paid from a petty cash fund.

Petty Cash Fund

The preferred system for a petty cash fund is the *imprest fund*. Literally, *imprest* means advanced in trust. A *fixed sum* is advanced to a designated petty cash fund custodian. At this point the fund would have cash equal to the imprest amount. The custodian makes cash payments out of this fund for minor items, obtaining a receipt on a petty cash voucher for each payment. Journal entries to record these payments are not made at the time the expenditure is made. These expenditures will not be recorded in the journal and ledger until the fund is replenished. Control over the cash in the petty cash fund is accomplished by the fact that the total of the cash and petty cash vouchers should be equal to the imprest amount at all times.

Periodically, the petty cash fund should be replenished. At that time, the receipted petty cash vouchers are "bought" from the custodian. That is, the custodian turns them in to the accounting department in exchange for sufficient cash to bring the cash in the fund back up to the imprest balance. The expenses represented by the petty cash vouchers are then debited and cash is credited. If the amount represented by the vouchers is different from the amount of cash necessary to bring the fund up to the proper imprest balance, an account entitled *Cash Over and Short* is used to balance the entry. The fund is again wholly cash. As the cycle starts over and cash payments are made from the fund, the fixed sum becomes a mixture of cash and receipted vouchers until the next replenishment is made. One caution about an imprest fund must be remembered. The fund must be replenished at an accounting period end in order for all the expenses to be properly recorded.

Bank Reconciliation

Daily receipts of cash are deposited in the bank intact. Depositing daily cash receipts intact means that no bills are paid out of the cash received from sales or collections. The total of all daily sales and collections is deposited in the bank at the end of each business day. All payments (except petty cash) are made by check. Accordingly, the Cash account should be equal to the bank balance. It rarely is, however, because of:

▶ *Timing differences*. For example, we credit (reduce) Cash at the moment we write a check. The bank doesn't reduce our account until the check reaches the bank for payment.

▶ *Actions by the bank not known to us*. For example, the bank may deduct a monthly service charge; the amount is not known until the monthly bank statement is received.

▶ *Errors*. Our accounting department (or the bank) may make an error in recording a deposit or a check.

The *bank reconciliation* is a statement that explains the specific differences between our Cash account and the bank's recorded balance shown on the monthly statement. The preferred form of bank reconciliation begins with the balance in Cash and the bank statement balance *(for the same date)* and adjusts each to the same amount. Refer to Figure 9-6 for an outline of the format of a bank reconciliation.

When the bank reconciliation shows identical amounts for adjusted book balance and adjusted bank balance, it is strong evidence that there are no errors in the Cash account. Every adjustment to the "balance per books" must be the subject of a journal entry. The adjustments to "balance per bank" do not require journal entries. Some, such as deposits in transit or outstanding checks, will clear automatically in a future period. Others must be returned to the bank for correction.

The key to preparing a bank statement reconciliation is recognizing when to add to or subtract from the book balance and the bank balance. For each item that could cause the two balances to be different, you should follow this line of thinking:

▶ Which balance (bank or books) is not reflecting the "true" cash balance because the item is not recorded or is incorrectly recorded? (For example, outstanding checks have not yet been reflected in the bank statement; therefore, it is the bank balance that should be adjusted.)

▶ Having decided which balance (bank or books) needs adjusting, then ask: Is that balance *as now stated* too high or too low? (To use outstanding checks as an example again, the bank balance is *now* too high. It will be reduced when they actually arrive at the bank. To adjust the bank balance, deduct them.)

In order to engage in this type of thinking, it is absolutely necessary that you understand the mechanics of bank transactions. *Ask questions about any item you do not understand.*

The Voucher System

The voucher system is designed to give better control over payments. Before any check can be written, a form known as a *voucher* must be approved by the person with authority to do so. Persons who prepare vouchers check such things as accuracy of prices and arithmetic on the dealer's bill or *invoice*. They also check the discount terms, compute the discount, and verify that the goods or services were received as authorized by the purchase order. Using account numbers from the chart of accounts, the person who prepares a voucher indicates on it the accounts to be *debited*. *Vouchers Payable,* a liability account, is *always* credited when a voucher is recorded.

The *voucher register* is a special journal. Together with the *check register* (another special journal), these journals replace the purchases journal and cash payments journal. Postings to ledger accounts are made from these two journals either in total or individually, as are postings from special journals. You should review posting procedures for special journals (Chapter 7) if you have any difficulty knowing when to post columns in total and when to post individual entries. Because *every entry* in the voucher register includes a *credit* to Vouchers Payable, there is a special column provided and only the total is posted. Entries that are made in the Other Accounts section (because there is no special column for them) are posted individually, as was the case with the cash payments journal. Note that the check register has only special columns. All monthly postings from it are postings of totals only. *Every entry* in the check register must include a *debit* to Vouchers Payable.

GUIDED STUDY OF THIS CHAPTER

A.   *Internal Control*

1. For good internal control over cash, *all* cash receipts should be _____ _____.

A1.   deposited in a bank daily

2. All payments should be made by check unless they are _____ _____.

A2.   minor items paid from a petty cash fund

3. Internal control over cash is so important because cash is _____ _____.

A3.   naturally vulnerable to theft or misuse

4. Having the same person receive cash and make entries into the cash receipts journal would be _____ (good/poor) internal control.

A4.   poor

5. Having two or more persons making cash sales from the same cash register drawer is _____ (good/poor) internal control.

A5.   poor

6. Should total cash receipts for any day be equal to the deposit to the bank account for that day? _____

A6.   Yes.

7. Wouldn't it be simpler to pay some local bills just by taking money out of the cash register and leaving a copy of the bill to show what the payment was for? _____ Explain.

_____

_____

A7.   Yes. However, it creates opportunities (and temptations) to employees to steal cash.

8. The safer way to handle small payments in cash is to use a _____ assigned to a single custodian.

A8.   petty cash fund

B.   *Petty Cash*

1. Figure 9-1 illustrates a petty cash voucher. What is the purpose of this voucher? _____

_____

B1.   To describe and give evidence of a payment.

B2.   Tom Dunlap.

B3.   Jim Brady.

B4.   When the fund is replenished.

B5.   Cash payments journal.

B6.   38

B7.   The receipted vouchers held by the custodian are exchanged for a check.

B8.   Cashes it at the bank and puts the cash in the petty cash fund.

B9.   451.50.

B10. 47.00.

B11. debited

2.   Who is the custodian of the petty cash fund? _____

3.   Who has received the payment and signed the receipt for it? _____

4.   This payment will be debited to Postage Expense. When? _____

5.   In what journal would you record the replenishment of the petty cash fund? _____ _____

6.   If a petty cash fund is $100 and there are receipted vouchers totaling $62 in the safe in which the fund is kept, there should also be $_____ in cash in the fund.

7.   Exactly what do we mean by *replenishment* of the petty cash fund? _____ _____ _____

8.   What does the custodian do with the check? _____ _____

9.   In the textbook example, what was the total amount of the petty cash vouchers turned in when the fund was replenished? $_____

10. What was the total amount of cash in the fund when the replenishment was made? $_____

11. The expenses represented by the petty cash vouchers are _____ in the journal entry.

12. Was the proper amount in the petty cash fund?_____ What was the difference? $_____ This amount is recorded to the account _____.

B 12.   No, 1.50, Cash
        Over and Short

13.   In the textbook journal entry to replenish High
      Company's petty cash fund, a debit of $1.50 is
      recorded to Cash Over and Short. What type
      of account is this? _____

      _____

      _____

B 13.   An expense if it has
        a debit balance; a
        revenue if it has a
        credit balance.

14.   Is it normal for persons handling cash to be
      over or short? _____ Explain. _____

      _____

      _____

B 14.   Yes. The amounts
        should be small
        relative to total
        cash handled.

15.   In case of an unreasonable cash overage or
      shortage, what action should a manager take?

      _____

      _____

B 15.   Investigate to
        determine and
        correct the cause.

C. *Bank Reconciliation*

1.   How often do banks provide statements to
     their depositors? _____

C 1.   Monthly.

2.   Figure 9-2 illustrates a typical check. What
     is the account number of this bank account?

     _____

C 2.   1239 876543.

3.   What does the term *payee* mean? _____

     _____

C 3.   It is the person to
       whose order the
       check is made
       payable.

4.   How does the payee exchange this check for
     cash? _____

C 4.   Takes it to any bank
       that will cash it.

5.   How does this depositor's account at Wachovia
     Bank and Trust Company get reduced when
     he writes a check? _____

     _____

     _____

     _____

     _____

     _____

C5.   The bank that cashes the check for the payee "sells" the check back to Wachovia. Wachovia then deducts the check amount from account number 1239 876543.

6.   Figure 9-5 shows the September 1985 bank statement for Clearwater Company. How many deposits were credited to this account in September? _____

C6.   Nine, including CM.

7.   Is Clearwater practicing good internal control by depositing receipts intact daily? _____

C7.   No.

8.   Clearwater Company had a balance of $_____ in its bank account on September 30, 1985.

C8.   204.24

9.   In Figure 9-5, the last transaction date is _____.

C9.   September 30, 1985

10.   The September bank statement (Figure 9-5) is reconciled with Clearwater's Cash account in Figure 9-7. On September 30, Clearwater's Cash account showed a debit balance of $_____.

C10.   41.58

11.   According to the text, the checks which were outstanding on August 31 were _____ through _____.

C11.   637, 644

12.   These checks had been credited to Clearwater's Cash account but had not reached the Wachovia Bank and Trust Company for payment by August 31.

C12.   No answer required.

13.   Check number 637 appears on the September bank statement (Figure 9-5) as being paid on September 3. Check number 644 cleared through the bank on _____.

C13.   September 4

14.   Check number 639 was paid by the bank on _____.

C14.   It has not been paid yet.

15.   Therefore, check number 639 is one of the _____ checks on September 30.

C15. outstanding

16. On August 31, 1985, there was one deposit in transit in the amount of $_____.

C16. 82.20

17. This $82.20 had been debited to Cash and deposited by Clearwater on August 30. It was recorded by the bank, however, on

_____.

C17. September 2 (See Figure 9-5.)

18. Clearwater's cash receipts journal indicates eight bank deposits made in September. How many of these eight are recorded on the September bank statement? _____

C18. Seven.

19. So the dollar amount of deposits recorded on Clearwater's books but not on the bank's books (in transit) on September 30 is $_____.

C19. 421.50

20. To adjust the bank balance of $204.24 to the correct amount, it is necessary to _____ (add/deduct) the deposit in transit.

C20. add

21. When the outstanding checks reach the bank for payment, they will _____ (reduce/increase) Clearwater's balance.

C21. reduce

22. So, they should be _____ (added to/deducted from) the bank statement balance.

C22. deducted from

23. When these adjustments are made to the bank statement, the adjusted bank balance (Figure 9-7) is $_____ on September 30, 1985.

C23. 513.72

24. Since Clearwater's Cash account has a balance of $_____, it must also be adjusted.

C24. 41.58

25. One of the items which requires adjustment is the collection of our customer's note by the bank.

C25. No answer required.

26. Clearwater Company had given a customer's note to the bank in the amount of $_____ to be collected by the bank.

C26. 500.00

27. If the customer who made the $500.00 note to Clearwater also had an account with Wachovia Bank and Trust Company, the bank could simply transfer $500.00 from the customer's account to Clearwater's account on September 16. To do this, the bank would record a _____ (debit/credit) memo against the *customer's* account.

C27. debit

28. To add $500.00 to Clearwater's account for this note, the bank recorded a _____ (debit/credit) memo.

C28. credit

29. For performing the service, the bank charged Clearwater $_____.

C29. 3.00

30. Thus, the bank has deposited the net amount of $_____ to Clearwater's account on _____ and issued a _____ memo.

C30. 497.00, September 16, credit

31. In effect, this transaction is the same as if the customer had paid the $500.00 in cash to Clearwater and Clearwater then immediately deposited it in the bank (except for the $3.00 collection fee).

C31. No answer required.

32. The bank statement showed $_____ in interest that had been earned on the account. Since the company did not know of this amount before the statement was received, it must be _____ (added to/ subtracted from) the book balance.

C32. 0.84, added to

33. An accounting error has been made with check number 640. The check was written in the amount of $_____ but was entered in the cash payments journal as $_____. Thus, $_____ will have to be _____ (added/subtracted) on the book side of the reconciliation.

C33. 200.16, 201.06, 0.90, added

34. Two other adjustments were needed. One was for the bank service charge of $_____ and was _____ (added/ subtracted).

C34. 5.40, subtracted

35. The other adjustment was for a/an _____ _____. $_____ was subtracted from the book side. It must be subtracted because _____

_____

_____

_____.

C35. customer's NSF check, 21.20, the bank has deducted the amount from our account when the check was dishonored by the maker's bank

36. When the adjustments to Clearwater's Cash account are added and deducted, the adjusted Cash balance should be $_____.

C36. 513.72

37. Is this amount the same as the adjusted bank balance? _____

C37. Yes.

38. Although the bank reconciliation statement is in balance, no change has yet been made to Clearwater's Cash account. To make such a change will require a series of _____ entries.

C38. journal

39. Is it correct that *every adjustment* made in the "Per Books" section of the bank reconciliation requires a journal entry on Clearwater's books? _____

C39. Yes.

40. There is something that every one of these journal entries will have in common. What is it? _____

_____

C40. Each one involves a debit or credit to Cash.

41. If the cash receipts and payments journals have not been closed and posted, the entries should be made there. However, if the cash journals have already been posted, the entries could be made in the _____ journal.

C41. general

42. Which of the items in the "Per Bank" section of the bank reconciliation require journal entries? _____

C42. None.

D.   *The Voucher System. A voucher is a locally designed form which serves as a check-off list to be gone over before a payment is made. It also shows which accounts should be debited with specific amounts from each payment. A person in authority approves the voucher for payment after various checks for accuracy and validity have been made.*

1.   Figure 9-8 illustrates a purchase order. This document authorizes Wheaton Company to

_____

_____ .

D1.   ship seat belt assemblies and mounts

2.   Figure 9-9 illustrates a typical voucher and Figure 9-10 an invoice. Wheaton Company's authority to ship and bill these items to Tennessee Aircraft Supply was Tennessee's purchase order number _____ .

D2.   09055

3.   The person approving this payment will do so by approving voucher number _____ .

D3.   314

4.   The due date on voucher 314 is 1/8/85. That is the date the check must be written. A payment date of 1/8/85 was chosen in order to _____

_____ .

D4.   take advantage of the 2 percent cash discount

5.   The Tennessee Aircraft Supply is using the gross procedure. Account number 501 is the Purchases account to be debited with $_____ .

D5.   3,500.00

6.   When this approved voucher is paid on 1/8/85, the actual amount of the check will be $_____ .

D6.   3,430.00

7.   The difference of $70.00 will be credited to the _____ account in the check register.

D7.   Purchases Discounts

8.   Let's study Figures 9-11 and 9-12. These figures show the voucher register and check register of the Tennessee Aircraft Supply. In the voucher register, the January 3 voucher to the Wheaton Company is obviously for merchandise for resale because _____

_____ .

D8.   the debit is to the
      Purchases account

9.   In the check register, we can see the journal-
      izing of payment to the Wheaton Company on
      January 8. Since there is a Purchases Dis-
      counts column in the check register, we know
      that Tennessee Aircraft Supply uses the
      _____ (gross/net) method of
      recording purchases.

D9.   gross

10.   In the voucher register, the credit to Vouchers
      Payable for the Wheaton Company purchase
      was in the amount of $_____ .

D10. 3,500

11.   In the check register, Vouchers Payable is
      debited with $_____ , but the amount
      of check number 709 is only $_____ .
      The difference of $70 is credited to the
      _____ account.

D11. 3,500, 3,430,
      Purchases Discounts

12.   Are the credit and debit (each of $3,500)
      posted individually to Vouchers Payable in
      the general ledger? _____

D12. No.

13.   How do these two entries get into the general
      ledger? _____
      _____
      _____

D13. They are part of the
      column total amounts
      that will be posted
      on January 31.

14.   In the voucher register, the notation (201)
      beneath the Vouchers Payable column means
      that $_____ has been _____
      (debited/credited) to Vouchers Payable.

D14. 22,324, credited

15.   In the check register, the notation (201)
      beneath the Vouchers Payable column means
      that $_____ has been _____
      (debited/credited) to Vouchers Payable.

D15. 13,154, debited

16.   Are all items in the check register posted in
      total? _____

D16. Yes.

17.   Are all items in the voucher register posted
      in total? _____

D17. No.

18.   For example, in the purchase from Dover
      Company on January 3, the $_____ entry
      to the _____ account
      was posted individually to account number
      _____ .

D18. 800, Office Equip-
      ment, 163

19. The symbol (X) below the total of $11,826 in
     the Other Accounts column of the voucher
     register means that $11,826 _____
     (was/was not) posted in total.

D19. was not

20. Since all column totals in the voucher register
     are not posted in total, is it necessary to add
     total debits and total credits to see if they are
     equal? _____ Explain. _____
     _____
     _____

D20. Yes. In this journal
      (as in all others)
      total debits must
      equal total credits.

21. Which vouchers in the Tennessee Aircraft
     Supply voucher register (Figure 9-11) are
     unpaid on January 31, 1985? _____
     _____

D21. Voucher nos. 316, 333,
      and 334. (There may
      be others; the total
      page is not shown.)

22. Where would those unpaid vouchers be physi-
     cally located? _____
     _____

D22. Attached to their
      respective invoices
      in the unpaid
      vouchers file.

23. Should the total of vouchers in the unpaid
     vouchers file on January 31 be equal to the
     balance of a specific general ledger account?
     _____

D23. Yes.

24. Which account? _____

D24. Vouchers Payable.

25. The major advantage of the voucher system
     is that _____
     _____
     _____
     _____.

D25. no check is allowed
      to be written except
      to pay an approved
      voucher; this im-
      proves control over
      cash

SELF TEST OF LEARNING GOAL ACHIEVEMENT

1. Washington Company's management has decided that it needs a petty cash fund of $500.00. On June 1, 1985, a check for $500.00 was given to Maria Ortega, who was appointed the fund custodian. On June 30, 1985, the fund contained $330.00 in currency and coins and receipted vouchers for:

Postage expense paid	$ 60.50
Sales travel expense (for subway tickets) . .	110.30

    Required:

    (1) Prepare journal entries for the establishment and replenishment of the fund.
    (2) Assuming that June is a typical month, comment on the size of the fund.

    (1)

    ## GENERAL JOURNAL

Date	Account Titles and Explanation	F	Debit	Credit

    (2)

2. Damon Dunson's Cash account has a balance of $582.00 on May 31, 1985. His bank statement on that date shows a balance of $834.50. Included in his statement are a group of deposits and check payments along with a $6.00 service charge. There is an item marked DM for $85.00 and John Gill's check in that amount, which he deposited last month, is returned stamped NSF. He also cannot find a deposit of $218.50 that he made on May 31 recorded on the statement. He has listed outstanding checks for a total of $517.00, but his bank reconciliation is out of balance. In matching cancelled checks with the check register, he finds that check no. 1685 in actual amount of $216.00 was recorded as $261.00 in payment of insurance expense on May 8.

Required:

(1)   Prepare a bank reconciliation.
(2)   Prepare general journal entries required.

(1)

(2)

GENERAL JOURNAL

Date	Account Titles and Explanation	F	Debit	Credit

3. The following transactions are to be entered in a check register, a voucher register similar to Figure 9-11, or both. For each of them, fill in the blank spaces in the form on the following page. Use the gross price method. Transaction 1 is done as a sample.

Transaction Number	Description
1	Merchandise is purchased on account for $5,000, terms 2/10, n/30. Voucher no. 321 is prepared for payment.
2	Voucher no. 322 is authorized to pay monthly rent of $350.
3	Voucher no. 323 is prepared to authorize payment of a $10,000 note plus $1,200 interest.
4	Check no. 1830 is issued to pay voucher no. 321 in time to take the cash discount.
5	Check no. 1831 is issued to pay voucher no. 322.
6	Arrangements are made to pay the interest and one-half the principle amount of the $10,000 note. A new note for $5,000 is issued for the balance. Voucher no. 323 is cancelled; vouchers no. 324 and 325 are issued to replace it.
7	Voucher no. 324 is paid by check.

SOLUTION FORM

Transaction Number	Entered in VR, CR, or Both	Columns in Which Entries Are Made and Amount of Each
1	VR	Voucher no. 321 Vouchers Payable Credit, $5,000 Purchases Debit, $5,000

ANSWERS TO LEARNING GOAL ACHIEVEMENT TEST

1.

(1)   GENERAL JOURNAL

Date		Account Titles and Explanation	F	Debit	Credit
1985					
Jun.	1	Petty Cash		500.00	
		Cash			500.00
		To establish petty cash fund.			
	30	Postage Expense		60.50	
		Sales Travel Expense		110.30	
		Cash Over and Short			0.80
		Cash			170.00
		To replenish the petty cash fund.			

(2)

Since $500.00 appears to be enough for about three months' petty cash needs, consideration should be given to reduction of the fund. About $200.00 should be enough. The remainder of the idle cash can be invested in a more productive asset. Also, too large a petty cash fund weakens internal control in that the custodian will need to seek replenishment (and thus be subject to review) less frequently.

2.

(1)   DAMON DUNSON
                              Bank Reconciliation
                              May 31, 1985

Balance per books, May 31		$ 582.00
Add: Error in check no. 1685		45.00
Subtotal		$ 627.00
Deduct: Bank service charge	$ 6.00	
Customer returned check	85.00	91.00
Adjusted balance per books, May 31		$ 536.00
Balance per bank statement, May 31		$ 834.50
Add: Deposit of May 31 in transit		218.50
Subtotal		$1,053.00
Deduct: Outstanding checks (per list)		517.00
Adjusted balance per bank, May 31		$ 536.00

(2)   GENERAL JOURNAL

Date		Account Titles and Explanation	F	Debit	Credit
1985					
May	31	Cash		45	
		Insurance Expense			45
		To correct error in entering			
		check no. 1685 on May 8.			
	31	Service Charge Expense		6	
		Accounts Receivable		85	
		Cash			91
		To record service charges for May			
		and returned customer check.			

3.
                                      SOLUTION FORM

Transaction Number	Entered in VR, CR, or Both	Columns in Which Entries Are Made and Amount of Each
1	VR	Voucher no. 321 Vouchers Payable Credit, $5,000 Purchases Debit, $5,000
2	VR	Voucher no. 322 Vouchers Payable Credit, $350 Other Accounts (Rent Expense) Debit, $350
3	VR	Voucher no. 322 Vouchers Payable Credit, $11,200 Other Accounts Debit: Notes Payable, $10,000 Interest Expense, $1,200
4	Both	Cash Credit, $4,900 Purchases Discounts Debit, $100 Vouchers Payable Debit, $4,900 In VR, date and check no. are entered in Paid column
5	Both	Cash Credit, $350 Vouchers Payable Debit, $350 In VR, date and check no. are entered in Paid column
6	VR	Voucher no. 324, 325 Vouchers Payable Credit, $6,200 Other Accounts (Notes Payable) Credit, $5,000 Other Accounts (Vouchers Payable) Debit, $11,200 Paid, "Cancelled by 324, 325"
7	Both	Cash Credit, $6,200 Vouchers Payable Debit, $6,200 In VR, date and check no. are entered in Paid column

Chapter 10
Short-Term Financing

■■■

EXPLANATION OF MAJOR CONCEPTS

Interest Computations

All interest in Chapter 10 is simple interest, and all rates are *annual rates*. The percent used is the fraction of 100 that is charged for the use of the specified amount of money *per year*. This is the reason for the T in the formula $I = PRT$. The principal times the rate--that is, PR--gives the amount of interest for one year. Because many interest-bearing papers are for periods greater than or less than one year, PR must also be multiplied by T. You should note that computations in this chapter use a 360-day year. In the $4,000, 16 percent, 90-day note that Joan Rockness gave Thomas Blocher (see Figure 10-1), T is expressed as 90/360, which has the effect of reducing the 16 percent of $4,000 to one-fourth of a year.

The regular interest formula computation ($I = PRT$) is usually made by students with a calculator. To compute interest on the note in Figure 10-1, punch in 4,000 x .16 x 90 ÷ 360 in that sequence. The result on your calculator is:

$$4,000 \times .16 = \qquad 640.$$
$$\times \quad 90 = 57,600.$$
$$\div \; 360 = \qquad 160.$$

Since the principal ($4,000) is stated in dollars, the resulting interest (I) of 160 is also dollars ($160). This is not the maturity value (the total amount to be paid when the note is due. The maturity value is the principal plus the interest. In formula form, it is $MV = P + I$. Since we already learned that $I = PRT$, these two terms can be used interchangeably. This leads to the formula $MV = P + PRT$. Factoring the P out of the right-hand side of the equation changes it to $MV = P(1+RT)$. Testing this formula against the Joan Rockness note in Figure 10-1, we find that $MV = \$4,000 [1 + (0.16 \times 90/360)] = \$4,000 (1.0 + 0.04) - \$4,000 (1.04) = \$4,160$, which is the same as $4,000 + $160.

Regardless of the method you use to compute interest or maturity value, it is essential that you understand exactly how it works and why. You can't concentrate on learning the accounting for notes if you can't do the arithmetic quickly and confidently.

Maturity Dates

The term of a note may be expressed in years, months, or days. The maturity date is the date on which payment of the note is due. For a note whose term is expressed in years or months, the maturity date is the corresponding date in the maturity year or month. In other words, a 3-month note dated March 25, 1985, would be due on June 25, 1985. For a note with a term expressed in days, it is necessary to count forward the exact number of days, *not* counting the date the note was made. For example, if the note dated March 25, 1985, was a 90-day note, the maturity date would be June 23, 1985, computed as follows:

```
March 26 thru 31 (31 - 25 = 6)  .     6 days
April . . . . . . . . . . . . .      30 days
May . . . . . . . . . . . . . .      31 days
    Total  . . . . . . . . . . .     67 days
June (90 - 67 = 23)  . . . . . .     23 days
    Total - term of note . . . . .   90 days
```

Since 67 days had run from when the note was made until the end of May, it required 23 additional days in June to complete the term. Also, note in the above computation that the date the note was made, March 25, was not counted, but that the date the note was due, June 23, was counted.

Notes Payable

To the maker of a note, it is a payable. Notes payable may be used to pay for assets or to borrow money. An interest-bearing note may be given for the principal amount with a specified rate of interest to be paid to maturity. The note illustrated in Figure 10-1 is this type. With such a note, the principal amount is recorded as a liability when the note is made, and interest expense is recorded when the note is paid at maturity. If the term of the note overlaps an accounting period end, an adjusting entry must be made to recognize the accrual of interest.

When money is borrowed, the note payable may be *discounted*--that is, the interest may be withheld when the money is borrowed. For a discounted note payable, the maturity value and the principal are the same. When the note payable is discounted, the amount of the discount is debited to Discount on Notes Payable. (Be careful in using this account. Students often confuse it with Notes Receivable Discounted, an account with totally different meaning.) Discount on Notes Payable is a contra liability account. On the balance sheet, it is deducted from the total principal amount of the notes payable. If the entire term of the note falls within one accounting period, the discount is transferred to interest expense at maturity. If the note does not mature in the period it is made, an adjustment is needed to recognize the amount of the discount that has become expense (expired) at the end of the accounting period. The remaining discount then becomes an expense in the next year.

If the entire term of the note falls within one accounting period, it is acceptable practice to debit the amount of the discount to interest expense. The reason is that all of the discount should be allocated to current period expense.

It should be remembered that whenever an interest-bearing note is outstanding at the end of an accounting period, an adjusting entry will be necessary to make sure the interest expense is stated properly. The amount of the interest is calculated as discussed earlier. The form of the adjusting entry will vary, depending on whether it is for a note bearing interest on the principal or a discounted note.

Notes Receivable

To Thomas Blocher, the note in Figure 10-1 is a note receivable. Often the accounting entries for notes receivable can be easily recognized as being the opposite of those made by the maker of a note payable. Two concepts that seem to bother students most about notes receivable are:

1. The accounting for a dishonored note (one the maker fails to pay when due) held by a payee.

2. The accounting for notes receivable that are discounted at a bank.

Dishonored Notes Receivable

As soon as a note reaches maturity, it loses its status as a negotiable instrument that can be passed on to another person (or bank) in exchange for something of value. If it is paid, its life cycle is over. If it is not paid, the debt still exists, but the life cycle of the note is over. A payee holding a dishonored note should recognize several things:

▶ The life cycle of the note receivable is over; Notes Receivable must be credited for the principal amount because a valid note receivable no longer exists.

▶ Interest has been earned. Even if not collected, the accrual basis of accounting requires the recognition of the amount of revenue earned. The amount of interest that should have been collected is credited to Interest Earned.

▶ The debt is neither cancelled nor uncollectible. The payee will take steps-- including legal action, if necessary--to collect the total debt. Thus, the amount of both the principal and interest should be debited to Accounts Receivable.

Notes Receivable Discounted

When the holder of a note receivable (the payee) needs immediate cash, he or she may discount it at a bank. This means that the holder sells the note to the bank at a price determined by the bank discount rate and the number of days left in the term (or life) of the note. In recording discounted notes, remember these points:

▶ The note is discounted at a bank discount rate applied to the *maturity value*-- not the principal--of the note. Thus, you must first compute maturity value before you can compute the amount of bank discount.

▶ The payee discounting a note receivable receives the proceeds. The *proceeds* is an amount equal to maturity value minus the discount. If proceeds is greater than the principal, interest has been earned and should be credited to Interest Earned in recording the discount transaction. If proceeds is less than the principal (and it can be if the bank charges a high rate of discount), expense has been incurred and Interest Expense should be debited in recording the transaction.

▶ Notes receivable are discounted conditionally. That is, the discounter agrees to pay the bank the full maturity value if the maker dishonors the note. To recognize this possibility (called a contingent liability), Notes Receivable is *not* credited when a note is discounted. The credit is to a contra asset account called Notes Receivable Discounted. At maturity date, the note is paid at the bank by the maker or the discounter. In either event, both the contingent liability and the asset, notes receivable, no longer exist. An accounting entry must be made to eliminate both from the books.

For example, calculation of the proceeds from a $1,000, 14 percent, 90-day note receivable, discounted at the bank at 15 percent after holding the note 30 days would be as follows:

Principal	$1,000.00
Interest ($1,000 x 0.14 x 90/360). .	+ 35.00
Maturity value	$1,035.00
Discount ($1,035 x 0.15 x 60/360) .	− 25.88
Proceeds	$1,009.12

Entries at Discounting

Cash	1,009.12	
Interest Earned		9.12
Notes Receivable Discounted . .		1,000.00

Entries at Maturity

Notes Receivable Discounted . . .	1,000.00	
Notes Receivable		1,000.00

If Dishonored

Accounts Receivable	1,035.00	
Cash		1,035.00

Recording Note Transactions

All journal entries in illustrations in Chapter 10 are in general journal form. In an accounting system that uses special journals, collections of notes receivable and proceeds of discounted notes (both receivable and payable) would be entered in the cash receipts journal. To simplify the presentation of solutions to problems, however, you should follow the practice in the text and use the general journal form for all entries unless instructed otherwise.

GUIDED STUDY OF THIS CHAPTER

A. Recording Note Transactions. Let's begin with a careful examination of Figure 10-1 to get a thorough understanding of the elements of a note.

1. Joan Rockness, the _____ is going to pay Thomas Blocher, the _____.

A1. maker, payee

2. $4,000 is the _____ or face value of this note.

A2. principal (Note the spelling of this word; it is *not* "principle.")

3. The date of the note is _____, and the term of the note is _____.

A3. April 19, 1985, 90 days

4. The maturity date of the note is _____ _____.

A4. July 18, 1985

5. On the books of Joan Rockness, this is a note _____.

A5. payable

6. On the books of Thomas Blocher, it is a note _____.

A6. receivable

7. The $160 interest that will be due at maturity is interest expense to Joan Rockness, but to Thomas Blocher it is interest _____.

A7. earned

8. A maker of a note must either receive an asset or cancel some other liability upon giving a note to a payee. If (contrary to the text illustration) Thomas Blocher loaned the $4,000 to Joan Rockness, the entry on her books would be:

Date		Account Titles	F	Debit	Credit

A8.

Date	Act. Tles.	F	Dr.	Cr.
1985				
Apr. 19	Cash		4,000	
	Notes			
	Payable			4,000

A9.

Date	Act. Tles.	F	Dr.	Cr.
1985				
Apr. 19	Notes			
	Receivable		4,000	
	Cash			4,000

A10. Office Equipment, Notes Payable

A11. 4,160, Cash

A12. Notes Payable, Interest Expense

A13. Accounts Payable

A14. Notes Payable

9. Thomas Blocher would record this transaction on his books as:

Date	Account Titles	F	Debit	Credit

10. In the Ace Company note payable illustration, the asset debited was _____ instead of Cash, but the liability account credited was still _____.

11. Interest is paid in addition to the principal at maturity date. The Ace Company paid Triangle Machine Company $160 interest on its 16 percent note for $4,000, causing the total payment to be $_____ credited to _____.

12. When Ace paid Triangle, a liability was reduced; a debit of $4,000 was recorded to _____. The $160 interest was debited to an expense account, _____.

13. Note the method used to record notes given in exchange for merchandise. When Ace Company purchased merchandise from Boone Company, the liability was first recorded as _____.

14. On the same date, the liability was changed to _____.

15. This purchase was "washed through" Accounts Payable so that Ace Company would have

_____
_____
_____.

A15. a complete record in the subsidiary ledger of all its transactions with Boone Company

16. Would the same procedure be used on the books of Boone Company? _____

A16. Yes.

17. Boone Company would record this sale as both a debit and a credit to _____

_____.

A17. Accounts Receivable

18. Ace Company could borrow money from the bank by giving the First National Bank a $12,000, 16 percent note, as illustrated in the text. A second way to borrow money is to _____ Ace's own noninterest-bearing note as was done on May 1 at the City National Bank.

A18. discount

19. The amount of cash given by the bank to a company (or person) discounting a note is called the _____.

A19. proceeds

20. Discount is *always* computed on maturity value. The maturity value of Ace's note was $_____ because it was noninterest-bearing.

A20. 12,000

21. The amount withheld by the lender is called the *discount*. Although discount is *always* ultimately debited to Interest Expense, it may be directly debited to the expense account only if the note will _____

_____.

A21. reach maturity date in the current accounting period

22. When Ace Company discounted a 60-day note payable on May 1, the amount of discount is debited to _____.

A22. Discount on Notes Payable

23. An entry is necessary on June 30, 1985, the maturity date, to recognize the fact that the discount has become interest expense.

A23. No answer required.

24. The Adjusto Company illustration provides an example of apportioning the discount. When an $18,000, 120-day, 16 percent note was discounted at the Bank of Rodin on December 16, 1985, Discount on Notes Payable was debited for $_____.

A24. 960

25. $960 is the total amount of Adjusto's interest expense on this note. However, only _____ of the 120 days are in the year 1985.

A25. fifteen

26. Accordingly, only $_____ should be debited to Interest Expense in the December 31, 1985, adjusting entry.

A26. 120

27. This leaves $_____ in the Discount on Notes Payable account. It is interest expense for the year _____, so another adjustment must be made on April 15, 1986 to include that amount in 1986 expense.

A27. 840, 1986

28. Notes Receivable may also be discounted but usually with an understanding that the company that does so will redeem the note at full maturity value if the maker does not pay it when it comes due. Notes receivable discounted are usually interest-bearing notes, but the discount rate charged by the bank may be different from the interest rate of the note.

A28. No answer required.

B. *Special Situations. Several special situations can arise in recording note transactions. One is the failure of the maker of the note to pay it when due.*

1. By failing to pay a note at the maturity date, a maker defaults on the payment or_____ the note.

B1. dishonors

2. A dishonored note is no longer a negotiable instrument, so it must be removed from the Notes Receivable account by a _____ (debit/credit).

B2. credit

3. The maturity value of the note is debited to

_____.

B3. Accounts Receivable

4. When Ronald Raymond dishonored his $4,000 note to the Potter Company, Accounts Receivable was debited with the $4,000 principal plus $160 interest = $4,160. The interest portion of the receivable is credited to

_____.

B4.   Interest Earned

5.   Should this note be written off as a bad debt?

_____

B5.   No. (Efforts will be made to collect it.)

6.   Another special situation that arises with both notes receivable and notes payable is the need for adjusting entries to accrue interest at the end of an accounting period on all notes not yet due. Accrued interest receivable gives rise to _____ (a revenue/an expense).

B6.   a revenue

7.   Accrued interest payable gives rise to _____

_____ .

B7.   an expense

8.   The amount to be accrued is interest from the date of the note to _____

_____ .

B8.   the end of the accounting period

9.   The Emerson Company is shown as having one note receivable on December 31, 1985. A note from Linda Wilson is a 16 percent, 150-day note for $3,660 dated November 1. On this note, exactly _____ days of interest should be recognized as income of 1985.

B9.   sixty (Twenty-nine in November and thirty-one in December.)

10.   Since this interest has not been recorded previously, a debit to the asset _____ _____ is needed.

B10.   Accrued Interest Receivable

11.   The credit is journalized to _____ _____; this adds $_____ to 1985 income.

B11.   Interest Earned, 97.60

12.   The total interest to be earned on the note for the entire term would be $_____ .

B12.   244.00

13.   Since $97.60 has been accrued as earned in 1985, the remaining $_____ will be recorded as earned when the note is collected on _____ .

B13.   146.40, March 31, 1986

14.   The total cash received on March 31, 1986, would be $_____ .

B14.   3,904.00

15.   Of the total, $_____ was the collection of 1985's interest, $_____ was 1986's interest, and $_____ was the principal.

B 15.   97.60, 146.40,
3,660.00

16.   Doesn't this procedure parallel the treatment of the Discounts on Notes Payable account?

B 16.   Yes. (However, one procedure records revenue, the other records expense.)

17.   A third special situation arises when customers' notes receivable are discounted at the bank. What would be a probable reason for discounting a customer's note receivable? _____

_____

B 17.   The company holding the note needs cash.

18.   Discount is computed on _____ value.

B 18.   maturity

19.   The maturity value of the note given by Edward Grande to the Fuller Company on April 19, 1985, is $6,000 + $_____ interest = $_____ .

B 19.   160, 6,160

20.   The discount period is the number of days that the bank will hold the note. May 1, the date of discount, _____ (does/ does not) count as one of these days.

B 20.   does not

21.   June 18, the due date, _____ (does/ does not) count as one of the days of the period of discount.

B 21.   does

22.   The amount of discount is

$$\frac{\$6,160}{1} \times \frac{15}{100} \times \frac{48}{360} = \$123.20.$$

The proceeds equal maturity value minus _____, so Fuller Company receives $6,160 − $123.20 = $_____ .

B 22.   discount, 6,036.80

23.   The amount received in excess of face value is credited to _____.

B 23.   Interest Earned

24.   In some cases, the proceeds may be less than face value. In that case, the difference would be debited to _____.

B 24.   Interest Expense

25.   When a business discounts a customer's note, it is usually with the requirement that the business must redeem the note if the customer fails to pay. This gives rise to a _____ liability.

B25. contingent

26. To show this contingent liability, we do not remove the note receivable from the books when it is discounted. Instead we credit a contra account, _____

_____.

B26. Notes Receivable Discounted

27. If Edward Grande pays the bank on the due date, an entry is required on the Fuller Company's books. What does this entry accomplish? _____

_____

B27. Removes the note receivable and the related contra account.

28. If Edward Grande fails to pay the note on June 18, the Fuller Company must buy it back from the bank at maturity value of $_____.

B28. 6,160

29. In this case, the bank charged a protest fee of $8. This fee is paid to the bank by_____

_____.

B29. the Fuller Company

30. Naturally, the Fuller Company would credit Cash with the full amount paid to the bank. That total is debited to _____

_____.

B30. Accounts Receivable

31. Students often ask why there is no Interest Earned entry on Fuller Company's books when this dishonored note is redeemed at maturity value. (There is an Interest Earned entry when a customer's note held by Fuller is dishonored.) What is the reason that no credit is made to Interest Earned when Fuller redeems Grande's note? _____

_____

_____

_____

_____

B31. The interest earned by Fuller was recorded at time of discount. All interest earned since that date has been earned by the bank, not by Fuller.

SELF TEST OF LEARNING GOAL ACHIEVEMENT

1. Rebecca Levin gives to Juan Garcia a 90-day note promising to pay him $10,000 with interest at 14 percent. The note is dated February 4, 1985. Answer the following:

    a. The maker is _____.

    b. The payee is _____.

    c. The term is _____.

    d. The maturity date is _____.

    e. The general formula to compute the interest is _____. In this case, the specific computation of interest is:

    f. The maturity value is:

    g. If Garcia discounts the note at the Bank of Commerce at 16 percent on April 5, 1985, the discount term is _____.

    h. The amount of discount is computed as:

    i. The proceeds to Garcia is in the amount of $_____.

    j. Therefore, Garcia has $_____ of interest _____ (earned/ expense) in the discount transaction.

    k. The journal entry for the discount transaction on Juan Garcia's books is:

GENERAL JOURNAL

Date		Account Titles and Explanation	F	Debit	Credit
1985					
Apr.	5				

l. The journal entry on Juan Garcia's books if Rebecca Levin pays the note at the bank on time is:

1985					

m. If she fails to pay and the bank adds a protest fee of $20, the entry(ies) required on Garcia's books is/are:

1985					

2. If Samual Jackson borrows $50,000 for his business by discounting a 90-day note at 15 percent at the West Bank on November 28, 1985, the journal entry on his books will be:

GENERAL JOURNAL

Date		Account Titles and Explanation	F	Debit	Credit
1985					
Nov.	28				

3. On December 31, 1985, Jackson's accountant must make an adjusting entry to apportion interest expense between 1985 and 1986. It is:

GENERAL JOURNAL

Date		Account Titles and Explanation	F	Debit	Credit
1985					
Dec.	31				

ANSWERS TO LEARNING GOAL ACHIEVEMENT TEST

1. a. Rebecca Levin
   b. Juan Garcia
   c. 90 days
   d. May 5, 1985
   e. I = PRT. $10,000 x 0.14 x 90/360 = $350.
   f. $10,000 + $350 = $10,350 OR $10,000 (1.035) = $10,350.
   g. 30 days
   h. $10,350 x 0.16 x 30/360 = $138.
   i. $10,212 = ($10,350 - $138)
   j. $212, earned
   k.

GENERAL JOURNAL

Date		Account Titles and Explanation	F	Debit	Credit
1985					
Apr.	5	Cash		10,212	
		Interest Earned			212
		Notes Receivable Discounted			10,000
		Discounted Levin note at 16			
		percent at Bank of Commerce.			

   l.

1985					
May	5	Notes Receivable Discounted		10,000	
		Notes Receivable			10,000
		To record maturity of Levin note.			

m.

1985					
May	5	Accounts Receivable		10,370	
		Cash			10,370
		Payment of dishonored Levin			
		note plus protest fee.			
	5	Notes Receivable Discounted		10,000	
		Notes Receivable			10,000
		To record maturity of Levin note.			

2.

GENERAL JOURNAL

Date		Account Titles and Explanation	F	Debit	Credit
1985					
Nov.	28	Cash		48,125	
		Discount on Notes Payable		1,875	
		Notes Payable			50,000
		Borrowing of $50,000 by			
		discounting note payable			
		at 15 percent.			

3.

GENERAL JOURNAL

Date		Account Titles and Explanation	F	Debit	Credit
1985					
Dec.	31	Interest Expense		687.50	
		Discount on Notes Payable			687.50
		To record expiration of			
		33 days' discount.			

Chapter 11
Accounts Receivable and Bad Debts

■■

EXPLANATION OF MAJOR CONCEPTS

Sources and Classification of Receivables

A receivable represents a claim against other entities for assets or services. There are two sources of these claims: trade--sale of goods or services, and nontrade--sources other than trade. Trade receivables may be of three types: accounts receivable, notes receivable, or credit card receivables. There are a wide variety of sources of nontrade receivables, such as loans to officers, accrued interest on notes receivable, and good-faith deposits made by customers.

Bad Debts Expense

Bad debts expense is the result of making sales on credit and being unable to collect them later. The expense could be recorded at the time an account is determined to be uncollectible. Such determinations, however, are usually made in accounting periods later than the one in which the sale was made. This causes revenue to be reported in one period and related expense to be reported in another.

Use of an estimate of bad debts expense as an adjusting entry at the end of each accounting period allows revenue and related expense to be assigned to the same period. To record an estimate of bad debts expense, however, requires the use of a contra asset account to Accounts Receivable. If Accounts Receivable were credited with estimated bad debts expense, it would not balance with its subsidiary ledger, since we do not know at the time of the adjustment just who's account is bad. Therefore, we credit a contra or valuation account to allow us to show the net or collectible amount on the balance sheet.

Allowance for Doubtful Accounts

Allowance for Doubtful Accounts is the contra asset account credited when estimated bad debts expense is recorded. This account serves two purposes:

1. As a contra account, it is deducted from trade receivables on the balance sheet. Thus, it causes receivables to be stated at their net realizable (or collectible) value--a more realistic asset valuation.

2. When accounts are actually determined to be uncollectible, it absorbs the debit for the account write-off. (Expense has already been debited with an estimated amount; often the expense debit was made in a prior period.)

Estimating the Expense

Two approaches can be taken to estimate bad debts expense. Either is acceptable, but once a method is chosen, it should be used consistently year after year.

▶ One method is the *income statement approach*. A company simply determines from past experience the percent of each year's net sales which became uncollectible. Then, for the adjusting entry, the current year's net sales are multiplied by the percentage, and that amount is debited to expense and credited to the allowance. The balance in the allowance account before adjustment is ignored. Thus, the amount of the adjustment has been determined using an income statement number, net sales.

▶ The other method is the *balance sheet method*. A study of the accounts receivable is made to estimate the amount of uncollectibles in them. This study may be done by dividing the individual receivables up into categories according to their age and multiplying each category by the appropriate percentage determined from past experience. Or, the balance in Accounts Receivable can be multiplied by a percentage determined from past experience. The amount determined in this analysis is what the balance in Allowance for Doubtful Accounts *ought to be*. The expense, then, is the amount needed to adjust the allowance to equal the estimated uncollectibles. Thus, the amount of the adjustment has been determined using balance sheet numbers, Accounts Receivable and Allowance for Doubtful Accounts.

The Direct Write-Off Method

The *direct write-off method* is a simple approach. No attempt is made to estimate in advance uncollectible accounts. When a specific account is identified as being uncollectible, the amount is debited to Bad Debts Expense and credited to Accounts Receivable. There is no adjusting entry made at the end of a year. Thus, there is a mismatching of revenue and expense under this method, and because of this the direct write-off method is not recommended.

Recording Transactions and Adjustments

Here are five suggestions to help you avoid errors that students seem to make most frequently:

1. The adjusting entry to record expense under the estimating method is always:

    Bad Debts Expense XXX
      Allowance for Doubtful Accounts . .   XXX

Never involve the Cash account in an end-of-year adjustment, and *never* involve Accounts Receivable in this one.

2. Every write-off of an uncollectibe account must credit Accounts Receivable.

3. Write-offs under the estimating (allowance) method *always* debit Allowance for Doubtful Accounts; write-offs under the direct write-off method *always* debit Bad Debts Expense.

4. Recoveries under the estimating (allowance) method *always* credit Allowance for Doubtful Accounts; recoveries under the direct write-off method *always* credit a revenue, Bad Debts Recovered.

5. In preparing an aging schedule, there must be a column for accounts not yet due. These are accounts less than thirty days old. It follows, then, that the age of an account in a past due column is thirty days plus the time in that column heading.

<u>Credit Card Sales</u>

Credit cards are issued by various types of institutions. The accounting for sales made to holders of these credit cards basically falls into two categories. The first is for sales on bank credit cards. The charge slips from these sales are accepted by the bank as if they were cash. The bank simply deducts a percentage from the total sale as a service fee. The entry to record these sales then is a debit to Cash for the net amount, a debit to Credit Card Fees Expense for the service fee, and a credit to Sales for the total.

The second category is sales with nonbank type cards, such as the green American Express. In this case, the charge slips are sent to the issuing institution for reimbursement. Again, the issuing institution charges a service fee and will reimburse only the amount of the sale less the service fee. The entry to record this type of sale is a debit to Accounts Receivable, Credit Cards for the net amount to be received; a debit to Credit Card Fees Expense for the service charge; and a credit to Sales for the total amount of the sale.

GUIDED STUDY OF THIS CHAPTER

A. Receivables. There are many types of receivables; all are assets. This chapter is concerned mainly with trade receivables that are current assets.

1. A trade receivable results from a _____ _____.

A1.   sale of goods or services to customers

2. The three major types of trade receivables are _____, _____, and _____.

A2. accounts receivable, notes receivable, credit card receivables

A3. Accounts

A4. Notes

A5. Credit card, credit cards

A6. should not

A7. should not

A8. As current liabilities.

A9. does

B1. Allowance for Doubtful Accounts

B2. Bad Debts Expense, Income Summary

3. _____ receivable are not supported by formal written promises to pay at a specific date.

4. _____ receivable are usually supported by written promises to pay at a specific date and often bear interest.

5. _____ receivables result from the acceptance of _____ where the resulting invoices are not accepted by banks for deposit.

6. Loans to officers and employees _____ (should/should not) be combined in the same accounts with trade receivables.

7. When some customers' accounts have credit balances (overpayments, returns, and so forth), the current asset, accounts receivable, _____ (should/should not) be shown in the balance sheet as the net figure.

8. How should credit balances in customers' accounts be reported in the balance sheet?

_____

9. If it is not so designated, the Accounts Receivable account _____ (does/ does not) represent trade receivables.

B. *Bad Debts Expense. When bad debts expense is estimated, it is recorded only once per year in an end-of-year adjusting entry.*

1. The account credited in this adjusting entry is

_____.

2. The debit in the adjusting entry is to an expense account, _____, which is then closed in the closing entries to the _____ account.

3. Allowance for Doubtful Accounts is not closed but is reported on the balance sheet as

_____.

B3.   a reduction from receivables (or from accounts receivable)

4.   The expense is reported in the _____ statement, where it is a deduction from revenues of the same period.

B4.   income

5.   As an individual's account actually is determined to be uncollectible, it is written off. This requires a reduction of Accounts Receivable which would be a _____ (debit/ credit).

B5.   credit

6.   The debit reduces the valuation account _____ .

B6.   Allowance for Doubtful Accounts

7.   Why isn't the write-off entry a debit to expense? _____

_____

_____

_____

B7.   Because estimated total expense has already been debited in the end-of-year adjusting entry.

8.   One approach to estimating bad debts expense is the income statement approach. The amount of expense debited in the end-of-year adjusting entry is a percent of _____ .

B8.   net sales (Sometimes net credit sales.)

9.   How is the rate (percent) of net sales decided upon? _____

_____

B9.   It is based on experience with losses in prior years.

10.   If there is a balance in the Allowance for Doubtful Accounts, what adjustment is made to the percent of net sales computed as bad debts expense? _____

B10.   None.

11.   Another approach is the balance sheet approach. In this method, we try to determine how much the Allowance for Doubtful Accounts ought to be at the end of each year. To do so, we analyze accounts receivable.

B11.   No answer required.

12.   Suppose it is determined that the Allowance for Doubtful Accounts ought to have a balance of $4,000 on December 31, 1985. If the account already has a credit balance of $500, we would need only $_____ more to bring it up to $4,000.

B 12. 3,500

13. But if it had a debit balance of $600, we would need a credit of $_____ to bring the account up to $4,000.

B 13. 4,600

14. So the debit to Bad Debts Expense under the balance sheet approach is the amount needed to bring the Allowance for Doubtful Accounts up to its _____.

B 14. desired balance

15. Does use of the balance sheet approach change the entries to write off uncollectible accounts?
_____

B 15. No. (They are the same under either approach.)

16. Let's study Figure 11-1. An amount will fall in the Not Yet Due column if it is less than
_____.

B 16. thirty days old

17. Any amount in the 1-30 column is between _____ and _____ days old.

B 17. thirty-one, sixty

18. Walter Arnold has amounts in more than one column. How can this happen? _____
_____

B 18. He has more than one unpaid purchase.

19. Allan Conlon has at least _____ unpaid purchases.

B 19. three

20. The number 52 at the bottom of the Not Yet Due column indicates that _____
_____.

B 20. 52 percent of total accounts receivable are not yet due

21. Could there be additional columns on this work sheet? _____ Explain. _____
_____
_____
_____

B 21. Yes. Instead of Over 90 Days Past Due, there could be columns for 91-120 Days Past Due, 121-150 days, and so on.

22. Of the $29,120 in accounts Not Yet Due, the John Rogers Company expects _____ percent to become uncollectible.

B22. 3

23. A different percentage is then applied against each column to determine the portion of those accounts estimated to be uncollectible. For the "Not Yet Due" column, the percentage is 3 percent, giving an estimated amount uncollectible of $_____.

B23. 873.60

24. Of the $16,240 that is 1-30 Days Past Due, John Rogers expects that _____ percent will become uncollectible.

B24. 4

25. As the accounts become older, John Rogers has found that the estimated percent uncollectible becomes _____ (smaller/ greater).

B25. greater

26. After estimating the dollar amount of uncollectible accounts in each segment, John Rogers Company believes that $_____ of its accounts receivable are uncollectible on December 31, 1985.

B26. 4,099.20

27. If the Allowance for Doubtful Accounts already has a credit balance of $150, only $_____ is needed to bring the allowance up to $4,099.20.

B27. 3,949.20

28. But if the Allowance for Doubtful Accounts had a debit balance of $300, it would require a credit of $_____ to bring the account up to $4,099.20.

B28. 4,399.20

29. The debit in the adjusting entry is always to the _____ account.

B29. Bad Debts Expense

30. So in the balance sheet approach, the amount of bad debts expense depends upon two factors. One is _____ _____ and the other is _____.

B30. the estimate of un- collectible accounts receivable, the balance in the allowance account

C. *Write-Off and Recovery. When an account is determined to be uncollectible, it is written off.*

1. Under the allowance (estimating) method, this requires a debit to _____ _____.

C1. Allowance for Doubtful Accounts

2. Accounts written off may later be wholly or partially recovered. If this happens, under the allowance method, there would be a credit to _____.

C2. Allowance for Doubtful Accounts

3. A second method of handling bad debts expense is to wait until they occur before recording them. In this case, there would be *no* end-of-year adjusting entries and *no* Allowance for Doubtful Accounts. This method is called the _____.

C3. direct write-off method

4. Under the direct write-off method, the account debited when an uncollectible is written off is

_____.

C4. Bad Debts Expense

5. A disadvantage of this method is that _____

_____

_____

_____.

C5. expense often falls into a year other than the one in which its related revenue was recognized

6. Under both the allowance method and the direct write-off method, _____

_____ is credited when an account is actually written off.

C6. Accounts Receivable

7. Since expense is debited on write-off under the direct write-off method, it is logical that a revenue would be credited for recoveries under this method. The revenue account credited is _____.

C7. Bad Debts Recovered

8. Figure 11-2 makes a complete comparison of the two methods and gives examples of transactions under each. It is worth careful study. Under the estimating method, bad debts expense for 1985 was $_____; under the direct write-off method, it was $_____.

C8. 5,060, 3,950

9. Under both methods, the accounts written off amounted to $_____.

C9. 3,950

10. Recoveries under both methods in 1985 were $_____.

C10. 250

11. Which method will report the recovery as a revenue? _____

C11. The direct write-off method.

12. Is the direct write-off method more accurate because the amount of expense recorded was equal to the uncollectible accounts written off? _____ Explain. _____

_____

_____

_____

C12. No. There are probably other amounts in 1985 credit sales that will become uncollectible in later years.

13. Assume that in Figure 11-2 the balance in Accounts Receivable on January 1, 1985, was $42,500. What is the Accounts Receivable balance on December 31, 1985? $_____

C13. 49,550 = ($42,500 + $510,000 - $495,000 - $4,000 - $3,950).

14. Under the direct write-off method of recognizing bad debts expense, accounts receivable would show on the December 31, 1985, balance sheet as:

Current assets:
Cash . . . . $XX,XXX
Accounts receivable . . . . . .   _____

C14.
Cash . . . . . . $XX,XXX
Accts. rec. . .   49,550

15. Under the allowance method of recognizing bad debts expense, the balance sheet would show (assume Allowance for Doubtful Accounts on January 1, 1985, to be a credit balance of $4,000):

Current assets:
Cash . . . . $XX,XXX
Accounts receivable . $_____

. .   _____   _____

C15.
Cash . . . . . $XX,XXX
Accts. rec. .$49,550
Dct: Allow.
    for d.a. . 5,360 44,190

16. Which method do you think gives the more realistic valuation to accounts receivable?

_____

Why? _____

_____

C16. The allowance method. Because it recognizes that the entire $49,550 will not be collected.

D. *Credit Card Sales. The introduction of internationally recognized credit cards allows a seller to sell on account without the risk of bad debt losses.*

D1.   The bank that issued the credit card.

D2.   It charges the seller a fee. (Also, there is an interest charge on unpaid balances.)

D3.   38,400.

D4.   40,000

D5.   Credit Card Fee Expense

D6.   Accounts Receivable, Credit Cards

D7.   same

D8.   current asset

D9.   No answer required.

1.   Who absorbs the bad debt expense when a bank credit card sale becomes uncollectible?

_____

2.   How does a credit card company compensate for its bad debt losses and still make a profit?

_____

_____

3.   Assume that a company makes sales of $40,000 in a day to customers who use bank credit cards. If the credit card companies charge an average of 4 percent, how much is the amount of the debit to Cash? $_____

4.   The credit to Sales is $_____.

5.   Therefore, a debit of $1,600 would be made to

_____.

6.   If the same facts had existed, but the sales had been made to customers who used nonbank cards, the debit for $38,400 would have been to _____.

7.   The rest of the entry to record the sales would have been the _____.

8.   Accounts Receivable, Credit Cards is classified on the balance sheet as a _____.

9.   It should be separated from other trade Accounts Receivable, however, because it is unlikely to have bad debt losses.

SELF TEST OF LEARNING GOAL ACHIEVEMENT

1. The following applies to Lloyd's Appliance Company:

	1983	1984	1985
Net credit sales	$200,000	$260,000	$360,000
Uncollectible accounts written-off . . .	600	3,200	4,200

When the business was formed in January 1983, Lewis Lloyd, the owner, estimated that bad debt losses would be 1 percent of net credit sales.

Required: Using that assumption, prepare general journal entries as of December 31 of each year to record (a) bad debts expense and (b) the write-offs for the year.

(1)
GENERAL JOURNAL

Date		Account Titles and Explanation	F	Debit	Credit

(2)   Do you consider Lloyd's estimate to be reasonably accurate? Explain.

(3)   Assume that 1986 sales are $400,000, accounts written off are $4,350, and analysis of accounts receivable on December 31, 1986, indicates that $5,200 is uncollectible. Change to the balance sheet approach and record the bad debts expense for 1986.

GENERAL JOURNAL

Date	Account Titles and Explanation	F	Debit	Credit

(4)   In a competitor's business, a bad debt of $900 written off in 1984 was recovered in 1985. The account credited was Bad Debts Recovered. What approach or method was the competitor using?

_____

(5)   If Lloyd's Appliance Company recovered an account in 1985 that has been written off in 1984, what account would be credited?

_____

2.   Wagner and Company had a balance of $74,500 in Accounts Receivable. Included as part of this balance are three customers who had overpaid their accounts by a total of $1,500. How should these facts be disclosed on Wagner's balance sheet?

3.   Bits and Bytes Shop has made the following credit sales on July 12, 1985:

To VISA and MasterCard customers .	$ 9,200
To American Express customers . . .	16,000

The credit card company's charge will be 5 percent of credit card sales. Record the credit sales for the day in a compound general journal entry.

GENERAL JOURNAL

Date		Account Titles and Explanation	F	Debit	Credit

ANSWERS TO LEARNING GOAL ACHIEVEMENT TEST

1.

(1)   GENERAL JOURNAL

Date		Account Titles and Explanation	F	Debit	Credit
1983		(a)			
Dec.	31	Bad Debts Expense		2,000	
		Allowance for Doubtful Accounts			2,000
		To estimate expense for 1983.			
		(b)			
	31	Allowance for Doubtful Accounts		600	
		Accounts Receivable			600
		To write off accounts.			
1984		(a)			
Dec.	31	Bad Debts Expense		2,600	
		Allowance for Doubtful Accounts			2,600
		To estimate expense for 1984.			
		(b)			
	31	Allowance for Doubtful Accounts		3,200	
		Accounts Receivable			3,200
		To write off accounts.			
1985		(a)			
Dec.	31	Bad Debts Expense		3,600	
		Allowance for Doubtful Accounts			3,600
		To estimate expense for 1985.			
		(b)			
	31	Allowance for Doubtful Accounts		4,200	
		Accounts Receivable			4,200
		To write off accounts.			

(2)   No, his estimate is probably too low. The business will begin 1986
       with only $200 in the allowance account. The balance at the beginning
       of a year should be adequate to cover prior year sales to be written
       off. Expense of 1983, 1984, and 1985 has probably been understated.

(3)   GENERAL JOURNAL

Date		Account Titles and Explanation	F	Debit	Credit
1986					
Dec.	31	Bad Debts Expense		9,350	
		Allowance for Doubtful Accounts			9,350
		To increase the allowance to $5,200.			

(4)   The direct write-off method.

(5)   Allowance for Doubtful Accounts.

2. Current assets:
    Cash . . . . $XX,XXX
    Accounts receivable   76,000

    Current liabilities:
    Accounts payable . . . . $XX,XXX
    Credit balances in customer accounts   1,500

3.

GENERAL JOURNAL

Date		Account Titles and Explanation	F	Debit	Credit
1985					
Jul.	12	Cash		8,740	
		Accounts Receivable, Credit Cards		15,200	
		Credit Card Fees Expense		1,260	
		Sales			25,200
		To record credit sales.			

Chapter 12
Inventories and
Cost of Goods Sold

■■

EXPLANATION OF MAJOR CONCEPTS

Basis of Inventory Valuation

Inventories should originally be recorded at cost. Cost is defined to include all expenditures necessary to get the merchandise in a saleable condition. Thus, it should include the invoice price of the merchandise minus any purchases discounts, plus transportation in and any other expenditures made to get the merchandise to the place of business.

Two Inventory Systems

There are two basic issues involved in the accounting for inventories. They are:

1. Item-by-item determination of quantities on hand at the end of an accounting period. This must be done by physical count if a periodic inventory system is used.

2. Item-by-item determination of historical cost. Since historical cost is the basis required by generally accepted accounting principles for recording assets, it would seem to be a simple matter to record the cost of each item and use it to place a valuation on the inventory. Usually this is not the case, as the following discussion explains.

Under the *periodic inventory system,* there is no running record maintained for items in the inventory. As described in Chapter 6, the physical count at the end of the accounting period establishes the quantity on hand. The quantity sold is then determined by the following computation:

Quantity on hand at beginning	XX
Plus quantity purchased during the period	XXX
Equals total quantity available for sale	XXX
Less quantity on hand at end	XX
Equals quantity sold	XXX

In Chapter 6, it was assumed that a cost valuation could be associated with each unit on hand. This method (called the *specific identification method*) is ideal if it is feasible. In some cases--say, with new cars on an automobile dealer's lot--

it is feasible. With most inventory items, the specific identification method is too costly or actually impossible to apply. Can you imagine using this method with a pile of oranges at a supermarket or with gasoline stored in an underground tank at the local service station? Accordingly, for the second step--determination of item-by-item historical cost--some assumptions must be made. These are explained after the perpetual system is discussed.

Under the *perpetual inventory system,* a continuous record of receipts and sales is maintained for units of each inventory item. In Chapter 12, this record is illustrated in the form of perpetual inventory cards or stock records--a common and popular device used by businesses. (Many companies with thousands of different items in stock maintain this continuous record by computer, but the basic idea is the same.) Maintenance of such a continuous record solves the problem of item-by-item determination of quantity on hand (although an annual count to verify the accuracy of stock records is still required). It does not, however, solve the second problem of placing a historical cost valuation on items on hand. When a customer selects a dozen oranges from the pile, which dozen did he or she take? Was it from those that were received on Wednesday at 48 cents per dozen or those received on Thursday at 51 cents per dozen? Or was it a combination of both? Even more impossible is the identification of cost of gasoline a customer pumps from the storage tank. Last month the station may have had four or five deliveries--all at different cost prices. In the storage tank, they are mixed together; we know how many gallons the customer pumped, but from which cost batch? Again, as in the periodic inventory system, some cost-flow assumptions must be made.

Cost-Flow Assumptions

We can make three basic assumptions about the flow of costs. You must under-stand that *they are assumptions. They may or may not represent the actual flow of goods.* The cost flow assumptions are:

▶ *First In, First Out (FIFO).* We assume that the oldest goods on hand are sold first. Thus, any items remaining on hand in inventory must be made up of the most recent purchases.

▶ *Last In, First Out (LIFO).* We assume that the newest goods on hand are sold first. Thus, any items remaining on hand must be made up of the earliest purchases, including the beginning inventory of the period.

▶ *Average.* The general idea of this assumption is that the cost of goods remaining on hand is an average of the cost of beginning inventory and pur-chases during the period. Under the periodic system, we apply a *weighted average* computation. Under the perpetual system, we use a *moving average* computation.

These cost-flow assumptions are used in both the periodic and perpetual inventory systems to determine (1) the valuation of ending inventory and (2) the cost of goods sold. The different assumptions usually yield different results. A manager must choose an assumption and apply it consistently from year to year. The assumption chosen *does not* relate to the physical flow of goods. Although it would be physically impossible for gasoline to flow through a storage tank in a FIFO or LIFO manner (gallons are mixed together), either FIFO or LIFO is an acceptable assumption for costing gasoline at a service station.

Journal Entries

When the periodic inventory system is used, journal entries to record the change in inventory balance are closing entries, as illustrated in Chapter 6. There is not a ledger account for cost of goods sold; it is determined by computation and automatically reduces income in the closing process. Under the perpetual inventory system, Cost of Goods Sold is a general ledger account that is debited with the *cost* of inventory items given up when sales are made. This account balance is closed into Income Summary at the end of the period to reduce net income. The comparison of journal entries made under the two systems in Figure 12-1 should be studied carefully. Both systems lead to the same net income under FIFO but not under LIFO or weighted average.

Lower of Cost or Market (LCM)

In order to present a conservative picture, inventory valuation may be reduced below cost if the market price should fall below the original cost. Three basic ways to compute LCM are presented in Chapter 12. Each of the three methods is an acceptable one. You should use the method that most properly reflects income under the circumstances. This is a matter of judgement by a trained accountant.

Estimating Inventories

There are many reasons that a business would need to estimate inventories. Perhaps monthly financial statements are desired. In many businesses, it is too expensive to make a physical count every month. Both the *retail method* and the *gross margin method* allow us to estimate the cost valuation of inventory at a specific date. They both require that we determine cost of goods as a percent of selling price, but in a slightly different way. You will find that the ability to estimate inventories under these two methods will be useful to you in several ways in the future. The gross margin method uses previously experienced cost percentages; the retail method uses the current year cost percent.

GUIDED STUDY OF THIS CHAPTER

> A. *Cost Assignment--Periodic System. The questions in this section use the chapter example, a stapler, stock number 802A. The same transactions are repeated for each assumption. In all cases, the basic task is to allocate the $596 cost of 230 staplers available for sale between (1) cost of 60 staplers remaining on hand and (2) cost of 170 staplers sold. Let's begin with FIFO.*

A1.   latest

1. Under the periodic system, there is no record of units sold; we know only that 60 staplers are on hand on April 30. If we assume that oldest goods are sold first, the 60 units remaining in stock on April 30 must have been the _____ (earliest/latest) purchased.

A2.   April 16, 2.80

2. Therefore, the 60 units on hand at April 30 must be from the purchase made on _____ at $_____ each.

A3.   2.80, 168

3. The April 30 inventory cost using the FIFO periodic assumption is 60 staplers at $_____ = $_____.

A4.   ending inventory

4. Cost of goods sold is equal to total available for sale minus _____.

A5.   596, 168, 428

5. So, under FIFO periodic, cost of goods sold is $_____ minus $_____ = $_____.

6. Cost of goods sold could also be computed by adding the cost of the batches we assumed to be sold. Under the FIFO assumption, we assume that sales included the entire beginning inventory (cost = $88), the entire April 5 pur-chase (cost = $312), and 10 staplers from the April 16 purchase (cost = $28). This cost of $88 + $312 + $28 = $_____, which _____ (is/is not) the same as we have already com-puted.

A6.   428, is

7. The LIFO assumption says that latest receipts are sold first. Therefore, the 60 staplers on hand on April 30 would be the _____ (oldest/newest) that we have.

A7.   oldest

8. The 60 oldest staplers would be _____ from _____ and _____ from the _____.

A8.   40, beginning inventory, 20, April 5 purchase

9. Thus, the LIFO periodic inventory is 40 staplers at $_____ plus 20 staplers at $_____ = $_____.

A9.   2.20, 2.60, 140

10. And cost of goods sold is $596 minus $140 = $_____.

A10. 456

11. Compute cost of goods sold by computing cost of individual batches of staplers assumed to have been sold.

A11. 70 x $2.80 = $196
      100 x 2.60 = 260
         Total   = $456

12. For weighted average, we compute the average cost of staplers available for sale. The total cost of staplers available for sale was $_____.

A12. 596

13. The total number of staplers available for sale was _____.

A13. 230

14. So the weighted average cost per stapler was $596 ÷ 230 = $_____.

A14. 2.5913043

15. Since several are involved, let's round to four decimal places. The April 30 inventory cost is assumed to be _____ staplers times $_____ = $_____.

A15. 60, 2.5913, 155.48

16. And cost of goods sold is $_____ minus $_____ = $_____.

A16. 596.00, 155.48, 440.52

17. Under each of the three methods, we apportioned total cost of goods available ($596) between the April 30 inventory (60 staplers) and cost of sales in April (170 staplers). Each of the three cost flow assumptions gave a different result.

A17. No answer required.

B. *Cost Assignment--Perpetual System. Under the perpetual system, a continuous record is kept for each stock item, but we still must make cost-flow assumptions. Again, they are FIFO, LIFO, and average. We will again use the transactions for the stapler, stock number 802A. Let's start with FIFO illustrated in Figure 12-4.*

1. This inventory card has three basic sections: Purchased, Sold, and _____.

B1. Balance

2. The Balance section shows units _____ _____.

B2.   remaining on hand

3.   Some parts have brackets around two or more lines. In the Balance section, the brackets mean that _____

_____ .

B3.   all bracketed batches are on hand

4.   In the Sold section, the brackets mean that

_____ .

B4.   all bracketed batches are sold

5.   There is no bracket in the Balance section around the 40 staplers on hand on April 1.

Why? _____

_____

B5.   Because the 40 units are a single batch purchased in March at $2.20 each.

6.   The inventory after the April 5 receipt is now made up of two batches whose total cost value is $_____ .

B6.   400

7.   On April 12, 110 staplers were sold. Why did we assume that these 110 staplers were made up of 40 at $2.20 and 70 at $2.60?

_____

_____

_____

_____

_____

B7.   The FIFO assumption that oldest are sold first uses up the 40 staplers in the April 1 inventory and assumes that the remaining 70 had to come from the April 5 purchase.

8.   The balance on hand after the sale of April 12 is _____ staplers at $_____ = $_____ .

B8.   50, 2.60, 130

9.   When the purchase of April 16 is received, the balance is increased by a second batch of _____ staplers at $_____ . The inventory cost valuation is now $_____ .

B9.   70, 2.80, 326

10.   In the sale of 60 on April 28, we assume that the 60 oldest staplers on hand are sold. Therefore, the sale includes only _____ staplers from the April 16 purchase, the $2.80 layer.

B10.   10

11.   The final inventory is 60 staplers (as we already know) at $_____ = $_____.

B11.   2.80, 168

12.   To obtain cost of goods sold, we can add the Total Cost column of the Sold section for a total of $_____. If you look back at FIFO applied on a periodic basis, the ending inventory balance was _____ (the same/different).

B12.   428, the same

13.   Consider Figure 12-5 which shows the same stapler recorded under the LIFO assumption. All entries are the same as FIFO down to

_____.

B13.   the sale on April 12

14.   Then, when the April 12 sale of 110 staplers is recorded, it is shown as a single batch of 110 at $2.60. Why? _____

_____

_____

_____

_____

B14.   LIFO assumes that sales are from the newest goods. The newest goods on April 12 are the batch received on April 5. (There are enough in that batch to cover the entire sale.)

15.   What batches are assumed to be left on hand after the April 12 sale? _____

_____

_____

_____

B15.   Forty staplers from April 1 inventory and 10 staplers from the receipt of April 5.

16.   The inventory valuation after the April 12 sale is 40 at $2.20 plus 10 at $2.60 = $_____.

B 16. 114

17. A receipt on April 16 adds a third batch to inventory, so we must bracket all three to show that the total inventory valuation is now $_____.

B 17. 310

18. Again, because of the LIFO assumption, the April 28 sale is assumed to come from the newest goods on hand. The 60 staplers sold, therefore, are assumed to be from the receipt of April 16. This leaves on hand _____ batches with a total cost valuation of $_____. By referring back to the LIFO periodic illustration, we note that applying LIFO to the perpetual system gives _____ _____ (the same/a different) amount for ending inventory.

B 18. three, 142, a different

19. Consider Figure 12-6. Under the moving average assumption, we *do not* need to keep batches separate. There will be no need for brackets. Each new receipt is added to the previous quantity on hand and a _____ _____ is computed if the purchase price is different from the unit price we now carry.

B 19. new unit price

20. The receipt of 120 staplers on April 5 increases the total units on hand to _____ and the total cost of units on hand to $_____.

B 20. 160, 400

21. The new average unit cost is $400 ÷ 160 = $_____.

B 21. 2.50

22. So, the next sale will be made at an assumed average cost of $_____ per stapler.

B 22. 2.50

23. Until a new receipt at a different unit price arrives, future sales will be recorded at the average cost of $_____ per stapler.

B 23. 2.50

24. A new receipt arrived on April 16 at a unit price of $2.80. We now have on hand _____ staplers with a total cost of $_____ attached to them.

B 24. 120, 321

25. A new unit cost must be computed (this is why the method is called moving average). It is $_____ ÷ _____ staplers = $_____.

B25. 321, 120, 2.675

26. The next sale is recorded at the new average cost, leaving an April 30 inventory of _____ staplers at $_____ = $_____.

B26. 60, 2.675, 160.50

C. *Comparison of Methods*

1. A comparison of FIFO periodic and FIFO perpetual shows that the April 30 inventory and cost of goods sold in April are _____ (the same/different) amounts under each method.

C1. the same (This will always be true for FIFO.)

2. A comparison of LIFO periodic and LIFO perpetual shows that results were _____ (the same/different).

C2. different (This is usually the case for LIFO.)

3. Weighted average (periodic) and moving average (perpetual) give _____ (the same/different) ending inventory and cost of goods sold.

C3. different (This is usually true for the average methods.)

4. Comparing the price of a stapler in the beginning inventory with the price per stapler for the purchases in April, would you say that prices are rising or falling? _____

C4. Rising.

5. FIFO assumes that oldest goods are sold first. Therefore, the April 30 inventory would be at the _____ (highest/lowest) prices.

C5. highest

6. On the other hand, LIFO assumes that newest goods are sold first. Under LIFO, the April 30 inventory would be at the _____ (highest/lowest) prices.

C6. lowest

7. By assigning a higher price to ending inventory, FIFO automatically assigns a _____ (higher/lower) price to cost of goods sold for April.

C7. lower

8. And a lower cost of goods sold means a _____ (higher/lower) profit would be shown under FIFO.

C8. higher

9. So, LIFO, with a lower profit, should cause the owner of a firm to pay _____ (more/less) income tax than FIFO.

C9.   less

10.   But remember that these transactions took place *during a period of rising prices*. Would it be accurate to expect the opposite results during a period of falling prices? _____

_____

C10.   Yes. The results would be exactly opposite.

D.   *Lower of Cost or Market (LCM)*

1.   Figure 12-8 illustrates the three methods of application of lower of cost or market. The total inventory value under the unit basis would be $_____.

D1.   5,725

2.   This total is obtained by first comparing the cost and the market price of each item. For Item A, total cost is $_____ and total market is $_____, so the lower is _____ at $_____.

D2.   1,000, 900, market, 900

3.   For Item B, cost is $_____ and market is $_____, so the lower is _____ at $_____.

D3.   800, 1,200, cost, 800

4.   This process is continued until the lower of cost or market is found for each item. On a unit basis, the LCM inventory valuation is the sum of these individual figures.

D4.   No answer required.

5.   To use the class or category basis, we compare the cost total and market total for each category. For Category X, LCM is _____ at $_____, and for Category Y, LCM is _____ at $_____.

D5.   cost, 1,800, market, 4,125

6.   So the LCM inventory valuation on a class or category basis is the sum of $_____ and $_____ = $_____.

D6.   1,800, 4,125, 5,925

7.   On the total inventory basis, we simply price the total inventory at cost and at market. Of these two figures, the lower is _____ at $_____.

D7.   market, 6,225

8.   Note that the unit basis provides the _____ (highest/lowest) valuation and the total inventory basis provides the _____ (highest/lowest) valuation.

D8.   lowest, highest
(This will always
be true.)

E.   *Estimating Inventories*

1.   The gross margin method of estimating inventories requires that you find cost of goods sold. If we know cost of goods sold, it can be subtracted from _____ _____ to find ending inventory at cost.

E1.   total goods available for sale

2.   In the textbook example, Lander Company has experienced a gross margin rate of _____ percent.

E2.   30

3.   If the gross margin equals 30 percent of sales, cost of goods sold must be 100 percent minus 30 percent = _____.

E3.   70 percent

4.   Sales of $160,000 times 70 percent means that cost of goods sold in 1985 was $_____.

E4.   112,000

5.   Another way to find this amount is to use the formula, sales minus _____ = cost of goods sold.

E5.   gross margin

6.   And gross margin = 30 percent of sales = 30 percent of $160,000 = $_____.

E6.   48,000

7.   Then cost of goods sold is sales of $160,000 minus gross margin of $48,000 = $_____.

E7.   112,000

8.   You may use either method to find cost of goods sold. Now you must find total goods available for sale. It is equal to _____ _____ plus net purchases.

E8.   beginning inventory

9.   For the Lander Company in 1985, this was $_____ plus $_____ = $_____.

E9.   20,000, 110,000 130,000

10.   Ending inventory is equal to total goods available for sale minus _____ _____.

E10.   cost of goods sold

11.   For the Lander Company, this is $_____ minus $_____ = $_____.

E11.   130,000, 112,000, 18,000

12.   The accuracy of the gross margin estimate depends on the accuracy of the estimate of gross margin percent.

E12.   No answer required.

13.   To use the retail method, it is necessary to record all receipts both at cost price and at

_____.

E13.   selling price or retail price

14.   In the example, the beginning inventory at cost is $20,000, but retail (or selling) price of this inventory is $_____.

E14.   30,000

15.   Purchases at cost must be net purchases (including transportation in). They were $180,000, but their retail price was $_____.

E15.   270,000

16.   Total goods available for sale cost $_____ and were recorded at a retail price of $_____.

E16.   200,000, 300,000

17.   The current cost as a percent of retail is $_____ ÷ $_____ = _____ percent.

E17.   200,000, 300,000, 66 2/3

18.   Actual sales at retail price are recorded in the Sales account. In this company, they are $_____.

E18.   258,000

19.   Total goods available for sale at retail price ($300,000) minus sales of $258,000 leaves an ending inventory at retail of $_____.

E19.   42,000

20.   To convert this figure to ending inventory at cost, we multiply it by the _____ percent, which is 66 2/3 percent.

E20.   cost

21.   Estimated inventory at cost = 66 2/3 percent times $_____ = $_____.

E21.   42,000, 28,000

22.   Does using the perpetual or estimating methods to find inventory values eliminate the need for physical count? _____ Explain. _____

_____

_____

_____

E22.   No. A physical count at least once per year is needed to check on other measures.

SELF TEST OF LEARNING GOAL ACHIEVEMENT

1. The following questions pertain to inventory systems. Each can be answered with the word *periodic* or *perpetual*.

    a. The beginning inventory is closed to Income Summary under a _____ system.

    b. Cost of goods sold is an account title under the _____ system.

    c. Transportation in cost is added to the Inventory account under the _____ system.

    d. The cost price of sales is deducted from the Inventory account under the _____ system.

    e. The purchases account is used only under the _____ system.

    f. Purchases discounts and purchases returns and allowances are credited to the Inventory account under the _____ system.

    g. Under the _____ system, Purchases Discounts is an account to be closed to Income Summary.

    h. The system that would be best for the Produce Department of a super-market is the _____ system.

    i. The system that would be best to record the inventory of repair parts for an airline is the _____ system.

    j. The higher degree of inventory control is found in the _____ system.

    k. The least expensive system to operate is the _____ system.

2. Record the receipt of a purchase of $1,000 of merchandise and the return of $200 in defective merchandise, using (a) the periodic system and (b) the perpetual system. Date all transactions May 10, 1985.

GENERAL JOURNAL

Date		Account Titles and Explanation	F	Debit	Credit
		(a)			

		(b)			

3. Assume the following activity for an inventory item in March 1985:

Mar. 1   Beginning balance, 100 pounds at $0.50.
    4   Sold 60 pounds.
   12   Received 100 pounds at $0.60.
   14   Sold 75 pounds.
   20   Received 50 pounds at $0.70.

Required: Compute ending inventory and cost of goods sold under periodic
(a) FIFO, (b) LIFO, and (c) weighted average.

(a)

(b)

(c)

4.   Lower of cost or market valuation can be computed on a unit, class, or total inventory basis.   The LCM valuations produced by each basis are:

(a)   Highest on the _____ basis.

(b)   Lowest on the _____ basis.

(c)   In between on the _____ basis.

5. Uber Company had a June 1, 1985, inventory valued at a cost of $1,500 and a retail price of $2,000. Purchases were $5,500 at cost and $8,000 at retail. Sales were $8,500. Estimate the June 30 inventory using the retail method.

6. Assume the same facts as in 5 above except that Uber Company has had an average gross margin percent of 40 percent for the past three years. Estimate the ending inventory using the gross margin method.

ANSWERS TO LEARNING GOAL ACHIEVEMENT TEST

1. a. periodic   g. periodic
    b. perpetual   h. periodic
    c. perpetual   i. perpetual
    d. perpetual   j. perpetual
    e. periodic   k. periodic
    f. perpetual

2.

GENERAL JOURNAL

Date		Account Titles and Explanation	F	Debit	Credit
1985		(a)			
May	10	Purchases		1,000	
		Accounts Payable			1,000
		Receipt of merchandise.			
	10	Accounts Payable		200	
		Purchases Returns and Allowances			200
		Return of defective goods.			
1985		(b)			
May	10	Merchandise Inventory		1,000	
		Accounts Payable			1,000
		Receipt of merchandise.			
	10	Accounts Payable		200	
		Merchandise Inventory			200
		Return of defective goods.			

3.   (a)   FIFO
Ending inventory:
    50 pounds at $0.70 = $35.00
    65 pounds at $0.60 = 39.00
    Total $74.00
Cost of goods sold:
   100 pounds at $0.50 = $50.00
    35 pounds at $0.60 = 21.00
    Total $71.00

   (b)   LIFO
Ending inventory:
   100 pounds at $0.50 = $50.00
    15 pounds at $0.60 =   9.00
    Total $59.00
Cost of goods sold:
    85 pounds at $0.60 = $51.00
    50 pounds at $0.70 = 35.00
    Total $86.00

(c)   Weighted average

	Pounds	Cost
Beginning inventory	100	$ 50.00
Purchases (100 pounds at $0.60)	100	60.00
(50 pounds at $0.70)	50	35.00
Total available for sale	250	$145.00

Weighted average unit price = $145.00 ÷ 250 = $0.58.
Ending inventory: 115 pounds at $0.58 = $66.70.
Cost of goods sold: 135 pounds at $0.58 = $78.30.

Note to student: In each case, ending inventory plus cost of goods sold = $145.00.

4. (a)   total
    (b)   unit
    (c)   class

5.

	Cost	Retail
Beginning inventory	$1,500	$ 2,000
Purchases	5,500	8,000
Total goods available for sale	$7,000	$10,000
Cost as a percent of retail	70%	
Sales		8,500
Ending inventory at retail		$ 1,500
Estimated inventory at cost ($1,500 x 0.70) . . .	$1,050	

6.   100% – 40% = 60% cost as a percent of sales.
     Cost of goods sold = $8,500 x 0.60 = $5,100.
     Ending inventory = $7,000 – $5,100 = $1,900.

Chapter 13
Property, Plant, and Equipment; Intangible Assets

■■

EXPLANATION OF MAJOR CONCEPTS

Long-Term Assets

Long-term assets (assets whose use will extend beyond one year) fall into three groups: tangible plant assets, natural resources, and intangible assets. The term *property, plant, and equipment* includes all plant assets and natural resources with tangible existence (meaning they have substance and can be touched). They are acquired for use in the regular operations of the business and will be used for more than one accounting period. Buildings, equipment, and delivery trucks would be examples of tangible plant assets. Intangible assets are those which which exist in concept but do not have substance in the sense that they can be touched or felt. They do, however, contribute to the operation of the business. Coal reserves and timber would be examples of natural resources. Patents, copyrights, and franchises would be examples of intangible assets. One thing common to all of these assets is a long useful life. All have *estimated useful lives* (EUL) extending over two or more accounting periods. Except for land, however, their useful lives are limited.

Long-term assets are recorded in the accounting records at their cost. This includes the purchase price less a cash discount, plus all other expenditures made to prepare the asset for use. These other expenditures should be reasonable and necessary, benefit the whole useful life, and be made before the asset is put into use. All costs debited to the asset account are said to be *capitalized*.

The major accounting problem with regard to a long-lived asset is to assign portions of its cost in some rational manner to the accounting periods over which it benefits the business. The process of allocating cost to accounting periods is called depreciation, depletion, or amortization. While the three terms cover the same basic concept, their specific meanings are different:

▶ *Depreciation* refers to the process of allocation of cost of *tangible,* long-lived assets to specific periods.

▶ *Depletion* refers to recording the consumption or extraction of natural resources.

223

▸ *Amortization* refers to recording the expiration of an intangible asset. However, amortization is sometimes used as a general term to describe all three concepts.

Depreciation Methods

There are several methods of computing depreciation. A company may choose any of them or may use a combination of methods. When a method is chosen for a specific plant asset (or group of assets), that method should be used consistently year after year. Two estimates must be made for each asset: estimated useful life and salvage value. *Estimated useful life* is the period of time over which the business plans to use the asset. *Salvage value* is the amount the business expects to recover from disposal at the end of the useful life. The methods of depreciation explained in the text are summarized here:

▸ *Straight line method* assumes that an equal share of depreciation expense is to be assigned to each accounting period. The formula is:

$$\frac{\text{Cost minus Salvage value}}{\text{EUL in years}} = \$ \text{ Depreciation per year.}$$

The *straight line percent* is another tool to compute annual costs. Straight line percent is:

$$\frac{100 \text{ percent}}{\text{EUL in years}} = \text{Annual straight line percent.}$$

(Cost minus Salvage value) x Annual straight line percent = $ Depreciation per year.

▸ *Production methods* assign expense to each period on the basis of amount of production per period. Two basic ones are:

1. *Working hours method,* in which EUL is estimated as a total number of working hours. For an aircraft engine it could be:

$$\frac{\text{Cost minus Salvage value}}{\text{Total flight hours of life}} = \text{Depreciation per flight hour.}$$

2. *Production units method,* in which EUL is estimated as total units of output. For a stamping machine this could be:

$$\frac{\text{Cost minus salvage value}}{\text{Total units machine can stamp}} = \text{Depreciation per unit.}$$

In either of the production methods, the depreciation expense of a period is the amount of work per period times the cost per working hour or cost per unit.

▸ *Accelerated methods* assign greater depreciation expense in earlier years of life. Two illustrated in Chapter 13 are:

1. *Declining balance method* which should be viewed as a *fixed percentage of declining balance*. The beginning point for this method is the straight line rate (explained earlier in this *Study Guide* section). Double-declining balance (or 200 percent-declining balance) uses twice the straight line rate applied to *carrying* value. Since carrying value equals cost minus accumulated depreciation, the carrying value gets smaller each year as accumulated depreciation increases. (Thus, the name, declining balance, is given to the method.) The 150 percent declining balance uses 1 1/2 times the straight line rate. You must be careful when using the declining balance method *not to deduct salvage value*. The rate chosen is applied to total carrying value. Also, you must be careful in the declining balance method not to take so much depreciation that the carrying value drops below the salvage value.

2. *Sum-of-the-years'-digits method* uses a fraction of the total digits in the years of EUL. The fraction applies each year's digit *in reverse order* as a percent of the total. You should learn and should use the arithmetic progression formula to compute the sum of the year's digits. It is:

$$\frac{n}{2}(n + 1) = \frac{n(n + 1)}{2} = n\frac{(n + 1)}{2} = SYD,$$

where n = estimated useful life. For example, if EUL is 8 years, then

$$\frac{8}{2}(8 + 1) = \frac{8(8 + 1)}{2} = 8\frac{(8 + 1)}{2} = 36 = SYD.$$

Then, to find depreciation, use cost minus salvage value. In the foregoing 8-year example, depreciation expense is:

First year   = 8/36 x (Cost minus Salvage value).
Second year = 7/36 x (Cost minus Salvage value).
Third year   = 6/36 x (Cost minus Salvage value).
.   .   .
.   .   .
.   .   .
Eighth year = 1/36 x (Cost minus Salvage value).

3. *Accelerated Cost Recovery* is a method permitted for tax reporting under the Economic Recovery Tax Act of 1981. Depreciable personal property falls into four cost recovery classes: three, five, ten, and fifteen year classes. Within each class the law provides a percentage of cost which can be deducted as depreciation in computing income tax liability.

Capital and Revenue Expenditures

Often it is necessary to make expenditures on a long-lived asset after it is put into use. These must be separated into capital and revenue expenditures. An expenditure made to an asset during its life is classified as a capital expenditure if it extends the useful life or increases the capacity of the asset. Capital expenditures are debited to Accumulated Depreciation if they are viewed as an extraordinary repair. Otherwise, they are debited to the asset account. If an expenditure does not qualify as a capital expenditure, it is classified as a revenue expenditure and debited to an expense account such as Repairs Expense.

Disposal and Trade-In

Most tangible plant or equipment items have some value at the end of their useful lives. Disposal by sale or scrapping often causes a gain or loss. If the amount recovered is greater than *book value* (cost minus accumulated depreciation), there is a gain. If the amount recovered is less than book value, there is a loss. Losses or gains from disposal by a means *other than trade-in* are always recorded and reported in the income statement. A loss account has a normal debit balance; a gain account a credit.

At the end of the EUL, assets are often traded in on new assets. The accounting for gains and losses is more complex in a trade-in situation. Two types of trade-in cases that must be distinguished are:

▶ *Trade-in on a similar asset*. The word *similar* has a broad interpretation here. Any asset that serves the same productive function is similar. Thus, the trade-in of a bookkeeping machine used to produce monthly bills on a small computer to produce bills (in addition to other functions) may be viewed as similar.

▶ *Trade-in on a dissimilar asset*. This would be the trade-in of an asset on another asset that performs an entirely different function. A grinding machine traded in on a parcel of land to be used as a parking lot would be viewed as a trade for a dissimilar asset.

The rules for recording a gain or loss on trade-ins are based on the concept that a trade-in on a similar asset is a continuation of the earnings process in which the old asset was engaged. A trade-in on a dissimilar item is viewed as the termination of the old earnings process. The rules are:

▶ Recognize all losses on trade-ins.
▶ Recognize gains on trade-ins for dissimilar items.
▶ Recognize gains on trade-ins for similar items only if you are the entity receiving the "boot" or amount of cash exchanged.

Depletion is used to record consumption of natural resources. Because the actual consumption is being recorded, production methods are usually used to record depletion cost. You should note that depletion--unlike depreciation--is not an expense immediately upon recording. Along with other production costs, it becomes part of the inventory; accordingly, it reduces income not as an expense but as part of cost of goods sold.

Amortization is usually computed by the straight line method. Intangible assets do not have salvage value; amortization, therefore, is computed on full cost.

GUIDED STUDY OF THIS CHAPTER

A. *Capital versus Revenue Expenditures*

1. A capital expenditure is an expenditure that increases the carrying value of a long-lived asset. The expenditure is said to be _____ rather than expensed.

A1. capitalized

2. In the purchase of a computer, expenditures could include (a) invoice cost less discount, (b) transportation in, (c) assembly, (d) installation, and (e) testing and trial runs. How many of these are capital expenditures?

   _____

A2. All of them.

3. A revenue expenditure is required to keep a piece of capital equipment operating. For example, a routine repair on this computer would be a _____ expenditure.

A3. revenue

4. An additional piece of equipment to enable the computer to do a larger job would be a _____ expenditure.

A4. capital

5. A major overhaul that extended the EUL of this computer would be a _____ expenditure.

A5. capital

6. Revenue expenditures are debited to *expense*, but capital expenditures are usually debited to _____.

A6. the asset

7. In some cases, capital expenditures that extend useful life may be viewed as cancellation of some of the depreciation. Some accountants debit these to _____ _____.

A7. Accumulated Depreciation

8. For example, if an overhaul added 2,000 flight hours to an aircraft engine, _____ _____ could be debited.

A8. Accumulated Depreciation--Engines

9. The purchase of a patent would be debited to the _____ account.

A9.   Patents

10.   If a delivery truck is bettered by having a hydraulic lift installed on it, the cost would be debited to _____.

A10.   Trucks

11.   Replacement of the broken headlight on the delivery truck would be debited to _____ _____.

A11.   Repairs Expense

12.   If a contractor offered to build a new toll booth for $4,500 and we built it ourselves at a cost of $4,150, we should debit the asset account with $_____.

A12.   4,150

B.   *Depreciation*

1.   Since depreciation is the allocation of cost to more than one accounting period, we must know how many periods to use. The life of an asset cannot be accurately known in advance, so we must establish an _____ _____.

B1.   estimated useful life (EUL)

2.   Also, since we expect to recover something (at least scrap value) on disposal of an asset, we must estimate the _____.

B2.   salvage value

3.   One method of computing depreciation does not require use of estimated salvage value. Which one is it? _____

B3.   Declining balance method.

4.   All methods require an estimate of _____ _____, and all but one an estimate of _____.

B4.   useful life, salvage value

5.   The simplest method is the straight line method. Following the formula in the textbook, compute the 1985 depreciation for a typewriter that cost $795 at the beginning of 1985 and has a salvage value of $45 and an EUL of ten years.

B5. $\dfrac{\$795 - \$45}{10} = \$75$

6.   The straight line percent for this typewriter is 100 percent divided by EUL = _____ percent.

B6.   10 (This can be computed as a decimal fraction by using 1 ÷ EUL.)

7.   Compute the straight line depreciation for 1985, using the straight line percent.

B7. 10 percent of
($795 − $45) = $75.

8. Suppose this same typewriter were to be depreciated by the double declining balance method. The rate would be _____ percent.

B8. 20

9. The 1985 depreciation would be 20 percent of $_____ = $_____.

B9. 795, 159

10. The carrying value for 1986 depreciation would be $795 minus $159 = $_____; the 1986 depreciation would be _____ percent of $_____ = $_____.

B10. 636, 20, 636, 127.20

11. Notice that the depreciation for 1986 is less than that for 1985 because we are using a fixed percent of a _____
_____.

B11. declining balance

12. Note in both cases illustrating DBM in the textbook that total depreciation never reduces the book value of the asset below the estimated salvage value. In case 1, this meant that no depreciation was taken in the last year of useful life. And in case 2, a switch was made to straight-line for the last two years.

B12. No answer required.

13. Let's use this same typewriter example and compute depreciation by the sum-of-the-years'-digits (SYD) method. The sum of the years' digits is _____ years.

B13. 55 [Computed as follows:
$\frac{10}{2}(10 + 1) = 55.$]

14. Assume that it had been purchased on January 11, 1985. Do we compute a full month for January? _____

B14. Yes.

15. So the 1985 depreciation using SYD is
_____ x ($795 − $45) = $_____.

B15. 10/55, 136.36

16. And for 1986, it is _____ x ($795 − $45) = $_____.

B16. 9/55, 122.73

17. At the end of ten years, 55/55 of ($795 − $45) will have been recorded, leaving $_____ of undepreciated cost.

B17. 45

18. Suppose this typewriter were estimated to have 10,000 hours of useful life. By the working hours method, we would depreciate $_____ per hour of use.

B 18.   0.075 (or 7 1/2
        cents)

19.   If it were used 1,800 hours in 1985, the depre-
        ciation charge would be $_____ x _____
        = $_____ .

B 19.   0.075, 1,800, 135

20.   Another way to compute the 1985 depreciation
        would be to note that 1,800/10,000 of its use-
        ful life was consumed in that year. Since
        that is _____ percent, we could say that the
        depreciation for 1985 = _____ percent of
        ($795 – $45) = $_____ .

B 20.   18, 18, 135

21.   Are both results the same? _____

B 21.   Yes.

22.   We could also use the units-of-output method
        with this typewriter. Suppose we estimate
        that it can type a total of 30,000 invoices in
        its EUL. The depreciation per invoice would
        be $_____ .

B 22.   0.025 (or 2 1/2
        cents)

23.   If it was used to produce 4,600 invoices in
        1985, the depreciation charge would be
        $_____ x _____ = $_____ .

B 23.   0.025, 4,600, 115

C.   *Accounting Entries. The entry to record
        annual depreciation is an adjusting entry. It
        would first have been recorded on the work
        sheet, and from the work sheet made into a
        general journal entry.*

1.   The entry to record the annual depreciation
        on the typewriter would debit the _____
        _____ account.

C 1.   Depreciation
        Expense--Office
        Equipment

2.   It would credit the _____
        _____ account.

C 2.   Accumulated Depre-
        ciation--Office
        Equipment

3.   At the end of 1985, the disposition of the
        expense account is that it is _____
        _____ .

C 3.   closed into Income
        Summary

4.   The expense amount appears in the _____
        statement.

C 4.   income

5.   The Accumulated Depreciation--Office Equip-
        ment account is closed into _____ .

C5. It is not closed.
(Did you get caught
on this one?)

6. It serves as a valuation (or contra) account to
_____ and reduces
the value of property, plant, and equipment on
the _____.

C6. Office Equipment,
balance sheet

7. The illustrations of asset disposal in the textbook begin with a $_____ truck that was
acquired on _____. The
truck has an EUL of _____ and
a salvage value of $_____.

C7. 18,000, January 3,
1985, five years,
zero

8. If sold on Oct. 1, 1989, the first task is to
record depreciation for the current year. The
last annual depreciation entry was an adjusting
entry made on _____.

C8. December 31, 1988

9. Depreciation for 3/4 year is $_____;
when that amount is recorded, _____
years of depreciation have been accumulated.

C9. 2,700, 4 3/4

10. The carrying value (or book value) on Oct. 1,
1989, is $_____, so that if the truck
were sold for $1,000, there would be a _____
(gain/loss) of $_____.

C10. 900, gain, 100

11. The Gain on Disposal of Equipment account is
closed into _____ and
reported on the _____
under the classification _____.

C11. Income Summary,
income statement,
other revenue

12. Example 2 shows the entry to record the sale
of this truck at a gain of $_____.

C12. 300

13. Example 3 shows the entry to record the sale
of the truck for $400. This produces a $500
_____.

C13. loss

14. The Loss on Disposal of Equipment account is
closed into _____
and reported in the income statement under
_____.

C14. Income Summary,
other expenses

15. In *all* entries for disposal, the asset account
is _____ (debited/credited) for the
full amount of cost, and the Accumulated
Depreciation is _____ (debited/
credited) for the amount of depreciation
recorded to date.

C15. credited, debited

16. In each example of disposal of this truck, the asset account was credited for $_____ and the Accumulated Depreciation account debited for $_____ .

C16. 18,000, 17,100

17. Whenever an asset is disposed of by sale, scrap, trade-in, or any other means, both the _____ and its _____ must be removed from the books.

C17. asset cost, accumulated depre-ciation

18. The method of recording asset trade-ins depends upon whether the asset is traded for a dissimilar or a similar asset. Which situation could prohibit the recording of a gain on disposal? _____

C18. Trade-in on a similar asset.

19. The textbook uses the example of a lathe traded in on a parcel of land. Is this trade for a similar or dissimilar asset? _____

C19. Dissimilar

20. To determine the amount of gain or loss, we must first determine the _____ value of the new asset.

C20. fair market

21. In the examples shown, the fair market value of the land is established at $_____ .

C21. 4,000

22. In example 1, the trade-in allowance for the lathe is $500; therefore, its fair market value must be $_____ .

C22. 500

23. Since the fair market value and book value are the same, there is no gain or loss.

C23. No answer required.

24. If a trade-in allowance of $500 is allowed on an asset with a list price of $4,000, the buyer will have to pay $_____ in cash.

C24. 3,500

25. In example 2, the list price of the land is still $4,000; the trade-in allowance is $_____ . Accordingly, there is a loss of $_____ .

C25. 400, 100

26. Example 3 holds the list price of the land at $_____ . Therefore, the $_____ trade-in allowance for the lathe brings a gain of $_____ .

C26.   4,000, 800, 300

27.   Where the trade-in is for a similar asset, a loss must be recognized, but a gain may not always be recognized. If the gain is not to be recognized, the new asset is recorded at the valuation of things given up to get it. This would be the book value of the old lathe plus _____

_____.

C27.   the cash paid

28.   If the trade-in for a similar asset results in a loss, the trade-in _____ (is/is not) recorded in the same manner as for a dissimilar asset.

C28.   is

29.   If the trade-in results in a gain and the trading entity *is paying* the boot (a cash payment), the gain _____ (is/is not) recognized.

C29.   is not

30.   In the example of the lathe traded for a new lathe at a gain, is the trading entity paying boot? _____

C30.   Yes.

31.   Therefore, instead of recording the gain, it must record the new lathe at a valuation equal to _____
plus cash paid.

C31.   the book value of the old lathe

32.   The book value of the old lathe is $_____.

C32.   500

33.   The cash paid is $_____, for a total valuation for the new asset of $_____ instead of $4,000.

C33.   3,200, 3,700

34.   The nonrecognition of the $300 gain reduces net income of 1987 (the trade-in year) by $_____.

C34.   300

35.   Is this unreported income compensated for in future years? _____ Explain. _____

_____

_____

_____

_____

_____

_____

_____

C35.   Yes. An asset costing $3,700 instead of $4,000 will be depreciated over its EUL. This means lower depreciation expense and higher net income = ($300 over the EUL).

D. *Depletion*

1.   The term *depletion* applies to _____ _____.

D1.   natural resources (or wasting assets)

2.   The output basis used to compute depletion is similar to the _____ methods of computing depreciation.

D2.   production

3.   In the textbook example, the depletion cost is $_____ per ton.

D3.   0.40

4.   The cost per ton is based on a mine that costs $_____, with the land expected to be resold for $_____ after the ore is removed.

D4.   180,000, 20,000

5.   The net value of the ore, therefore, must be $_____.

D5.   160,000

6. $160,000 ÷ 400,000 tons = $_____ per ton.

D6.   0.40

7.   The 10,000 tons of ore removed in this period represent a cost of $0.40 x 10,000 = $_____.

D7.   4,000

8.   The depletion cost of $4,000 is not expense; instead it becomes a part of the cost of _____ awaiting sale.

D8.   inventory (or ore inventory)

9.   Since only 8,000 tons (or 8/10) of the ore mined has been sold, _____ tons remain in inventory as an asset.

D9.   2,000

10.   The inventory valuation included not only depletion costs but other production costs such as _____.

D10.   wages of miners

11.   When $10,000 of production costs are added to the depletion, the cost per ton becomes ($4,000 depletion + $10,000 production cost) ÷ 10,000 tons = $_____.

D11.   1.40

12.   8,000 tons costing $1.40 were sold for a cost of goods sold of $_____.

D12. 11,200

D13. 2,800

D14. 800 (This is a
critical question.
If you missed it,
you need some more
study of depletion.)

E1. straight line

E2. expense

E3. the asset account

E4. most representative
of the period
benefited

E5. above normal

E6. purchase of all or
part of a business

E7. expenses

13. This leaves 2,000 tons in inventory at the end of the period with a cost valuation of $_____.

14. Of this $2,800 inventory value, $_____ is depletion cost.

E. *Amortization*

1. The _____ method is used to compute amortization.

2. As is the case with depreciation, the amortization charge is debited to an _____ account.

3. Unlike depreciation, however, a contra account is not used. In the annual adjusting entry to recognize amortization, the credit is to _____

   _____.

4. Intangible assets may be amortized over their legal lives or estimated useful lives, whichever is _____

   _____.

5. Goodwill is the ability of a firm to generate _____ net income.

6. It can be recorded on the books only as the result of the _____

   _____.

7. Business people sometimes argue that research and development costs should be treated as capital expenditures. *FASB Statement No. 2* requires that most be treated as _____.

SELF TEST OF LEARNING GOAL ACHIEVEMENT

1. Record depreciation for the year 1985 on a computer purchased on January 4, 1985, at a cost of $50,000 and a salvage value of $2,000 at the end of its eight-year EUL using:

    a. Straight line method.
    b. Double declining balance method.
    c. Sum-of-the-years'-digits method.
    d. Production method with an EUL of 32,000 hours with 3,500 hours of operation in 1985.

GENERAL JOURNAL

Date	Account Titles and Explanation	F	Debit	Credit

2. On January 4, 1988, a machine is traded for a similar new machine that has a fair market value of $60,000. These accounts appear on the books of the trading entity:

	Balance
Machine	$50,000
Accumulated Depreciation--Machine . .	41,000

Required: Give general journal entries to record the trade-in if:
(1) A trade-in allowance of $5,000 is received on the used asset and the balance is paid in cash.
(2) A trade-in allowance of $12,000 is received on the used asset and the balance is paid in cash.

GENERAL JOURNAL

Date		Account Titles and Explanation	F	Debit	Credit

3. Compute depletion cost of 30,000 barrels of oil extracted from a well that had an original cost of $12,000,000, no salvage value, and is expected to produce 400,000 barrels of oil before it is exhausted.

4. Duterium Company had purchased a delivery truck on January 3, 1983, for $10,000. They estimated the useful life to be 10 years and the salvage value $1,000.

   a. Assume that on January 5, 1985, they spent $2,000 to increase the capacity of the cargo area. This expenditure would be considered a _____ expenditure and would be debited to _____.

   b. Assume that on March 8, 1985, they spent $1,500 on a major overhaul that extended the useful life of the truck by 2 years. This expenditure would be considered a _____ expenditure and would be debited to _____.

   c. Assume that on October 28, 1985, they spent $800 to replace the worn out tires. This would be considered a _____ expenditure and would be debited to _____.

ANSWERS TO LEARNING GOAL ACHIEVEMENT TEST

1.

GENERAL JOURNAL

Date		Account Titles and Explanation	F	Debit	Credit
1985		(a)			
Dec.	31	Depreciation Expense--Computer		6,000	
		Accumulated Depreciation--Computer			6,000
		1985 depreciation by S/L method.			
		(b)			
Dec.	31	Depreciation Expense--Computer		12,500	
		Accumulated Depreciation--Computer			12,500
		1985 depreciation expense by			
		DDB = (2 x 0.125 x $50,000).			
		(c)			
Dec.	31	Depreciation Expense--Computer		10,667	
		Accumulated Depreciation--Computer			10,667
		1985 depreciation by SYD =			
		(8/36 x $48,000).			

		(d)			
Dec.	31	Depreciation Expense--Computer		5,250	
		Accumulated Depreciation--Computer			5,250
		1985 depreciation for 3,500 hours			
		at $1.50 per hour = ($48,000 ÷			
		32,000 hours).			

2.

GENERAL JOURNAL

Date		Account Titles and Explanation	F	Debit	Credit
1988		(1)			
Jan.	4	Machine		60,000	
		Accumulated Depreciation--Machine		41,000	
		Loss on Disposal of Machine		4,000	
		Machine			50,000
		Cash			55,000
		To record trade-in for similar			
		asset at a loss.			
		(2)			
Jan.	4	Machine		57,000	
		Accumulated Depreciation--Machine		41,000	
		Machine			50,000
		Cash			48,000
		To record trade-in for similar			
		asset at nonrecognized gain.			
		New machine = $48,000 + $9,000.			

3. $12,000,000 ÷ 400,000 barrels = $30 per barrel, and
   30,000 barrels x $30 = $900,000 depletion cost.

4. a. capital, Trucks
   b. capital, Accumulated Depreciation--Trucks
   c. revenue, Repair Expense--Trucks

Appendix to Part Three
Compound Interest and
Application

■■■

EXPLANATION OF MAJOR CONCEPTS

A Comparison of Simple Interest and Compound Interest

Simple interest is interest computed only on the principle. Compound interest is interest computed on the principal plus prior periods interest. In other words, with compound interest, each period the interest is not paid but is added to the principal, and the next period the sum earns interest. A simple illustration will help show the difference. Assume that $1,000.00 was invested in an account for 4 months at 12 percent. If it earned simple interest, the calculation of the interest would be as follows:

$$\$1,000.00 \times .12 \times (4/12) = \$40.00$$

If the amount had been invested in an account at the same rate of interest, but the interest was compounded monthly, the interest calculation would have been as follows:

$$
\begin{aligned}
\$1,000.00 \times .12 \times (1/12) &= \$10.00 \\
\$1,010.00 \times .12 \times (1/12) &= 10.10 \\
\$1,020.10 \times .12 \times (1/12) &= 10.20 \\
\$1,030.30 \times .12 \times (1/12) &= \underline{10.30} \\
\text{Total} &\quad \underline{\$40.60}
\end{aligned}
$$

When money is loaned or invested at compound interest, the interest accumulated for a period is not paid but is added to the principal amount. For the next period, the same interest rate is applied to the greater principal, yielding a larger amount of interest than the prior period. This amount is again added to the principal, creating a greater amount to be multiplied by the same rate, and the cycle continues for period after period until the end of the specified term. We can see in this illustration that simple interest at 12 percent for 4 months on $1,000.00 was $40.00. Interest compounded monthly at 12 percent for 4 months gave $40.60 in interest or $0.60 more interest. The important concept here is that interest is constantly being added back to the principal so that interest is being earned on the original principal plus the periodic interest additions. This concept is referred to as the *time value of money*.

Banks compound interest in savings accounts. Certain other types of investments can earn compound interest. For this reason, business people compare
simple interest investments with their equivalents in compound interest yields to
make decisions. Although bonds issued by corporations to borrow money actually
carry simple interest at an annual rate, investors make a compound interest calculation to determine how much to invest. Choices among investments in plant or in
equipment are often made on the basis of comparisons with their compound interest
returns to the company. If you are to understand these topics, you must master
compound interest techniques first.

Types of Compound Interest Calculations

In the Appendix, the time value of money is used in connection with four basic
computations. Each of the four is briefly commented on in this section.

Compound Future Amount of a Single Sum. When the $1,000.00 principal is
added to the interest shown in the previous section, the amount becomes $1,040.60
= ($1,000.00 + $40.60). This compound amount is the dollar value to which a single
sum of $1,000.00 will grow in four months at a given interest rate (12 percent) and
a given frequency of compounding (monthly). The more frequent the compounding,
the faster the amount will grow. Thus, $1,000.00 compounded daily at the annual
rate of 12 percent will grow to a future sum greater than $1,040.60 in four months
because the interest is added back more times.

Present Value of a Single Sum. Any computation that allows us to determine
a compound future amount can be worked backward. The process of working
backward from a future sum to find what earlier amount was compounded to produce it is called *discounting*. The amount that was used to begin the compounding
(the original principal) is called the *present value*. In our example, we know that
the present value (today) of $1,040.60 four months from today is $1,000.00 if the
annual interest rate is 12 percent and the compounding is done monthly. If only
the future amount is known, we can compute the present value for any given
annual interest rate and number of compounding periods.

Compound Future Amount of an Ordinary Annuity. An *annuity* is a type of
investment in which periodic deposits are added to an original sum in addition to
the compound interest. Thus, an annuity grows in two ways: (1) by the addition
of compound interest and (2) by the addition of periodic additional deposits. Of
course, an annuity will grow to a much greater amount than a single sum given the
same interest rate and compounding periods. The additional deposits are called
rents. When the rents are deposited at the end of each period, the annuity is
called an *ordinary annuity*. Other types of annuities are not discussed in this
book.

Present Value of an Ordinary Annuity. There are instances in which a person
(or business) would like to invest a single sum now and withdraw periodic amounts
from it over periods of time. For example, a company may buy a machine now for
$100,000 that will increase net income by $5,000 per month over its estimated useful life. The monthly earnings are really periodic withdrawals instead of deposits;
they are still called rents. The $100,000 investment required to earn them is the

present value of the investment in an ordinary annuity. Often the amounts of withdrawals are known (as is the case with interest on corporate bonds) but the present value is not known. It can be computed for any given rate of interest, amounts of each rent, and frequency of withdrawals.

Compound Interest Tables

As explained in the Appendix, there are formulas for the computation of each of the four compound interest computations. You should understand the idea that underlies each formula, but it is not necessary to memorize them. The tables in the back of the textbook provide factors for each of the four basic computations. The factors in each of these tables represent the formula applied to the number 1. Accordingly, you can use the tables in two steps as follows:

1. Determine the appropriate table to use. (This isn't easy; students find it useful to draw time lines or other diagrams and label them to see exactly what type of situation exists.)

2. When the proper table has been chosen, multiply (or divide) by the factor for n and i for the given situation. In doing this, remember that n is the number of periods in the future sum or present value of an amount and the number of rents for an annuity. The symbol i represents the *interest rate per period*, not the annual rate. In the case of 12 percent compounded monthly, $i = 1$ percent.

GUIDED STUDY OF THIS CHAPTER

	A. Simple and Compound Interest
	1. In the formula for simple interest (I = PRT), P is the _____.
A1. principal amount of the loan	2. R is the rate per _____.
A2. year	3. And T is the time at interest stated as a fraction (or multiple) of a _____.
A3. year	4. To apply the formula, the textbook uses an example of Joan Rockness and Thomas Chope. Which one is borrowing the $10,000? _____ _____.
A4. Joan Rockness.	5. The term of the loan is 90 days; therefore T = _____.
A5. 90/360 or 1/4	6. The principal amount of this note is $_____.

A6.   10,000

A7.   principal + interest

A8.   10,400

A9.   future

A10.   400

A11.   Yes. Because it is
original principal x
rate x time.

A12.   416. Because last
quarter's interest
was added to the
principal, making
it larger.

A13.   10,400

A14.   For the total term
of the loan.

A15. $10,000 + ($10,000 x
0.16 x 1) = $11,600.

7.   The maturity value = P + PRT, which is simply
a way of saying _____.

8.   The maturity value of the Rockness note to
Chope is $_____.

9.   A compound amount is the sum to which a
present amount will grow at a given date in
the _____.

10.   The table in Figure AIII-1 shows a compound
interest computation. For the first quarter,
the amount of interest is $_____.

11.   Is this the same as it would be under simple
interest for 1/4 year? _____ Why or why
not? _____

_____

12.   In the second quarter at the same rate, the
interest is now $_____ instead of $400.
How is this possible? _____

_____

_____

13.   In other words, in the second quarter,
$_____ is multiplied by 16 percent x
1/4 to equal $416 instead of $400.

14.   Each quarter the principal (multiplied by 16
percent x 1/4) becomes larger. How long will
this continue? _____

_____

15.   In Figure AIII-1 the future amount at the end
of a year is $11,698.59. Compute the amount
it would be (its maturity value) at the end of
a year using simple interest.

_____

16.   At compound interest the loan has earned
$98.59 more than it would at simple interest
because _____

_____

_____.

A 16. the future amount
       at the end of each
       quarter becomes
       the new principal

B 1.   left, right

B 2.   four

B 3.   16 percent

B 4.   4 percent, 16

B 5. $P(1 + i)^n$

B 6.   one (or 1)

B 7.   1.810639

B 8. i

B 9.   end

B 10. 18,106.39, 1989

B. Compound Interest Techniques

1. Time lines are frequently helpful to picture the characteristics of a situation. One is used with future amount; time flows from _____ to

    _____.

2. The situation is an example of the future amount of a single sum of $10,000 compounded annually at 16 percent for _____ years.

3. Since each compounding period is exactly one year, i is the same as the annual rate or

    _____.

4. If compounding were quarterly for this four-year period, i would become _____ and n would be _____.

5. The general formula for the amount a is $a =$

    _____.

6. To apply this general formula, we would have $10,000 x (1.16)^4$. But we don't have to use the formula (and raise 1.16 to the fourth power) because the compound interest table has already solved the formula for the amount of _____.

7. A portion of the table reproduced in Figure AIII-3 shows that $1(1.16)^4 =$ _____.

8. To use any table, carefully determine the values of n and i. Then go down the n column to locate the desired number of periods and across the table at that point to the column for the desired amount of _____.

9. In the present value of a single given sum, the known amount is the amount that will be on deposit at the _____ of the time period.

10. In the text illustration, $_____ is to be in the fund on Dec. 31, _____.

11. The present value is to be determined as of Dec. 31, _____, or for a period of _____ years.

B 11. 1985, four

12. The present value of $1 for 4 periods at 16 percent is $_____ .

B 12. 0.552291

13. If the present value of $1.00 is $0.552291, then the present value of $18,106.39 is $_____ .

B 13. $10,000.00 = ($18,106.39 x 0.552291)

14. An annuity is _____

_____

_____ .

B 14. a series of equal payments or rents made at regular intervals with interest compounded

15. If a person made _____ deposits to an account each period and the account earns _____ interest, the amount that would be in the account five years from now would be _____

_____ .

B 15. equal, compound, the future value of an ordinary annuity

16. In future amount of annuity illustration, the amount to be deposited each period is $_____ , the interest rate per period is _____ percent, and the number of rents is _____ each _____ apart.

B 16. 10,000, 16, 4, 1 year

17. The future value of an annuity of $1 for four years is $_____ .

B 17. 5.066496

18. Thus, the future value of an annuity of $10,000 at 16 percent for four years is $_____ .

B 18. 50,664.96

19. In the present value of an annuity, the amount of the rents is _____ (known/ unknown) and we want to calculate the _____

_____

_____ .

B 19. known, amount which is available one period before the first rent

20. In the illustration we want to know the amount which must be available on _____ to permit four withdrawals of $_____ each on Dec. 31, 198___ through 198___ .

B 20. Jan. 1, 1985, 10,000, 5, 8

21. The amount which satisfies these conditions is $_____ . It was found by _____ _____ $10,000 by the factor _____ .

B21.   27,981.81,
      multiplying
      2.798181

C.   *Use of Present Value Tables*

1.   Tables exist for each of the four basic types of compound interest situations and various values of n and i.   The next several frames will explore the use of these tables.

C1.   No answer required.

2.   A person wants to have $18,000 available five years from today.   She can do so by depositing a single sum today that will grow to $18,000; that deposit made today is called the _____ _____ of a future amount.

C2.   present value

3.   If money is worth 16 percent compounded quarterly, i is _____ percent.

C3.   4

4.   Remember that 16 percent is the annual rate; i is the *rate per period,* so we must divide the annual rate by _____ periods per year.

C4.   four

5.   Because the total term is five years, n is

      _____.

C5.   twenty

6.   Look up the table factor in the table for the present value of a single future amount for $n = 20$ and $i = 4$ percent; the factor is

      _____.

C6.   0.456387

7.   This is the amount that will grow to a future amount of _____.

C7.   one (or 1)

8.   But she needs $18,000 or $18,000 times 0.456387 = $_____.

C8.   8,214.97

9.   This seems unbelievable; let's check it.   To determine the future amount to which $8,214.97 would grow in five years if compounded quarterly at an annual rate of 16 percent, we would use the table for _____

      _____.

C9.   the future amount of a single sum

10.   In that table, the factor for $n = 20$ and $i = 4$ percent is _____.

C10.   2.191123

11.   And $8,214.97 x 2.191123 = $_____.

C11. 18,000 (rounded)

12. Jane wants to deposit an amount now to make twenty withdrawals of $1,000 at the end of each quarter for the next five years. Are we viewing a present value or a future amount situation? _____

C12. Present value.

13. Is this a single sum or an annuity? _____

_____

14. So we need the table for the _____

_____.

C13. An annuity.

C14. present value of an ordinary annuity

15. Assume that money is still worth an annual rate of 16 percent compounded quarterly. The values of *n* and *i* are _____ and

_____.

C15. 20, 4 percent

16. In this case (an annuity), *n* is the _____ _____; we must count the rents (withdrawals).

C16. number of rents

17. Look up the table factor; it is _____.

C17. 13.590326

18. This, in dollars, is the amount that Jane must deposit now to withdraw $_____ per period for twenty periods.

C18. 1

19. To withdraw $1,000 per period, Jane must deposit 1,000 times that amount or $_____.

C19. 13,590.33

20. The steps in dealing with compound interest situations require that we first determine whether we are seeking an unknown_____ _____ or _____.

C20. future amount, present value

21. Then we must determine whether we are dealing with a single sum or an _____.

C21. annuity

22. These two steps lead us to the correct table. Now it is necessary to determine the values of _____ and _____.

C22. *n, i*

23. Having found the correct table and determined the values of *n* and *i,* we locate the factor in the *i* column on the *n*th line and apply it to our known amount.

C23. No answer required.

24. Usually, we must multiply--but sometimes it is necessary to divide--by the table factor. For example, if the present or future values of an annuity are known but the amount of each rent is unknown, we must _____ by the table factor.

C24. divide

D. *Applications of Compound Interest*

1. In installment payments, the amount borrowed or the price of the item purchased represents the _____ value of _____.

D1. present, an annuity

2. To determine the amount of the installment payments, you would _____ the purchase price by the factor.

D2. divide

3. In recording the receipt of cash, the accountant would split the payment between _____ and _____.

D3. principal, interest

SELF TEST OF LEARNING GOAL ACHIEVEMENT

1. Compute the maturity values of the following loans at simple interest:

   a. $1,000 loaned on January 4, 1985, for three months at 14 percent:

   b. $3,000 loaned on April 11, 1985, for four months at 15 percent:

   c. $10,000 loaned for 180 days at 18 percent:

2. Using the compound interest tables, solve the following problems (show *n* and *i* in each case):

a. Determine the amount to which $1,000 will grow in three years at 18 percent per year compounded monthly.

b. Determine the amount to be deposited now to allow twenty quarterly withdrawals of $3,000 each with money worth 20 percent per year compounded quarterly.

c. Shelly Lair began to receive a Christmas bonus of $2,000 a year at the end of 1983. She investest each bonus in a savings plan that pays 12 percent per year compounded annually. How much was in her fund immediately after she deposited her 1987 bonus?

d. The town of Sibley must pay off a debt of $500,000 on December 31, 1995. The town council voted to accumulate a fund by making semiannual deposits into a plan that will earn 12 percent per year compounded semiannually. The first deposit is to be made on July 1, 1986. What is the amount of each deposit?

ANSWERS TO LEARNING GOAL ACHIEVEMENT TEST

1. a. $1,000 x 0.14 x 90/360 = $35 interest; and $1,000 + $35 = $1,035.

   b. $3,000 x 0.15 x 122/360 = $152.50 interest; and $3,000 + $152.50 = $3,152.50.   (*Note:* This four month period has 122 actual days.)

   c. $10,000 x 0.18 x 180/360 = $900 interest; and $10,000 + $900 = $10,900.

2. a. $n = 36.$
        $i = 1\ 1/2\%.$
        $1,000 x 1.709140 = $1,709.14.

   b. $n = 20.$
        $i = 5\%.$
        $3,000 x 12.462210 = $37,386.63.

   c. $n = 5.$
        $i = 12\%.$
        $2,000 x 6.352847 = $12,705.69.

   d. $n = 20.$
        $i = 6\%.$
        $500,000 ÷ 36.785591 = $13,592.28.

Chapter 14
Financial Reporting: Concepts and Price-Level Issues

■■

EXPLANATION OF MAJOR CONCEPTS

Purpose of Financial Statements

The basic purpose of financial statements is to provide both internal and external users with information that is useful in making economic decisions. Financial statements reflect a combination of recorded facts, accounting conventions, and personal judgments. In using financial statements, the reader must recognize that the personal judgments of management have an effect on the information shown. Also, it is important to understand the accounting conventions which have gone into the presentation. This is one of the reasons you are studying accounting. Many of these conventions have been set forth by several major authoritative accounting bodies.

Authoritative Bodies

Three authoritative bodies have had a significant influence on the establishment of accounting standards: the American Institute of Certified Public Accountants, the Financial Accounting Standards Board, and the Securities and Exchange Commission. The AICPA was very active in the setting of standards until 1973 when the FASB came into existence. The principal pronouncements of the AICPA which affected financial reporting were the *Accounting Research Bulletins* and the *Accounting Principles Board Opinions*.

In 1972 the FASB was created as an independent, standard setting body. Through their staff, the FASB researches issues of financial reporting and makes pronouncements regarding reporting practices. Today they are the primary non-governmental body which deals with the practices and procedures of financial reporting in the United States. Many of the accounting methods which you are studying in this course have been established by the FASB. Recently, a Government Accounting Standards Board was established to provide the same authority for accounting by governmental units.

The SEC also plays a role in the establishment of accounting standards. They have the authority to prescribe accounting methods for firms whose stocks and bonds are sold on the stock exchanges. Their primary concern is the fairness and accuracy of public disclosure. To this goal, they require detailed reporting by these companies to the SEC quarterly and annually.

The Conceptual Framework of Accounting

Recently, the FASB has been involved with a project to create an overall "Conceptual Framework of Accounting." This project has resulted in the issuance of several *Concept Statements* which are intended to provide the framework within which accounting standards are to be set.

Generally Accepted Accounting Principles

Over the years the accounting profession has developed a set of standards which are called *generally accepted accounting principles*. The principles which were discussed in the chapter are as follows:

Entity--separate accounting records are to be kept for each business.

Going Concern--an entity will continue to operate indefinitely.

Consistency--the same procedures should be followed every period.

Conservatism--the procedure which produces the least favorable immediate result is usually chosen.

Periodicity--financial statements are prepared for regularly specified time periods.

Objective Evidence--amounts recorded in accounting records should be supported by source documents.

Materiality--accounting treatment of an item too small to influence a decision need not follow prescribed standards.

Full Disclosure--financial statements should report all significant information.

Historical Cost--assets are recorded at the actual cost incurred.

Stable Dollar--the dollar is used as the unit of measure without adjustment for changes in price levels.

Revenue Realization--revenue is recognized in the accounting records according to one of the following methods:

Point of Sale

Collection Method--cost recovery or installment basis.

Percentage of Completion

Matching Expense and Revenue--expenses incurred in the generation of revenue should be matched against those revenues.

Extraordinary Items

In order to make accurate projections using accounting information, the user must be able to distinguish between activities which will be likely to continue and those which are unique to the current period. Accountants believe that this need is best met by segregating extraordinary items in the income statement. An extraordinary item is a gain or loss, which is unusual in the type of business and occurs very infrequently. Thus, the income statement, in the top section, calculates income from continuing operations and then reflects extraordinary gains and losses in calculating net income. Although the bottom line net income is the business's overall net income for the year, the net income from recurring operations is more appropriate for predictive purposes.

Price-Level Changes

Current standards require external financial reporting to be based on historical cost. Since 1979, the FASB has required that certain large companies include as supplemental information the effects of changes in price levels on income measurement. During the current period of experimentation, two alternative methods are required. The first adjusts for general price-level changes, and the second adjusts to the current cost of the specific item.

The purpose of general price-level adjustments is to restate historical costs in terms of dollars of a common purchasing power. Thus, it restates the financial statements for the general effects of inflation. Historical cost items are categorized as either monetary or nonmonetary. Monetary items are those in which the dollar amount exchanged or to be exchanged is fixed. Examples include accounts receivable and payable, notes payable, and bonds payable. Holding monetary items during a period of changing prices will cause a purchasing power gain or loss. If the monetary liabilities exceed the monetary assets during a period of inflation, a purchasing power gain will be experienced. And a purchasing power loss will be experienced if monetary assets exceed monetary liabilities. Nonmonetary items are the other balance sheet items.

Nonmonetary items must be adjusted for statement presentation. They are multiplied by a ratio of the Consumer Price Index on the date we wish to convert to over the index on the date the item was acquired.

The other alternative is current cost accounting. This method attempts to take into consideration the effects of inflation on specific items used in the business. This is done by adjusting the cost of nonmonetary items to the amount that they would cost at the time the adjustments are being made.

GUIDED STUDY OF THIS CHAPTER

A. *Financial Reporting Concepts and Authoritative Bodies*

1. The basic purpose of financial statements is to

_____

_____

_____.

A1. transmit to interested groups information that is useful in making economic decisions

2. Financial statements reflect a combination of

_____, _____

_____, and _____

_____.

A2. recorded facts, accounting conventions, personal judgements

3. A fundamental guideline that serves to determine whether or not an accounting alternative is acceptable is called an _____

_____.

A3. accounting standard

4. The authoritative body that published the *Accounting Principles Board Opinions* is the

_____.

A4. AICPA

5. The current nongovernmental standard setting body is the _____.

A5. FASB

6. The major pronouncements of the FASB are the

_____.

A6. *Statements of Standards*

7. Recently, the Financial Accounting Foundation created a second board called the _____ to make pronouncements for governmental units.

A7. GASB

8. The major governmental body that makes accounting rules governing external reporting is the _____

_____.

A8. Securities and Exchange Commission

9. The organization whose research and publication activities are directed toward the managerial accountant is the _____

_____.

A9. National Association of Accountants

B. *Generally Accepted Accounting Principles*

1. The principle which suggests that the alternative accounting procedure chosen should present the least favorable result is the _____ principle.

B1. conservatism

2. _____ assumes that the entity will continue indefinitely.

B2.   Going concern

B3.   Full disclosure

B4.   entity

B5.   consistency

B6.   Historical cost

B7.   materiality

B8.   point of sale

B9.   percentage of
completion

B10.   installment basis

B11.   matching

3. _____ dictates that
all significant financial and economic information should be reported.

4. The principle which requires that a separate
set of books be kept for each business enter-
prise is the _____ principle.

5. The principle which requires that the same
accounting procedures be followed each period
is the _____ principle.

6. _____ requires that
assets be recorded at their incurred cost.

7. The _____ principle
suggests that an item small enough that it
would not influence a decision based upon the
statements may be treated in a manner different from principle.

8. The revenue realization method which dictates
that revenue be recorded when the service is
performed or the goods delivered is the
_____ method.

9. The revenue recognition method which uses the
proportion of total costs incurred to determine
the revenue recorded is the _____
_____ method.

10. A method of revenue recognition often used by
retail stores recognizes a portion of each dollar
collected as a return of cost and a portion as
gross margin. This method is known as the

_____.

11. Under the _____ principle,
the expenses incurred to generate revenue
should be recorded in the same period as the
revenues.

C. *Reporting Issues*

1. A gain or loss which is unusual in nature and
occurs infrequently is called an _____

_____.

C1. extraordinary item

2. Extraordinary items are reported in a separate section of the income statement at the _____ _____ (top/bottom) of the income statement.

C2. bottom

3. This presentation allows the identification of a separate income number before extraordinary items which is more useful for _____ about income in the future years.

C3. predictions

4. The ability of each dollar to buy fewer goods and services is known as _____.

C4. inflation

5. _____ describes a condition when the prices of goods and services are dropping.

C5. Deflation

6. The reporting alternative to historical cost which adjusts the financial statements for the general effects of inflation is called _____ _____.

C6. general price-level adjusted accounting

7. The alternative which adjusts for the price-level changes of specific items is called _____.

C7. current cost accounting

8. If a parcel of land were shown in the financial statements at the price which would have to be paid today, the firm would be using _____ _____.

C8. current cost accounting

9. When statements are adjusted for inflation, the amounts in the ledger _____ (are/ are not) changed.

C9. are not

10. General price-level accounting uses the _____ _____.

C10. Consumer Price Index for All Urban Consumers

11. The general formula to convert historical cost amounts for general price levels multiplies historical cost by a ratio of the index on the date converted _____ (TO/FROM) over the index on the date converted _____ (TO/FROM).

C11.   TO, FROM

12.   A parcel of land costing $20,000 was bought when the CPI-U was 120, and it is to be shown on a balance sheet when the index is 150. The adjusted amount would be $_____.

C12.   25,000 = ($20,000 x 150/120)

13.   Items which are fixed in terms of the total number of dollars that will be collected on assets or paid on liabilities, regardless of changes in the price level, are called _____ items.

C13.   monetary

14.   Since monetary items are fixed in amount and are not affected by inflation, no adjustement is necessary.

C14.   No answer required.

15.   During a period of inflation, a purchasing power _____ (gain/loss) arises from holding monetary assets.

C15.   loss

16.   And, during a period of inflation, a purchasing power _____ arises from holding monetary liabilities.

C16.   gain

17.   Items whose amount is not fixed contractually and thus whose balance is not stated in terms of current dollars are known as _____ _____ items.

C17.   nonmonetary

18.   Nonmonetary items _____ (require/ do not require) adjustment by the use of the indexes.

C18.   require

19.   Refering to Figure 14-2, the net income which would have been reported on the traditional income statement would have been $_____.

C19.   9,000,000

20.   Since the net sales amounts in all three columns are the same, it can be inferred that the amounts are being adjusted to _____ _____ (average-for-the-year/ end-of-year) dollars.

C20.   average for-the-year

21.   Income adjusted for general inflation shows a _____.

C21.   loss

22.   Since the loss shown under adjustment for current cost is greater than general inflation, specific items in this company were _____ (more/less) severely affected by inflation.

C22. more

23. The company experienced a purchasing power _____. This means that they must have had a net monetary _____ (asset/liability) position.

C23. gain, liability

24. Depreciation and amortization expense was higher on an adjusted basis than on a historical cost basis because price-level changes have caused the value of property, plant, and equipment to _____ (increase/decrease).

C24. increase

25. The appendix to the chapter shows a portion of the financial statements of General Motors Corporation. The net income reported in their historical cost income statement was $_____. Adjusted for the general effects of inflation, their net income would have been $_____. On a current cost basis, it would have been $_____.

C25. 333,400,000,
       -833,300,000,
       -688,800,000

26. Adjusted for the effects of general inflation, the dividends per share have been _____ (increasing/decreasing).

C26. decreasing

SELF TEST OF LEARNING GOAL ACHIEVEMENT

1. Match the letter of the description with the proper generally accepted accounting principle.

    _____ Entity
    _____ Going concern
    _____ Consistency
    _____ Conservatism
    _____ Periodicity
    _____ Objective evidence
    _____ Materiality
    _____ Full disclosure
    _____ Historical cost
    _____ Stable dollar
    _____ Matching

    a. Financial statements are prepared at regular time intervals during the lifetime of a company.
    b. The same accounting procedures should be followed year after year.
    c. A separate set of records should be kept for each business.
    d. Small dollar amounts need not follow generally accepted accounting principles.
    e. Expenses incurred in generating revenues should be recorded in the same period as the revenues.
    f. Financial statements should report all significant financial and economic events.
    g. The dollar is significantly free from changes in purchasing power to be used as the measuring unit.
    h. The amount used in the recording of a transaction is the amount incurred.
    i. It is assumed that a business will continue to operate indefinitely.
    j. Amounts used in recording transactions should be based on source documents.
    k. Using the alternative which will give the least favorable immediate results.

2. The Bargain Basement sold a television set for $400 which had cost them $300. For each of the following months calculate the amount of gross margin that will be recognized on the installment basis given the amount received from the customer.

    a. March, $50.00

    b. April, $75.00

    c. May, $100.00

3. The Bellview Company bought three identical assets at a cost of $20,000 each in 1970, 1978, and 1980 when the CPI–U was 120, 150, and 175, respectively. If the index is now 210, show the calculation of the total amount that would appear on a balance sheet adjusted for general price-level changes.

ANSWERS TO LEARNING GOAL ACHIEVEMENT TEST

1. c, i, b, k, a, j, d, f, h, g, e.

2. a. $50.00 x [($400 – $300)/$400] = $12.50.

    b. $75.00 x .25 = $18.75.

    c. $100.00 x .25 = $25.00.

3. $20,000 x 210/120 = $35,000
    $20,000 x 210/150 = 28,000
    $20,000 x 210/175 = 24,000
                TOTAL $87,000

Chapter 15
Partnership Accounting

■■■

EXPLANATION OF MAJOR CONCEPTS

Forms of Business

The three major forms of business in the United States are the single proprietorship, the partnership, and the corporation.

Single proprietorship. Owned by one person, a single proprietorship is the simplest form of business. Up to this point in the textbook, the primary focus has been on the single proprietorship.

Partnership. A partnership is a voluntary association of two or more persons to carry on a business for profit. The partnership is a popular form of business for professionals such as lawyers or accountants. Partnerships are formed by written or verbal agreement. Although there are no formal procedures (such as filing of applications with the state to form the business), there are state laws that regulate the relationships of partners with each other and with the public. The laws affecting partnerships are the same in most states because they have adopted a model law called the *Uniform Partnership Act.*

Because they pool financial resources and the borrowing power of more than one person, partnerships can raise more capital than proprietorships. They can also bring together in the same business a greater variety of talent. Against those advantages certain disadvantages must be weighed. Each partner is personally liable for the debts of the firm and must secure agreement of other partners for certain actions such as selling a portion of his or her interest.

The income tax status is similar to that for proprietorships. Partners include their individual shares of partnership income and deductions in their personal income tax returns.

Corporation. A corporation is, in the eyes of the law, a "fictitious person." A state creates a legal entity by issuing to a group of incorporators a certificate called a *corporate charter*. A corporation may be owned by a large number of persons who invest in it and receive *shares of capital stock*. These shares of ownership may be sold to any other person without obtaining permission of the corporation or any of its other owners. The focus of the remaining chapters in the textbook is on corporations. Chapter 15, however, concentrates on accounting techniques that are unique to partnerships.

Division of Profits

In computing the division of profits of a partnership, there are some common errors which students tend to make. The following points will help you to avoid them:

▶ The division of profits is a computation *leading up to* a single journal entry-- closing of the Income Summary to the capital accounts. It is *not* the journal entry, and elements of the computation *do not* appear in any journal entry.

▶ Any formula that the partners agree to use to divide profits is possible. When the formula contains interest allowances or salary allowances, these items are *not* expenses. Remember that they are simply part of a formula; they are not part of the journal entry.

▶ Often a formula will provide that a residual amount be divided in some ratio. If other allowances are greater than net income, this residual will be a *negative figure*. Treat it as a negative figure--allocate it, and add it in as a negative figure.

▶ The drawing accounts have no relation to profit division. The partners' with-drawals are completely unrelated to any salary allowances and are not expense. Ignore the drawing accounts when dividing profits.

▶ Once the division of profits has been computed, make a compound general journal entry to close net income into the capital accounts *(not to close capital)* as follows:

```
Income Summary  . . . . . . . . . . . . . . . . .      xxx
     Partner A, Capital . . . . . . . . . . . . . . .           xx
     Partner B, Capital . . . . . . . . . . . . . . .           xx
     Partner C, Capital . . . . . . . . . . . . . . .           xx
          To close the Income Summary account.
```

▶ Finally, remember that drawing has no effect on income. Close the drawing accounts separately into the capital accounts.

You should take the time at this point to review the four examples which appear in the text of the division of profits under various situations.

Changes in Capital Structure

New partners may come into the business; existing partners may die or with-draw. When this happens, the existing partnership is *dissolved,* and a new one takes its place. To an external viewer (except for a possible change in the business name), a partnership dissolution is not noticeable. To the part-ners, however, it may mean some reassignment of capital balances or at least the creation of new ones. As you work with the many possible ways to record admission or retirement of a partner, try this process of analytical reasoning:

Net assets = Total assets - Total liabilities = Total partners' equity.

Follow these steps:

1. Determine the amount of net assets before the change.

2. Determine the amount of net assets after the change. It can be (a) any amount the partners agree it should be or (b) equal to old net assets plus assets contributed by the new partner (or minus assets removed by a retiring partner).

3. Using these data, determine the effect on each partner's capital balance (called that partner's interest).

Again, review of the examples in the text is recommended at this point.

Liquidation of Partnership

An entirely different type of dissolution occurs when a partnership is liquidated. In this case, the assets are all sold or collected so that cash becomes the only asset (a process called *realization*). Then the cash is paid to the equity claimants. The creditors are paid in full before any cash is distributed to partners; remaining cash is then paid out to partners, and the business ceases to operate. Again, here are some points to help you:

▸ There are almost always gains and losses in the realization process. These gains and losses are credited (if gains) or debited (if losses) to the partners' capital accounts *in their profit-sharing ratio*. Losses must be shared in the same ratio as profits.

▸ When realization is complete and creditors are paid, the remaining cash belongs to the partners. It is paid to them in accordance with their remaining capital balances--*not* in accordance with profit-sharing ratios.

▸ A partner could develop a debit (negative) balance in the realization process. This is called a *deficiency*. Deficient partners must pay in the amount of any deficiency to bring their capital balances up to zero. If a partner cannot do so, this is another loss to be shared among the remaining partners in the profit-sharing ratios that they bear to each other. It is important to grasp this last point. Suppose A, B, and C share profits on a 3:2:1 basis. This means that A takes 3/6 or 50 percent; B takes 2/6 or 33 1/3 percent; and C takes 1/6 or 16 2/3 percent. If B becomes deficient, A and C stand 3:1. A must absorb 3/4 or 75 percent, and C must absorb 1/4 or 25 percent.

Let's look at these concepts in more detail in the guided study.

GUIDED STUDY OF THIS CHAPTER

A. Division of Profits. The public accounting firm of Carter and Foley is used in the textbook to illustrate division of profits.

1. In example 1, they share profits on what basis?

   _____

A1.   Equally.

2. To divide a net income of $67,000, each partner's capital account is credited with $_____ .

A2.   33,500

3. Assume they also had equal withdrawals of $12,000 per year. Is this because of the profit-sharing ratio? _____ Explain.

   _____

   _____

   _____

A3.   No. The amount each withdraws is a matter for a separate agreement.

4. Could Kay Carter withdraw more than her share of the profits for the year? _____
   Explain._____

   _____

   _____

A4.   Yes. There is no relationship between profit-sharing formulas and drawings.

5. Suppose that Carter and Foley had a net loss of $12,500 in 1985 instead of a net income. How would this affect the capital accounts?

   _____

A5.   It would reduce them.

6. Ann Foley began the year with less capital than Kay Carter ($47,500 compared to $62,500). Should Foley, therefore, absorb less of a $12,500 loss? _____ Explain.

   _____

   _____

   _____

A6.   No. Losses are shared in the same ratio as profits; in this case, equally or $6,250 each.

7. Move to example 2. The formula has been changed to include an interest allowance of 20 percent. On what is the 20 percent based?

   _____

A7. Beginning-of-year capital balances.

8. Since total beginning-of-year capital balances are $110,000, it is obvious that total interest credit of 20 percent will be $_____.

A8. 22,000

9. With an assumed net income of $67,000 in 1985, the residual is _____ (positive/ negative).

A9. positive

10. The residual $45,000 is divided on a 2:1 ratio. This means that _____ gets 2/3 and _____ gets 1/3.

A10. Carter, Foley

11. But the journal entry does not close out 2/3 and 1/3 of the Income Summary, respectively.

Why? _____

_____

A11. Because of the different interest allowances added in.

12. Example 3 adds a new dimension to the formula. What is it? _____

A12. A salary allowance.

13. Does the salary allowance determine how much Kay Carter may withdraw during the year?

_____ Explain. _____

_____

A13. No. The amount each can draw is a separate agreement.

14. Do the salary allowances reduce net income?

_____ Explain. _____

_____

A14. No. They are simply a part of the profit-sharing formula.

15. In example 3, is the residual (remainder) divided on a 2:1 ratio? _____ Does it have to be? _____ Explain. _____

_____

_____

A15. Yes. No. It can be divided any way the partners agree in advance to do so.

16. In example 3, the assumed profit is again $67,000. How much of it is debited to Salaries Expense? _____

A16. None. (If you missed this, you'd better go back to A7 and repeat.)

17. Move to example 4. How much is the assumed net income for the year? $_____

A17.   22,000.

18.   How much is allocated (in total) to salary allowances and interest allowances? $_____.

A18.   40,000.

19.   This leaves a residual of $22,000 – $40,000 = $18,000 _____ (negative/positive).

A19.   negative

20.   Using the 2:1 division of the residual, Kay Carter would be allocated $_____ and Ann Foley would be allocated $_____.

A20.   (12,000), (6,000)

21.   If the ratio of the residual had been 4:1, Kay Carter would have been allocated $_____ of it.

A21.   14,400

22.   Remember that the purpose of the computation for division of net income is to make a single journal entry to close the Income Summary account. Do not try to inject the interest allowances, salary allowances, or residual into journal entries.

A22.   No answer required.

23.   In the statement of partner's equity, each partner would _____ _____, and there would be a _____ column.

A23.   have a separate column, total

B.   *Changes in Capital Structure. Probably the most complex entries to reflect changes in capital structure are to record the admission of a new partner because there are so many ways to accomplish it.*

1.   In the textbook example, Arthur Allen and Brian Barnes are partners, with capital balances of $_____ and $_____, respectively.

B1.   30,000, 42,000

2.   This means that net assets of the partnership are $_____.

B2.   72,000

3.   They agree to admit Charles Cahn as a third partner. In the first example, Allen sells _____ of his interest to Cahn for $_____.

B3.   1/2, 18,000

4.   What is the net asset value of 1/2 of Allen's interest? $_____

B4.   15,000.

5.   What happens to the additional $3,000 =
($18,000 - $15,000)? _____

_____

B5.   It is a personal gain
to Allen.

6.   Does Cahn pay any money to the partnership?
_____ Explain. _____

_____

B6.   No. It is an outright
purchase of part of
Allen's ownership.

7.   Then why is a journal entry needed on the
partnership books? _____

_____

B7.   It is still necessary
to record the changes
in capital.

8.   Another way for a new partner to join a partnership is to invest cash or other assets to
acquire an interest (share of ownership).
Does this *always* cause an increase in net
assets? _____

B8.   Yes.

9.   Look at example 1. Allen and Barnes are partners; their capital balances are $30,000 and
$42,000, respectively. Total net assets before
admission of Cahn are $_____.

B9.   72,000

10.   Cahn desires to own 1/3 of the business. To
do so, he must invest an amount equal to
exactly _____ the combined capital balances
of the other two partners.

B10.   1/2

11.   This amount is $36,000; when added to present
net assets, the new total net assets is
$_____.

B11.   108,000

12.   And 1/3 of $108,000 (Cahn's interest) is
$_____.

B12.   36,000

13.   Admission of a new partner is a time of negotiation. Sometimes the new partner may be
required to invest more or less than the exact
book value needed to change net assets to
bring about the desired changes in shares of
ownership. Two methods to account for such
a situation are the goodwill method and the
bonus method. Both produce the same *relative*
shares of ownership among the partners, but
they produce different amounts in the capital
accounts.

B13. No answer required.

14. Example 2 covers the goodwill methods. Goodwill is an _____ asset.

B14. intangible

15. If the partners decide to recognize goodwill, the total net assets will be _____ (increased/decreased) by the amount of goodwill.

B15. increased

16. The increase will be _____ (in addition to/part of) any cash invested by the new partner.

B16. in addition to

17. Goodwill can be viewed as being contributed to the new partnership by _____ (old/new/either) partner(s).

B17. either

18. If the goodwill is attributed to the old partners, it is divided among their capital accounts according to the _____

_____.

B18. profit-and-loss sharing ratio

19. If to the new partner, the amount of goodwill decided upon is credited to his or her capital account in addition to the _____

_____.

B19. cash invested

20. In the case of goodwill to the old partners, the new partner's investment is equal to his interest of the agreed upon total capital.

B20. No answer required.

21. In the illustration, Cahn invested $_____ of agreed upon total capital of $_____. This ratio was equal to his interest in total capital. Thus, the _____ (old/new) partner(s) receive(s) the goodwill.

B21. 40,000, 120,000, old

22. In the next illustration, Cahn contributes an amount _____ (less than/equal to) his share of the agreed upon total capital. Thus, the goodwill goes to the _____ (old/new) partner(s).

B22. less, new

23. Cahn, in this case, will be credited with the difference between his _____ and his share of the agreed upon total capital.

B23. contribution

24. Study carefully both instances in example 2. The amount of goodwill is determined by

_____.

B24. negotiation (agree-ment between the partners)

25. Example 3 moves to the bonus methods. As in goodwill, an extra credit may be given to either the old or new partner(s). The account balances will be different from the goodwill method because the only new asset added is the _____.

B25. cash invested by the new partner

26. And if old partners want to give credit to the new partner greater than the cash invested, they must _____

_____.

B26. reduce their capital account balances

27. How do the old partners divide this reduction of capital balances? _____

_____

B27. It is in profit-and-loss-sharing ratios.

C. *Retirement or Death of a Partner.   This is a situation somewhat the reverse of admission of a new partner.*

1. If a partner retires either voluntarily, with permission of the other partners, or involun-tarily (for example, by death), assets should be adjusted to _____

_____.

C1. their current market value

2. Why is this necessary? _____

_____

_____

_____

_____

C2. Any increases or decreases in value occurred while the retiring partner was in the firm, and he or she should partici-pate in them.

3. How does a retiring partner participate in gains or losses due to changes in asset values?

_____

_____

_____

_____

C3.   By debits or credits to capital accounts of all partners in the profit-and-loss-sharing ratio.

C4.   24,000

C5.   Because they share profits equally.

C6.   12,000

C7.   8,000, 4,000

C8.   No answer required.

D1.   the conversion of all noncash assets to cash

D2.   profit-and-loss-sharing ratio

D3.   creditors

D4.   cash

D5.   No. (An exception could be a debt owed by the firm to one of the part-ners.)

4.   Before Fred Thomas retired from the firm of Rhodes, Wills, and Thomas, the land and building were appraised at $_____ more than their book value.

5.   Why was $8,000 credited to each partner?

_____

6.   If the ratio had been 3:2:1, Kirsten Rhodes would be credited with $_____ in her capital account.

7.   And Wills and Thomas would be credited with $_____ and $_____, respec-tively.

8.   It would also be normal to close the books and update all partners' capital accounts with operating profit or loss in case of the death of a partner. In a voluntary withdrawal, this process might be avoided by negotiation.

D.   *Liquidation*

1.   Liquidation involves the process of realization, which is _____

_____.

2.   In the process of realization, losses and gains are reflected in capital accounts in accordance with the _____.

3.   The first cash distribution is the payment to

_____.

4.   When realization and payment to creditors are complete, the only remaining asset is _____.

5.   Are there any remaining liabilities? _____

6.   Therefore, total cash = total _____

_____.

D6. partners' equity

7. Since the partners' capital accounts have been debited and credited with losses and gains, do they now reflect the profit-and-loss-sharing ratio? _____ Explain. _____

_____

D7. No. They reflect each partner's amount of ownership.

8. Could some be negative (debit balance) capital accounts? _____

D8. Yes.

9. A debit balance in the capital account is called a _____.

D9. deficiency

10. What should happen to eliminate a deficiency?

_____

_____

D10. The deficient partner should pay in that amount to the firm.

11. If he or she is unable to pay, how is the deficiency eliminated? _____

_____

D11. The other partners must reduce their capital accounts.

12. How do they share this capital reduction?

_____

_____

D12. In their remaining profit-and-loss-sharing ratio.

13. When liquidation cash is finally paid to partners, is it paid in the profit-and-loss-sharing ratio? _____

D13. No.

14. How are the amounts to each partner determined? _____

_____

D14. Each is entitled to withdraw his or her capital balance.

SELF TEST OF LEARNING GOAL ACHIEVEMENT

1. Herman Sanderson and Alice Jones are partners with capital balances as follows on January 1, 1985:

    Sanderson, capital $80,000
    Jones, capital   60,000

    They share profits as follows:

	Sanderson	Jones
Salary allowances	$15,000	$30,000
Interest on beginning-of-year balance	10%	10%
Residual (remainder)	70%	30%

    Required: Show computations to divide net income for 1985 under each of the following assumptions:

    (a) There is a net income of $100,000.

(b)　There is a net income of $50,000.

(c)　There is a net loss of $10,000.

2.　Maria Randado and Jim Hall are partners who share profits 2:1, respectively. Randado's capital balance is $60,000; Hall's is $40,000. They agree to admit Rita Guerra to their law firm. Show general journal entries to admit Guerra under each of the following independent possible agreements:

a. She is to pay Hall $50,000 for 1/2 his interest.
b. She is to invest $50,000 for a 1/3 interest.
c. She is to invest $65,000 for a 1/3 interest with total capital to be
    $165,000.
d. She is to invest $40,000 for a 1/3 interest with total capital to be
    $150,000.   There is no bonus.

GENERAL JOURNAL

Date		Account Titles and Explanation	F	Debit	Credit

3. Dan Donver, Marcia Marin, and Sam Nevada are equal partners with capital balances after closing the books on December 31, 1985, as follows:

    Donver $32,600
    Marin   40,000
    Nevada   15,300

They agree that Nevada will leave the firm as of December 31, 1985. An appraisal finds the inventory overvalued by $5,000 and the building under-valued by $20,000. They share profits equally.

Required: Record the necessary journal entries for Nevada's retirement from the firm by withdrawing cash.

GENERAL JOURNAL

Date	Account Titles and Explanation	F	Debit	Credit

4. Assume that the firm of Donver, Marin, and Nevada (Question 3) is to liquidate on December 31, 1985. In addition to the capital balances shown in Question 3, there are cash of $15,000, liabilities of $5,000, and other assets of $77,900. The other assets are sold for $38,900 cash. Prepare a statement of liquidation.

ANSWERS TO LEARNING GOAL ACHIEVEMENT TEST

1. (a)

	Sanderson	Jones	Total
Salary allowances	$15,000	$30,000	$ 45,000
Interest allowances	8,000	6,000	14,000
Remainder ($100,000 − $45,000 − $14,000)			
70% to Sanderson	28,700		28,700
30% to Jones		12,300	12,300
Totals	$51,700	$48,300	$100,000

(b)

	Sanderson	Jones	Total
Salary allowances	$15,000	$30,000	$45,000
Interest allowances	8,000	6,000	14,000
Total allowances	$23,000	$36,000	$59,000
Excess of allowances over income			
Allowances $59,000			
Net income 50,000			
Excess divided 70:30	(6,300)	(2,700)	(9,000)
Totals	$16,700	$33,300	$50,000

(c)

	Sanderson	Jones	Total
Total allowances (as before) . .	$ 23,000	$36,000	$ 59,000
Excess of allowances over income			
Allowances $59,000			
Net income (loss) . . . . . (10,000)			
Excess divided 70:30	(48,300)	(20,700)	(69,000)
Totals	$(25,300)	$15,300	$(10,000)

2.

GENERAL JOURNAL

Date		Account Titles and Explanation	F	Debit	Credit
	a.	Jim Hall, Capital		20,000	
		Rita Guerra, Capital			20,000
		Purchase of 1/2 of Hall's			
		interest.			
	b.	Cash		50,000	
		Rita Guerra, Capital			50,000
		Admission to 1/3 interest			
		by investment.			
	c.	Cash		65,000	
		Maria Randado, Capital			6,667
		Jim Hall, Capital			3,333
		Rita Guerra, Capital			55,000
		Admission to 1/3 interest			
		by investment (rounded).			
	d.	Cash		40,000	
		Goodwill		10,000	
		Rita Guerra, Capital			50,000
		Admission to 1/3 interest			
		by investment.			

3.

GENERAL JOURNAL

Date		Account Titles and Explanation	F	Debit	Credit
1985					
Dec.	31	Building		20,000	
		Inventory			5,000
		Dan Donver, Capital			5,000
		Marcia Marin, Capital			5,000
		Sam Nevada, Capital			5,000
		Revaluation of assets.			
	31	Sam Nevada, Capital		20,300	
		Cash			20,300
		Retirement of partner.			

4.

DONVER, MARIN, AND NEVADA
Statement of Partnership Liquidation
For the Month of December 1985

	Cash	Other Assets	Liabilities	Capital Donver	Marin	Nevada
Balances before realization	$15,000	$77,900	$5,000	$32,600	$40,000	$15,300
Sale of assets	38,900	(77,900)		(13,000)	(13,000)	(13,000)
Balances	$53,900	$ 0	$5,000	$19,600	$27,000	$ 2,300
Payment of liabilities .	(5,000)		(5,000)	0	0	0
Balances	$48,900		$ 0	$19,600	$27,000	$ 2,300
Cash to partners . . .	(48,900)			(19,600)	(27,000)	(2,300)

Chapter 16
Corporations:
Paid-In Capital

■■■

EXPLANATION OF MAJOR CONCEPTS

Corporations

A corporation is, in the eyes of the law, a "fictitious person." A state creates a legal entity by issuing to a group of incorporators a certificate called a *corporate charter*. A corporation may be owned by a large number of persons who invest in it and receive *shares of capital stock*. These shares of ownership may be sold to any other person without obtaining permission of the corporation or any of its other owners.

Corporations have the ability to raise vast sums of money. Another advantage is that the individual owners are not liable for the debts of the corporation. This enables the shareholders (owners) to invest any amount they desire in a business without the risk of losing a large amount of their personal wealth if the business fails. Since corporations are legal entities, they are required to pay federal and state income tax on their earnings.

Paid-In Capital--General

Assets that are invested in a business are known as *paid-in capital*. A corporation has several types of paid-in capital, including:

▶ Cash paid to the corporation in exchange for shares of its stock.

▶ Assets other than cash given to the corporation in exchange for shares of its stock.

▶ Amounts received from reissuance of shares of its own stock that have been:

  ● Repurchased by the corporation and then reissued at a higher price.
  ● Donated to the corporation by shareholders and reissued to new shareholders.

▶ The value of property such as land donated to a corporation to get it to build a plant in a certain community.

279

Chapter 16 discusses these types of paid-in capital and the accounting for transactions that bring paid-in capital to the corporation.

Issuance of Stock

The two basic types of capital stock are preferred and common stock. *Preferred stock* has certain advantages, such as a stipulated rate of dividends that must be paid before any other dividends are paid. However, the residual ownership stock is *common stock*. Under most circumstances, it is the common stockholders who have the right to vote for election of directors and on other important matters. If a company experiences fast growth, it is the value of common stock that will increase rapidly on the market--not the preferred.

The stock of corporations usually has a par value or a stated value. When the corporation issues its stock, most state laws require that the amount of assets received in exchange for it be equal to or greater than *par* or *stated value*. The amount of the par or stated value is credited to an account called Preferred Stock or Common Stock, as appropriate. Amounts received in excess of par or stated value of common stock cause a credit to be made to an account called Paid-in Capital--Excess over Par Value, Common (or Preferred, if appropriate). Another name for this account is Premium on Common Stock (or Premium on Preferred Stock). It is very important that you bear in mind that the accounts being credited on issuance of stock are owner's equity accounts. *They show ownership claims generated by investment.* The assets that are invested are debited to asset accounts.

Some investors *subscribe* for capital stock, meaning that the investor signs a contract agreeing to invest in a specified number of shares at a specified price. Usually a down payment is made, with dates set for payment of remaining installments later. In addition to the debit to Cash for the down payment, there is a debit to the current asset account Subscriptions Receivable for the balance due. Remember that *Subscriptions Receivable* is an asset; it is not part of the owner's equity. Owner's equity is created when stock is subscribed. The amount of new owners' equity equal to par value of the subscribed stock is credited to *Common Stock Subscribed* (or Preferred Stock Subscribed, if appropriate). This account is a temporary paid-in capital account. It simply shows par value of subscribed but unpaid shares, and amounts in it will be transferred to the Common Stock (or Preferred Stock, if appropriate) account when the subscription is paid up and the stock is issued. If subscriptions are received at a price higher than par or stated value, the excess is credited directly to the Excess over Par or Stated Value account.

Value Terms

The value terms explained in this chapter are extremely important. You should take time to understand them clearly now rather than be confused by them later.

▶ *Par value* is an arbitrary amount per share established in the corporate charter as the lowest amount an investor is allowed to pay in to receive a share of ownership. It is usually set at a relatively low figure for common stock. Dan River Inc. has $5 par value common stock.

▶ *Stated value* is an amount per share assigned by the corporation's board of directors to take the place of par value. In states that authorize the issuance of no-par value stock, a corporation may choose not to have a par value assigned. For accounting purposes, you may treat stated value as if it were par.

▶ *Market value* is the price of a share of stock bought on the stock market. It is in no way related to par value. Market values change daily.

GUIDED STUDY OF THIS CHAPTER

A. Value of Stock. Let's work first to understand the meaning of the different types of value attributed to a share of stock.

1. If Khell Corporation issues 1,000 shares of stock to John Smith at $12 a share, its market value at that time is $_____ per share.

A1.   12

2. If John Smith sells 100 shares ten months later for $1,950, its market value has risen to $_____ a share.

A2.   19.50

3. Market value, then, is the _____

_____.

A3.   amount for which a share of stock can be sold

4. If the charter places an arbitrary amount of $5 per share as the minimum for which Kheel Corporation can issue its stock, the $5 is _____ value.

A4.   par

5. Market value of a stock changes daily. Does par value also change? _____

A5.   No.

6. Some states authorize the issuance of no-par value stock. If the Kheel Corporation's stock is no-par, Kheel's directors may assign a _____ value to each share.

A6.   stated

7. For all recording of stock issuances, stated value is treated the same as _____ value.

A7.   par

8.   Which of these capital stock values change because of economic conditions, politics, or investors' expectations? _____

_____

A8.   Only the market value.

9.   Are changes in market value recorded in the corporate accounts? _____

A9.   No.

10.   If Kheel Corporation issued 1,000 shares of $10 par value common stock, the value recorded in the account Common Stock is

_____.

A10.   par value

11.   If the stock is issued at 25 (meaning $25 per share), the excess is $_____ per share.

A11.   15

12.   The $15 excess x 1,000 shares = $_____ is credited to the _____

_____ account.

A12.   15,000, Paid-in Capital--Excess over Par Value, Common

13.   Another account title used for the excess is

_____.

A13.   Premium on Common Stock

B.   *Paid-In Capital Transactions*

1.   Sometimes attorneys or accountants who perform services in getting a corporation organized are paid in stock instead of cash for their services. The account debited in such a transaction is _____.

B1.   Organization Costs

2.   Is this an expense account? _____ Explain.

_____

B2.   No. It is an intangible asset.

3.   Kheel Corporation was authorized to issue 50,000 shares of $10 par value common stock. The organizers (Example A-3) charged $10,000 for their services but accepted 1,000 shares of stock instead. The debit of $10,000 was to _____.

B3.   Organization Costs

4.   The credit in this transaction was to _____

_____.

B4. Common Stock

5. Suppose that this bill were in the amount of $12,000 and they accepted 1,000 shares of stock instead. The amount of debit to Organization Costs would be $_____.

B5. 12,000

6. The credit to Common Stock would be for $_____.

B6. 10,000

7. The remaining $2,000 would be credited to

_____

_____.

B7. Paid-in Capital--
Excess over Par
Value, Common

8. Some stock issuances are made by the subscription process. A *subscription* is an agreement to invest in a stipulated number of shares at a specified price. Let's follow the Kheel Corporation illustration in the textbook step by step.

B8. No answer required.

9. On Nov. 2, 1986, subscriptions were received for 10,000 shares at $10.50. The first entry records the total subscription and debits

_____

for $105,000.

B9. Subscriptions
Receivable--Common

10. Subscriptions Receivable--Common is a _____ _____ account.

B10. current asset

11. The par value (10,000 shares x $10) = $100,000 is credited to _____.

B11. Common Stock
Subscribed

12. Common Stock Subscribed is an _____ _____ account of a temporary nature.

B12. owners' equity

13. When the stock is issued, we will close this account and transfer the $100,000 credit to

_____.

B13. Common Stock

14. However, if we should prepare a balance sheet before the stock is issued, we would include Common Stock Subscribed in the _____ _____ section.

B14. paid-in capital

15. The subscription price of $10.50 exceeded par value by $_____ per share.

B15.   0.50

16.   10,000 shares x \$0.50 = \$5,000 was credited to the _____

_____ account.

B16.   Paid-in Capital--
        Excess over Par
        Value, Common

17.   Payment was made on December 2 and the asset _____
is reduced to zero.

B17.   Subscriptions
        Receivable--Common

18.   After the stock was paid for, Kheel Corporation issued the stock certificates on December 2. The amount in Common Stock subscribed was transferred to _____.

B18.   Common Stock

19.   At the time of issuance on December 2, was action necessary to record the excess? _____

Explain. _____

_____

B19.   No. That entry was
        made on Nov. 2 when
        the subscription was
        received.

20.   Subscribers who do not complete their payments are said to be in *default*. In such a situation, Kheel Corporation has several options, depending on state law. One option is to resell the shares and refund to the original subscribers any amounts of unpaid subscriptions recovered. Another is to issue to subscribers a smaller number of shares at \$10.50 up to any amounts they have already paid.

B20.   No answer required.

21.   To attract industry that will provide jobs for local people, cities or towns may donate land or buildings to a corporation. These assets are a source of *paid-in capital,* but the donors do not ask for owners' equity in return. Accordingly, the equity of present owners is increased. The account credited to show this increase in owners' equity is _____

_____.

B21.   Paid-in Capital--
        Donations

22.   The donated assets are debited in the amount of _____.

B22.   fair market value

SELF TEST OF LEARNING GOAL ACHIEVEMENT

1. List five things that make a corporation different from other forms of business:

    (1) _____

    _____

    (2) _____

    _____

    (3) _____

    _____

    (4) _____

    _____

    (5) _____

    _____

2. List three major sources of paid-in capital of a corporation:

    (1) _____

    _____

    (2) _____

    _____

    (3) _____

    _____

3. Opposite each of the following descriptions, indicate whether it is more likely to apply to preferred or to common stock:

    a. Has a specified dividend rate. _____

    b. Votes to elect directors. _____

    c. Is usually denied voting rights. _____

    d. Has first claim on dividends if any dividends are to be paid. _____

    e. Is the class that will exist if only one type of stock is issued. _____

    f. Is often restricted to a specific dividend rate. _____

    g. If the corporation were to be liquidated:

       (1) Has first claim (after creditors) on remaining assets up to a specified amount. _____

       (2) Has the residual claim against all other assets. _____

4. Opposite each of the following descriptions indicate whether it is most likely to apply to par, stated, or market value:

   a. The value per share set forth in the corporate charter. _____
   b. The value per share assigned by directors as a basis for recording stock on the books. _____
   c. The minimum amount per share that must be paid in to the corporation on issuance of stock. _____
   d. The actual amount per share paid in to the corporation on issuance of stock. _____
   e. The amount you would pay to buy a share of Eastern Airlines stock on the stock market. _____

5. Ebony Company is authorized to issue 1,000,000 shares of $2 par value common stock and 500,000 shares of $50 par value preferred stock. Record in the general journal the following events that occurred in July 1985.

Jul.	7	Issued 1,000 shares of common stock at $18 per share for cash.
	7	Issued 1,000 shares of preferred stock at $52 per share for cash.
	8	Received subscriptions for 10,000 shares of common stock at $18 per share with a 40 percent down payment.
	28	Collected the unpaid balance due under the subscription contract and issued the stock.

GENERAL JOURNAL

Date	Account Titles and Explanation	F	Debit	Credit

ANSWERS TO LEARNING GOAL ACHIEVEMENT TEST

1. (1) It is a legal entity.
   (2) The owners' liability for business debts is limited.
   (3) It can raise more capital than other forms.
   (4) Its ownership shares are readily transferrable.
   (5) It must pay income tax.

2. (1) Par value paid in for capital stock.
   (2) Excess over par value paid in for capital stock.
   (3) Donated capital.

3. a. Preferred   e. Common
    b. Common   f. Preferred
    c. Preferred   g. (1) Preferred
    d. Preferred   (2) Common

4. a. Par   d. Market
    b. Stated   e. Market
    c. Par

5.

GENERAL JOURNAL

Date		Account Titles and Explanation	F	Debit	Credit
1985					
Jul.	7	Cash		18,000	
		Common Stock			2,000
		Paid-in Capital--Excess over			
		Par Value, Common			16,000
		Issuance of 1,000 shares at $18.			
	7	Cash		52,000	
		Preferred Stock			50,000
		Paid-in Capital--Excess over			
		Par Value, Preferred			2,000
		Issuance of 1,000 shares at $52.			
	8	Subscriptions Receivable--Common		180,000	
		Common Stock Subscribed			20,000
		Paid-in Capital--Excess over			
		Par Value, Common			160,000
		Received subscriptions for			
		10,000 shares at $18.			
	8	Cash		72,000	
		Subscriptions Receivable--Common			72,000
		40 percent down payment.			
	28	Cash		108,000	
		Subscriptions Receivable--Common			108,000
		Collected unpaid balance.			
	28	Common Stock Subscribed		20,000	
		Common Stock			20,000
		Issued 10,000 shares.			

Chapter 17
Corporations:
Retained Earnings, Dividends,
Treasury Stock, and Other
Equity Issues

■■■

EXPLANATION OF MAJOR CONCEPTS

Stockholders' Equity

As you study stockholders' equity accounts in more detail, bear in mind that *none of them represents anything of value in the corporation*. The things of value are on the left-hand side of the equation, A = L + OE. Many of the titles of stockholders' equity accounts sound as if they are assets, and students often become confused as to their real meaning. Just remember that they are *merely subdivisions of the OE term* in the equation. OE in a corporation is subdivided by source to meet requirements of law of the various states that charter corporations. The accounts for these subdivisions, however, continue to represent owners' claims against assets of a corporation; some, such as Treasury Stock, are contra owners' equity accounts but that does not give them value (so they are not assets).

Retained Earnings

In a corporation, the Income Summary is closed to Retained Earnings. Amounts of dividends paid out to stockholders are also closed to Retained Earnings, so that the balance in this account represents ownership claims that have accumulated through profitable operations where profits have not been passed out to the owners.

In some states, this amount is legally a limit to dividends that can be paid. Even if it is not a legal limit, prudent directors do not feel that they should make payouts to owners that amount to a return of investment and, therefore, view retained earnings as a limit on ability to pay dividends. In some situations it is desirable to reduce dividend-paying ability below the balance in the Retained Earnings account. To do so, the directors order restrictions in specific amounts for specific purposes. The basic entry is the same for all restrictions. It is

```
Retained Earnings . . . . . . . . . . . . . . . . . . . . . XXXXX
     Retained Earnings Restricted for (Purpose). . . . . . .      XXXXX
          To restrict retained earnings for (name of purpose).
```

The result of such an entry is to reduce the balance in the Retained Earnings account, thus reducing ability to pay dividends. There is no decrease in total retained earnings, and there is no change in assets. When the reason for the restriction no longer exists, the entry is reversed and the restricted amount is restored to the Retained Earnings account.

Dividends

Dividends may be paid out in cash or in property. They are paid only if the corporation's board of directors meets and authorizes a dividend (a declaration). Boards of most large corporations declare a cash dividend quarterly. When a dividend is declared, the three important dates are: date of declaration, date of record, and date of payment.

▶ *Date of declaration* is the date the directors meet and declare a dividend. On this date, a legal liability exists to pay the declared dividend, so an entry is made to record it as follows:

```
Dividends--Common Stock . . . . . . . . . . . . .     XXXXX
   Dividends Payable--Common Stock . . . . . . . .             XXXXX
      To record declaration this date of a
      dividend of X cents a share, payable
      (date) to stockholders of record (date).
```

▶ *Date of record* is the date that determines who gets the dividend. Any person who buys a share of stock in time to be recorded on the corporation's stockholders' ledger by the date of record will receive the dividend. This is true even if that person buys the share after the dividend has been declared. No entry is required in the corporation's accounts on the date of record.

▶ *Date of payment* is the date when the checks are to be delivered to stockholders. (One large corporation has printed on the outside of envelopes in which dividend checks are mailed, "POSTMASTER: DELIVER ON (date)." When the dividend checks are prepared and mailed, the journal entry is as follows:

```
Dividends Payable--Common . . . . . . . . . . . .     XXXXX
   Cash . . . . . . . . . . . . . . . . . . . . . .             XXXXX
      To record payment of dividend number xxx.
```

If dividends are declared quarterly, the Dividends account is debited four times per year with dividend declarations. In the end-of-year closing entries, it is closed to Retained Earnings. This entry parallels the closing of drawing accounts in proprietorships and partnerships.

Preferred stock certificates usually carry a stipulated dividend rate. If the preferred stock has a par or stated value, the rate is shown as a percent of par. If it is no-par value stock, the rate is shown in dollars (such as $3.20 preferred). In either case, the rate is an annual one. Quarterly declarations on preferred would be one-fourth the annual rate. Preferred stock may be *cumulative,* which means that dividends in arrears (that is, not declared when due) must be caught up before the directors can declare current dividends on any stock. Arrearages are not liabilities, and no journal entries are needed to record them, but they cannot be overlooked if a current dividend is considered.

Usually, preferred stockholders are limited to their stipulated dividend rate, while companies pay increased dividends (and sometimes extra dividends) to common stockholders. There will be some work on this in the Guided Study section of the chapter.

A *stock dividend* is not just another name for a cash dividend on the corporation's stock. Instead, it is an actual distribution of additional shares of stock to existing shareholders without any additional investment on their part. A stock dividend *does not reduce assets* and, therefore, does not reduce total stockholders' equity. It does reduce retained earnings and increase paid-in capital by the same amount. On the books of the corporation, the result is simply a transfer of some amount of retained earnings to paid-in capital accounts. As in cash dividends, there are three dates. Entries are slightly different. For example, the entries for a small stock dividend (see textbook for definition) would be:

▶ Date of declaration.
   Stock Dividends--Common Stock
     (or Retained Earnings) . . . . Market Value
       Stock Dividend to Be Issued--Common .   Par Value
       Paid-in Capital--Excess over Par
         from Stock Dividend . . . .   Difference

▶ Date of record.
   No entry.

▶ Date of issuance.
   Stock Dividend to Be Issued--Common . . . Par Value
      Common Stock . . . .   Par Value

A *stock split* is a technique whereby a company forces the price of its stock down. This is done by recalling the currently outstanding stock and issuing to the owners a multiple number of shares of reduced par value. For example, if a company has outstanding 50,000 shares of $10 par value common stock, they can declare a 2-for-1 stock split. They will call in all the $10 par stock and reissue to the same owners 100,000 shares of $5 par value common stock. This should cause the market price of the stock to drop about one-half.

Treasury Stock

Treasury stock is the name given to a corporation's own shares that have been reacquired but not cancelled. They are held by the corporation temporarily and will be reissued. The Treasury Stock account is debited at cost when treasury stock is purchased. This account is not an asset; it does not represent a thing of value. It does represent a temporary refund of investment to some stockholders and is a contra account to total paid-in capital and retained earnings. When treasury stock is reissued, the Treasury Stock account must be credited at cost for the shares reissued. Any amounts received upon reissuance in excess of that cost constitute additional paid-in capital--not a gain. If it is reissued below cost, the corporation has suffered a permanent reduction of paid-in capital--not a loss. The details of the various entries will be looked at in detail in the guided study.

Book Value of Common Stock

The book value of common stock is the proportion of stockholders' equity attributable to one share of common stock. If there is only one class of stock outstanding, it is the total stockholders' equity divided by the number of shares of common stock. If there is more than common stock outstanding, the portion of stockholders' equity attributable to the other classes of stock must be subtracted from total stockholders' equity before dividing by the number of common shares.

GUIDED STUDY OF THIS CHAPTER

A. Retained Earnings

1. Retained Earnings has a normal _____ (debit/credit) balance. Why? _____
_____

A1. credit, Because it is an owners' equity account.

2. Its balance is increased by _____.

A2. net income

3. Its balance is most commonly decreased by
_____.

A3. dividends

4. A corporation's ability to pay dividends is limited by the amount of cash it has; it is also limited by the balance in _____
_____.

A4. Retained Earnings

5. Suppose that a corporation wants to impose a voluntary restriction on dividend payments to retain cash for plant expansion. Its directors could _____ retained earnings.

A5.   restrict

6.   When the directors took such action, the accountant would debit Retained Earnings (to reduce it) and credit an account called

_____

_____ .

A6.   Retained Earnings-- Restricted for Plant Expansion

7.   Will this action provide funds for plant expansion? _____ Explain. _____

_____

_____

A7.   No. It limits dividends, but cash can be used for any other purpose.

8.   What would be a good way to build up money for plant expansion? _____

_____

_____

A8.   Create a special cash fund and make periodic deposits into it.

9.   Are the amounts of restricted retained earnings reported on the balance sheet? _____

A9.   Yes.

10.   How? _____

_____

_____

A10.   As separate amounts in the retained earnings part of the stockholders' equity section.

B.   *Dividends*

1.   National Ore Company's dividend, illustrated in the textbook, was declared on _____

_____ .

B1.   December 14, 1985

2.   If you buy 200 shares of National's common stock on December 20, 1985, you will receive a dividend of $_____ on _____ .

B2.   95, January 15, 1986

3.   December 31, 1985, is the date of _____ .

B3.   record

4.   If 200 shares of National common are bought on the stock exchange on January 5, 1986, who gets the dividend (the buyer or the seller)?

_____ Why? _____

_____

B4. The seller. The date of record is past.

5. The buyer is said to have bought the stock _____.

B5. ex-dividend

6. Elmer Corporation is used to illustrate a dividend declaration and payment. It has only one type of stock outstanding, which must be _____ stock.

B6. common

7. If Elmer had more than one type of stock, there would be a separate Dividends account and a separate _____ Payable account for each type.

B7. Dividends

8. What effect does the declaration by Elmer on January 7 have on total assets? _____

B8. None.

9. What effect does the payment on January 28 have on total assets? _____

_____

B9. Reduces them by $3,000.

10. If four quarterly dividends are declared and paid in 1985, total assets will be reduced by $12,000, and stockholders' equity will be _____ by $12,000.

B10. reduced

11. Is the Dividends account closed into Income Summary? _____

B11. No.

12. Then dividends _____ (do/do not) change net income.

B12. do not

13. Then how does the Dividends account actually reduce stockholders' equity? _____

_____

B13. By being closed into Retained Earnings.

14. Let's move to the illustration of dividends on preferred stock in the textbook. Columbia Corporation has outstanding _____ shares of cumulative preferred.

B14. 1,000

15. The preferred stock has a par value of $_____ per share.

B15. 100

16. What is the dividend rate on preferred?

_____

B 16. 15 percent.

17. The preferred dividend *per share* of stock is 15 percent x $_____ par value = $_____ per year.

B 17. 100, 15

18. Since the arrearage on preferred is $15,000, the amount paid to preferred in 1984 must have been $_____ and to common $_____.

B 18. zero, zero

19. If $52,000 in dividends is to be paid in 1985, the first $_____ is assigned to preferred to cover the _____.

B 19. 15,000, arrearage

20. The next $_____ must be assigned to _____ to cover the _____ _____.

B 20. 15,000, preferred, current dividend

21. The remaining amount goes to common stockholders, who will receive $_____.

B 21. 22,000

22. Let's study stock dividends. A stock dividend is one in which the corporation _____ (does/does not) distribute assets to stockholders.

B 22. does not

23. In issuing a stock dividend, the corporation distributes _____ _____.

B 23. additional shares of its own stock

24. The AICPA defines a small stock dividend as one that will not affect the market value of stock. A small stock dividend should not be greater than _____ percent of outstanding shares.

B 24. 25

25. A large stock dividend is expected to affect the market value of the stock by driving it _____ (up/down).

B 25. down (Many more shares will be available to the same number of buyers.)

26. When issuing a small stock dividend, a corporation should reduce retained earnings by the _____ _____.

B 26. market value of the stock

27. The Peet Corporation stock dividend was a _____ percent dividend and is, therefore, a _____ stock dividend.

B27. 10, small

B28. 60,000

B29. 10, 50,000

B30. 2

B31. 10,000, Paid-in
      Capital--Excess
      of Par Value on
      Stock Dividends

B32. 200,000

B33. 500,000

B34. Common Stock

B35. 200,000

B36. None.

B37. None.

28. Since Peet stock is selling for $12 a share, 5,000 shares x $12 = $_____ is to be moved from retained earnings to paid-in capital.

29. Of this amount, par value = 5,000 shares x $_____ = $_____ is transferred to Common Stock when the dividend is issued.

30. The difference between market value and par value is $_____ a share.

31. This amount x 5,000 shares = $_____ to be moved to the _____

_____.

32. Suppose Peet Corporation had enough retained earnings and were to issue a 100 percent stock dividend. The number of shares outstanding would then be _____ shares.

33. It would be necessary that Peet have a balance of at least $_____ in Retained Earnings.

34. The ultimate effect of a 100 percent stock dividend would be to transfer $500,000 from Retained Earnings to _____.

35. Suppose Peet Corporation were to issue a 2-for-1 stock split instead of a 100 percent stock dividend. How many shares of stock would then be outstanding? _____

36. This gives the same number of shares as a 100 percent stock dividend. How much would a 2-for-1 split reduce Retained Earnings? $_____

37. How much would the 2-for-1 split increase the Common Stock account? $_____

38. How can the number of shares outstanding be doubled without increasing the Common Stock account? _____

_____

B 38. By reducing Peet's par value from $10 to $5 a share.

39. To summarize, a *stock dividend* leaves par value the same, reduces retained earnings, and increases capital stock. Total stockholders' equity is unchanged. A *stock split* reduces par value and increases number of shares. It does not change the Retained Earnings or Capital Stock account balances. Total stockholders' equity is also unchanged.

B 39. No answer required.

C. *Treasury Stock and Other Issues.*

1. In the Ell Corporation example, 200 shares of Ell's own stock is purchased at $5.50 a share. What is the par value of Ell stock? $_____

C 1. 5 per share.

2. What is the market value on August 5, 1985? $_____

C 2. 5.50.

3. Is par value considered in the journal entry to record the purchase? _____ Is market value? _____ Explain. _____

_____

_____

_____

_____

_____

C 3. No. Yes. Since Ell Corporation intends to hold the stock for a temporary period, it will not cancel it. It will record the purchase in Treasury Stock at cost (which is obviously market value).

4. Is the Treasury Stock account an asset? _____ Explain. _____

_____

C 4. No. It is a reduction in stockholders' equity.

5. What is the market value of Ell stock on October 5? $_____

C 5. 6.50 a share.

6. Is the Treasury Stock account credited for the market value when 50 shares are reissued on October 5? _____

C6.   No.

C7.   Cost.

C8.   No.

C9.   Ell did not dispose of an asset. The $50 in excess of cost is additional paid-in capital.

C10.   Paid-in Capital from Treasury Stock Transactions, Common

C11.   They are deducted from total paid-in capital and retained earnings.

C12.   Their cost of $825.

7.   What is the basis for the credit of $275?

   _____

8.   Since the 50 shares were sold at $50 above cost, has Ell Corporation made a gain on disposal? _____

9.   Why not? _____

   _____

   _____

10.   The account to be credited for the $50 difference is _____

   _____.

11.   When a balance sheet is prepared, how are the 150 shares still held as treasury stock shown on it? _____

   _____

   _____

12.   At what amount? _____

13.   If treasury stock is reissued below cost, what account or accounts absorb the difference?

   _____

   _____

   _____

   _____

   _____

   _____

   _____

   _____

C13. Paid-in Capital from Treasury Stock Transactions if it has a balance. (See Ell entry of Nov. 4.) If that account cannot absorb the difference, then other paid-in excess pertaining to the same stock or Retained Earnings. (See Ell entry of Nov. 29.)

14. Book value is not a very meaningful concept because it does not reflect actual market conditions. To determine book value per common share, the liquidation claims of preferred stock are deducted from net assets. The remainder-- book value of assets assigned to common stock-- is divided by the number of common shares outstanding.

C14. No answer required.

15. Included in liquidation claims of preferred stock are the current dividend and any dividends in _____ if the preferred stock is cumulative.

C15. arrears

16. Note that book value per share is computed by dividing the net assets by the _____ (actual/weighted average) number of shares outstanding.

C16. actual

17. Earnings per share (EPS) is considered by many to be an important indicator of market value of a stock. EPS really means earnings per share of _____ stock.

C17. common

18. Before computing EPS, dividends to _____ _____ must be deducted from net income.

C18. preferred stock-holders

19. Then EPS equals net income available to common stockholders divided by the weighted average of _____ _____.

C19. common shares outstanding during the year

20. Because corporations issue many types of securities (for example, bonds that holders can exchange for common stock), it is possible that the number of common shares outstanding could increase suddenly. An increase in the number of shares outstanding would be expected to cause EPS to _____ (increase/decrease).

C20. decrease

21. Accordingly, *APB Opinion No. 15* requires companies that have outstanding securities that could dilute the EPS figure to report two amounts for EPS. The amount of EPS without considering the potential of such securities is called *primary* earnings per share. When the effect of such securities is included, the figure is called *fully diluted* earnings per share.

C21. No answer required.

22. When the number of shares of stock outstanding during the year changes, the end-of-year number of shares _____ (is/is not) the same as the weighted average.

C22. is not

23. Careful study of the Bern Company's stockholders' equity section of the balance sheet at the end of Chapter 17 is very important to you. Some of the important ideas are identified by number and explained. By learning this model, you will be able to solve many of the exercises and problems more quickly and accurately.

C23. No answer required.

SELF TEST OF LEARNING GOAL ACHIEVEMENT

1. Which of the following are paid-in capital accounts?

   a. Common Stock.
   b. Preferred Stock.
   c. Common Stock Subscribed.
   d. Subscriptions Receivable--Common.
   e. Paid-in Capital--Donations.
   f. Treasury Stock.
   g. Retained Earnings--Restricted for Plant Expansion.
   h. Stock Dividend to Be Issued.
   i. Dividends.
   j. Retained Earnings.

2. Vista Corporation had the following capital structure before declaring its first quarterly dividend in 1985:

Stockholders' equity

8 percent preferred stock, $50 par value, 100,000 shares authorized and outstanding	$5,000,000
Common stock, $2 par value, 5,000,000 shares authorized, 1,000,000 shares issued and outstanding	2,000,000
Retained earnings	2,500,000
Total stockholders' equity	$9,500,000

On March 15, 1985, the directors vote to declare a *quarterly* dividend of $560,000.

Required: Show computations for journal entries to record the declaration of this dividend under each of the following possible independent situations. Do not make the entries, but compute the amounts payable to each class of stock.

a.   The preferred stock is cumulative with no dividends in arrears.

b.   The preferred stock is cumulative with dividends in arrears for the last quarter of 1984.

a.

b.

3. Assume that the Vista Corporation (Question 2) declared the regular quarterly cash dividend of $100,000 to preferred and a 10 percent stock dividend to common on March 15, 1985. The market value of common stock is $20 a share. Record, in general journal form, the declaration of both dividends.

GENERAL JOURNAL

Date		Account Titles and Explanation	F	Debit	Credit

4. Assume that Vista Corporation (Question 2) purchased 10,000 shares of its common stock on the stock exchange at $20 per share on May 10, 1985. On July 18, 1985, the company resold 5,000 of these shares at $23 per share. Then on October 18, 1985, the company resold the remaining 5,000 shares at $19 per share. Record all these transactions.

GENERAL JOURNAL

Date	Account Titles and Explanation	F	Debit	Credit

5. Assume the same facts as in Question 4, except that the reissuance of 5,000 shares on October 18 was at $15 per share instead of $19. Record only the October 18 transaction.

GENERAL JOURNAL

Date		Account Titles and Explanation	F	Debit	Credit

6. Assume that liquidation value of Vista Corporation's preferred stock (Question 2) is $52 per share. Compute the book value per share of common.

ANSWERS TO LEARNING GOAL ACHIEVEMENT TEST

1. a, b, c, e, h

2.

		Preferred	Common

a.

First quarter to preferred $100,000

Remainder to common. $460,000

   Totals $100,000 $460,000

b.

1984 arrears (1/4 x 8% x $5,000,000) $100,000

First quarter 1985 (1/4 x 8% x $5,000,000)   100,000

Remainder to common. $360,000

   Totals $200,000 $360,000

3.

GENERAL JOURNAL

Date		Account Titles and Explanation	F	Debit	Credit
1985					
Mar.	15	Dividends--Preferred		100,000	
		Retained Earnings (or Stock			
		Dividends--Common)		2,000,000	
		Dividends Payable--Preferred			100,000
		Stock Dividend to Be Issued,			
		Common			200,000
		Paid-in Capital--Excess of Par			
		Value on Stock Dividends, Common			1,800,000
		Declaration of regular quarterly			
		preferred dividend and a 10			
		percent stock dividend on			
		common.			

4.

GENERAL JOURNAL

Date		Account Titles and Explanation	F	Debit	Credit
1985					
May	10	Treasury Stock--Common		200,000	
		Cash			200,000
		Purchase of 10,000 shares of			
		Vista common stock at $20.			
Jul.	18	Cash		115,000	
		Treasury Stock--Common			100,000
		Paid-in Capital from Treasury Stock			
		Transactions--Common			15,000
		Reissuance of 5,000 shares at $23.			
Oct.	18	Cash		95,000	
		Paid-in Capital from Treasury Stock			
		Transactions--Common		5,000	
		Treasury Stock--Common			100,000
		Reissuance of 5,000 shares at $19.			

5.

GENERAL JOURNAL

Date		Account Titles and Explanation	F	Debit	Credit
1985					
Oct.	18	Cash		75,000	
		Paid-in Capital from Treasury Stock			
		Transactions--Common		15,000	
		Retained Earnings		10,000	
		Treasury Stock--Common			100,000
		Reissuance of 5,000 shares at $15.			

6. Net assets (same as total stockholders' equity) $9,500,000
    Net assets assigned to preferred (100,000 x $52)   5,200,000
    Net assets available to common $4,300,000

    Book value ($4,300,000 ÷ 1,000,000 shares) $4.30

Chapter 18
Bonds Payable and Other Long-Term Liabilities

■■

EXPLANATION OF MAJOR CONCEPTS

Bonds Payable

The issuance of bonds by a corporation creates a long-term liability. Accounting for bonds differs from the accounting for capital stock in three ways:

▶ The money received is *borrowed*, not invested.

▶ There is a *legal obligation to pay interest* periodically. Unlike payment of dividends, payment of bond interest is not a matter for the directors to decide. It must be done. Also, interest *is* an expense; dividends are not.

▶ The *face value* of bonds payable is due to be repaid on the maturity date.

Bonds are often issued at a *premium* (more than face value) or at a *discount* (less than face value). The reason for a premium is that the contract rate of interest carried on the bond is too high. Because the bond interest rate is higher than the market rate, bond buyers (lenders) bid against each other to get the opportunity to earn this better-than-normal interest. This will force the price of the bond up above face value. On the other hand, if bonds carry a rate of interest that is less than the market rate, the bond buyers (lenders) will refuse to pay face value for the bond, forcing the price down below face value. The exact price--whether below or above face value--is determined by a compound interest computation. It is the price that will bring to the buyers, in true interest, exactly what they believe the correct rate to be. Regardless of the price at which bonds are issued, *the interest is computed and paid on face value.* For most corporate bonds, interest is paid twice a year.

Meaning of Amortization

If an investor buys one $1,000 face value, ten-year, 12% bond at 105, that investor is paying a premium. Since *105 means 105 percent of face value,* the investor will pay 5 percent (or $50) more than will be repaid ten years later. The investor pays in (lends) $1,050 to the corporation. At the end of ten years, the corporation must repay only the face value ($1,000). The $50 premium is not a revenue, because a corporation doesn't earn money by borrowing. Instead *it is a reduction in interest expense*.   (Remember that the reason the premium was paid is that the bond interest rate is higher than the market rate.)   It would be contrary to the standard of matching expense and revenue to record this $50 reduction in interest expense in any single year.   It should be spread across the ten-year life of the bond.   Accordingly, each time the corporation records interest expense, a portion of the premium should be amortized adjusting the interest expense.   This portion is found by dividing the premium, $50, by the number of semiannual interest payments, 20, or $2.50 per payment.   The entry to record a semiannual interest on the bond would be:

Bond Interest Expense	57.50	
Premium on Bonds Payable	2.50	
Cash		60.00

In this way, the interest reduction is divided into an equal amount for each year of the life of the bonds.   This method of amortization is the *straight line method*. It works in the same way that straight line depreciation works.

Suppose that the $1,000 bond were issued at 97.   This means that the corporation receives only $970 but must repay $1,000 at the end of ten years.   The additional $30 that is paid back is, in effect, *additional interest expense*.   Again, it would be wrong to allow this extra interest expense to be recorded against a single year.   The semiannual entry to record the interest would include the amortization of a proportionate amount of the discount.   The amount of the amortization can be found by dividing the discount, $30, by the number of interest payments in the life of the bonds, 20, or $1.50 per six-month period.

Bond Interest Expense	61.50	
Discount on Bonds Payable		1.50
Cash		60.00

Notice in both cases the amount of cash was determined using the face amount of the bond, $1,000, and the face rate, 12%, for one-half year.   Also, note that when the maturity date of the bonds is reached, the amortization process has brought the premium or discount account to a zero balance.

The Interest Method of Amortization

To understand the concept of amortization, you should first concentrate on the straight line method of amortization.   However, if this method provides a materially different amount of interest expense in an accounting period, *APB Opinion No. 21* requires the use of the interest method of amortization.   The interest method is very simple to use if you will note these points:

► A constant market rate of interest is the rate used each six months.

► This interest rate multiplied by the carrying value of the bonds gives the amount of interest expense.

▶ The cash interest paid is calculated using the face amount of the bonds and the face interest rate.

▶ The difference between the interest expense and the interest paid gives the amount of amortization.

▶ The carrying value is changed each six months by the *deduction* of the amount of premium amortized or the *addition* of the amount of discount amortized.

Let's go back to our previous examples. A $1,000 bond bought at 105 has a beginning carrying value of $1,050 = (face value + premium). Suppose it were a 12 percent bond, while the true market rate of interest is 11 percent. The semi-annual interest paid is $1,000 x 0.12 ÷ 2 = $60. (This is really 6 percent each six months.) To compute the interest expense and premium amortization for the first six months, use the carrying value times the market rate or:

$1,050 x 0.11 ÷ 2 = $57.75 = Interest expense.
This is really 5 1/2 percent each six months.

Interest paid – Interest expense = Amortization of premium.
$60 – $57.75 = $2.25.

The carrying value for the next six-month period is reduced to:
$1,050.00 – $2.25 = $1,047.75.

The interest expense is:
$1,047.75 x 0.055 = $57.63.

Interest paid – Interest expense = Amortization of premium.
$60 – $57.63 = $2.37.

The total amortization for the first year is $4.62 = ($2.25 + $2.37). Under the straight line method, it was $5. In each of the remaining nine years, the straight line amortization will continue to be $5, while the interest method amortization will increase. In later years, it will be greater than the straight line amount, but the total amortized in ten years will be the same.

The Price of a Bond

In the foregoing examples, we have used a bond issued at 105 to illustrate the concept of amortization and the two methods of computing interest expense and amortization. While the issue price of $1,050 = ($1,000 x 1.05) is convenient to illustrate the ideas, it is not an accurate issue price for a 12 percent bond for which the market rate of interest is 11 percent. Let's now calculate what the actual issue price should have been.

The issue price of this bond is made up of two distinct elements:

▶ The present value of the face amount ($1,000) to be repaid to the bond purchaser ten years from now.

▶ The present value of twenty interest payments of $60 each.

They are computed as follows by using table factors from the compound interest tables for the present value of an amount (the face value) and the present value of an annuity (the interest):

Present value of face = $1,000 x 0.342729 . . . . $ 342.73
Present value of interest = $60 x 11.950382 . . . .   717.02
    Actual price of bond to yield 11 percent $1,059.75

The price at which the bond would be issued is the sum of its two elements-- in this case, $1,059.75.

Accrued Interest on Bonds

Bond interest is paid at specified dates each six months--say, for example, April 1 and October 1. The interest paid to each bondholder on those dates is for a *full six months*. A bondholder who has owned a bond for only two months before an interest date will still receive a check for six months' interest. (Other- wise, issuers of bonds would have the problem of making payments of interest for partial periods. This would be too expensive, even if it were possible.) To com- pensate for payments that are greater than interest actually earned, buyers of bonds must *buy the interest that has accrued since the last interest date*. In the example just used, a bondholder who bought a bond on August 1 must buy four months of accrued interest (April, May, June, and July). On October 1, that bondholder will receive a check for six months' interest--the period April 1 to October 1. The bond was held for only two months (August and September); the check represents interest earned for those two months plus a refund of the accrued interest for the previous four months that was bought. This practice of buying interest accrued since the last interest date is followed in all cases. It is used when a company issues bonds between interest dates; it is also used when bondholders sell bonds to each other on the bond market.

Shortened Amortization Periods

When a bond issue is not floated on the authorization date, the actual life of the bonds will be *less than* the authorized life. A corporation may be authorized to issue twenty-year bonds. The twenty-year period starts to run *at date of authori- zation*. But the company may not issue the bonds (or at least part of them) for a year after authorization. Since these bonds will have only nineteen years of life remaining when issued, any premium or discount must be amortized over nineteen years instead of twenty. A good way to compute amortization is to convert re- maining life into months and determine amount of amortization per month. Thus,

$$\frac{\text{Premium or Discount}}{19 \text{ years}} = \frac{\text{Premium or Discount}}{228 \text{ months}} = \text{Monthly amortization.}$$

GUIDED STUDY OF THIS CHAPTER

A. Bonds Payable

A1.   many years

1.   Bonds are a certificate of debt that may not be due for _____.

A2.   long-term liabilities

2.   Bonds Payable, therefore, are shown as _____ on the balance sheet.

A3.   semiannually (or each six months)

3.   Bonds carry provisions for interest; interest is paid _____.

A4.   indenture

4.   A contract between the bondholders and the company is called the bond _____.

A5.   stockholders

5.   Before a corporation floats a bond issue, it must obtain approval of the _____.

A6.   face

6.   The denomination of a bond (or amount to be repaid when due) is the _____ value.

A7.   face

7.   Interest is a percent of _____ value.

A8.   face value

8.   Bonds issued for an amount of money equal to _____ are said to be issued at 100 or at par.

A9.   premium

9.   Bonds issued for more than face value are said to be issued at a _____.

A10.   Bond Interest Expense

10.   The cost of bond interest is debited to an expense account called _____ _____.

A11.   200,000

11.   In the Amerson Corporation (Example A in the textbook), face value of the bonds issued is $_____.

A12.   16, 32,000

12.   The interest rate of _____ percent means that Amerson Company must pay interest of $_____ per year.

13.   The first interest payment date is _____ _____ at which time Bond Interest Expense is debited for _____ months of interest = $_____.

A13. October 1, 1985, six, 16,000

14. Financial statements must be made on December 31, 1985, but the next interest payment is not due until _____.

A14. April 1, 1986

15. So, on December 31, 1985, an adjusting entry must be made to record _____ _____.

A15. accrued interest

16. This makes the total of Bond Interest Expense equal to $_____ for the year 1985.

A16. 24,000

17. The $24,000 balance in Bond Interest Expense is closed into _____ during the closing entries.

A17. Income Summary

18. This causes net income to be _____ (reduced/increased) by $24,000.

A18. reduced

B. *Bonds at a Premium or Discount*

1. Example B-1 shows bonds issued at a premium of $_____.

B1. 2,981.16

2. The Bonkers Corporation bonds mature in _____ years.

B2. twenty

3. The amount of premium to be amortized each interest date is $2,981.16 ÷ 40 = $_____ (assume straight line).

B3. 74.53

4. So the straight line amortization will change expense by $_____ (rounded).

B4. 74.53

5. The premium amortization will _____ (reduce/increase) 1985 interest expense.

B5. reduce

6. The amount of interest to be paid by Bonkers in 1985 is $_____.

B6. 8,250

7. The amortization of premium will cause interest expense to be reduced by $74.53 so that the expense is $_____.

B7. 8,175.47

8. In 1985 only one-half year's interest expense was recorded. How much will be paid in 1986? $_____ How much is interest expense in 1986? $_____

B8. 16,500, 16,350.94

B9. 16

B10. 18

B11. discount

B12. 181,742.91

B13. twenty

B14. 912.85

B15. 200,000, 0.08,
16,000

B16.
Interest paid . $16,000.00
Discount amort.   912.85
   Expense. . . $16,912.85

B17. increases

---

9. Example B-2 is a new situation. The interest paid on the Davidson Company bonds is at the rate of _____ percent.

10. The market rate of interest for this type of bond is _____ percent.

11. Since the nominal rate on the bonds is lower than the market rate, the bond buyers will compensate for the difference by paying a price resulting in a _____ (premium/discount).

12. The carrying value of the Davidson Company bonds immediately after issue is $_____.

13. To compute amortization of discount for a six-month period by the straight line method, we would divide the discount by _____ interest periods.

14. The result is $18,257.09 ÷ 20 = $_____.

15. The interest paid each six months is
$_____ x _____ = $_____.

16. Compute interest expense for the last half of 1985:

17. So discount amortization _____ (increases/decreases) interest expense.

18. Let's use the interest method to amortize the premium on bonds in Example C-1. They were sold to yield an annual rate of _____ percent.

B 18. 16

19. This is the equivalent of _____ percent semi-annually.

B 19. 8

20. Interest expense for the last six months of 1985 is $102,981.16 x 0.08 = $_____.

B 20. 8,238.49

21. Note that the _____ of $102,981.16 was multiplied by one-half the annual *effective* interest rate to determine interest expense.

B 21. carrying value

22. But the amount of interest paid is $_____ multiplied by one-half the annual nominal rate or _____ percent.

B 22. 100,000, 8 1/4

23. Compute it:

B 23. $100,000 x 0.0825 = $8,250.

24. Now compute the amount of amortization for 1985:

B 24.
Paid $8,250.00
Expense . . .   8,238.49
Amort. . . . . $ 11.51

25. Compute carrying value to be used for the first six months' interest computation in 1986:

B 25.
Old value $102,981.16
Amort.   11.51
New value $102,969.65

26. Use it to compute interest expense for the first six months of 1986:

B26. $102,969.65 × 0.08 = $8,237.57.

27. Interest expense in the second six-month period is _____ (greater/smaller) than in the first period.

B27. smaller

28. Will it continue to become smaller each six-month period hereafter? _____ Why or why not? _____

_____

_____

_____

B28. Yes. Because a constant rate of interest (8 percent) is applied to a decreasing carrying value.

29. Then the amortization will grow _____ (larger/smaller) each six-month period.

B29. larger

30. Example C-2 is for $_____ in bonds issued at a discount of $_____. This would make the carrying value $_____.

B30. 200,000, 18,257.09, 181,742.91

31. The interest expense for the last six months of 1985 computed by the interest method is $_____ × _____ = $_____.

B31. 181,742.91 × 0.09 = 16,356.86

32. Under the interest method of amortization, the amount of interest to be paid in this period is $_____.

B32. 16,000

33. Amortization of discount = $_____ − $_____ = $_____.

B33. 16,356.86 − 16,000 = 356.86

34. The new carrying value for computing expense in 1986 is $_____.

B34. 182,099.77

35. And the interest expense for the first half of 1986 is $_____ × _____ = $_____.

B35. 182,099.77 × 0.09 = 16,388.98

36. Is this greater or less than for the first six-month period? _____

B36. Greater.

37. Will it continue to increase each six-month period? _____ Why or why not?

_____

_____

_____

_____

B37. Yes. Because a constant rate of interest (9 percent) is being multiplied by an increasing carrying value.

38. Will the amortization of discount also increase? _____

B38. Yes.

39. Look at Figures 18-6 and 18-8. Note in both premium and discount situations the amount of amortization each period is the same under the straight line method. In Figure 18-6 the amount of amortization of premium under the interest method _____ (increases/decreases) as time passes.

B39. increases

40. In Figure 18-8 the amount of amortization of discount under the interest method _____ (increases/decreases) as time passes.

B40. increases

41. Does this indicate that amortization of both premium and discount increase interest expense? _____

B41. No.

42. Go back and look at the examples we used. In all cases, amortization of premium _____ interest expense, and amortization of discount _____ it. Don't memorize this. Keep studying these examples until you understand why the above statement is true once you have the correct answers in it.

B42. decreases, increases

C. *Bonds Issued Between Interest Dates*

1. When bonds are issued between interest dates, the amount of cash interest which has accrued since the last interest date is collected by the issuer. In the illustration, this was $_____.

C1.   12,000

2. This $12,000 is the interest from _____ _____ to _____, the date of issue.

C2. April 1, 1985,
June 1, 1985

C3. 420,000, 12,000,
432,000

C4. six, four

3. The bonds were issued at a price of
$_____, or a premium, plus the
accrued interest of $_____, for a
total cash received of $_____.

4. On the first interest payment date, _____
months interest will be paid. This includes
the $12,000 of accrued interest and the
interest expense for _____ months.

SELF TEST OF LEARNING GOAL ACHIEVEMENT

1. What are at least three major differences between bonds payable and preferred stock?

_____
_____
_____
_____
_____
_____
_____

2. Brazoria Corporation issued $100,000 of 12 percent bonds at a price to yield 14 percent on April 1, 1985. The bonds mature in ten years. Interest is payable April 1 and October 1.

a. Show a general journal entry for the issuance. In your explanation, show how the issue price was computed.

GENERAL JOURNAL

Date		Account Titles and Explanation	F	Debit	Credit

b. Show a general journal entry for payment of interest and straight line amortization on October 1, 1985.

c. Show a general journal entry for payment of interest and amortization by the interest method on October 1, 1985.

3. On April 1, 1987, Brazoria Corporation made the regular interest payment and straight line amortization entry on its bonds. It then retired all the bonds by purchase on the market for $90,000 cash. Show a general journal entry for the early retirement.

GENERAL JOURNAL

Date	Account Titles and Explanation	F	Debit	Credit

4. Baytown Corporation has a bond issue of $50,000 due in five years. The company will make five annual deposits into a sinking fund that is guaranteed to earn 10 percent simple interest per year. Each annual deposit plus earnings must equal $10,000. Show general journal entries for the deposits for the first two years, beginning December 31, 1985.

GENERAL JOURNAL

Date		Account Titles and Explanation	F	Debit	Credit

ANSWERS TO LEARNING GOAL ACHIEVEMENT TEST

1. Bonds are debt; preferred stock is owners' equity. Bond interest must be paid each period; preferred stock dividends may be passed (not declared). Bond interest is tax deductible; preferred dividends are not. Bonds have a limited life; preferred stock does not.

2.

a.

GENERAL JOURNAL

Date		Account Titles and Explanation	F	Debit	Credit
1985					
Apr.	1	Cash		89,405.98	
		Discount on Bonds Payable		10,594.02	
		Bonds Payable			100,000.00
		Issuance of 10-year, 12 percent			
		bonds to yield 14 percent, as			
		follows:			
		PV of face:			
		$100,000 x 0.258419 = $25,841.90			
		PV of interest:			
		$6,000 x 10.594014 = 63,564.08			
		Issue price $89,405.98			

b.

Oct.	1	Interest Expense		6,529.70	
		Discount on Bonds Payable			529.70
		Cash			6,000.00
		Payment of interest and amortiza-			
		tion of discount. Amortization =			
		$10,594.02 ÷ 20.			

c.

Oct.	1	Interest Expense		6,258.42	
		Discount on Bonds Payable			258.42
		Cash			6,000.00
		Payment of interest and amortiza-			
		tion of discount. Interest =			
		$89,405.98 x 0.07.			

3.

GENERAL JOURNAL

Date		Account Titles and Explanation	F	Debit	Credit
1987					
Apr.	1	Bonds Payable		100,000.00	
		Discount on Bonds Payable			8,475.22
		Gain on Retirement of Bonds			1,524.78
		Cash			90,000.00
		To record retirement by purchase			
		at 90. Carrying value =			
		$89,405.98 + ($529.70 x 4) =			
		$91,524.78.			

4.

GENERAL JOURNAL

Date		Account Titles and Explanation	F	Debit	Credit
1985					
Dec.	31	Bond Sinking Fund		10,000	
		Cash			10,000
		First annual deposit.			
1986					
Dec.	31	Bond Sinking Fund		10,000	
		Cash			9,000
		Bond Interest Earned			1,000
		Second annual deposit and			
		fund earnings.			

Chapter 19
Temporary and Long-Term Investments

■■■

EXPLANATION OF MAJOR CONCEPTS

Types of Investments

A business may invest in bonds of governments or corporations. A business may also invest in common and preferred stocks of corporations. These bonds and stocks all fall under the general term *securities*. If a security is actively bought and sold on the stock exchanges or through securities dealers, it is called a *marketable security,* meaning simply that it can be resold readily.

Investments in marketable securities are current assets *if it is the intent of management that the investment be a temporary one.* If securities invested in are not marketable or if the intent of management is to hold them for a long term, they are not current assets. Short-term investments are carried in the accounts Temporary Investments in Bonds or Temporary Investments in Stocks. Long-term investments are carried in the accounts Investments in Stocks or Investments in Bonds.

Some Accounting Procedures

Accounting procedures for short-term and long-term investments are similar in that all purchases of either type are initially debited to the asset account at full cost (including brokerage fees). Some specific techniques you should note carefully are:

▶ Interest on bonds accrues, and end-of-period adjusting entries are needed to recognize such accruals and the interest associated with them.

▶ Dividends on stocks do not accrue and should not be recorded on the books of an investor before they are declared.

▶ Premiums or discounts on bonds are part of the bonds' cost and are not carried in a separate premium or discount account.

▶ Bond premiums or discounts on temporary short-term investments are not amortized. We do not know how long they will be held and have no specific time period over which to compute amortization.

▶ Bond premiums or discounts on long-term investments are amortized. We use the *remaining life to maturity date* as the period over which the amortization is computed. In this textbook, the straight line method and the interest method are explained.

▶ Long-term investments in stocks are accounted for by two different methods. If we hold less than 20 percent of the voting stock of a company, the *cost method* should be used to account for the investment. If we hold 20 percent or more of the voting stock of a company, the *equity method* should be used to account for the investment.

Valuation of Investments (Appendix 19.1)

Although initially recorded at cost, investments in marketable securities should be carried at the lower of cost or market on a "total portfolio" basis. This involves the use of a contra valuation account that is revised by an annual adjusting entry to update the carrying value. If marketable securities fall below cost, a loss is recorded and shown in the income statement. Recoveries of market value are shown as gains--also in the income statement. An *unrealized* loss or gain is one that has been recorded in the books on market quotations. When investments in marketable securities are sold, *realized* losses or gains occur.

GUIDED STUDY OF THIS CHAPTER

	A. Temporary Investments
	1. A security is marketable when it _____ _____.
A1. can be resold readily	2. Whether an investment in a marketable security is a current asset or not depends upon the _____.
A2. intent of management	3. A marketable security purchased as a current asset is debited to the _____ or the _____ account.
A3. Temporary Invest-ments in Bonds, Temporary Invest-ments in Stocks	4. Premiums paid on bonds and brokerage fees paid to purchase them _____ (are/ are not) part of the cost.

A4. are

5. The cost of the Bylinski Corporation's investment in Shields Company bonds (illustrated first in the chapter) includes face value of $_____ + premium of $_____ + brokerage fees of $_____.

A5. 30,000, 600, 60

6. Bond interest is a legal liability. Bylinski Corporation should record an adjusting entry on December 31, 1985, to accrue $_____ of interest earned in 1985 on the Shields bonds.

A6. 2,100

7. Therefore, when payment is received on January 1, 1986, the credit is not to a revenue account but to _____

_____.

A7. Accrued Bond Interest Receivable

8. When Bylinski needed cash and sold the bonds on February 1, 1986, they were sold at a loss of $_____.

A8. 135

9. However, interest was earned for six months in 1985 and for one month in 1986 at $350 per month, for a total of $_____.

A9. 2,450

10. The interest of $2,450 minus the loss on disposal of $135 gives a net return of $_____ for the seven-month period.

A10. 2,315

11. In the Bowen Corporation illustration, another temporary investment is recorded; this time in preferred stock. A dividend on July 1, 1983, brought in earnings of $_____.

A11. 300

12. The Edwin stock was sold in September before another quarterly dividend had been declared. Was the accrued dividend sold along with the 200 shares of stock? _____ Explain. _____

_____

A12. No. Dividends do not accrue. (It is likely, however, that public expectation of a dividend drove the price up from 105 to 106 1/2.)

13. The dividends earned of $_____ + the gain on disposal of $_____ gave a total earnings of $_____ for holding this stock for five and one-half months.

A13.   300, 192, 492

14.   If the accounting standard of full disclosure is followed, the balance sheet would report temporary investments at cost but would also disclose the _____.

A14.   market value
(See Appendix 19.1.)

B.   *Long-Term Investments. Among the many types of long-term investments that an entity can hold, emphasis in Chapter 19 is on investments in stocks and bonds.*

1.   Investment in the stock of another company may be for the purpose of earning dividends. A frequent reason to buy shares of voting stock of another company, however, is to gain _____.

B1.   control

2.   *APB Opinion No. 18* states that a company holding less than _____ percent of the voting stock of another firm is *not* assumed to have significant influence.

B2.   20

3.   If a company has less than 20 percent of the voting stock of another, the _____ method of accounting for the investment should be used.

B3.   cost

4.   Under the cost method, the _____ _____ account is debited with total cost of the investment.

B4.   Investment in Stocks

5.   As in temporary securities, cost includes all costs to buy the stock, including the price paid plus _____.

B5.   brokerage fees

6.   In the Phyllis Corporation's July 1 purchase, cost included 10,000 shares at $_____ per share = $_____ + $_____ brokerage fees, for a total cost of $_____.

B6.   10.50, 105,000, 440, 105,440

7.   Under the cost method, the Investment in Stocks account was debited for $_____. This debit balance _____ (will/ will not) change unless some of the stock is sold or more is bought.

B7.   105,440, will not

8.   As dividends are received, they are credited to the _____ account.

B8.   Dividends Earned

9.   Thus, the only form of income on the invest- ment in David Corporation stock is
_____.

B9.   dividends

10.   When David Corporation issued a 100-percent *stock* dividend, was this considered to be revenue? _____

B10.   No.

11.   The original cost per share of Lot No. 1 of David Corporation stock was $105,440 ÷ _____ shares = $_____.

B11.   10,000, 10.544

12.   After receipt of the stock dividend, the new cost basis per share is $105,440 ÷ _____ shares = $_____.

B12.   20,000, 5.272

13.   If Phyllis Corporation were to sell 100 shares from Lot No. 1 at $5.50, would there be a gain or a loss? _____

B13.   Gain.

14.   Compute it on the specific identification basis.

B14.   100 ($5.50 − $5.272) = $22.80.

15.   Would a 2-for-1 stock split also have provided an additional 30,000 shares of David stock to Phyllis Corporation? _____

B15.   Yes.

16.   What difference would there be on Phyllis Corporation's books between recording a 100-percent stock dividend and a 2-for-1 stock split by David Company? _____

B16.   None.

17.   When _____ percent or more of the voting stock of a company is owned, ability to influence is presumed. *APB Opinion No. 18* then requires the _____ method of accounting for the investment.

B17.   20, equity

18.   The Parento Corporation purchased 40 percent of Sunno Corporation stock. It is assumed that Parento _____ (can/can't) exercise influence over Sunno.

B18.   can

19.   Therefore, Parento must use the _____ method.

B 19. equity

20. The August 8 dividend is viewed as a reduction of Parento's investment (not as revenue). It is credited to Investment in Stocks, but why only $8,000 of the $20,000 dividend?

_____

_____

_____

B 20. Parento only owns 40 percent of Sunno stock and received only 40 percent of the total dividend.

21. Under the equity method, an investor corporation considers that its investment increases as the retained earnings of the investee increases. When Sunno earned $80,000 in 1985, how much did its retained earnings increase? $_____

B 21. 80,000.

22. Parento Corporation should increase its investment account by _____ percent of Sunno's earnings or by $_____ .

B 22. 40, 32,000

23. Is this reported as income in Parento's income statement? _____

B 23. Yes.

24. In 1986 Sunno had a loss of $3,000; Sunno's retained earnings decreased. How does Parento Corporation reflect this loss in its books? _____

_____

_____

B 24. By a decrease in Investment in Stocks and a debit to Investor's Share of Investee Loss.

25. Is Parento's share of the loss (_____ percent of $3,000 = $_____) reported in its income statement for 1986? _____

B 25. 40, 1,200, Yes.

26. Companies also invest in bonds of other companies. The primary reason for an insurance company to do this on a long-term basis is probably to _____ .

B 26. earn bond interest

27. If bonds are purchased as temporary investments, any premium or discount _____ (is/is not) amortized.

B 27. is not

28. When bonds are purchased for a long-term investment, premium or discount _____ (is/is not) amortized.

B28. is

29. The period used for amortization is the _____

_____

_____ .

B29. remaining life to
maturity of the
bonds

30. In example A, the Global Finance Corporation's
purchase of Windham Corporation bonds does
not require amortization entries because _____

_____ .

B30. there was no premium
or discount

31. In example B, when Douglass Corporation paid
$318,613.52 for $300,000 of Rice Corporation
bonds, the premium was $_____ .

B31. 18,613.52

32. The investor _____ (does/does not)
show the premium in a separate account.

B32. does not

33. Douglass will amortize this premium over a
period of _____ .

B33. fifteen years

34. Fifteen years = _____ semiannual periods,
so the amount of straight line amortization
per *semiannual* period is $_____ .

B34. 30, 620.45 =
(18,613.52 ÷ 30)

35. The amortization of premium on investment
recognizes that Douglass Corporation will be
repaid $18,613.52 _____ (more/less)
than they paid for the bonds.

B35. less

36. Therefore, amortization should _____
(increase/decrease) Bond Interest Earned by
$_____ per semiannual period.

B36. decrease, 620.45

37. At the date of maturity, the Rice bonds will
be worth exactly $_____ .

B37. 300,000

38. So, the amortization entry is reducing the
carrying value by $620.45 for six months.
On June 30, 2000, the balance in the Investment in Bonds account will be $_____ .

B38. 300,000

39. The Rice Corporation bonds carry a nominal
interest rate of 15 percent, so the corporation receives $_____ per year in
interest payments.

B39. 45,000

40. However, because Douglass Corporation paid $18,613.52 more for the bonds than will be repaid to them, their true rate of interest is _____ (more/less) than 15 percent.

B40. less

41. Actually, the amount of premium paid was a result of the true market rate of interest for these bonds. It was _____ percent.

B41. 14

42. In example B-2, the bonds were purchased at a _____.

B42. discount

43. Britton paid $_____ for the bonds, giving a discount of $_____.

B43. 380,363.61, 19,636.39

44. Since there are _____ years remaining to maturity, each six months $_____ discount will be amortized.

B44. 10, 981.82 = (19,636.39 ÷ 20)

45. Since Britton Corporation will receive _____ (more/less) back from Carson at maturity, Bond Interest Earned will be _____ than the cash received.

B45. more, greater

46. If the interest method is used to amortize the premium (see example C-1), the first amortization entry will credit Bond Interest Earned with $22,302.95 = $_____ x _____ percent.

B46. 318,613.52, 7

47. The rate of 7 percent is one-half (or six months) of the _____ rate of interest.

B47. market (or effective)

48. The amount $318,613.52 is the _____ _____ before the first amortization entry.

B48. carrying value

49. Does the amortization entry reduce the Premium on Bonds account? _____

B49. No. (There is no such account; investments are recorded at full cost.)

50. What account does the amortization amount reduce? _____

B50. Investment in Bonds

51. The carrying value for computing the next interest expense on June 30, 1986, is $_____ = $_____ − $_____.

B 51. 318,416.47,
       318,613.52,
       197.05

52. Notice that the difference in the amount of the amortization for the first year between the straight line and interest methods is 204.2 percent. But the difference in interest expense is _____ percent. (See Figure 19-1.)

B 52. 1.9

53. Would this difference of 1.9 percent be considered material? _____

B 53. Probably not.

54. If the difference is considered to be immaterial (as it appears to be in this case), *APB Opinion No. 21* would allow the use of either method of amortization. In example C-2, an investment in bonds is made at a discount. You should follow the illustration carefully, noting that the investor records at cost and does not use a separate account for the discount element. Amortization entries debiting the investment account will increase it to face value by maturity date.

B 54. No answer required.

C. *Investment in Bonds between Interest Dates*

1. If a bond investment is purchased between interest dates, the investor must also purchase the _____ .

C 1. accrued interest

2. Is the accrued interest amortized? _____

Explain. _____

_____

C 2. No. It is repaid to the investor in the first interest payment.

3. Are bonds purchased between interest dates subject to premium or discount? _____

C 3. Yes.

4. What is the difference in amortization procedures when bonds are purchased at a premium or discount between interest dates? _____

_____

_____

_____

_____

_____

C4.   Recording proce-
dures are the same.
The amortization
period is only the
remaining life of
the bond issue.

5.   The Dawson Corporation investment in Eason
debenture bonds was made when the Eason
bonds had only _____ months of life until
maturity date.

C5.   100

6.   Therefore, the $20,000 premium must be
amortized at the rate of $_____ per month.

C6.   200 = ($20,000 ÷ 100)

7.   4/100 x $20,000, used to compute four months'
amortization, is the same as 4 x $_____ .

C7.   200

8.   Dawson Corporation's effective rate of interest
is _____ (more/less) than the
nominal rate of 15 percent carried by the
Carson bonds.

C8.   less

D.   *Valuation. Since* Appendix 19.1 *discusses
valuation of investments in marketable securities in complete detail, no questions and
answers are provided here. The FASB has
stated that lower of cost or market should be
used for valuation of marketable securities on
the balance sheet. The FASB has prescribed
a "total portfolio" approach to computation of
LCM. You should study the examples in the
appendix carefully, noting that changes in
market value can bring about unrealized losses
and gains that are reported in the income statement. Please note also that the LCM valuation
can never rise above cost--that is, there will
never be a debit balance in the Valuation
Allowance account.*

SELF TEST OF LEARNING GOAL ACHIEVEMENT

1.   Fill in the blank spaces in the following statements about investments made by
the Newport Corporation:

   a.   A purchase of 1,000 shares of Exxon Corporation common stock as a use
of excess cash would be a _____ investment if
Newport's management intends to sell the stock as soon as it needs the
cash.

   b.   Newport Corporation would use the _____ method to account for
dividends received.

   c.   This means that dividends received would be credited to the _____
_____ account.

d. Suppose Newport Corporation bought 40,000 shares of Alvino Corporation's 100,000 total shares of common stock as a long-term investment. This investment should be accounted for by the _____ method.

e. In this case, dividends received should be credited to the _____ _____ account.

f. How should Alvino's reported net income of $60,000 in 1985 be recorded on Newport Corporation's books? _____

_____

_____

g. If Exxon stock (bought in item a) has a higher market price at the end of the year than Newport paid for it, what adjustment must be made? _____

h. If Exxon stock is lower at the end of the year than Newport's cost, what adjustment should be made? _____

_____

_____

i. Is Exxon stock a marketable security? _____

j. Investments in marketable securities should be valued on the balance sheet at _____

_____.

2. Raccoon River Corporation is offering $100,000 of ten-year, 16 percent bonds to the public. The current market rate for this type of bond is 14 percent.

a. Compute the price that ought to be paid by an investor.

b. Why do these bonds sell at a premium? _____

_____

_____

c.   Assume that the bonds are bought on the authorization date of March 1, 1985. Show the general journal entry on the books of the investor to record the purchase.

GENERAL JOURNAL

Date	Account Titles and Explanation	F	Debit	Credit

d.   Show a general journal entry to record the receipt of interest and amortization of premium by the straight line method on September 1, 1985.

e. Show a general journal entry to record the receipt of interest and amortization of premium by the interest method on September 1, 1985.

f. Show a general journal entry to record accrued interest and amortization of discount by the straight line method on December 31, 1985.

g. Show a general journal entry to record accrued interest and amortization of discount by the interest method on December 31, 1985.

3. (Appendix) Goldstein Company purchased three temporary investments in marketable securities in 1985. On December 31, 1985, values were as follows:

	Cost	Market Value
Krypton common stock	$8,000	$7,500
Xenon common stock	6,000	7,000
Neon common stock	6,000	4,700

a. Compute the amount of unrealized loss or gain on these stocks.

b. On December 31, 1986, the investment values were:

	Cost	Market Value
Krypton common stock	$8,000	$7,600
Xenon common stock	6,000	7,200
Neon common stock	6,000	5,600

What is the unrealized gain or loss for 1986?

ANSWERS TO LEARNING GOAL ACHIEVEMENT TEST

1. a. temporary
    b. cost
    c. Dividends Earned
    d. equity
    e. Investment in Stocks
    f. Forty percent ($24,000) should be debited to Investment in Stocks and credited to Investor's Share of Investee Income.
    g. None.
    h. A contra account should be used to record the difference with a debit to an unrealized loss account.
    i. Yes.
    j. the lower of cost or market on a "total portfolio" basis.

2. a.

PV of face ($100,000 x 0.258419)	$ 25,841.90
PV of interest ($8,000 x 10.594014)	84,752.11
Price to be paid	$110,594.01

    b. Because they carry a rate that is higher than the market rate for this type of bond.

    c.

GENERAL JOURNAL

Date		Account Titles and Explanation	F	Debit	Credit
1985					
Mar.	1	Investment in Bonds--Bonds of			
		Raccoon River Corporation		110,594.01	
		Cash			110,594.01
		Investment in 16 percent			
		bonds to yield 14 percent.			

d.

Date		Account Titles and Explanation	F	Debit	Credit
1985					
Sep.	1	Cash		8,000.00	
		Investment in Bonds--Bonds of			
		Raccoon River Corporation			529.70
		Bond Interest Earned			7,470.30
		Receipt of interest and amortiza-			
		tion of six months' premium.			

e.

Date		Account Titles and Explanation	F	Debit	Credit
1985					
Sep.	1	Cash		8,000.00	
		Investment in Bonds--Bonds of			
		Raccoon River Corporation			258.42
		Bond Interest Earned			7,741.58
		Receipt of interest and amortiza-			
		tion of six months' premium.			

f.

1985					
Dec.	31	Accrued Bond Interest Receivable		5,333.33	
		Investment in Bonds--Bonds of			
		Raccoon River Corporation			353.13
		Bond Interest Earned			4,980.20
		Accrual of interest and amortiza-			
		tion of four months' premium.			

g.

1985					
Dec.	31	Accrued Bond Interest Receivable		5,333.33	
		Investment in Bonds--Bonds of			
		Raccoon River Corporation			184.34
		Bond Interest Earned			5,148.99
		Accrual of interest and amortiza-			
		tion of four months' premium.			

3. a. Total cost $20,000
        Total market value   19,200
            Unrealized loss . . . . $ 800

    b. Market value end of 1986 . . . . $20,400
        Market value end of 1985   19,200
            Recovery in 1986 . . . . $ 1,200

However, the unrealized gain is only $800 because the valuation is not allowed to be recorded at greater than cost.

Chapter 20
Statement of Changes in
Financial Position

■■■

EXPLANATION OF MAJOR CONCEPTS

What the Statement Is

The three major financial statements that we have studied up to now do not tell
the reader in detail where a company received its financial resources and what it
did with them. This fourth major financial statement--the statement of changes
in financial position--rounds out the set of major financial reports by reporting
on *the flow of resources in and out of the firm*. It shows what caused financial
resources to increase and what caused them to decrease in a given period. Figure
20-1 shows diagramatically how the statement of changes in financial position fits
into the set of financial statements.

Appendix B to the textbook shows the 1982 statement of changes in financial
position of Dennison Manufacturing Company. This statement shows (as does the
income statement) that Dennison's financial resources were increased in 1982 by a
net income of $20,637,000. But the total increase in cash was a much smaller
amount ($9,113,000). A study of Dennison's statement of changes in financial
position explains this difference. There was some change in long-term debt, an
increase of $2,500,000. Note that this statement does not simply report the amount
of change; it shows separately the fund inflows and outflows. For Dennison the
major item is a total of $23,206,000 used to purchase property, plant, and equip-
ment. Other sources and uses of funds shown account for the net increase of
$9,113,000.

This statement provides useful information, and it is the purpose of Chapter 20
to enable you to understand it. Before leaving Appendix B, however, let's consider the idea of working capital.

Working Capital

Working capital is a dollar amount. It is equal to current assets minus current
liabilities. A current asset is cash or an asset that is expected to be turned into
cash in one year (or in the business operating cycle if longer than a year).
Current liabilities are liabilities that will be satisfied with current assets.
(Usually you can expect them to be due for payment within a year.) An equation to help you remember the meaning of working capital is:

$$CA - CL = WC,$$
$$\text{where } CA = \text{Total current assets,}$$
$$CL = \text{Total current liabilities,}$$
$$WC = \text{Working capital.}$$

Dennison's statement of changes in financial position is a slightly different form of the statement shown in the textbook. However, the change in working capital can still be calculated by reference to the balance sheet. Trace the following calculation to the statements.

Working capital 1982 (215,220,000 – 93,755,000) $121,465,000
Working capital 1981 (207,305,000 – 84,606,000) . . . . . . <u>122,699,000</u>
   Decrease in working capital . . . . <u>$ 1,234,000</u>

Before we get into the preparation of the statement, let's take the time to think through the effect of changes in the amounts of current assets and liabilities and the resulting effect on working capital. Let's think through the changes with the following steps:

▶ CA – CL = WC.

▶ If an element of CA decreases, there is less to subtract CL from. Accordingly, WC decreases.

▶ If an item of CL decreases, there is less to subtract from CA. Accordingly, WC increases.

▶ Following this reasoning, we can establish this pattern of effect on working capital when one of its elements changes:

Change in Element of WC	Effect on WC = CA – CL	
	Increase	*Decrease*
↑ in CA	↑	
↓ in CA		↓
↑ in CL		↓
↓ in CL	↑	

Test this idea for yourself with a few simple equations. Let CA = 20 and CL = 10. The equation for working capital is 20 – 10 = 10. Now decrease CA to 15; the result is 15 – 10 = 5, and WC has decreased as our table predicted it would. Take time to stop here and make up some examples of your own; notice how each follows the pattern in the table.

To summarize, there are two broad ideas we have been developing:

▶ The first part of the statement (known as Part A in the textbook) tells a reader *why* working capital or cash changed.

▶ The second part of the statement (known as Part B in the textbook) tells a reader *how* working capital or cash changed.

The two parts provide a complete picture that is not provided in any other financial statement. This information is needed by financial analysts.

Concepts of Funds

There can be several definitions of *funds*. The funds concept we have just examined (WC = CA - CL) is a popular one. A broader and more informative definition of funds is *all financial resources*. This definition describes funds as any financial resource available to the business. Even when it is used as the basis for the statement of changes in financial position, Part B must still show the changes that occurred in working capital components. In some cases, cash may be so important to a business that cash is used as the definition of funds, as in Dennison's case.

Preparation of the Statement

The first step in preparing a statement of changes in financial position is to prepare Part B. We do this by comparison of end-of-year data for each current asset and each current liability. In this comparison, we observe the pattern shown earlier in the table to compute the net increase or net decrease in working capital.

The second step is to explain the causes of this net increase or net decrease in working capital. Before considering techniques of explaining the net change, examine Figure 20-3. This figure shows that the only type of transaction that can *cause* a change in working capital must cross the open space between working capital components and nonworking capital components. This is really a simple idea. Nonworking capital components are all balance sheet items except current assets or current liabilities. *Therefore, the cause of working capital changes lies in nonworking capital items*. Go back to the use of simple equations to test this idea and let CA = 20 and CL = 10. Again WC = 20 - 10 = 10. Now try some examples:

▶ Pay an account payable of 3. The transaction reduces cash (a current asset) and accounts payable (a current liability). The equation is now 17 - 7 = 10, and WC is unchanged.

▶ Collect an account receivable of 4. The transaction increases cash (a current asset) and decreases accounts receivable (a current asset). The net change in total current assets is zero, and the original equation remains 20 - 10 = 10, with WC unchanged.

▶ Buy a machine for 7. The transaction reduces cash (a current asset) and increases machinery (not a current asset). The original equation changes to 13 - 10 = 3, and WC is changed.

Make some of your own tests. Notice that every time the transaction involves both a current and a noncurrent item WC will change. When it is between current items only or noncurrent items only, WC does not change. Therefore, the key to explaining why WC changed--and this is what Part A of the statement does--lies in an analysis of changes in noncurrent items.

Funds from Operations

The beginning point in the preparation is to determine the amount of funds provided by operations. The largest source of funds from operations is the net
income, but it needs to be adjusted to the funds concept being used. Many items
increase or decrease net income but do not have any effect on working capital or
cash. Probably the most obvious one is depreciation. While deducted as an
expense in the income statement, depreciation has no effect on working capital
or cash. The entry to record depreciation for a period may be:

> Depreciation Expense   100
> Accumulated Depreciation   100

Neither account is an element of CA - CL = WC, so depreciation is called a
nonworking capital charge to net income. It must be added back to net income
to determine the amount of working capital provided by operations. There are
also nonworking capital credits that increase net income but do not have any
effect on working capital. These must be deducted. Figure 20-7 shows some
examples of nonworking capital charges and credits. Don't try to memorize
them; instead, jot down the original journal entries to record them so that
you can see how they changed net income without changing working capital.

Techniques of Preparing the Statement

The chapter begins by describing the simple analytical approach to the preparation of the statement. This method will work in the simple cases, but as noncurrent accounts have more and more transactions affecting them, it becomes
cumbersome. The other method shown in the chapter is called the work sheet
approach. It essentially utilizes the same approach, but in a more organized
manner.

The work sheet approach begins by setting up a four-column work sheet.
The first column is for the beginning balances, the second and third columns
are used to reconstruct the transactions which changed the account balances,
and the fourth column is for the ending balances. The first step in the preparation is to enter the beginning and ending balances of the balance sheet
accounts in the first and fourth columns, respectively. All accounts on the
balance sheet are not entered. The current asset and current liability accounts
are replaced by the one number, working capital. This is entered on the first
line of the work sheet.

The lower half of the work sheet is divided into two sections, one for
sources and the other for uses. If the transaction required a credit to explain
the change in a noncurrent account, it will require that a debit be entered in
the bottom half to balance. Debits represent sources. On the other hand, if
a transaction required a debit to explain the change in a noncurrent account,
a credit would be entered in the bottom half of the work sheet as a use of
financial resources.

After the work sheet is set up in this manner, the next step is to go through and reconstruct all of the transactions which explain the changes in the noncurrent account balances. Normally, this is done by starting with net income. Since net income is closed to retained earnings, it is entered on the retained earnings line as a credit. The offsetting debit is then put in the lower half of the statement as a source from operations. After this is entered, the remaining changes in non-current accounts are explained through entries.

When all of the changes in noncurrent accounts have been explained, the debit and credit columns for the bottom half of the work sheet are subtotaled. These subtotals are the total sources and uses of financial resources. The difference between the two subtotals should be the same as the change in working capital. An entry (z) is placed on the first line to explain the change in that item, and the offsetting debit or credit should cause the subtotals in the bottom half of the work sheet to balance.

Cash Basis Statement

The cash basis is becoming a very popular definition of all financial resources. The statement is very similar to the working capital basis. The principal differ-ence is in the calculation of cash provided by operations. All of the nonworking capital charges and credits are still shown as adjustments to net income. In addi-tion, all of the changes in noncash working capital accounts are also used as adjustments to net income. *Decreases in current assets and increases in current liabilities are added, and increases in current assets and decreases in current liabilities are subtracted.* The rest of Part A will be the same as under the working capital approach.

Part B is much more straightforward under the cash approach. The beginning balance in cash is simply subtracted from the ending balance to arrive at the change in cash. This form of the statement of changes in financial position is becoming more popular as the cost of money increases. An example of this form is shown in Appendix B with the Dennison Manufacturing Company's statements.

GUIDED STUDY OF THIS CHAPTER

A. *Working Capital Provided by Operations. An important primary source of working capital is regular operations.*

1. Working capital provided by operations _____ (is/is not) equal to net income.

A1.   is not

2. The determination of net income includes items which _____ (do/do not) affect working capital.

A2.   do not

3. Figure 20-4 shows the CHL company's net income was $_____ .

A3.   1,500

4.   Included in operating expenses is _____ _____, which does not affect working capital.

A4.   depreciation--
machinery

5.   Depreciation _____ (increases/ decreases) net income and _____ (increases/decreases) machinery.

A5.   decreases, decreases

6.   Since neither of these accounts are current assets or current liabilities, working capital _____ (is/is not) changed by depreciation expense.

A6.   is not

7.   Therefore, in the calculation of the change in working capital due to operations, depreciation _____ (would/would not) be subtracted. See Figure 20-5.

A7.   would not

8.   Figure 20-6 shows the indirect method for calculating working capital provided by operations. To the net income of $_____, nonworking capital charges to operations are _____, and nonworking capital credits to operations are _____.

A8.   1,500, added,
subtracted

9.   There is _____ nonworking capital charge and _____ nonworking capital credits.

A9.   one, no

10.   The nonworking capital charge to operations is _____. It reduced _____ but did not reduce _____; therefore, it needs to be _____ back to eliminate the effect of its subtraction on the income statement.

A10.   depreciation expense,
net income, working
capital, added

11.   Nonworking capital charges to operations are expenses or reductions in revenues, and non-working capital credits are revenues or reductions in expenses which affected net income but did not affect working capital. They are added or subtracted to remove the affect of their subtraction or addition on the income statement.

A11.   No answer required.

B. *Simple Analytical Approach.* *Example 1 uses the simple analytical approach to the preparation of a statement of changes in financial position.*

1. All of CHL Company's account balances on December 31, 1984, (the beginning of the year) were _____.

B1.   0

2. Thus, the December 31, 1985, (ending) balances represent the _____ in the account during the year. See Figure 20-8.

B2.   change

3. The first step in the preparation of a statement of changes in financial position is to prepare a schedule of _____ which _____ will become Part _____ of the statement.

B3.   changes in working capital components, B

4. Cash _____ by $_____, and since cash is a current asset, this means the working capital also _____ by $_____.

B4.   increased, 25,600 increased, 25,600

5. Accounts payable _____ by $_____, and since accounts payable is a current liability, this means that working capital _____ by $_____.

B5.   increased, 4,710, decreased, 4,710

6. Thus, we see that when a current asset increases, working capital _____. And, when a current liability increases, working capital _____.

B6.   increases, decreases

7. The opposite must also be true. When a current asset decreases, working capital must _____. And, when a current liability decreases, working capital must _____.

B7.   decrease, increase

8. From Figure 20-9, we can see that the total increases in working capital were $_____, and the total decreases were $_____. Thus, the net _____ in working capital was $_____.

B8.   45,660, 10,560, increase, 35,100

9. When Part A of the statement is completed, it must show the same _____ _____.

B9.   change in working
      capital

10.   In preparing Part A, one analyzes the changes
      in _____ accounts.

B10. noncurrent

11.   First it is necessary to calculate the working
      capital provided by _____.

B11. operations

12.   The income statement of the CHL Company
      showed net income of $_____.

B12. 1,500

13.   To this we must _____ depreciation
      expense, because it is an item which reduced
      net income but did not affect working capital.

B13. add

14.   This would make working capital from opera-
      tions: $_____ + $_____ =
      $_____.

B14. 1,500, 2,100, 3,600

15.   Referring back to Figure 20-8, next we identify
      the _____ (current/non-
      current) accounts which have changed.

B15. noncurrent

16.   The following noncurrent accounts have
      changed: _____, _____

      _____, and _____

      _____.

B16. Machinery, Common
      Stock, Retained
      Earnings

17.   Machinery _____ by $_____,
      which means we must have _____
      machinery. If we assume that it had been
      bought with cash, working capital would have
      had to _____ (increase/decrease)
      because of the transaction.

B17. increased, 21,000,
      purchased, decrease

18.   When a transaction crosses the working capital
      line and causes working capital to decrease,
      this is a _____ (source/use) of finan-
      cial resources.

B18. use

19.   The Common Stock account _____
      by $_____. If we assume that the other
      half of the entry was to Cash, this would have
      caused working capital to _____.

B19. increased, 53,500,
      increase

20.   Thus, when a transaction crosses the working
      capital line and causes working capital to
      increase, it is a _____ (source/use)
      of financial resources.

B20. source

21. Retained Earnings _____ by $_____. This change actually resulted because of _____ events.

B21. increased, 500, two

22. The two events were _____ _____ and _____.

B22. closing of net income from income summary, declaration of dividends

23. Net income caused Retained Earnings to _____ and has already been shown in financial resources provided by operations.

B23. increase

24. The declaration of dividends caused Retained Earnings to _____ and working capital to _____.

B24. decrease, decrease

25. Thus, declaration of dividends would be shown as a _____ of financial resources.

B25. use

26. By referring to Figure 20-10, we can see that each of these items has been placed on the statement in accordance with the analysis you have just made. Total financial resources provided were $_____.

B26. 57,100

27. Total financial resources used were $_____.

B27. 22,000

28. Therefore, the _____ is the net _____ in working capital.

B28. difference, increase

C. *Work Sheet Approach. Example 2 illustrates a more complex situation and the use of a work sheet for gathering the information for Part A of the statement of changes in financial position.*

1. Figure 20-11 shows the balance sheet data for December 31, _____ and _____, the second year of operation for CHL Company.

C1. 1985, 1986

2. The first step is again the preparation of the _____ _____.

C2.   schedule of changes in working capital components

3.   The method of analysis is the same as that used in example 1. Notice in Figure 20-13 that notes payable, a current liability, _____ (increased/decreased) during 1986, which caused an _____ in working capital.

C3.   decreased, increase

4.   The net increase in working capital for the year ended December 31, 1986, for CHL Company was $_____. The next step is to find the causes of this change in working capital. We will look for it in the working capital provided by operations and in the

_____.

C4.   228,100, noncurrent accounts

5.   This is done in the preparation of the work sheet. The first step in this is shown in Figure 20-14.

C5.   No answer required.

6.   The first step in setting up the work sheet is to enter the beginning and ending amount of _____ on the first line of the work sheet.

C6.   working capital

7.   The rest of the accounts and balances listed in the first and fourth amount columns are the beginning and ending balances of the _____

_____.

C7.   noncurrent accounts

8.   In the lower half of the work sheet, space has been provided to list the _____ of financial resources and the _____ of financial resources.

C8.   sources, uses

9.   What is the working capital on December 31, 1985? $_____

C9.   35,100.

10.   What is the working capital balance on December 31, 1985? $_____

C10.   263,200.

11.   Where is it shown in the work sheet in Figure 20-14? _____

_____

C11.   On the same line as the beginning balance.

12.   And $263,200 - $35,100 = $_____, which is _____

_____.

C12. 228,100, the increase in working capital

13. In the bottom half of the work sheet, we gather sources and uses of working capital by reconstructing the events that caused it to change. The beginning point is always net income or net loss, which in 1986 was $_____.

C13. 120,000

14. Because it was a source, $120,000 is shown in the Debit (source) column. It also increased the _____ account.

C14. Retained Earnings

15. Note the other part of entry (a) is a _____ (debit/credit) to Retained Earnings.

C15. credit

16. Items (d) and (j) are adjustments to net income. They are called _____ _____ charges and credits to net income.

C16. nonworking capital

17. Trace items (d) and (j) through. For each debit there is a matching _____.

C17. credit

18. Every entry on the work sheet is explained in detail; follow each of them through. The Sources and Uses columns collect information to prepare Part A of the statement. What is the amount of working capital provided by operations? $_____

C18. 131,100.

19. Let's trace a couple of entries through. First, look at the common stock account. The beginning balance was $_____, and the ending balance was $_____.

C19. 53,500, 153,500

20. Thus, the common stock account increased, which would most likely have occurred because of the _____ of stock.

C20. issuance

21. In the stock issuance transaction, a second account changed, _____ _____.

C21. Paid-in Capital-- Excess over Par, Common

22. This account went from $_____ on December 31, 1985, to $_____ on December 31, 1986.

C22. 0, 2,000

23. Since the two accounts changed due to the issuance of the stock, the amount received must have been $_____.

C23. 102,000

24. In order to explain the change in the accounts in the top half of the work sheet, _____ (debits/credits) have been entered.

C24. credits

25. Therefore, to maintain equality of debits and credits, a _____ will have to be entered in the bottom half of the work sheet.

C25. debit

26. Debits entered in the bottom half represent _____ of financial resources.

C26. sources

27. Look also at Retained Earnings. One amount has already been entered into that line (a), net income. Since this does not fully explain the change of $_____ , more entries are required.

C27. 30,000

28. Entry (i) was for the restriction of $_____ in retained earnings. Since this entry did not cross the working capital line, it _____ (is/is not) a source or use of financial resources.

C28. 50,000, is not

29. The other entry, (b), was for the declaration of _____ of $_____ . This is entered as a _____ on the Retained Earnings line because it _____ (increases/decreases) retained earnings.

C29. dividends, 40,000, debit, decreases

30. To balance the entry a _____ is needed in the lower half of the work sheet.

C30. credit

31. Credits represent _____ of financial resources, so it is entered in that portion of the work sheet.

C31. uses

32. Note that when all entries are made the two columns in the upper half of the work sheet balance with totals of $_____ .

C32. 694,100

33. The amount $694,100 is not significant except as a balancing figure. Note also that differences in all beginning and ending noncurrent balances are explained. For example, in Machinery, $21,000 + $175,000 = $_____ .

C33. 196,000

34. Try the same thing in all other noncurrent accounts. Has each change been explained? _____

C34. Yes.

35. The amount that brings the entire work sheet into balance is item (z). This item is the

   _____.

C35. increase in working capital

36. If the work sheet is not in balance after inserting item (z), there must be more changes that have not been entered.

C36. No answer required.

37. The work sheet is now used to prepare Part A of the statement of changes in financial position. Move to Figure 20-16, and trace every dollar amount back to the work sheet.

C37. No answer required, but do this carefully.

38. Now, how do we prepare Part B of Figure 20-11?

   _____

   _____

C38. It has already been done to determine the change in working capital.

D. *All Financial Resources--Cash Basis*

1. Instead of interpreting *all financial resources* as working capital, it can also be interpreted as _____.

D1. cash

2. The approach to the preparation of the statement of changes in financial position on a cash basis is very similar to working capital except that we are attempting to explain the causes of the change in _____.

D2. cash

3. Part B of the statement simply subtracts the _____ cash balance from the _____ cash balance.

D3. beginning, ending

4. The other major difference is in calculating the cash provided by _____.

D4. operations

5. In Figure 20-18 we see that additions are for _____ and the deductions are for _____.

D5. noncash charges against operations, noncash credits to operations

6. Noncash charges to operations include not only depreciation expense, like the working capital approach, but also _____ in current _____ and decreases in current assets.

D6.   increases, liabilities

7.   Noncash credits to operations include similar items as the working capital approach, and also _____ in current assets and decreases in current _____ .

D7.   increases, liabilities

8.   The Athens Corporation had net income of $_____ , but operations generated a cash _____ of $_____ .

D8.   237,000, increase, 217,000

9.   By studying Figure 20-19 we can see that the rest of the statement looks much the same as the working capital approach. The cash basis is becoming quite popular and is very helpful to management, especially during periods of high interest rates when cash management is very important.

D9.   No answer required.

SELF TEST OF LEARNING GOAL ACHIEVEMENT

1.   Pierre Corporation had the following in its trial balances:

	1985	1984
Cash	$100	$ 90
Accounts Receivable	60	70
Inventory	200	180
Accounts Payable	40	50
Notes Payable (due in 60 days)	80	100

a.   What is the amount of working capital in 1985? $_____
In 1984? $_____

b.   Show the amount of working capital change as follows:

	Change in Working Capital	
	Increase	*Decrease*
Cash		
Accounts Receivable		
Inventory		
Accounts Payable		
Notes Payable		

2. For each of the following transactions, indicate in the space provided whether it would be a *source, use, neither,* or *both* of working capital and of all financial resources.

		Working Capital	All Financial Resources
a.	Sale of a used delivery van for cash.	_____	_____
b.	Issuance of bonds for cash at discount.	_____	_____
c.	Issuance of bonds in exchange for a building with no cash involved.	_____	_____
d.	Declaration of a cash dividend.	_____	_____
e.	Declaration of a stock dividend.	_____	_____
f.	Payment of an account payable.	_____	_____
g.	Conversion by bondholders of convertible bonds into common stock.	_____	_____
h.	Restriction of retained earnings for plant expansion.	_____	_____
i.	Payment of cash dividend that was declared last year.	_____	_____
j.	Collection of a 90-day note receivable.	_____	_____

3. For each of the following items, indicate in the blank space provided whether it should be *added* to or *deducted* from net income to determine funds provided by operations.

a.	Depreciation expense	_____
b.	Gain on sale of building	_____
c.	Amortization of premium on bonds payable	_____
d.	Amortization of discount on bonds payable	_____
e.	Loss on sale of machinery	_____
f.	Amortization of premium element in investment in bonds	_____
g.	Amortization of discount element in investment in bonds	_____

4. Use the general journal form of entry to show how each transaction on the following page would be entered into a work sheet. Use the all financial resources basis. The following sample is provided: (Use the accounts Operating Summary and Financial Resources Summary for the part of the entry to appear in the lower half of the work sheet.

Sample: Net income for the year is $90,000.

Operating Summary	90,000	
Retained Earnings		90,000

a.   Depreciation expense on machinery for the year was $30,000.
b.   Cash dividends declared during the year were $25,000.
c.   A truck that originally cost $20,000 and had accumulated depreciation of $18,000 was sold for $2,500 cash.
d.   Bonds with a face value of $100,000 were issued in exchange for land and a building. The land and building had fair market values of $20,000 and $85,000, respectively.
e.   The total amortization of premium on bonds payable was $2,700.
f.   10,000 shares of $3 par value common stock were issued for cash at $12 per share.

T ACCOUNT ENTRIES IN GENERAL JOURNAL FORM

Item	Account Titles	Debit	Credit
a.			

ANSWERS TO LEARNING GOAL ACHIEVEMENT TEST

1. a.   1985 = $100 + $60 + $200 − $40 − $80 = $240.
        1984 = $90 + $70 + $180 − $50 − $100 = $190.

   b.

	Change in Working Capital	
	Increase	*Decrease*
Cash.	$10	
Accounts Receivable		$10
Inventory	20	
Accounts Payable	10	
Notes Payable	20	

2.

	Working Capital	All Financial Resources
a.	source	source
b.	source	source
c.	neither	both
d.	use	use
e.	neither	neither
f.	neither	neither
g.	neither	both
h.	neither	neither
i.	neither	neither
j.	neither	neither

3. a.   added
   b.   deducted
   c.   deducted
   d.   added
   e.   added
   f.   added
   g.   deducted

4.

T ACCOUNT ENTRIES IN GENERAL JOURNAL FORM

Item	Account Titles	Debit	Credit
a.	Operating Summary	30,000	
	Accumulated Depreciation--Machinery		30,000
b.	Retained Earnings	25,000	
	Financial Resources Summary		25,000
c.	Financial Resources Summary	2,500	
	Accumulated Depreciation--Trucks	18,000	
	Trucks		20,000
	Operating Summary		500
d. (1)	Financial Resources Summary	105,000	
	Bonds Payable		100,000
	Premium on Bonds Payable		5,000
(2)	Land	20,000	
	Buildings	85,000	
	Financial Resources Summary		105,000
e.	Premium on Bonds Payable	2,700	
	Operating Summary		2,700
f.	Financial Resources Summary	120,000	
	Common Stock		30,000
	Paid-in Capital--Excess over Par		
	Value, Common		90,000

Note to Student: These entries are made only for analysis of summary transactions that changed financial resources. They are never entered in the
entity's journal or in its ledger accounts.

Chapter 21
Analysis and Interpretation
of Financial Statements

■■■

EXPLANATION OF MAJOR CONCEPTS

Income and Retained Earnings Disclosure

To make possible a more useful comparison of net operating margin, certain items of a revenue and expense nature are considered to be nonoperating (or not ordinary) items. One category of these items is extraordinary items. This topic was discussed in Chapter 14, and its placement with other items is shown in Figure 21-1. A second type of nonoperating item is discontinued operations. When a company drops a segment of its business whose operations form a separate major line of the business, special reporting should be made. The profit or loss earned on that segment during the period should be reported separately from continuing operations. To include it with regular operations would be misleading, because the reader cannot expect those results to appear again in the future. The reporting on discontinued operations should also include the gain or loss from the disposal of the assets of the deleted segment.

In the reporting of both extraordinary items and discontinued operations, the income tax consequences of these events should be reported with the event. This will mean that the number reported as income tax on the income statement applies only to the net income from continuing operations. This practice is known as *intraperiod tax allocation*.

A third category of items deserving special attention is called prior-period adjustments. Prior-period adjustments are *not* reported on the income statement; they are shown on the retained earnings statement as an adjustment to the beginning-of-period retained earnings. Prior-period adjustments are even more rare than extraordinary items. A *prior-period adjustment* must be a correction of an error in financial statements of some accounting period before the current one.

Percentage Analysis

It is difficult to make useful comparisons of financial statement data when only dollar amounts are shown. A way to overcome this problem is to change the dollar amounts to percentages. Then we can compare several years in a single entity (or could compare several companies in the same year). In *horizontal analysis,* data from a designated year—called the base year—are used as a measure against which to judge all other years. For the chosen base year, each statement item is designated as 100 percent. The same items for other years are expressed as percentages of the base-year item. This type of horizontal analysis is called *trend percentages*. In another type of horizontal analysis, the amount of change from one year to the next is expressed as a percent of the earlier (or base) year. This type analysis is called *percent of change*. In both cases, the percentages are computed across a span of years; this is why the term *horizontal analysis* is used.

In *vertical analysis,* a financial statement amount is chosen as the base (that is, 100 percent), and all other amounts in that statement are expressed as a percent of the base. *Net sales* is used as the base for vertical analysis of an income statement. In the balance sheet, there are two bases, but both are the same amount. Each dollar amount in the assets section is expressed as a percent of total assets (the base). In the other portion of the balance sheet, total liabilities and stockholders' equity is the base amount.

In either horizontal or vertical analysis, remember that you are expressing some amount as a percent of a base amount. The resulting percent is always equal to the designated item *divided by the base amount*.

Percentage analysis helps comparative statements take on real meaning to you. Look for changing relationships. Ask questions such as: What items changed? Is the change favorable or unfavorable in terms of operating results? What could be some of the causes of the change? Is corrective action in order? Or is the change obviously a temporary one?

Ratio Analysis

A ratio is a fraction or the relationship of one number to another. Ratio analysis is another tool which can be used to make financial statements more useful. It is best to aim for understanding of the meaning of a ratio rather than simply to memorize a formula for it. To say that the working capital ratio equals current assets divided by current liabilities doesn't mean much. But to say that the current ratio tells us how many times the current assets could cover (or liquidate) the current liabilities, really helps us comprehend what it means.

There is an important key to remember in computing ratios. Whenever one part of the ratio is an income statement number (a number measuring activity for a period of time) and the other part is a balance sheet number (a number measuring status at a point in time), the balance sheet number must be expressed as the average-for-the-year amount. For example, if net income (which spans a year) is expressed in ratio to total assets, you should use the average total assets. The easy way is to add the ending year assets for both years and divide by 2. Remember that no one ratio or set of ratios gives an answer. Each is just one of several pieces of evidence of the financial well-being of an entity, and points to the need for further investigation and analysis.

GUIDED STUDY OF THIS CHAPTER

A. Horizontal Analysis

1. In comparative statements, the _____ (latest/earliest) year is presented first. (See Figure 21-4.)

A1.   latest

2. Each statement is presented in a single column. Since there must be subtotals, a single line is drawn under each subtotal. It means that amount is "stored" to be used with a later subtotal.

A2.   No answer required.

3. In Figure 21-4 total current assets of the Morco Company in 1985 were $_____.

A3.   111,000

4. This amount will be added to $_____ to determine total assets.

A4.   146,000

5. Therefore, both the current assets amount and the property, plant, and equipment amount were "stored" to be added for total assets of $_____.

A5.   257,000

6. Figure 21-4 is a form of horizontal analysis using only two years. The base year is _____.

A6.   1984

7. Cash _____ (increased/ decreased) by $16,000 during 1985.

A7.   increased

8. The $16,000 increase is expressed as a percent of the base amount of $_____.

A8.   16,000

9. $16,000 ÷ $16,000 = _____ = _____ %.

A10.   1.0, 100

10. Notes payable decreased by $1,000. Since the base amount for notes payable is $_____, the percent of decrease is _____ percent.

A10.   20,000, 5 = ($1,000 ÷ $20,000)

11. Let's examine current assets. Do the individual percents of increase or decrease add up to equal the percent of increase in total current assets? _____

A11.   No.

12. Also, does the 42.3 percent increase in total current assets minus the 3.3 percent decrease in property, plant, and equipment equal the percent of change in total assets in 1985? _____

A12. No.

13. So, in *horizontal analysis, we cannot* add per-cent of change figures in a statement to get meaningful subtotals as we can with the dollar amounts.

A13. No answer required.

14. Let's move to Figure 21-5. Which increased more, the sales or the cost of goods sold?

_____

A14. The cost of goods sold.

15. Do you consider this to be a favorable result? _____ What could be some reasons for it?

_____

_____

_____

_____

_____

A15. No. Cost prices of merchandise could be rising faster than retail prices, there could be errors in inventory, or per-haps merchandise is being stolen.

16. There is a _____ percent increase in miscellaneous general expense. Do you con-sider this important enough for management to investigate? _____ Explain. _____

_____

_____

_____

A16. 21.4, Yes. The dollar amount is small, but it may be a clue to an expense that is getting out of hand.

17. What do you think is the reason for the 3.8 percent increase in insurance costs? _____

_____

_____

_____

A17. Probably because of additional insurance on inventories needed to support a larger amount of sales.

18. To be sure that you understand percent of change, compute the 55.6 percent increase in earnings per share.

A18.
1985 . . . . $0.28
1984 . . . .   0.18
Increase $0.10

$$\frac{\text{Increase}}{\text{Base}} = \frac{\$0.10}{\$0.18} =$$

0.556 = 55.6%.

A19. 1982

A20.
$$\frac{1984}{1982} = \frac{\$69,600}{\$60,000} =$$

1.16 = 116%.

A21. 116

A22. 120

A23. Yes. Greater sales
with a lower increase
in cost of merchan-
dise means a greater
gross margin.

A24. 110. Favorably, the
result should be an
improved profit.

A25. 168 percent.

A26. No. There was a
decrease in 1983.

19. Where there are more than two years, a trend
percent can be computed. In Figures 21-6 and
21-7, the base year *for each item* is _____ .

20. Compute the 116 percent trend percentage for
cost of goods sold in 1984.

21. In other words, the 1984 cost of goods sold
has risen to _____ percent of the 1982
amount.

22. In the same year, sales rose to _____ percent of 1982.

23. Is this a favorable sign? _____ Explain.

_____

_____

_____

24. Also, selling expense rose to _____ percent
in 1984. How does this compare with the
increased sales? _____

_____

25. What is the 1984 net income before taxes as a
percent of 1982? _____

26. Does Figure 21-7 convey a picture of steady
growth since 1982? _____ Explain. _____

_____

B. *Vertical Analysis.   Vertical analysis uses a single amount for the base in each year.*

B1.   total assets

1.   In Figure 21-8 the base for the assets section is _____.

B2.   12.5

2.   In 1985 cash is _____ percent of total assets.

3.   Compute this percent.

B3.
$$\frac{\$32,000}{\$257,000} = 0.1245 \text{ or } 12.5\%.$$

4.   Total current assets make up _____ percent of the total assets of Morco Company in 1985.

B4.   43.2

5.   Compute this figure.

B5.
$$\frac{\$111,000}{\$257,000} = 0.4319 \text{ or } 43.2\%.$$

6.   Add the common-size percentages for the three current assets in 1985.   Their sum is _____ percent.

B6.   43.2 = (12.5 percent + 13.2 percent + 17.5 percent)

7.   Unlike horizontal analysis, vertical analysis does allow us to obtain common-size percentage subtotals by addition or subtraction.   For example, current assets of _____ percent + property, plant, and equipment of _____ percent = 100 percent = total assets in 1985.

B7.   43.2, 56.8

8.   Before leaving the balance sheet, let's examine a few changes.   Do the stockholders own a greater or a smaller percent of the total assets in 1985 than in 1984? _____

B8.   Greater.

9.   How do current assets as a percent of total assets in 1985 compare with the same ratio for 1984? _____

_____

B9. Current assets are a greater share of total assets in 1985.

10. Why do you suppose the net (or carrying value) of the building and store equipment is a smaller percent of total assets in 1985 than they were in 1984? _____

_____

B10. Because of increases in the accumulated depreciation (not shown here).

11. Figure 21-9 shows common-size amounts for the income statement. The base is _____.

B11. net sales

12. Cost of goods sold went up from _____ percent of net sales in 1984 to _____ percent in 1985.

B12. 60.9, 62.4

13. Compute the 62.4 percent amount for 1985.

B13.

$$\frac{\$123,000}{\$197,000} = 0.624 \text{ or } 62.4\%.$$

14. Would you expect the gross margin percent in 1985 to increase or to decrease? _____

B14. To decrease.

15. The gross margin percent is _____ percent in 1985 compared to _____ percent in 1984.

B15. 37.6, 39.1

16. The _____ percent increase in cost of goods sold as a percent of sales is _____ (a favorable/an unfavorable) change.

B16. 1.5, an unfavorable

17. This increase in cost of goods sold could be offset by reduction of operating costs. Selling expenses as a percent of sales _____ (increased/decreased) by _____ percent.

B17. decreased, 3.0

18. General and administrative expenses as a percent of sales _____ by _____ percent.

B18. decreased, 2.1

19. So total operating expenses as a percent of sales _____ by _____ percent.

B 19.   decreased, 5.1

20.   Note again that this common-size percentage may be obtained by addition. Show how:

_____

B 20.   3.0% + 2.1% = 5.1%.

21.   The same common-size percentages can be used to make a graphic presentation of what happened *to each dollar of revenue*. For example, in 1985

Operating Income =

$_____

B 21.   0.209.

22.   If a segment of the revenue dollar equal to total salaries expense in 1985 were shown, it would be _____ cents.

B 22.   13.
(Sales salaries $0.093
Gen. salaries   0.037
Total salaries $0.130)

C.   *Ratio Analysis. A ratio is a comparison of one value to another value.*

1.   Any fraction _____ (would/ would not) be a ratio.

C 1.   would

2.   Thus 1/2 is _____ in ratio to _____.

C 2.   1, 2

3.   And 1/2 could also be stated as _____ as a percent of _____.

C 3.   1, 2

4.   Ratio analysis allows us to compare certain important relationships among financial statement items. For example, the current ratio expresses _____ in ratio to _____.

C 4.   current assets, current liabilities

5.   In 1985 Morco Company has a current ratio of 1.96, which is the same as 1.96/_____.

C 5.   1

6.   We can say that current assets in 1985 are 196 percent of current liabilities. We more frequently say that they are _____ times current liabilities.

C 6.   1.96

7.   Such a ratio is also expressed as _____ to 1.

C7.   1.96

8.   Quick assets consist of _____

_____ .

C8.   cash, temporary
       investments, and
       receivables

9.   The acid-test ratio is a _____ (more/less)
      strict test of current debt-paying ability than
      the current ratio.

C9.   more

10.   Different ratios give evidence of various
       strengths and weaknesses. For example, if
       Morco Company makes sales on a 2/10, n/30
       basis, fifty-six days' sales uncollected is
       _____ (a favorable/
       an unfavorable) indicator.

C10.   an unfavorable

11.   Is the 1985 number of days' sales uncollected
       an improvement over 1984? _____

C11.   Yes.

12.   Morco's inventory turnover was _____ times
       in 1985. If Morco Company were a food store,
       would this be a favorable indicator? _____

C12.   3.0, No.

13.   An inventory turnover of 3.0 times per year
       means that Morco carries about _____
       months' stock.

C13.   four

14.   Some disadvantages of carrying *too much* stock
       are _____

_____

_____

_____

_____ .

C14.   higher carrying
       costs (insurance,
       storage costs),
       danger of items
       becoming obsolete,
       loss of the cash
       invested in inventory
       to more profitable
       investment

15.   Some disadvantages of carrying *too little* stock
       are _____

_____

_____

_____

_____ .

C15. lost sales opportunities, lost customers,
extra costs of rush
orders and premium
transportation (such
as air freight)

16. Many other ratios are explained in Chapter 21. Only by use of all of them to get a total picture can a good financial analysis of a firm be made.

C16. No answer required.

17. To summarize, answer these with the textbook closed. In horizontal analysis, the base amount is the amount for a specific _____. In vertical analysis, the base amount is the amount of a specific _____ in a year. Common-size percentages are a tool for _____ analysis. Trend percentages are a tool for _____ analysis.

C17. year, item, vertical, horizontal

18. As a final reminder, you should know how to compute and interpret each ratio in Figure 21-11.

C18. No answer required.

SELF TEST OF LEARNING GOAL ACHIEVEMENT

1. *Use of Financial Statements*. The following pertain to the use of financial statements by both internal and external users.

   a. Opposite each financial statement user, indicate a type of decision to be made based on the financial statements of Morco Company:

User	Decision
An officer of a bank	_____
	_____
	_____
	_____
	_____
	_____
	_____
A Morco stockholder	_____
	_____
	_____
	_____

User	Decision
A vendor that is accepting a large order from Morco . . .	_____
	_____
	_____
	_____
	_____
	_____
The vice president for production planning	_____
	_____
	_____
	_____
	_____
	_____
The board of directors as a group	_____
	_____
	_____
	_____
	_____
	_____

b. An income statement shows a loss from riot damages has reduced net income from $91,000 to $81,000. Compute net income as a percent of sales before and after the extraordinary item, if sales are $390,000.

Before   After

c. Is the extraordinary item expected to occur again? _____

d. Then, the more realistic rate of return on sales is _____ percent.

e.   Why is a prior-period adjustment not reported in the income statement?

_____

_____

_____

f.   What is the reason for intraperiod tax allocations? _____

_____

_____

2.   Following are some selected figures from income statements and balance sheets of an industrial company:

| | Figures in Thousands of Dollars | | | |
	1985	1984	1983	1982
Sales	$330,195	$285,659	$247,113	$178,664
Net income	10,439	9,385	8,598	5,867
Total assets	138,684	122,477	111,457	88,690
Stockholders' equity . .	65,407	57,152	49,956	41,193

a.   Using 1984 as the base year, compute the percent of change in 1985 for each item.

b. Using the earliest year as the base year, convert all items to trend percentages. Round to the nearest percent.

c. Compute a common-size percent for net income, for stockholders' equity,
and for total liabilities for each year. Carry each percent to two decimal
places.

d. Compute the rate of return on stockholders' equity for 1985, 1984, and 1983.

e. Using all the data that you have generated in this problem, make a recommendation as to whether an investment in its common stock is advisable. Give reasons.

3. Write out the formula for computing each of the following:

   a. Merchandise inventory turnover.
   b. Average number of days' sales uncollected.
   c. Acid-test ratio.
   d. Current ratio.
   e. Price-earnings ratio.
   f. Number of times bond interest earned.
   g. Sales to property, plant, and equipment.
   h. Earnings per share of common stock.

ANSWERS TO LEARNING GOAL ACHIEVEMENT TEST

1. a.   (These are some possible decisions.)

User	Decision
An officer of a bank	Whether to make a specific loan to Morco, whether to grant an extended line of credit, the limits to be placed on the loan or line of credit, what collateral to require, and what interest rate to charge.
A Morco stockholder	Whether to hold, buy more, or to sell his or her shares.
A vendor that is accepting a large order from Morco . . .	Whether to require total payment in advance, a partial down payment, a note, or to sell on open account to Morco.
The vice president for production planning	Which products shall be produced in greater quantity, cut back, or discontinued. What capital equipment or plant expansion projects should be undertaken.
The board of directors as a group	Whether to make changes in the management, declare a dividend (and, if so, of how much), or propose a bond issue to the stockholders.

b.

Before

$$\frac{\$91,000}{\$390,000} = 23\ 1/3\%.$$

After

$$\frac{\$81,000}{\$390,000} = 20.77\%.$$

c.   No.
d.   23 1/3
e.   Because it is a matter that is totally unrelated to the current net income; it is related to a past period, and its effect is already in retained earnings.
f.   So that a statement reader can determine the net (or after-tax) effect of a gain or loss.

2. a.

Sales in 1985	$330,195	$\frac{\$44,536}{\$285,659} = 15.59\%.$
Sales in 1984	285,659	
Increase	$ 44,536	

Net income in 1985	$ 10,439	$\frac{\$1,054}{\$9,385} = 11.23\%.$
Net income in 1984	9,385	
Increase	$ 1,054	

Total assets in 1985	$138,684	$\dfrac{\$16,207}{\$122,477} = 13.23\%.$
Total assets in 1984	122,477	
Increase	$ 16,207	

Stockholders' equity in 1985 . .	$ 65,407	$\dfrac{\$8,255}{\$57,152} = 14.44\%.$
Stockholders' equity in 1984 . .	57,152	
Increase	$ 8,255	

b.

	1985	1984	1983	1982
Sales	185%	160%	138%	100%
Net income	178	160	147	100
Total assets	156	138	126	100
Stockholders' equity	159	139	121	100

c.

	1985	1984	1983	1982
Net income	3.16%	3.29%	3.48%	3.28%
Stockholders' equity[a]	47.16	46.66	44.82	46.45
Total liabilities[b]	52.84	53.34	55.18	53.55

a) Remember A = L + OE, so Total liabilities + Stockholders' equity = Total assets.
b) Common-size percent for stockholders' equity + Common-size percent for total liabilities = 100%.

d. 1985: $\dfrac{\text{Net income}}{\text{Average SE}} = \dfrac{\$10,439}{\dfrac{\$65,407 + \$57,152}{2}} = 17.04\%.$

1984: $\dfrac{\$9,385}{\dfrac{\$57,142 + \$49,956}{2}} = 17.53\%.$

1983: $\dfrac{\$8,598}{\dfrac{\$49,956 + \$41,193}{2}} = 18.87\%.$

e. This company is certainly growing. Until 1985 its net income grew at a faster rate than sales--a favorable sign. Another favorable item is the company's ability to generate sales at a greater rate than it needed to increase assets. Net income as a percent of average stockholders' equity has declined slightly in the past three years, but stockholders' equity has increased rapidly, providing a larger base for this ratio. These results generally point toward a favorable decision to invest, but additional analyses should be made.

3.

a. Merchandise inventory turnover $= \dfrac{\text{Cost of goods sold}}{\text{Average inventory}}$.

b. Average number of days' sales uncollected $= \dfrac{\text{Average accounts receivable}}{\text{Net credit sales per day}}$.

c. Acid-test ratio $= \dfrac{\text{Quick current assets}}{\text{Current liabilities}}$.

d. Current ratio $= \dfrac{\text{Current assets}}{\text{Current liabilities}}$.

e. Price-earnings ratio $= \dfrac{\text{Market price per share}}{\text{Earnings per share}}$.

f. Number of times bond interest earned $= \dfrac{\text{Net income + Income taxes + Annual bond interest expense}}{\text{Annual bond interest expense}}$.

g. Sales to property, plant, and equipment $= \dfrac{\text{Net sales}}{\text{Average property, plant, and equipment (net)}}$.

h. Earnings per share of common stock $= \dfrac{\text{Net income − Annual preferred dividend}}{\text{Average outstanding common shares}}$.

Chapter 22
Branch Accounting and Consolidated Statements

■■■

EXPLANATION OF MAJOR CONCEPTS

Reciprocal Accounts

Business growth is often accomplished by either opening new branches or divisions or by buying existing companies. When this occurs, it will either be helpful or required to have a separate set of accounting records at each of the locations. In this case, there will be an account on each set of books which represents a common element and would offset each other if the books were combined. These accounts are called *reciprocal accounts*. When the amounts from each set of books are combined for the purpose of financial statement presentation, the reciprocal amounts must be eliminated so as not to double count the element represented.

Branch Accounting

When a business expands by opening a branch, there is still only one entity, but it will often be helpful for management decision making to have a separate set of records at each branch as well as the home office. On the branch's books, there will be an account entitled *Home Office* which represents the home office's equity in the branch. As an equity account, it has a credit balance. The reciprocal account on the home office's books is titled with the branch's name and represents the home office's investment in the branch. As an investment account, it has a debit balance. The investment on one set of books is equal to the equity on the other set of books and represents the same thing, and therefore must be eliminated when the books are combined to produce firm financial statements.

A review of the use of these accounts will be done in the "Guided Study" section. One note in these entries should help you. Remember that whenever there is an entry on one set of books to the Home Office or Branch account, there must be an entry on the other set of books for the same amount. These two accounts must always be kept in balance.

Parent-Subsidiary Relationship

When an investor owns more than 50 percent of the stock of an investee corporation, a *parent-subsidiary relationship* has been created. It is assumed that the investor can control the investee. When a parent-subsidiary relationship exists, the companies are known as *affiliates*. Each of the corporations is still a legally separate entity and maintains a totally separate set of accounting records. However, from an external reporting perspective, it is often more informative to combine the records and present *consolidated financial statements*. In such a case, we are viewing the *economic entity* as more important than the *legal entity*.

Again, in this situation, reciprocal accounts exist and must be eliminated when the amounts are combined for reporting. One set of reciprocal accounts will be the Investment account on the parent's books and the stockholders' equity accounts on the subsidiary's books. The investment represents an interest in all or part of the subsidiary's equity which is expressed in their stockholders' equity accounts. Thus, the balances are measuring the same element and would have to be eliminated in order not to double count the item.

Other reciprocal accounts may exist if the two companies engage in transactions with one another. For example, if the parent loans the subsidiary money, the parent's books would show a receivable and the subsidiary's books would show a payable. From a legal perspective, this is accurate because they are separate legal entities. But from an economic perspective, an entity cannot owe itself money. Thus, for consolidated statements the reciprocal amounts must be eliminated. Other types of reciprocal amounts can arise. For example, if the subsidiary sells to the parent, some of the sales on the subsidiary's records measure the same event as some of the purchases on the parent's books. And since we cannot sell to ourselves, they must be eliminated.

Minority Interest

If the parent owns less than 100 percent of the outstanding stock of the subsidiary, the outside owner's share of the stockholders' equity of the subsidiary is termed *minority interest*. This proportion of the stockholders' equity of the subsidiary is shown on the consolidated balance sheet between liabilities and stockholders' equity.

International Accounting (Appendix)

Many companies today operate in more than one country. Two basic financial reporting issues arise when international transactions involve dealings in more than one national currency. One of these involves the translation of financial statement items from foreign currencies into the *reporting currency* used in the combined statements. The other is the problem of accounting for fluctuations in the value of the foreign currency in respect to the *functional currency* during the period of time that a transaction is being completed; for example, between the sale and the collection. A *functional currency* is the currency in which assets, liabilities, revenues, and expenses are measured.

GUIDED STUDY OF THIS CHAPTER

A. *Branch Accounting*

1. Accounts in two sets of books that represent common elements and would offset each other if the books were combined are called

   _____.

A1.   reciprocal accounts

2. In the chapter illustration, the account on the home office's books is entitled _____ _____ and has a _____ balance.

A2.   Fullerton Branch, debit

3. The account on the branch's books is entitled _____ and has a _____ balance.

A3.   Home Office, credit

4. The Home Office account is in essence the owner's equity account on the branch's records, and the Branch account on the home office's books is in essence the investment account.

A4.   No answer required.

5. The balances in these two accounts, although opposite, are _____.

A5.   equal

6. When the home office transfers assets to the branch, the asset accounts are _____ and the Branch account is _____ on the home office's books. (See Figure 22-2.)

A6.   credited, debited

7. On the branch's books, the assets are _____ and the Home Office account is _____. (See Figure 22-2.)

A7.   debited, credited

8. Transactions engaged in solely by the branch are recorded _____

   _____.

A8.   only on the branch's books

9. When the home office pays an expense for the branch, the home office _____ the Branch account, and the branch _____ the expense account and _____ the Home Office account. (See Figure 22-2.)

A9. debits, debits, credits

A10. No answer required.

A11. Income Summary

A12. Home Office

A13. debiting, crediting

A14. 56,400, 56,400

A15. eliminated

A16. 563,500, 56,400, 563,500

B1. control

B2. parent, subsidiary

B3. affiliates

10. Note that whenever the Home Office or Branch account is involved, there are entries on both sets of books.

11. At the end of the accounting period, the branch closes their revenue and expense accounts to

_____. (See Figure 22-3.)

12. The Income Summary account is then closed to the _____ account.

13. Since the Home Office account was involved, there must also be an entry on the home office's books _____ the Branch account and _____ Branch Income.

14. When all of the entries have been posted on both sets of books, the balance in the Branch account is $_____, and the balance in the Home Office account is $_____. (See Figure 22-4.)

15. When the work sheet for a combined balance sheet is prepared, the Branch account and the Home Office account will be _____.

16. Thus, even though the home office's total assets are $_____ and the Fullerton Branch's total assets are $_____, the total combined assets are only $_____.

B. *Parent-Subsidiary Relationships*

1. When an investor owns 50 percent or more of the outstanding stock of the investee, it is presumed that the investor has the ability to _____ the investee.

2. At this point, the investor is known as the _____, and the investee is a _____.

3. The group is known as _____.

4. In these cases, the operating results and financial position is often more meaningful if it is presented for the _____ entity instead of the _____ entity.

B4.   economic, legal

5.   Statements presented for the economic entity are known as _____ financial statements.

B5.   consolidated

6.   In a parent-subsidiary relationship, reciprocal accounts again exist. On the parent's books, the reciprocal account is entitled _____ _____.

B6.   Investment in Company S

7.   On the subsidiary's books, the reciprocal accounts would be the _____ account and the _____ account.

B7.   Common Stock, Retained Earnings

8.   When the parent owned 100 percent of the subsidiary's outstanding stock, the _____ account will be eliminated against the stockholders' equity of the subsidiary.

B8.   Investment

9.   The eliminations which are made on the work sheet for consolidated statements _____ _____ (are/are never) journalized on the books of either corporation.

B9.   are never

10.   In looking at Figure 22-8, the total assets on the consolidated balance sheet are _____ _____ (equal/not equal) to the sum of the assets of the parent and the subsidiary.

B10.   not equal

11.   In a parent-subsidiary relationship, other reciprocal accounts can arise. In example 2, an intercompany _____ occurred.

B11.   loan

12.   On the books of the parent, there was a _____.

B12.   note receivable

13.   On the books of the subsidiary, there was a _____.

B13.   note payable

14.   When the two businesses are viewed as a single economic entity, there _____ (is/is not) a loan.

B14.   is not

15.   Therefore, the note receivable and note payable must be _____ to prepare a consolidated balance sheet.

B15. eliminated

16. In example 2, the _____
     still must be eliminated against the _____
     _____ and _____
     of the subsidiary.

B16. Investment in
      Company S, Common
      Stock, Retained
      Earnings

17. Income and expense items may also be recipro-
     cal. In example 3, _____
     on the books of the subsidiary and _____
     _____ on the books of the
     parent are reciprocal.

B17. Interest Expense,
      Interest Earned

18. If both of these were to appear on the con-
     solidated income statement, it would be mis-
     leading. Thus, the $_____ must be
     eliminated.

B18. 1,500

19. The Investment in Company S and the Common
     Stock and Retained Earnings of the subsidiary
     must also still be _____.

B19. eliminated

20. Two things must be kept in mind when pre-
     paring consolidated financial statements. The
     only events that change the status of the
     economic entity are transactions with _____
     _____ businesses.

B20. outside

21. And, elimination entries on the work sheet are
     for purposes of preparing consolidated state-
     ments only. They _____ (are/
     are never) reflected in the accounting records
     of any of the affiliates.

B21. are never

C. *International Accounting (Appendix)*

1. In an international transaction, if the buyer
    pays in a foreign currency, the seller then
    must use the foreign currency to purchase
    dollars. The transaction in which the dollars
    are purchased is called a _____
    _____.

C1. foreign currency
     exchange

2. The currency in which an entity measures its
    assets, liabilities, revenues, and expenses is
    called the _____.

C2. functional currency

3. The currency in which an entity reports the
    combined results of its domestic and foreign
    operations is called the _____
    _____.

C3.   reporting currency

4.   When the reporting currency and the functional currency are not the same, translation into the reporting currency results in _____ _____.

C4.   foreign exchange gains and losses

5.   In the text example of the translation of a specific transaction, Alabama Corporation made a sale in _____.

C5.   France

6.   Alabama Corporation's functional currency was _____.

C6.   francs

7.   The 2,000,000 franc sale must be translated into _____ to be recorded on Alabama's books. This was done by multiplying by the number of dollars it took to buy a franc, $_____.

C7.   dollars, 0.15

8.   Thus, the sale will be recorded at _____ francs x $_____ or $_____.

C8.   2,000,000, 0.15, 300,000

9.   As of December 31, 1985, the exchange rate had risen so that it now took $_____ to buy one franc.

C9.   0.16 2/3

10.   Therefore, the 2,000,000 francs that Alabama will receive will buy more dollars. 2,000,000 francs x $_____ equals $_____.

C10.   0.16 2/3, 333,333.33

11.   Thus, Alabama has experienced a foreign currency exchange gain of $_____.

C11.   33,333.33

12.   When the receivable was actually paid on Jan. 15, 1986, the exchange rate had dropped to $_____ per franc.

C12.   0.135

13.   Since December 31, 1985, Alabama has experienced a foreign currency exchange _____, because the 2,000,000 francs they will receive will buy fewer dollars.

C13.   loss

SELF TEST OF LEARNING GOAL ACHIEVEMENT

1. Record the following transactions of the Thornton Company and its Wakonda branch on the books of both the home office and the branch. The company uses the periodic inventory system.

    Jun. 1   The main store transferred $4,000 in cash and merchandise with a cost of $9,500 to the Wakonda branch.

    3   The branch purchased $8,000 worth of merchandise on account.

    5   Monthly rent of $500 was paid for the branch by the home office.

    6   Branch cash sales of $6,000 were recorded.

    7   Paid $5,000 on account for June 3 purchase.

    8   The branch paid salaries of $600 (ignore payroll taxes).

    9   The branch deposited $2,000 in the home office's checking account.

Home Office

GENERAL JOURNAL

Date		Account Titles and Explanation	F	Debit	Credit

Wakonda Branch

GENERAL JOURNAL

Date		Account Titles and Explanation	F	Debit	Credit

2. List four reasons for business acquisitions.

(1) _____

(2) _____

(3) _____

(4) _____

3. On December 31, 1985, the accounts of the Catalina Corporation and its wholly-owned subsidiary, Capri Corporation, showed the following balances:

Account Title	Catalina	Capri
Cash	$ 50,000	$10,000
Accounts Receivable from Capri	4,000	0
Accounts Receivable--Other	12,000	6,000
Investment in Capri	94,000	0
Property, Plant, and Equipment	120,000	90,000
Accounts Payable to Catalina	0	4,000
Accounts Payable--Other	30,000	8,000
Common Stock	150,000	60,000
Retained Earnings	100,000	34,000

Enter the balances on a work sheet to prepare consolidated financial statements and complete the work sheet. Also prepare the consolidated balance sheet.

CATALINA CORPORATION AND SUBSIDIARY CAPRI Work Sheet for Consolidated Statements December 31, 1985					
Account Title	Catalina	Capri	Eliminations Debit	Eliminations Credit	Consolidated Trial Balance

4. (Appendix) The Iowa Grain Marketing Co-Op sold a load of grain to a
    Japanese importer for 5,000,000 yen on September 10, 1985, when the
    exchange rate was $0.004 = 1 yen. On October 28, 1985, they received
    payment in yen. The exchange rate on that date was $0.0045 = 1 yen.
    Prepare general journal entries to record the sale and collection, assuming
    that the reporting currency of Iowa Grain is the dollar.

GENERAL JOURNAL

Date		Account Titles and Explanation	F	Debit	Credit

ANSWERS TO LEARNING GOAL ACHIEVEMENT TEST

1. *Home Office*

GENERAL JOURNAL

Date		Account Titles and Explanation	F	Debit	Credit
1985					
Jun.	1	Wakonda Branch		13,500	
		Cash			4,000
		Shipments to Wakonda			9,500
	3	No entry required.			
	5	Wakonda Branch		500	
		Cash			500
	6	No entry required.			
	7	No entry required.			
	8	No entry required.			
	9	Cash		2,000	
		Wakonda Branch			2,000

Wakonda Branch

GENERAL JOURNAL

Date		Account Titles and Explanation	F	Debit	Credit
1985					
Jun.	1	Cash		4,000	
		Shipments from Home Office		9,500	
		Home Office			13,500
	3	Purchases		8,000	
		Accounts Payable			8,000
	5	Rent Expense		500	
		Home Office			500
	6	Cash		6,000	
		Sales			6,000
	7	Accounts Payable		5,000	
		Cash			5,000
	8	Wages Expense		600	
		Cash			600
	9	Home Office		2,000	
		Cash			2,000

2. Possible answers include:

   Opening new markets
   Establish a fair market share in new products
   Achieve growth
   Complement existing operations
   Diversify into nonrelated fields
   Improve overall profitability

3.

			Eliminations		Consoli-dated Trial Balance
Account Titles	Catalina	Capri	Debit	Credit	
Debit Accounts					
Cash	50,000	10,000			60,000
Accounts Receivable--Capri	4,000	0		(b) 4,000	0
Accounts Receivable--Other	12,000	6,000			18,000
Investment in Capri	94,000	0		(a)94,000	0
Property, Plant, and Equipment	120,000	90,000			210,000
	280,000	106,000			288,000
Credit Accounts					
Accounts Payable--Catalina	0	4,000	(b) 4,000		0
Accounts Payable--Other	30,000	8,000			38,000
Common Stock	150,000	60,000	(a)60,000		150,000
Retained Earnings	100,000	34,000	(a)34,000		100,000
	280,000	106,000	98,000	98,000	288,000

CATALINA CORPORATION AND SUBSIDIARY CAPRI
Work Sheet for Consolidated Statements
December 31, 1985

CATALINA CORPORATION
Consolidated Balance Sheet
December 31, 1985

Cash	$ 60,000	Accounts Payable .	$ 38,000
Accounts Receivable	18,000	Common Stock . . .	150,000
Property, Plant, and Equipment .	210,000	Retained Earnings .	100,000
Total Assets	$288,000	Total Equities . . .	$288,000

4.

GENERAL JOURNAL

Date		Account Titles and Explanation	F	Debit	Credit
1985					
Sep.	10	Accounts Receivable		20,000	
		Sales			20,000
Oct.	28	Cash		22,500	
		Foreign Currency Exchange Gain			2,500
		Accounts Receivable			20,000

Chapter 23
Accounting for a Manufacturing Firm

■■

EXPLANATION OF MAJOR CONCEPTS

Accounting Differences in a Manufacturing Firm

When a merchandising firm sells a product, it is selling the labor, materials, and manufacturing costs of another firm. These elements are built into the cost of each inventory item, but they are not visible. A merchandising firm simply records its purchases *at cost* without having to be concerned with how the cost was determined. However, a firm that manufactures the products it sells must, in its accounting system, be able to determine product cost by *identifying and summarizing* basic cost elements.

In a general manufacturing accounting system, a *schedule of cost of goods manufactured* is the financial statement that identifies and summarizes the cost of making the product. As indicated in Figure 23-3, this schedule provides the information about the cost of additions to the stock of goods for sale. In a merchandising firm, net purchases is comparable to this item (see Figure 23-2).

A different view must be taken of costs in a manufacturing firm. Those costs that are incurred to manufacture the product are called *inventoriable costs*. Instead of being treated as expenses and closed into the Income Summary, inventoriable costs become part of the *finished goods inventory*--an asset. As the items of product in finished goods inventory are actually sold, their cost becomes part of cost of goods sold. At that time, they reduce income.

Certain other costs are not incurred to manufacture the product. These are *period expenses;* they are included in the income statement and reduce income when they are incurred.

Inventories

A merchandising company has three major inventory accounts--materials, work-in-process, and finished goods. Materials inventory is composed of the cost of materials and parts used in the manufacture of the product. Some of the materials become a part of the final product and others are used in the factory. Work-in-process inventory is the costs incurred in the manufacture of partial completed units of product up to the date of measurement. These are units which were begun during the current accounting period and will probably be completed during the next accounting period. Finished goods inventory is composed of the total cost of making the units of product that have been completed but have not yet been sold.

Cost of Goods Manufactured

Three basic elements of manufacturing cost include materials used, direct labor incurred, and manufacturing overhead.

▶ *Materials Used.* If a periodic inventory system is the method of accounting for materials inventory, this amount must be computed. The computation is a simple one that is used often in accounting. Think of it in this way:

What you started with (beginning inventory)	$ XXXX
Add what you added to it (net purchases)	XXXXX
Equals total materials available to be used	$XXXXX
Deduct what you ended with (ending inventory) . .	XXX
Equals what you consumed (materials used)	$XXXXX

▶ *Direct Labor.* The salaries and wages of people who work at making the product are covered by the term *direct labor*. Other people may work in the factory but not directly on the product (janitors, timekeepers, foremen, and other supporting personnel). Salaries and wages of these people are called *indirect labor* and are a part of manufacturing overhead.

▶ *Manufacturing Overhead.* In addition to materials used and direct labor, many other manufacturing costs are incurred in producing a product. Such things as factory rent; depreciation of factory equipment; indirect labor; and heat, light, and power are only a few examples. The term for these costs is *manufacturing overhead*.

The total of the three elements of cost for any period--say for a month--is termed the *total manufacturing costs of the period*. This is not, however, the amount added to finished goods inventory. At the end of each period, there is partly finished work at several points in the factory. These partly finished items are considered to be "in process." The costs invested in them are inventoriable costs. Therefore, the total of these costs is called *work-in-process inventory*. To determine the cost of the goods added to the stock of finished goods, we must consider the changes in work-in-process inventory. We can use a computation like the one for materials used.

What you started with (beginning work in process)	$ XXXX
Add costs added (total manufacturing costs)	XXXXXX
Equals total work in process during period	$XXXXXX
Deduct what you ended with (ending work in process) . . .	XXXX
Equals what you added to finished goods (cost of goods manufactured).	$XXXXXX

The Work Sheet

A work sheet is of great value in a manufacturing firm. However, a new set of columns with the title *Manufacturing* must be added to the standard format (see Figure 23-6). These columns are used to develop the cost of goods manufactured. Note carefully these points about Figure 23-6:

▶ Inventories are not the subject of adjusting entries. Each ending amount is entered as a debit in the balance sheet column and as a credit in the column which it affects. Materials and work-in-process inventories affect cost of goods manufactured; finished goods affects income.

▶ No Adjusted Trial Balance column is used by Cola Manufacturing Company, but the adjusted trial balance amounts are extended across to the columns which they affect. Notice that this includes beginning inventories.

▶ The cost of goods manufactured *is always the difference* between total debits and total credits in the Manufacturing column. (If any work is done at all, debits must be greater.) That figure is entered *twice*--as a balancing credit in the Manufacturing column and as a debit in the Income Summary column.

▶ From this point, the work sheet is balanced in the same manner as other work sheets. Its columns then provide data for the schedules and financial statements, the adjusting entries, and the closing entries.

Financial Statements

The financial statements of a manufacturing company are similar to that of a merchandising company. A new schedule computes the cost of goods manufactured and supports that number in the cost of goods sold section of the income statement. On the income statement, operating expenses are divided into two groups-- selling, and general and administrative. The balance sheet, current asset section, will show three inventories instead of the one in a merchandising company.

Accounting Entries

There are a few differences in the accounting entries during the period. The purchases accounts are used to record the acquisition of materials. And, instead of expense accounts for factory labor and other factory costs, these are debited to accounts such as direct labor, indirect labor, depreciation, factory rent, etc. Notice that these accounts do not have the word expense in the title and, in fact, they are not expense accounts. They represent product costs and will become a part of finished goods. As the products are sold, these costs will become a period cost as a part of cost of goods sold.

The Closing Process

The closing entries for a manufacturing firm must include closing of all manufacturing accounts. A new account, *Manufacturing Summary,* is used to do this.

The balance in the Manufacturing Summary is the cost of goods manufactured. It is closed to Income Summary. Closing of the manufacturing accounts of Cola Manufacturing Company are illustrated in the textbook. Take time to compare them with the Manufacturing column of Cola's work sheet. You will find that the accounts are taken directly from the work sheet.

GUIDED STUDY OF THIS CHAPTER

A.   *The Manufacturing Process and Cost of Goods Manufactured*

1.   A firm that makes and sells a product is termed a _____.

A1.   manufacturing firm

2.   Costs which become a part of the cost of the product are _____.

A2.   product costs (or inventoriable costs)

3.   These costs become a part of _____ _____ when the product is sold.

A3.   cost of goods sold

4.   A manufacturing company has _____ major inventory accounts.

A4.   three

5.   Materials and parts used in making the product are _____.

A5.   materials inventory

6.   The stock of completed products ready for sale are _____.

A6.   finished goods inventory

7.   The sum to date of costs invested in partly completed products in the manufacturing process is _____ _____.

A7.   work-in-process inventory

8.   The amount in a manufacturing firm which compares to net purchases in a merchandising firm is _____.

A8.   cost of goods manufactured

9.   Cost of goods manufactured is the sum of _____, _____ _____, and _____ _____.

A9.   materials used, direct labor, manufacturing overhead

10.   Materials used is found by adding _____ _____ and _____ _____, and deducting _____.

A10.   beginning materials inventory, net cost of materials purchased, ending materials inventory

11.   Wages paid to factory workers who work on the product are _____.

A11.   direct labor

12.   Other factory wages are _____ _____.

A12.   indirect labor

13.   Indirect labor is a part of _____ _____.

A13.   manufacturing overhead

14.   Factory rent, machinery depreciation, heat, light, and power are items of _____ _____.

A14.   manufacturing overhead

B.   *The Work Sheet. Let's use Figure 23-6 as a focal point for study.*

1.   The amounts in the Trial Balance columns were taken from the _____ _____.

B1.   general ledger accounts

2.   The trial balance figures represent account balances in every account in Cola Manufacturing Company's general ledger before the _____ _____ process on December 31, 1985.

B2.   adjustment

3.   Accounts such as Cash, Accounts Receivable, and Prepaid Insurance are _____ accounts.

B3.   asset

4.   Materials Purchased, Direct Labor, and Indirect Labor are examples of _____ accounts.

B4.   manufacturing

5.   Sales, Bad Debts Expense, and Advertising Expenses are _____ accounts.

B5.   income statement
(or revenue and
expense)

6.   Heat, Light, and Power is an account that must
be allocated between the _____
and _____ columns.

B6.   Manufacturing,
Income Statement

7.   Cola Manufacturing Company does not use an
Adjusted Trial Balance column. Accordingly,
the amounts extended across the work sheet
will be the Trial Balance amounts plus or minus
the _____ amounts.

B7.   Adjustments

8.   Amounts that are part of the manufacturing
process will be extended to the _____
_____ column.

B8.   Manufacturing

9.   Is materials inventory an amount that enters
into the manufacturing process? _____

B9.   Yes.

10.   Why? _____
_____
_____

B10.   Because it is a part
of the computation
of materials used
(see Figure 23-4).

11.   What other work sheet items are part of the
computation of materials used? _____
_____
_____
_____
_____
_____

B11.   Materials purchases,
transportation in
(not shown in text-
book example),
materials--purchases
returns and allow-
ances, materials--
purchases discounts,
ending materials
inventory.

12.   Does the cost of materials used show as a
separate amount on the work sheet? _____
Explain. _____
_____
_____

B12.   No. The amount
must be computed
as in Figure 23-4.

13.   In addition to materials used, what other major
costs of manufacturing are required to produce
a product? _____
_____

B 13. Direct labor and manufacturing overhead.

14. Direct labor is labor that is performed _____ _____.

B 14. directly on product production

15. Wages for a machine operator who is boring holes in a metal brace for a school desk _____ (are/are not) classified as direct labor cost.

16. Wages for the factory supplies storekeeper _____ (are/are not) classified as direct labor cost.

B 15. are

B 16. are not

17. What classification is given to costs for factory personnel who do not perform direct labor?

_____

B 17. Indirect labor.

18. Indirect labor is one of many costs in the manufacturing process that fall into the major category called _____

_____.

B 18. manufacturing overhead

19. Manufacturing overhead consists of all production costs that are not classified as _____ _____ or _____ _____.

B 19. materials used, direct labor

20. Give some examples of manufacturing overhead costs incurred by Cola Manufacturing Company.

_____

_____

_____

_____

B 20. Indirect labor; rent; heat, light, and power; insurance; depreciation-- machinery and equipment

21. On the work sheet, the groups of items extended to the Manufacturing column are (1) the amounts reflecting cost of materials used, (2) _____, (3) _____ _____ items, and (4) _____.

B 21. direct labor, manufacturing overhead, work-in-process inventory

22. After the ending materials inventory and work-in-process inventory are entered in the Manufacturing column, the total debits will be _____ (greater than/less than/equal to) the total credits.

B22. greater than

B23. goods manufactured

B24. debit, Income
Statement

B25. materials used

B26. manufacturing
overhead

B27. schedule of cost of
goods manufactured

B28. expense

B29. cost of goods
manufactured

B30. merchandise
purchases

B31. No answer required.

23. The balancing amount in that column is called the cost of _____.

24. It is inserted in the work sheet on the credit side of the Manufacturing column as a balancing amount and on the _____ side of the _____ column.

25. At this point, stop and note how every amount in the Manufacturing column is used in the *schedule of cost of goods manufactured* (Figure 23-7). For example, the first debit amount ($58,300) is used in Figure 23-7 to compute _____.

26. The last debit amount ($10,200) is part of the

_____.

27. A major purpose of the Manufacturing columns of the work sheet is to provide information to prepare the _____

_____.

28. The beginning and ending finished goods inventory amounts, revenue account balances, and _____ account balances are extended to the Income Statement column.

29. The amounts in the Income Statement column are used in a similar manner to prepare the income statement (Figure 23-8). An amount found in this statement that is not found in the income statement of a nonmanufacturing firm is the _____

_____.

30. Cost of goods manufactured in Cola Manufacturing Company serves the same purpose in the income statement as _____ _____ does in a merchandising firm.

31. The balance sheet can be prepared from the work sheet in the same manner that the balance sheet for any other firm is prepared.

C. *Allocations of Cost.* *Some costs are in support of manufacturing operations and selling and general operations at the same time.* *A study made in Cola Manufacturing Company in 1984 provides a basis for allocation of such costs.*

1. One of these costs, insurance on the building, is an element of _____ _____ and of periodic expense.

C1.　manufacturing overhead

2. The total rent in 1985 was $_____. It covers the factory, salesroom, and general offices of the company.

C2.　12,000

3. The plant study showed that manufacturing operation uses _____ percent of the building floor space, so it is charged with $_____ of the total 1985 rent cost.

C3.　80, 9,600

4. Selling operations use _____ percent of the floor space, so that $1,800 of the rent appears on the income statement as _____ _____.

C4.　15, selling expense

5. The remaining 5 percent of the rent, or $_____, appears as a general and administrative expense.

C5.　600

6. On the work sheet, two rent expense items are extended to the _____ column.

C6.　Income Statement

7. The letter (S) after $1,800 means that it is a _____ expense.

C7.　selling

8. The letter (G) after $600 means that it is a _____ expense.

C8.　general and administrative

9. Other such common costs must also be allocated. The base chosen for allocation should be that which provides the fairest allocation.

C9.　No answer required.

D. *Closing Entries.* *In general, the closing process in a manufacturing firm follows the same concepts as the closing process in a merchandising firm.* *The one major difference, however, is that it has an additional step in the process.*

D1.   Manufacturing
       Summary

D2.   Income Summary

D3.   229,845

D4.   cost of goods
       manufactured (See
       Figure 23-7.)

D5.   Retained Earnings

D6.   333,795,
       Manufacturing Debit

D7.   debits

D8.   credit

D9.   103,950

D10.   goods manufactured

1. First, the accounts that pertain to the manu-
    facturing process are closed into the _____
    _____ account.

2. Then the Manufacturing Summary and the
    various income statement accounts are closed
    into the _____
    account.

3. The debit balance in Manufacturing Summary
    that is closed into Cola Manufacturing Com-
    pany's Income Summary is $_____.

4. This amount is called the _____
    _____.

5. As a last step, Income Summary and Dividends
    (if any) are closed into _____
    _____.

6. Note the first closing entry of Cola's general
    journal. The *debit* amount of $_____
    came from the total of the _____
    _____ column of the work sheet.

7. Each *credit* in that entry matches (and is,
    therefore, closing) the individual _____
    (credits/debits) in the Manufacturing column
    of the work sheet.

8. Each debit in the second closing entry matches
    an individual _____ in the Manu-
    facturing columns of the work sheet.

9. The credit to Manufacturing Summary of
    $_____ is the first subtotal in the
    Manufacturing Credit column of the work
    sheet.

10. In the third closing entry, the cost of _____
    _____ again comes
    from the work sheet.

E. *Summary*

1. In accounting for operations in the Cola Manu-
    facturing Company, a _____
    inventory system is used for materials inven-
    tory and for finished goods inventory.

E1.   periodic

2.   Therefore, the cost of materials _____ and the cost of _____ sold must be computed.

E2.   used, goods

3.   However, a work sheet can be used to bring together the costs of manufacturing and other costs of operations. This is a helpful tool in preparing:
    a.   the schedule of cost of goods manufactured,
    b.   the financial statements,
    c.   the adjusting entries, and
    d.   the closing entries.

E3.   No answer required.

SELF TEST OF LEARNING GOAL ACHIEVEMENT

1.   The following data apply to operations of the Augie Corporation during October 1985:

Sales $268,000
Finished goods inventory, October 1   42,000
Finished goods inventory, October 31   46,000
Cost of goods manufactured   160,000
Operating expenses   56,000

Required: Prepare an income statement for October.

2. The materials inventory at Galesburg Company on June 1, 1985, was valued at $22,000. Materials purchases in June were $78,000, of which $3,000 were returned as unsatisfactory. Transportation in on materials was $2,000. The valuation placed on the June 30, 1985, materials inventory was $20,000. Compute the cost of materials used in June.

3. The following data apply to operations of Cedar River Manufacturers in February 1985:

Work-in-process inventory, February 1	$ 62,500
Work-in-process inventory, February 28	47,000
Direct labor cost	146,200
Indirect labor cost	29,550
Materials used	92,150
Depreciation of factory machinery	6,200
Factory insurance cost	15,200
Sales salaries	18,000
Delivery cost (of finished goods sold)	3,200
Amortization of machinery patents	2,500
Small tools used	5,120
Factory heat, light, and power	6,000

Required: Prepare a schedule of cost of goods manufactured in February.

4. Clay Manufacturing Company had three costs in the Adjusted Trial Balance columns of the work sheet which apply to three functions. They are shown along with the allocation basis chosen by the accountant, as follows:

Item	Amount	Allocation Basis
Insurance	$12,000	Value of equipment
Building rent	18,000	Floor space
Heat, light, and power	6,000	Actual usage

The following information is also available:

	Factory	Sales	General
Space occupied . .	7,500 sq. ft.	1,000 sq. ft.	1,500 sq. ft.
Equipment value. .	$80,000	$10,000	$10,000
Power usage . . .	7,000 kw.	1,500 kw.	1,500 kw.

Required: Compute the allocations of each cost to manufacturing overhead, selling expense, and general and administrative expense. Use the following form:

CLAY MANUFACTURING COMPANY
Allocations of Cost

Item	Total	Manufacturing Overhead		General and Administrative Expense		Selling Expense	
		%	Amount	%	Amount	%	Amount

ANSWERS TO LEARNING GOAL ACHIEVEMENT TEST

1.
AUGIE CORPORATION
Income Statement
For the Month Ended October 31, 1985

Sales		$268,000
Cost of goods sold:		
Finished goods inventory, October 1	$ 42,000	
Add: Cost of goods manufactured	160,000	
Total goods available for sale	$202,000	
Deduct: Finished goods inventory, October 31 . . .	46,000	156,000
Gross margin on sales		$112,000
Deduct: Operating expenses		56,000
Net income		$ 56,000

2.
GALESBURG COMPANY
Computation of Materials Used
For the Month Ended June 30, 1985

Materials inventory, June 1		$22,000
Add: Materials purchases	$78,000	
Transporation in	2,000	
Gross delivered cost of purchases	$80,000	
Deduct: Materials purchases returns and allowances .	3,000	
Net cost of materials		77,000
Total materials available for use		$99,000
Deduct: Materials inventory, June 30		20,000
Materials used		$79,000

3.

CEDAR RIVER MANUFACTURERS
Schedule of Cost of Goods Manufactured
For the Month Ended February 28, 1985

Work-in-process inventory, February 1			$ 62,500
Add: Materials used		$ 92,150	
Direct labor		146,200	
Manufacturing overhead:			
Indirect labor	$29,550		
Depreciation of machinery	6,200		
Factory insurance	15,200		
Amortization of patents	2,500		
Small tools used	5,120		
Heat, light, and power	6,000	64,570	
Total manufacturing costs.			302,920
Total			$365,420
Deduct: Work-in-process inventory,			
February 28			47,000
Cost of goods manufactured			$318,420

4.

CLAY MANUFACTURING COMPANY
Allocations of Cost

Item	Total	Manufacturing Overhead %	Amount	General and Administrative Expense %	Amount	Selling Expense %	Amount
Insurance	$12,000	80	$ 9,600	10	$1,200	10	$1,200
Building rent	18,000	75	13,500	10	1,800	15	2,700
Heat, light, and power	6,000	70	4,200	15	900	15	900

Chapter 24
Job Order
Cost Accounting

■■

EXPLANATION OF MAJOR CONCEPTS

Cost Accounting

There are two major objectives of a cost accounting system. One objective is to *determine unit costs* of making products so that sales prices can be established. Another objective is to *control costs*. To enable management to do a better job in both the foregoing areas, a cost accounting system provides information that can be incorporated into frequent reports for management. Therefore, cost accounting serves users of accounting information *inside the entity*.

The flow of costs through the cost accounting system parallels the movement of goods through the manufacturing process. Costs are first accumulated in accounts which describe their nature. They are then transferred to work-in-process inventory. And when the goods are completed and physically moved to the warehouse, the costs are transferred to finished goods inventory.

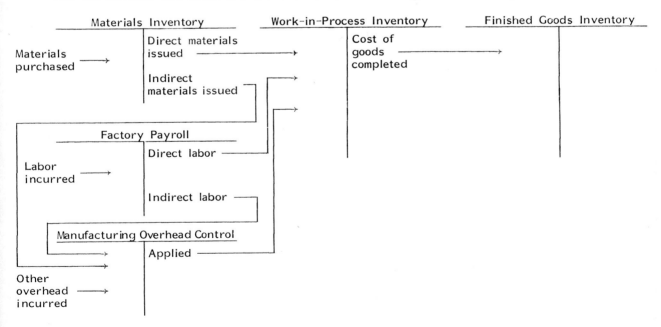

There are two basic cost accounting systems. One system--called *job order cost accounting*--is described in this chapter. The other system--called *process cost accounting*--is described in Chapter 25.

Inventories

As in accounting for a general manufacturing firm, cost accounting recognizes three inventories. A separate general ledger account is maintained for Materials Inventory, Work-in-Process Inventory, and Finished Goods Inventory. The periodic inventory system is not adequate, however, for cost accounting. Perpetual inventory records are needed for materials and for finished goods. In a job order cost system, the work-in-process inventory has a subsidiary record--the cost sheets. There will be one cost sheet for each job in production. As a subsidiary ledger, the details of all debits to work-in-process inventory in the general ledger are also posted to the appropriate job cost sheet. This allows the cost of each job to be accumulated as it is being manufactured. When a job is complete, the cost sheet is removed and totaled and that total cost is transferred to finished goods inventory. Often the journal entries to the general ledger accounts are done in summary form at the end of a week or month.

Cost Sheets

The cost sheets are at the heart of a job order cost system. Suppose that a builder of bridges has several bridges under construction at the same time. Each bridge will be assigned a job number, and a separate cost sheet will be maintained for each job. The job number will be recorded on the cost sheet. Each time labor is used at one of the bridges, a *time ticket* showing the job number must be prepared and recorded on the cost sheet. Each time material is issued for use at one of the bridges, the job number must be shown on the *materials requisition* and recorded on the cost sheet. Manufacturing overhead is allocated (or applied) to jobs (and recorded on the cost sheets) by using an overhead rate that has been determined in advance. The total of all cost sheet charges for incomplete jobs represents the cost value of work in process at any specific time.

Overhead Rates and Application

There are several ways in which overhead costs are incurred in production operations. Some types of transactions that are debited to Manufacturing Overhead Control are:

- ▶ Issues of indirect materials to production.
- ▶ Use of indirect labor.
- ▶ Adjusting entries to record depreciation of equipment used in production.
- ▶ Purchase of heat, light, power, or insurance.

Many of these costs fluctuate from month to month, but it is desirable that they be charged to production steadily. So that each job will reflect its fair share of manufacturing overhead costs, a rate for the accounting period is determined in advance. Using this predetermined overhead rate, manufacturing overhead is *applied* to jobs (that is, debited to Work-in-Process Inventory). Direct materials cost and direct labor cost charged to each job are based on actual tracing of these costs to the job. Manufacturing overhead costs, however, cannot be traced to a job; instead they must be allocated.

The *predetermined overhead rate* is based on the budgeted overhead cost for planned future production and an estimated volume factor that reflects the same planned future production. For example, often the annual estimated manufacturing overhead is divided by the estimate of direct labor hours to be used for the same period. This will give a dollar amount of overhead to be applied to a job for each direct labor hour worked on that job. Other volume factors such as machine hours or direct labor dollars can also be used.

The total amount of overhead applied to jobs during a period will seldom equal the actual overhead incurred. Since overhead incurred has been debited to Manufacturing Overhead Control and overhead applied has been credited to the same account, there will often be a balance in Manufacturing Overhead Control at the end of the period. This represents underapplied (debit) or overapplied (credit) manufacturing overhead. In the final month of the accounting year, probably with adjusting entries, this balance will be transferred (closed) to the Cost of Goods Sold account.

GUIDED STUDY OF THIS CHAPTER

A. Nature of Cost Accounting

1. The Cola Manufacturing Company (illustrated in Chapter 23) knew that cost of goods manu-factured was $229,845. If that company makes only one product, can it determine the cost per unit of product? _____

A1. Yes.

2. How would this be done? _____

_____

_____

A2. By dividing $229,845 by the number of units produced.

3. Suppose Cola produced several different products. Could it determine the unit cost of each?_____

A3. No.

4. With a job order cost accounting system, can a firm determine the cost of each unit of product produced? _____

A4. Yes.

5. How is this done? _____

_____

_____

A5. By establishing a record to record costs of each unit (or batch of identical units).

A6. cost sheet

A7. A perpetual inventory system, a method of identifying labor and materials with specific work done, budgets or estimates of future costs, and a manufacturing overhead rate.

A8. No. Cost of goods manufactured is computed in the cost accounting records. (A work sheet may be used, however, to determine net income and to make adjusting entries, closing entries, and financial statements.)

A9. No. As indicated in A8, cost of goods manufactured is computed from the cost accounting records.

A10. selling, costs

6. This record is called a job _____ _____.

7. What are some specific requirements in a cost accounting system that are not required in accounting for general manufacturing operations? _____
_____
_____
_____
_____

8. Is a work sheet used to compute cost of goods manufactured? _____ Explain. _____
_____
_____
_____
_____
_____

9. Is the Manufacturing Summary account required? _____ Explain. _____
_____
_____
_____
_____

10. The advantages of a cost accounting system include the ability to determine unit costs so that a better job can be done of establishing _____ prices and controlling _____.

B1.   stock item

B2.   subsidiary ledger

B3.   materials
       requisition

B4.   J. Seibert, 2

B5.   That the material
       has been received
       in Department 2.

B6.   62

B7.   21A, 22B

B8.   October 4

C1.   identified directly
       with specific jobs

C2.   time tickets

B.   *Materials*

1.   In a perpetual inventory system for materials,
     a separate stock record is maintained for each

     _____ .

2.   In Figure 24-2 the Materials Inventory account
     in the general ledger is a controlling account.
     The individual stock records make up a

     _____ .

3.   Materials are issued from the stockroom upon
     presentation of an approved _____

     _____ .

4.   Figure 24-3 illustrates materials requisition
     number 00326. It was approved by _____
     _____ in Department _____ .

5.   What does O. Haines' signature on this requi-
     sition mean? _____

     _____

6.   These gaskets and couplings will be used on
     job number _____ .

7.   A copy of requisition number 00326 will be
     used to reduce the balance of stock numbers
     _____ and _____ on the stock record cards.

8.   The stock record card will show these items
     issued as of _____ , 1985.

C.   *Labor*

1.   Direct labor is that work which can be _____

     _____ .

2.   The amount and cost of direct labor used on a
     job can be determined from the _____

     _____ .

3.   In Figure 24-6 a time ticket is shown.
     Employee _____ worked
     all day on October 4, 1985, on job number _____ .

C3.   John Seibert, 62

4.   At Seibert's rate of pay, job number 62 will be charged with $_____ for his work on October 4, 1985.

C4.   80

5.   That John Seibert worked _____ hours on job 62 was certified by the foreman _____

_____.

C5.   eight, Angie Smith

D.   *Manufacturing Overhead*

1.   The Whittier Company computes the manufacturing overhead rate using _____ _____ as a base.

D1.   direct labor hours

2.   To determine the rate for 1985, it is necessary to estimate *at the beginning of the year* the dollar amount of _____

_____.

D2.   manufacturing overhead cost

3.   It is also necessary to estimate the number of _____ that will be used in 1985.

D3.   direct labor hours

4.   The financial plan for 1985 (of which these estimates are a part) is called the _____.

D4.   budget

5.   Whittier estimates that its 1985 manufacturing overhead cost will be $_____ (page 853).

D5.   800,000

6.   The company has a production plan calling for _____ direct labor hours.

D6.   200,000

7.   The cost divided by the base = $_____ per direct labor hour.

D7.   4

8.   For each direct labor hour worked, $4 of manufacturing overhead will be applied to the _____ account.

D8.   Work-in-Process Inventory

9.   If less than 200,000 direct labor hours are worked in 1985, overhead will probably be _____ (overapplied/ underapplied).

D9.   underapplied

D10.   actual overhead
       costs are kept
       below $800,000

E1.   two power brake
       assemblies

E2.   2

E3.   Three.

E4.   Fifty.

E5.   Eight.

E6.   No answer required.

E7.   direct labor hours

E8.   1,574,787

10.   It may be possible for Whittier Company to work fewer than 200,000 direct labor hours and still not have underapplied overhead if

       _____

       _____.

E.   *The Cost Sheets. Figure 24-5 illustrates the cost sheet for job number 62.*

1.   This job number calls for the manufacture of

      _____.

2.   Therefore, to know the cost of one brake assembly, we will need to divide total job cost by _____.

3.   How many issues of material were made to this job? _____

4.   How many direct labor hours were used on it?

      _____

5.   How many time tickets were charged to job 62?

      _____

6.   On October 5, 6, and 9, two time tickets were recorded in a single entry. It appears that the accountant is gathering them into daily batches and recording them at the end of each day.

7.   At Whittier Company, overhead is applied on the basis of _____.

8.   The total cost of this job was $_____, which means that each power brake is assigned a cost of $_____.

F.   *Accounting Entries. In a cost accounting system, the costs actually flow through various accounts as assets until they ultimately become the cost of goods sold. Figure 24-1 diagrams this flow for a job order cost accounting system.*

F1.   Work-in-Process
Inventory

F2.   Manufacturing
Overhead Control

F3.   applied

F4.   Work-in-Process
Inventory, Manu-
facturing Overhead
Control

F5.   applied

F6.   Finished Goods
Inventory

F7.   Cost of Goods Sold

F8.   1,200, 787, 413

F9.   operating expenses

F10.   34 = ($413 ÷ $1,200)

1. Materials used in production that can be
identified directly with the job are *not* debited
to an expense account but to the asset _____

_____.

2. Materials used in production that cannot be
associated with a specific job are also *not*
debited to an expense account but to _____

_____.

3. Manufacturing Overhead Control accumulates
costs that are moved into Work-in-Process
Inventory when they are _____
at a predetermined rate.

4. Labor costs in production are *not* debited to
an expense account either. They are cleared
through the Factory Payroll account and move
into _____

or _____.

5. Even if debited to Manufacturing Overhead
Control, indirect labor ultimately flows into
Work-in-Process Inventory when overhead
is _____.

6. As work on the job is completed, the Work-in-
Process Inventory is credited for its cost and
_____ is
debited.

7. These costs still retain asset status in
Finished Goods Inventory until sold. At
that point, they lose asset status and are
debited to _____.

8. Whittier sold one of the power brakes for
$_____.   Since they cost $_____
each, the gross margin on the sale of one
brake would be $_____.

9. The gross margin on all sales must be large
enough to cover _____
and provide a net income.

10. Whittier's gross margin rate on these power
brakes is _____ percent.

SELF TEST OF LEARNING GOAL ACHIEVEMENT

1. The following statements pertain to cost accounting systems in general. Fill in the blanks with the most appropriate term to complete each statement.

   a. Two major aims of a cost accounting system are to enable management to establish _____ and to _____.

   b. The two basic types of cost accounting systems are the _____ cost system and the _____ cost system.

   c. The _____ inventory system is generally not suitable for a cost accounting system. With a cost accounting system, both materials and finished goods inventories would normally be recorded using a _____ inventory system.

   d. Under a cost accounting system, costs of work that is currently being performed are debited to an account called _____
   _____.

   e. Materials issued to production are recorded on a document called a _____.

   f. In the journal, materials issued to production are debited to the _____ account.

   g. Manufacturing overhead debited to Work-in-Process Inventory is said to be _____.

   h. As work is completed, it is recorded in the journal with a debit to the _____ account and a credit to the _____ account.

2. Antelope Island Company had $40,000 of materials purchases on account in June 1985. Issues to production were as follows:

   Job order 1056 . . . . $8,350
   Job order 1057   6,210
   Job order 1058   2,620
   Indirect materials   1,270

   Required: Prepare summary end-of-month general journal entries to record the purchases and issues.

GENERAL JOURNAL

Date	Account Titles and Explanation	F	Debit	Credit

3. Waco Corporation budgeted for $800,000 of manufacturing overhead costs in 1985; the production plan was to use 100,000 direct labor hours for that year. The actual overhead cost was $789,000, and actual direct labor hours used were 98,000.

Required:

a. Compute the predetermined 1985 manufacturing overhead rate.

b. Prepare a December 31, 1985, summary journal entry to record manufacturing overhead applied to production in 1985.

GENERAL JOURNAL

Date	Account Titles and Explanation	F	Debit	Credit

c. Calculate the amount by which manufacturing overhead will be over or
    underapplied.

4. Lakeland Shipbuilding Company incurred the following costs during the first
    week of August 1985 in work on a new job order number CVA63:

Aug. 1   Issued materials on requisition 0171 at a cost of $2,670.

     1   Direct labor on time tickets 784 and 785 amounted to sixteen hours
          at $9 per hour.

     2   Issued materials on requisition 0185 at a cost of $7,360.

     2   Direct labor on time tickets 792, 793, and 794 amounted to twenty
          hours at $9 per hour.

     3   Direct labor on time tickets 812, 813, and 814 amounted to twenty-
          four hours at $9 per hour.

     4   Direct labor on time ticket 820 of six hours at $10 per hour completed
          the job.

     4   Manufacturing overhead was recorded at the rate of $8 per direct
          labor hour.

   Required: Design a cost sheet for job number CVA63, and record these
                 charges on it. The job was to repair one boat.

5. Appel Company worked on three jobs in November 1985. All three jobs had been started in October, and on November 1 had accumulated costs as follows:

	Materials	Labor	Overhead
Job no. 870	$ 2,100	$ 800	$ 1,200
Job no. 871	81,500	9,790	14,685
Job no. 872	15,230	1,410	2,115

November costs were as follows:

	Materials	Labor	Overhead
Job no. 870	$31,850	$8,200	$12,300
Job no. 871	0	3,200	4,800
Job no. 872	6,250	2,100	3,150

Jobs no. 871 and 872 were completed in November; job 870 was still in process on November 30.

Required: Prepare summary end-of-month general journal entries to record the costs charged to production in November and the completion and transfer to finished goods of jobs no. 871 and 872.

GENERAL JOURNAL

Date		Account Titles and Explanation	F	Debit	Credit

ANSWERS TO LEARNING GOAL ACHIEVEMENT TEST

1. a. selling prices, control costs
   b. job order, process
   c. periodic, perpetual
   d. Work-in-Process Inventory
   e. materials requisition
   f. Work-in-Process Inventory
   g. applied
   h. Finished Goods Inventory, Work-in-Process Inventory

2.

GENERAL JOURNAL

Date		Account Titles and Explanation	F	Debit	Credit
1985					
Jun.	30	Materials Inventory		40,000	
		Accounts Payable			40,000
		Purchases in June.			
	30	Work-in-Process Inventory		17,180	
		Manufacturing Overhead Control		1,270	
		Materials Inventory			18,450
		Issues to production in June.			

3. a. $800,000 \div 100,000 = $8.00 per direct labor hour.

b.   ### GENERAL JOURNAL

Date		Account Titles and Explanation	F	Debit	Credit
1985					
Dec.	31	Work-in-Process Inventory		784,000	
		Manufacturing Overhead Control			784,000
		To apply overhead for 98,000			
		hours at $8.00.			

c. $5,000 underapplied.

Manufacturing Overhead Control

789,000	784,000
Bal. 5,000	

4.

LAKELAND SHIPBUILDING COMPANY
Cost Sheet

Description: Repair 1 boat   Job No. CVA63
Date started: August 1, 1985   Date completed: Aug. 4, 1985

Materials			Direct Labor			
Date	Requis. No.	Amount	Date	Time Ticket No.	Hours	Amount
8-1	0171	2,670	8-1	784,785	16	144
8-2	0185	7,360	8-2	792, 793, 794	20	180
			8-3	812, 813, 814	24	216
			8-4	820	6	60

Summary
Materials $10,030
Direct Labor   600
Manufacturing overhead   528
Total cost $11,158

5.

GENERAL JOURNAL

Date		Account Titles and Explanation	F	Debit	Credit
1985					
Nov.	30	Work-in-Process Inventory		38,100	
		Materials Inventory			38,100
		Issuance to production.			
	30	Work-in-Process Inventory		13,500	
		Factory Payroll			13,500
		Direct labor for November.			
	30	Work-in-Process Inventory		20,250	
		Manufacturing Overhead Control			20,250
		Overhead applied in November.			
	30	Finished Goods Inventory		144,230	
		Work-in-Process Inventory			144,230
		Completion of jobs 871 and 872.			

Chapter 25
Process Cost
Accounting

■■

EXPLANATION OF MAJOR CONCEPTS

The Process Cost Accounting System

Some manufacturing firms produce large quantities of identical products (for example, computer chips). In such firms, the product usually must pass through a series of processes (or departments) as it is made. In each process, a specialized operation takes place; usually some additional material is added. The final process is often a finishing or packaging operation from which the product is transferred to the finished goods storeroom. Each process, termed a *cost center,* may be a separate department or there may be more than one process in a department.

Process cost accounting systems are designed to fit this method of production. Necessary features of such a system are:

▶ A perpetual inventory system for materials inventory.

▶ A separate Work-in-Process Inventory account for each process.

▶ A system to identify direct materials and direct labor used in each process.

▶ A rate to apply manufacturing overhead to each process.

▶ A method of counting production (in units) in each process so that unit costs can be computed by dividing units produced into total costs.

▶ Journal entries to recognize the transfer of costs through processes, with each process (or department) adding on a bit of cost.

Equivalent Units

The costs in a process (or department) during an accounting period represent work done to:

1. Complete items that were in the beginning work-in-process inventory.

419

2. Start additional units and complete some of these.

3. Start other units which are partially completed as of the end of the period. These units are in ending work-in-process inventory.

The equivalent in whole units of the combination of the work described in the foregoing paragraph is called *equivalent units of work* done. It is the amount of whole units that would have been produced by this combination of work if it had been possible to concentrate the effort on producing whole units. In actual practice, however, we must use some of the effort to complete the beginning inventory. And, in many cases it is not physically possible to have all the units started in a period completed by the end of the period. Therefore, we compute the number of equivalent whole units that could have been produced with the same amount of work effort. For example, if 100 physical units are all 40 percent completed, the accountant assumes for purposes of cost computation that this is the same as 40 equivalent units 100 percent complete. Where material and labor are not added at the same rate, equivalent units must be computed separately for those items. If the overhead is applied with direct labor as a base, the equivalent units of overhead and labor will be the same. (That is the case with all illustrations and problems in this chapter.)

Cost of Production Report

There is not a separation of work into job orders in a process manufacturing system. Accordingly, cost sheets are not used in a process cost accounting system. Direct labor and direct materials are identified with processes (or departments) and overhead is applied on the work done in each process (or department). Unit costs of labor, materials, and overhead are computed for each process (or department) by dividing total costs of the element (for example, total labor costs) by the equivalent units produced. This computation is summarized in a four-step calculation outlined below:

1. The *quantity schedule,* which shows the number of physical units that were worked on in the process and what happened to them--completed or remaining in process.

2. Computation of *equivalent units,* which shows the number of equivalent whole units which could have been produced with the effort outlined in the quantity schedule.

3. The *unit cost computation,* which shows the dollar costs of materials, labor, and overhead per equivalent unit for the current period.

4. The *accumulated cost distribution,* which shows the assignment of costs incurred to the units which were completed and transferred and to the units remaining in ending work-in-process inventory.

Based upon these computations a *monthly cost of production report* is prepared. It is composed of three major sections:

1. The *quantity schedule,* which shows the number of *whole units* that were available to work on and what was done with them.

2. The *cost schedule,* which shows dollar costs of materials, labor, and overhead.

3. Computation of equivalent units and unit costs.

The cost of production report serves as the basis for journal entries to record the flow of costs into and between departments. For the *final department* in the production flow, the cost of production report shows the cost of the transfer of goods completed this period and sent to the finished goods storeroom. In this sense, cost of production reports replace the cost sheets of a job order cost system.

Work Flow

Since cost flows in a process cost system follow the flow of work, it is important that you have a clear picture of the work and cost flow in each process manufacturing system. Students often benefit by drawing a diagram such as the one in Figure 25-1 or in Figure 25-2. Note carefully that costs accumulate as units move through the departments on the way to completion and consequent storage in the finished goods inventory.

GUIDED STUDY OF THIS CHAPTER

A. *Quantity Schedules. The essential concepts of a process cost accounting system are contained in the illustration in the textbook. Let's use the Pompano Chemical Company to begin our study.*

1. Browardmint passes through two departments as it is produced. Which department works on the product first? _____

A1. Cooking.

2. After the cooking process is done, the incomplete product moves to the _____ Department.

A2. Finishing

3. Upon completion of the finishing process, the completed product, Browardmint, is transferred to the _____ inventory storeroom.

A3. finished goods

4. On July 1, 1985, the partially completed products on hand (beginning work-in-process inventory) in each department were: Cooking, _____ units; Finishing, _____ units.

A4.   0, 4,000

5.   The 4,000 units on hand in Finishing were
_____ percent complete as to labor and overhead.

A5.   75

6.   We are not concerned with percent of materials
in the beginning inventory in Finishing. It is
obviously zero because _____

_____.

A6.   no materials are
added in Finishing

7.   Quantity schedules are computed on the basis
of whole units; the *percent of completion is
ignored*. The Cooking Department must
account for zero units in the beginning inventory plus _____ new units started in
July.

A7.   50,000

8.   The Cooking Department has accounted for
50,000 units by transfer of _____ units
to the Finishing Department plus _____
units still in process in Cooking on July 31.

A8.   40,000, 10,000

9.   Verify with Figure 25-4 the quantity schedule
for Cooking. Then verify it again in the cost
of production report (Figure 25-7).

A9.   No answer required.

10.   The Finishing Department must account for the
_____ units received from Cooking
during July plus the _____ units in
its July 1 work-in-process inventory.

A10.   40,000, 4,000

11.   This total of _____ units is accounted
for by _____ units of completed
Browardmint transferred to finished goods
plus _____ units in process on July 31.

A11.   44,000, 38,000,
6,000

12.   As you did for Cooking, check Figures 25-8
and 25-12 to verify the quantity schedule for
the Finishing Department. Do the quantities
agree? _____

A12.   Yes.

B.   *Equivalent Units. To study computation of
equivalent units, let's begin with the Cooking
Department.*

1.   The beginning work-in-process inventory (on
July 1) in Cooking was _____ units.

B1.   0

2.   Therefore, the work done in July to complete the beginning inventory was the equivalent of _____ units.

B2.   0

3.   A beginning inventory of zero indicates that all of the _____ units transferred to Finishing were started in July and worked through to completion in July.

B3.   40,000

4.   These are called units "started and finished" during the period. The quantity can always be computed by subtracting the number of units in the beginning inventory from the number of units _____ of the department.

B4.   transferred out

5.   The Cooking Department also performed work on units in its ending (July 31) work-in-process inventory. _____ percent of the materials have been added.

B5.   100

6.   _____ units in the ending inventory with 100 percent of materials added is equivalent to _____ units of materials.

B6.   10,000, 10,000

7.   So, total equivalent units of materials in Cooking is _____ started and finished plus _____ in ending inventory = _____ units.

B7.   40,000, 10,000
        50,000

8.   Units "started and finished" are the same for labor and overhead as for materials, so that amount is _____ units.

B8.   40,000

9.   The ending inventory in Cooking is _____ percent complete as to labor and overhead.

B9.   40

10.   _____ percent of 10,000 ending inventory units is the equivalent of _____ units of labor and overhead for Cooking in July.

B10.   40, 4,000

11.   Total equivalent units of labor and overhead for Cooking is _____.

B11.   44,000

12.   Equivalent units are computed only to enable us to compute unit cost. Since there was no materials cost in the Finishing Department, we do not need to compute equivalent units of materials. (In Figure 25-9, it is computed as zero.)

B12.   No answer required.

13.   In the Finishing Department, we do need to compute equivalent units for labor and overhead. Finishing began July with _____ units in process.

B13.   4,000

14.   These 4,000 units were _____ percent complete on July 1, leaving _____ percent or the equivalent of _____ units of labor and overhead to complete in July.

B14.   75, 25, 1,000

15.   Of the _____ units transferred out of Finishing, _____ must have come from the beginning inventory of work in process.

B15.   38,000, 4,000

16.   This means that _____ units were started in July and finished in July in Finishing. These units are in addition to the 4,000 units from beginning inventory which were completed.

B16.   34,000

17.   Finishing's quantity schedule shows an inventory of _____ units in process on July 31. They were _____ complete.

B17.   6,000, 1/3

18.   A third of 6,000 units = _____ equivalent units of labor and overhead in Finishing's July 31 work-in-process inventory.

B18.   2,000

19.   Total equivalent units of labor and overhead in Finishing = _____ + _____ + _____ = _____ .

B19.   1,000, 34,000, 2,000, 37,000

C.   *Unit Cost. Unit costs should be computed separately for each cost element.*

1.   In the Cooking Department, total materials costs incurred during the month of July were $_____ .

C1.   10,000

2.   This $10,000 total cost divided by _____ equivalent units of *materials* in Cooking indicates a cost of $_____ per unit for materials in that department in July.

C2.   50,000, 0.20

3.   Total labor cost incurred during July of $_____ divided by _____ equivalent units of *labor* indicates a unit cost of $_____ for July in Cooking for labor.

C3. 13,200, 44,000,
     0.30

4. Total overhead cost applied of $_____
    in Cooking in July divided by _____
    equivalent units of *overhead* indicates a
    $_____ per unit cost of overhead.

C4. 11,000, 44,000,
     0.25

5. Unit costs of $_____ (materials) +
    $_____ (labor) + $_____ (overhead) =
    $_____ total unit cost of production in
    July.

C5. 0.20, 0.30,
     0.25, 0.75

6. Note here a *very important point*. The $0.75
    per unit cost in cooking *applies only to work
    done in July*. If there had been a beginning
    inventory in process on July 1, its value would
    have represented work done in June. Unit
    costs in June are *unlikely* to be the same as
    in July.

C6. No answer required.

7. Since all 40,000 units transferred from Cooking
    to Finishing in July were "started and finished"
    units, they are transferred at July's unit price
    of $0.75 for a total cost of $_____.

C7. 30,000

8. In Figure 25-7, the $30,000 cost of work trans-
    ferred to the Finishing Department is shown.
    The remainder of Cooking's $_____
    total July cost is accounted for by $_____
    of cost in the ending work-in-process inven-
    tory.

C8. 34,200, 4,200

9. Let's verify the ending inventory cost. It is
    composed of 10,000 units with _____ percent
    of material at a unit cost of $_____ =
    $_____.

C9. 100, 0.20, 2,000

10. The 10,000 units are _____ percent complete
    as to labor at a unit cost of $_____ =
    $_____.

C10. 40, 0.30, 1,200

11. And the 10,000 units are also _____ percent
    complete as to overhead at a unit cost of
    $_____ = $_____.

C11. 40, 0.25, 1,000

12. So that total costs in the July 31 work-in-
    process inventory in Cooking are $_____
    (materials) + $_____ (labor) +
    $_____ (overhead) = $_____.

C12. 2,000, 1,200,
     1,000, 4,200

13. In Figure 25-11, the July 31 work-in-process
    inventory in Finishing is shown as $_____.

C13. 6,020

14. *Here is another very important point.* In all departments (or processes) *after the first one,* a product carries *prior department costs.* In the Finishing Department, every unit already has prior department costs of $_____ .

C14. 0.75

15. In computing the ending inventory of work in process in Finishing on July 31, we must add prior department costs of $0.75 per unit to unit costs of labor of $_____ and overhead of $_____ .

C15. 0.40, 0.36

16. In the Finishing Department, _____ units with prior department costs of $0.75 per unit = $_____ of prior department costs in Finishing's July 31 work-in-process inventory.

C16. 6,000, 4,500

17. These same 6,000 units (that are 1/3 complete) have the equivalent of _____ units of Finishing Labor at $_____ = $_____ .

C17. 2,000, 0.40, 800

18. And they have the equivalent of 6,000 x 1/3 = _____ units of Finishing overhead at $_____ = $_____ .

C18. 2,000, 0.36, 720

19. The total cost attached to ending work-in-process inventory in Finishing is $_____ (prior department cost) + $_____ (labor) + $_____ (overhead) = $_____ .

C19. 4,500, 800,
      720, 6,020

20. The beginning inventory cost of $_____ in Finishing is added to $760 of July costs to obtain the cost of those 4,000 units transferred to finished goods inventory.

C20. 5,300

21. Why isn't prior department cost added to the beginning inventory to obtain total cost of those 4,000 units? _____

_____

_____

C21. Prior department cost is already included in the $5,300 value. (Remember that we added it to ending inventory of July. The same thing was done at the end of June.)

D1. source documents from the factory

D2. cost of production reports

D3. debits to overhead (indirect materials, indirect labor, depreciation, and purchased overhead items), purchases of material, recording of the payroll, and sales of finished goods

D4. Jul. 31, 30,000, transferred to next department

D5. 57,400 Finished Goods Inventory, Yes.

D. *Journal Entries. Journal entries must record two major cost flows: (1) The flow of costs (materials, labor, and overhead) into processes (or departments) and (2) the flow of total costs from one department to the next and ultimately to Finished Goods Inventory and Cost of Goods Sold.*

1. The basis for the journal entries for the flow of costs into departmental Work-in-Process Inventory accounts is the _____

_____.

2. The basis for journal entries for the flow of costs from one department to the next is the

_____.

3. Journal entries that cannot be based on the cost of production reports but must be made from other source documents include _____

_____

_____

_____

_____

_____.

4. The entry recording the transfer of costs from the Cooking Department to the Finishing Department was dated _____ and was for $_____. This was the amount shown on the cost of production report labeled as _____.

5. Using the cost of production report for the Finishing Department, the cost transferred to finished goods was $_____. Is this the amount used for the July 31 journal entry crediting Work-in-Process--Finishing Department and debiting _____

_____ ? _____

SELF TEST OF LEARNING GOAL ACHIEVEMENT

1. Sun Saver Company manufactures a solar panel in three departments as follows:

    a. Department 1 assembles a frame and fits into it the collector mechanism with all parts included except collector cells.
    b. Department 2 then subjects the assembled panel and mechanism to a series of tests and makes necessary adjustments.
    c. Department 3 paints and coats the exposed portions of the panel with a special weather resistant compound. As a final step, the collector cells are installed. The panels are then complete.

    Required: Draw a diagram to show the accumulation of costs in this production sequence. Show at which points various components of cost are added.

2. Blackstone Corporation had the following production record in its Binding Department in May 1985:

    Beginning inventory, 2,500 units 40 percent complete as to materials and 20 percent complete as to labor and overhead. Ending inventory was 6,000 units that were 100 percent complete as to materials and 70 percent complete as to labor and overhead. There were 42,000 units transferred to the next department.

    Required: Compute the equivalent units of work done in the Binding Department in May.

3. Sandusky Bay Company's Cleaning Department produced equivalent units of product in July 1985 as follows:

Materials	29,450 units
Labor and overhead	32,100 units

    July production costs were:

Materials	$20,615
Labor	11,235
Overhead	19,260

    Ending inventory was 3,000 units that were 100 percent complete as to materials and 60 percent complete as to labor and overhead.

    Required:

    a. Compute unit costs for July.

b. Compute the valuation of the July 31 work-in-process inventory in this this department. There were no prior department costs.

4. Following is information taken from various records of the Hartford Company for September 1985:

Materials issued:
  To Mixing Department . . . . $ 10,670
  To Finishing Department   6,175
Direct labor recorded in the factory:
  Payroll account:
  For Mixing Department   52,000
  For Blending Department   47,210
  For Finishing Department   12,815
Manufacturing overhead applied:
  In Mixing Department   36,400
  In Blending Department   33,047
  In Finishing Department   8,970
Transfers between departments:
  Mixing to Blending   98,470
  Blending to Finishing   175,710
  Finishing to finished goods storeroom   202,140

Sales for the month made on account were 90,000 units at a selling price of $4.50 each; their cost was $3.00 each.

Required: Record the September events in summary general journal entries dated September 30, 1985.

GENERAL JOURNAL

Date		Account Titles and Explanation	F	Debit	Credit

GENERAL JOURNAL

Date	Account Titles and Explanation	F	Debit	Credit

ANSWERS TO LEARNING GOAL ACHIEVEMENT TEST

1.

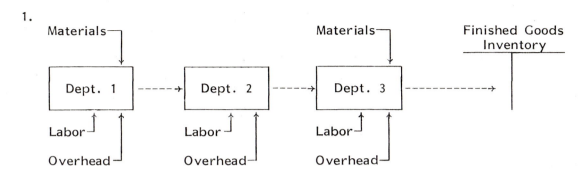

2.

	Materials	Labor and Overhead
To complete beginning inventory:		
Materials = 2,500 x 0.60	1,500	
L + O = 2,500 x 0.80		2,000
Started and finished = 42,000 - 2,500	39,500	39,500
Work on ending inventory:		
Materials = 6,000 x 1.0	6,000	
L + O = 6,000 x 0.70		4,200
Total equivalent units	47,000	45,700

3. a.
Materials = \$20,615 ÷ 29,450 = \$0.70.
Labor = \$11,235 ÷ 32,100 = \$0.35.
Overhead = \$19,260 ÷ 32,100 = \$0.60.

b.
Ending inventory:

Materials = 3,000 x 1.0 x \$0.70	\$2,100
Labor = 3,000 x 0.60 x \$0.35	630
Overhead = 3,000 x 0.60 x \$0.60	1,080
Total.	\$3,810

4.

GENERAL JOURNAL   Page 30

Date		Account Titles and Explanation	F	Debit	Credit
1985					
Sep.	30	Work in Process--Mixing		10,670	
		Work in Process--Finishing		6,175	
		Materials Inventory			16,845
		Issuance of materials to			
		production in September.			
	30	Work in Process--Mixing		52,000	
		Work in Process--Blending		47,210	
		Work in Process--Finishing		12,815	
		Factory Payroll			112,025
		Direct labor used in September.			
	30	Work in Process--Mixing		36,400	
		Work in Process--Blending		33,047	
		Work in Process--Finishing		8,970	
		Manufacturing Overhead Control			78,417
		Overhead applied to			
		production in September.			

GENERAL JOURNAL   Page 31

Date		Account Titles and Explanation	F	Debit	Credit
1985					
Sep.	30	Work in Process--Blending		98,470	
		Work in Process--Mixing			98,470
		Cost of units transferred			
		in September.			
	30	Work in Process--Finishing		175,710	
		Work in Process--Blending			175,710
		Cost of goods transferred			
		in September.			
	30	Finished Goods Inventory		202,140	
		Work in Process--Finishing			202,140
		Cost of goods completed			
		in September.			
	30	Accounts Receivable		405,000	
		Sales			405,000
		Sale of 90,000 units at $4.50 each.			
	30	Cost of Goods Sold		270,000	
		Finished Goods Inventory			270,000
		Cost of 90,000 units			
		sold in September.			

Chapter 26
Forecasting and Budgeting:
The Flexible Budget

■■■

EXPLANATION OF MAJOR CONCEPTS

Cost Behavior

Certain types of costs tend to follow specific patterns. *Fixed costs* are those whose total remains the same when volume of production or other activity changes. *Total variable costs* rise or fall directly with increases or decreases in volume. They are usually pictured as follows:

Some costs fit neither the variable nor fixed categories. These fall into two groups—stepped semivariable and mixed semivariable. These costs are neither constant nor do they vary in direct proportion to volume. In practice, these latter two types of costs are split into their variable and fixed components. *Relevant volume range* is simply the distance along the volume axis where costs can be predicted to follow a definite pattern.

Costs such as direct labor, direct materials, consumption of supplies, use of small tools, or sales commissions tend to be variable. Building depreciation, property taxes, or the salaries of night security patrol personnel are usually fixed. It is important to be able to classify each type of cost as fixed or variable so that the planned expenditures can be adjusted as levels of volume change. Some costs—for example, heat, light, and power—are partly fixed and partly variable. Techniques exist for separating these into fixed and variable components. Such techniques are not explained in this textbook, but are usually covered in a course in cost accounting.

Budgets

You must recognize that budgets (or financial plans) are prepared ahead of time (that is, to cover a future period) and are interrelated. Each specific budget depends upon others. The materials purchases budget is based on production predicted in the production budget. In turn, the production budget is based on predicted sales in the sales budget. Although we think of them as financial plans, most budgets are expressed in terms of both dollars and units of resources (materials, labor hours, quantity of product, and so on).

We have earlier recognized the need for budgets in connection with the computation of the manufacturing overhead rate. From the illustration in Chapter 26, it is obvious that budgets are needed to plan production schedules, purchases of materials, requirements for labor, need for salespersons, and even to plan for investment of cash or borrowing of cash.

Cash Forecasts

Most cash forecasts include collections from sales (both cash sales and sales on account) and payments for purchases as the major cash inflow and outflow, respectively. There is usually a pattern to such collections and payments that repeats itself month after month. It is often useful to you to prepare separate schedules of collections of accounts receivable and payments on accounts payable. Summary figures from these schedules can then be incorporated into the cash forecast.

Responsibility Accounting

Responsibility accounting traces costs to specific segments of the business supervised by one person. Then periodically these actual costs are compared to the budget. If the budget used was for a level of activity different from that actually experienced, the comparison would be meaningless for control purposes. Thus, it is desirable to adjust budgets to levels of production actually attained. The process of adjusting a budget, called a flexible budget, is illustrated here. Remember, it is the total variable costs that are expected to change if actual results are not equal to budgeted activity. Assume the following budget for 100 hours of work:

Fixed manufacturing overhead costs	$100
Variable manufacturing overhead costs	100
Total budget	$200

Each type of cost is at the rate of $1 per hour *as planned in the budget*. But if only 90 hours are worked (90 percent of normal), the variable costs would be expected to be 90 percent of $100 or 90 hours x $1. The fixed costs are *not* expected to change. The adjusted budget is:

Fixed manufacturing overhead costs	$100
Variable manufacturing overhead costs	90
Adjusted budget	$190

A *flexible budget* is a plan that predicts costs at various volume levels. To adjust from one volume level to another, it is necessary to recognize that variable costs are expected to change in direct proportion to changes in volume, while fixed costs remain the same. This simple concept is the key to flexible budgeting. You must be sure it is understood now; similar adjustments are made in Chapter 27.

Direct Costing (Appendix 26.1)

Direct costing is a method of accounting for the cost of production in which only the variable manufacturing costs are assigned to the product as inventoriable costs. All fixed manufacturing costs are assigned as expense to the period in which they are incurred. This method permits an income statement which is presented in a way which reveals the *contribution margin*--the excess of revenues over variable costs.

The format of a direct costing income statement is as follows:

Sales	$X
Less: Cost of goods sold (variable costs only)	X
Gross contribution margin	$X
Less: Variable operating expenses	X
Contribution margin	$X
Less: Fixed costs and expenses	X
Net income	$X

The difference in the net income reported using direct costing and the net income reported using full absorption costing--the method learned in earlier chapters--is the amount of fixed manufacturing costs which are in the beginning and ending inventories.

Under absorption costing, fixed costs in beginning inventory are actually fixed manufacturing costs incurred last period and carried forward to this accounting period as a part of inventory cost. These fixed costs become a part of this period's cost of goods sold. The fixed manufacturing costs in ending inventory are some of this period's fixed costs which are included in inventory which is subtracted in calculating cost of goods sold. These latter costs will be carried forward to next period when they will be released. Under direct costing, all fixed manufacturing costs are subtracted in calculating net income during the period that they are incurred.

Cost-Volume-Profit Analysis (Appendix 26.1)

Cost-volume-profit analysis is a tool which allows the manager to answer "what if" questions about the interrelationships between costs, production and sales volume, and profits. For example, what will happen to profits if fixed costs increase, or what will happen to profits if volume decreases? Cost-volume-profit analysis requires a good understanding of the differences between variable and fixed costs and the effects of volume on each of these types of costs. If you have had trouble with this, go back and review cost behavior.

At the heart of cost-volume-profit analysis is the concept of contribution margin. *Contribution margin* is the excess of selling price over variable cost. When contribution margin is stated as a dollar amount, it is the selling price per unit minus the variable cost per unit. Contribution margin can also be stated as a percent. In this case, it is computed by dividing sales minus variable costs by sales (contribution margin in dollars divided by sales). This can be done either on a unit basis or a total basis with the same result.

The simplest case of c-v-p analysis is break-even. The break-even point is the volume at which neither a profit or loss is incurred. This is the point at which the total contribution margin (sales – variable costs) exactly covers, or is equal to, the fixed costs. Mathematically, break-even is equal to fixed costs divided by unit contribution margin. If the contribution margin is stated as a dollar amount, break-even will be in terms of units of sales. If the contribution margin is stated as a percent, break-even will be in terms of total sales dollars.

By adding desired profit to fixed costs in the numerator, the analysis is extended to what is called cost-volume-profit analysis. So, total fixed costs plus desired profit divided by unit contribution margin is equal to the sales level necessary to earn the desired profit. This form of analysis is the most useful, in that we may change any one of the variables--total fixed costs, sales price per unit, variable cost per unit, or desired profit--and see what happens to the sales volume necessary to achieve the desired results.

Cost-volume-profit analysis has one additional tool called margin of safety. *Margin of safety* is the dollar volume of sales above the break-even point. Thus, it is the amount by which sales could decline before a company reached the break-even point.

GUIDED STUDY OF THIS CHAPTER

A. *The Budget Process. Budgets are prepared in advance of an operating period and form a plan of operations to be followed. The overall budget is really a structure of interrelated budgets.*

1. The basic or first budget to be prepared in a commercial firm is the _____ budget.

A1.   sales

2. Figure 26-4 illustrates a summary of Upstate Manufacturing Company's sales budget. In actual practice, this budget would be supported by a group of sales plans showing sales by

_____

_____ .

A2. districts or territories (and perhaps by divisions of the company or by specific salespeople).

A3. cash

A4. production

A5. 345,000, income statement

A6. 2,360, 2,000

A7. 20

A8. 1,800, 20

A9. 640

A10. beginning inventory

3. The dollar figures from the sales budget can be used in making the _____ forecast.

4. The quantity figures from the sales budget can be used to prepare the _____ budget.

5. The total sales target of $_____ will also be used in preparing the projected

_____ .

6. Turning to Figure 26-5, we see a total requirement for Style I hats of _____ in the first quarter of 1985; _____ of these are for anticipated sales.

7. The amount of 360 is required to be in stock at the end of the first quarter because Upstate's experience has indicated that it needs to start each quarter with _____ percent of anticipated sales on hand.

8. The sales budget (Figure 26-4) plans for sales of _____ Style I hats in the second quarter; 360 is _____ percent of those planned sales.

9. Since Upstate plans to sell 3,200 hats in the third quarter, it wants to have _____ on hand at the end of the second quarter.

10. After determining total requirements for sales in a quarter and inventory at the end of a quarter, we deduct the expected _____ _____ to know how many units to produce.

11. Figure 26-6 combines into one budget what would really be three separate budgets. Let's concentrate on the labor portion first. Labor hours required in the first quarter of 1985 to manufacture Style I hats are _____.

A11.   196

A12.   1/10

A13.   1,960

A14.   196

A15.   1/4

A16.   2,900

A17.   725

A18.   921

A19.   8

A20.   8, 7,368

A21.   4,160, 15,000

A22.   2,080, 2

A23.   3,000, 5

12.   We can compute this figure by using the stand-ard requirements (Figure 26-3) and the produc-tion budget (Figure 26-5). Each Style I hat requires _____ labor hours.

13.   Upstate plans to produce _____ Style I hats in the first quarter of 1985.

14.   So, 1/10 x 1,960 = _____ direct labor hours.

15.   Each Style II hat requires _____ labor hours.

16.   Upstate plans to produce _____ Style II hats in the first quarter of 1985.

17.   So, 1/4 x 2,900 = _____ direct labor hours for Style II hats (see Figure 26-6).

18.   Total direct labor hours for the first quarter are 196 + 725 = _____ .

19.   The expected cost per direct labor hour is $_____ .

20.   So, $_____ x 921 hours = $_____ expected (or budgeted) direct labor cost for the first quarter of 1985.

21.   Material costs can be computed in the same manner. For example, Upstate expects to use _____ feet of plastic in the *second* quarter for Style I hats and _____ feet of plastic for Style II hats.

22.   The amount for Style I hats (4,160 feet) is needed because Upstate plans to produce _____ in the second quarter, and they require _____ feet of plastic per hat.

23.   Upstate plans to use 15,000 feet of plastic to produce _____ Style II hats in the second quarter, and they require _____ feet per hat.

24.   Total requirements for plastic in the second quarter are _____ feet at $_____ per foot = $_____ .

A24. 19,160, 0.30, 5,748

25. You should follow through each of Upstate's other budgets to be sure you understand the source of the amounts. For example, in Figure 26-7, how was the $600 variable selling expense amount for Style II hats in the first quarter computed? _____

_____

A25. Sales of 3,000 hats x $0.20 per hat = $600.

26. In Figure 26-10 Upstate projects a profit that is reasonably close to their profit target of 12 percent. If the projected profit had turned out to be only 10 percent, what actions should Upstate's management consider? _____

_____

_____

A26. They might look for ways to reduce cost or consider a small increase in selling price.

27. Let's go back and review the overall budget process in Figure 26-2. The four budgets which are based upon the sales budget are

_____,

_____,

_____,

and _____.

A27. cash forecast, production budget, general and administrative expense budget, selling expense budget

28. The three budgets which are based on the production are _____,

_____ and

_____.

A28. direct labor budget, materials budget, manufacturing overhead budget

B. Responsibility Accounting. A natural outgrowth of the budget process is responsibility accounting.

1. Does responsibility accounting require additional accounts in the accounting system?

_____ Explain. _____

_____

_____

_____

_____

B1.   Yes. The existing accounts must be subdivided to collect information at the lowest level of management responsibility desired by the company.

2.   Would budgets also be subdivided? _____
Explain. _____
_____
_____
_____

B2.   Yes. Budgets would be prepared in detail down to the lowest level of management responsibility decided on by the company.

3.   What advantage does this subdivision of budget and accounting data bring to a firm? _____
_____
_____
_____
_____

B3.   Managers at several levels of responsibility will have reports of planned performance compared with actual performance.

4.   If actual performance in a division or department is at variance with the budget plan, the responsible manager should _____
_____
_____.

B4.   explain the reasons and take corrective action where necessary

5.   The budget to which actual performance is compared should be a budget adjusted to
_____
_____.

B5.   the level of production actually attained

6.   This type of budget is called a _____
_____.

B6.   flexible budget

C.   *Flexible Budget*

1.   A flexible budget is a series of budgets adjusted to _____
_____.

C1.   various levels of operation

2.   If total volume of production activity increases, total variable costs are expected to _____ (increase/decrease).

C2.   increase

C3.   remain the same

C4.   variable

C5.   1,000

C6.   945, 90, 1,050, 100

C7.   Because the fixed
      costs are not
      reduced.

C8.   261 = ($300 x .87)

C9.   1,913.50 = [($1,050 x
      .87) + $1,000]

C10. 93

C11. 300

C12. variable

3.   If total volume of production increases, total fixed costs are expected to _____ _____.

4.   Accordingly, to adjust a budget to different levels of production requires an adjustment of _____ costs.

5.   Figure 26-12 shows a flexible budget for Upstate Manufacturing Company at four possible production levels. At each level the fixed costs are $_____.

6.   Total variable costs of $_____ at the 90 percent level are _____ percent of the total variable costs of $_____ at the _____ percent level.

7.   However, total budgeted costs of $1,945 at the 90 percent level *are not* 90 percent of the total budget of $2,050 at the 100 percent level. Why not?_____

8.   Suppose the actual level of operations for the quarter ending June 30, 1985, at Upstate were 87 percent of the plan. The expected expenditure for factory supplies is $_____.

9.   The total budgeted costs at 87 percent would be $_____.

10. Figure 26-13 shows a performance report assuming that Upstate operated at _____ percent of the planned level.

11. The adjusted amount for factory supplies ($279) is 93 percent of the planned amount of $_____.

12. This item is adjusted because factory supplies is a _____ cost.

13. The total adjusted budget is not 93 percent of plan because _____ _____.

C 13.   fixed costs did
not change

14.   The performance report in Figure 26-13 is an example of responsibility accounting. In the variance column, U means that the variance is _____.

C 14.   unfavorable

15.   F means that the variance is _____.

C 15.   favorable

D.   *Direct Costing (Appendix 26.1)*

1.   Under direct costing, only the _____ manufacturing costs are assigned to the product as inventoriable costs.

D 1.   variable

2.   This would mean that cost of goods sold would be made up of only _____ costs.

D 2.   variable

3.   Fixed manufacturing costs would be deducted in the year they were incurred as a _____

_____.

D 3.   period expense

4.   Finished goods inventory would include only _____ manufacturing costs.

D 4.   variable

5.   In the direct costing income statement for William Woods Company (Figure A26-2), the cost of goods manufactured was equal to the _____ units produced times the $10 per unit _____ cost.

D 5.   20,000, variable

6.   In Figure A26-3, the ending inventory for May was determined by multiplying the _____ units in ending inventory by $_____, the _____ manufacturing cost per unit.

D 6.   3,000, 10,
variable

7.   Under absorption costing, Figure A26-4, the ending inventory included not only the $30,000 in variable manufacturing costs but also $_____ in fixed manufacturing costs.

D 7.   15,000

8.   Since 3,000 of the 20,000 units produced had not been sold, _____ of the $100,000 in fixed manufacturing costs were also included in ending inventory.

D8.   3/20

D9.   15,000

D10.   equal

D11.   15,000, fixed

D12.   lower

D13.   higher

D14.   No answer required.

E1.   volume, fixed,
      variable, profit

E2.   break-even

E3.   zero

9.   By comparing Figures A26-3 and A26-4, we can see that the difference in net income for May was $_____ .

10.   This was _____ to the fixed costs included in ending inventory under absorption costing.

11.   Note also the difference in net income for June was $_____ . This was equal to the _____ manufacturing costs in beginning inventory.

12.   In May when more units were produced than were sold, direct costing net income was _____ (lower/higher) than absorption costing.

13.   And in June when more units were sold than were produced, direct costing net income was

      _____ .

14.   This was because some of May's fixed manufacturing costs were included in ending inventory under absorption costing. Thus, they did not reduce May's income but did reduce June's income when they became a part of cost of goods sold.

E.   *Cost-Volume-Profit Analysis*

1.   Cost-volume-profit analysis allows the manager to ask questions such as: How will changes in _____ of sales, _____ costs, or _____ costs affect our _____ ?

2.   The simplest form of cost-volume-profit analysis is _____ .

3.   Break-even seeks to determine the volume of sales at which profits will be _____ .

4.   Profits will be zero when _____ costs are exactly equal to the total _____

      _____ .

E4.   fixed, contribution margin

5.   Thus, the volume of sales necessary to break even can be found by dividing the total _____ by the _____ _____ per unit.

E5.   fixed costs, contribution margin

6.   In the case of the William Woods Company, the selling price per unit was $_____ and the variable cost per unit was $_____.

E6.   30, 12

7.   Thus, the contribution margin would be $_____.

E7.   18 = ($30 - $12)

8.   The sales volume necessary to break even, 11,666 2/3, was then found by dividing $_____ by $_____.

E8.   210,000, 18

9.   In this case, it is impossible to produce a fractional unit, so the break-even volume would be stated as _____ units. This would actually give a slight profit of $6, an amount equal to the contribution margin on 1/3 of a unit.

E9.   11,667

10.   The break-even point in terms of a volume stated in sales dollars can be found by dividing the total fixed costs by the _____.

E10.   contribution margin percent

11.   The contribution margin percent is equal to the _____ divided by the _____.

E11.   contribution margin, selling price

12.   For the William Woods Company, this would be $_____ divided by $_____, or _____ percent.

E12.   18, 30, 60

13.   Calculating the break-even sales volume in dollars, $_____ divided by _____ gives a volume of $_____.

E13.   210,000, .60, 350,000

14.   Using the more extended model of cost-volume-profit analysis, _____ is introduced.

E14.   desired profit

15.   The model now becomes the sales volume necessary to earn a desired profit which is equal to _____ plus _____ divided by _____.

E15.   total fixed costs, desired profit, contribution margin

16.   So for William Woods Company to earn a profit of $100,000, they would have to sell _____ units.

E16.   17,222.222

17.   This was found by dividing $_____ plus the desired profit of $100,000 by $_____ .

E17.   210,000, 18

18.   The necessary sales volume in dollars could have been found by dividing the same numerator by _____ .

E18.   .60 (the contribution margin ratio)

19.   Cost-volume-profit analysis can also be used to solve all types of "what if" questions. For example, in the William Woods case, if the fixed costs were to increase by $36,000, what would happen to sales volume necessary to earn the desired profit of $100,000? _____

_____

_____

_____

_____

E19.   It would increase by 2,000 units. Fixed costs are now $246,000 and desired profit is $100,000. Dividing this by $18, gives 19,222.222.

SELF TEST OF LEARNING GOAL ACHIEVEMENT

1.   Indicate whether each of the following costs is more likely to be a fixed cost or a variable cost:

   a.   Direct labor. _____
   b.   Department supervisor's salary. _____
   c.   Materials used. _____
   d.   Building depreciation (straight line). _____
   e.   Machinery depreciation (production hours method). _____
   f.   Machinery depreciation (double-declining balance). _____
   g.   Property tax. _____
   h.   Oil for factory machinery. _____
   i.   Small tools used. _____
   j.   Transportation of products between departments. _____

2. Pass-A-Grille Beach Manufacturing Company has prepared a sales budget for 1986. Without referring to the textbook, complete this diagram of the budget structure.

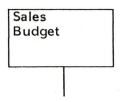

3. Palma Sola Company plans to sell 30,000 units of elpam in the first quarter of 1986 and 40,000 units in the second quarter. It is estimated that inventory on January 1, 1986, will be 3,000 units. It is company policy to end each quarter with 10 percent of the next quarter's sales on hand. How many units of elpam should they plan to produce in the first quarter of 1986?

4. Uni Company has found that 30 percent of its sales are made for cash, 25 percent more are collected in the month of sale, 40 percent in the month following sale, and 3 percent in the second month following sale. The remainder are never collected. Sales for the last quarter of 1985 were: October, $50,000; November, $52,000; December, $60,000. How much cash from sales should Uni expect to collect in December?

5. The manager of Department A had the following manufacturing overhead budget for October 1985:

Direct labor hours	2,000
Variable costs	$18,000
Fixed costs	20,000
Total costs	$38,000

The department was required to work 1,900 hours and experienced actual costs of $37,450. The production superintendent is pleased with the $550 cost savings. Is the happiness justified? Support your answer with computations.

6.   (Appendix 26.1) Umkc Company had no beginning inventory of finished goods on January 1, 1985. During 1985, they produced 30,000 and sold 28,000 at $30 each. Manufacturing costs for 1985 were as follows:

Materials	$150,000
Direct labor	240,000
Manufacturing Overhead	180,000
Selling expenses	60,000
Administrative expenses	80,000

Two-thirds of the manufacturing overhead was fixed, one-half of the selling expenses were fixed, and all of the administrative expenses were fixed. Prepare a direct costing and full absorption costing income statement.

6.   continued

6. continued

7. (Appendix 26.1) The Durango Company makes and sells a product with a selling price of $10 per unit and variable costs per unit of $6. Their anticipated fixed costs totaled $180,000.

    a. Compute the break-even point.

       In units:

       In dollars:

    b. If they desired to earn a profit of $80,000, what would be the necessary sales volume in units?

    c. If the fixed costs were to increase to $210,000, by how much would the volume change to continue to earn a profit of $80,000?

ANSWERS TO LEARNING GOAL ACHIEVEMENT TEST

1. a. Variable.   f. Fixed.
   b. Fixed.   g. Fixed.
   c. Variable.   h. Variable.
   d. Fixed.   i. Variable.
   e. Variable.   j. Variable.

2.

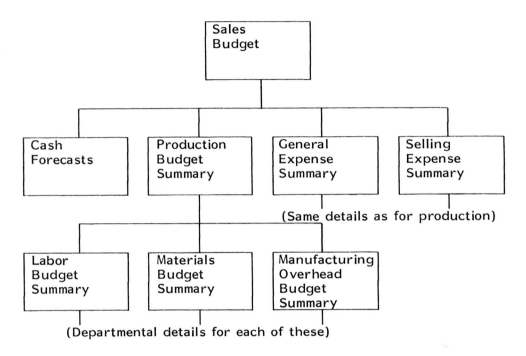

(Same details as for production)

(Departmental details for each of these)

3.

	Units
Required for sales	30,000
Required for ending inventory	4,000
Total required	34,000
Deduct January 1 inventory	3,000
Production requirements	31,000

4.

From December cash sales	$18,000
From December credit sales	15,000
From November sales	20,800
From October sales	1,500
Total December collections	$55,300

5. No. By adjusting the budget to the actual level of production achieved, it can be seen that the department should have incurred costs of $37,100. They have incurred costs of $37,450 or $350 more than was justified.

Adjusted budget:

Variable costs [($18,000 ÷ 2,000) x 1,900]	$17,100
Fixed costs (no change)	20,000
Adjusted budget	$37,100
Actual costs	37,450
Unfavorable variance	$ 350

6. Direct costing

UMKC COMPANY
Income Statement
For the Year Ended December 31, 1985

Sales		$840,000
Cost of goods sold:		
Finished goods inventory, January 1	$ 0	
Cost of goods manufactured	450,000	
	$450,000	
Finished goods inventory, December 31	30,000	420,000
Gross contribution margin		$420,000
Variable operating expenses:		
Selling		30,000
Contribution margin		$390,000
Fixed costs and expenses:		
Manufacturing	$120,000	
Selling	30,000	
Administrative	80,000	230,000
Net income		$160,000

Absorption

UMKC COMPANY
Income Statement
For the Year Ended December 31, 1985

Sales		$840,000
Cost of goods sold:		
Finished goods inventory, January 1	$ 0	
Cost of goods manufactured	570,000	
	$570,000	
Finished goods inventory, December 31	38,000	532,000
Gross margin		$308,000
Operating expenses:		
Selling	$ 60,000	
Administrative	80,000	140,000
Net income		$168,000

7. a.   In units:

$180,000 ÷ ($10 - $6) = 45,000 units

   In dollars:

$180,000 ÷ (.40) = $450,000

   b.   ($180,000 + $80,000) ÷ $4 = 65,000 units

   c.   ($210,000 + $80,000) ÷ $4 = 72,500 units
72,500 units - 65,000 units = 7,500 unit increase

Chapter 27
Standard Cost Accounting

■■

EXPLANATION OF MAJOR CONCEPTS

Standard Costs

A *standard* is what something ought to be under a given set of circumstances. If
a student is expected to complete a test in one hour, then one hour is the standard
time for that test. If he or she is expected to write the answers on four pages,
then four pages is the standard quantity of paper for the test. If the instructor
has made the test so that a good student should answer correctly 8 out of 10 questions on the test, the standard for performance is 80 percent. The student may
finish the test in fifty minutes (a *favorable variance* from the standard time quantity).

In production operations, standards are determined by engineering studies on
the jobs to be performed. Then standards can be established for costs of materials, labor, and overhead. Standards can also be established for usage of materials
and labor and amount of overhead applied. There is no set of standards that will
suit all companies. Each company must study its own operations and set its own
standards. For example, a set of standards for the production of one unit of
product might appear as follows:

> Materials:
>   2 pounds of material at $3.50 per pound
> Labor:
>   3 hours of direct labor at $8.00 per hour
> Manufacturing Overhead:
>   3 hours of direct labor at $12.00 per hour

Notice that for materials and labor there is a quantity of input which should be
used and an amount that should be paid for each unit of material or labor.
Also, note that when manufacturing overhead is being applied based on direct
labor, the quantity (number of direct labor hours) is the same as for direct
labor. The price per labor hour is different because it is an application rate
not a pay rate.

In production operations, the engineering studies lead to establishment of a
set of standards for each unit of product. These are set forth on a *standard
cost card* (or a *specification*) for each product. Costs can then be recorded

in the accounts at standard cost--that is, Work-in-Process Inventory and Finished Goods Inventory are debited with what costs ought to be. The deviations from standard cost are recorded in variance accounts. Management can look for the causes of variance from standard and take action to correct the cause if necessary.

Computation of Variances

A *variance* is a deviation from standard. For materials and labor, variances tend to match the type of standard. Because each has (1) a price standard and (2) a quantity standard, it follows that there would be a price and a quantity variance for each. Variances are either favorable or unfavorable. For example, an *unfavorable* materials purchase price variance would indicate that the price paid for materials is greater than the standard. A *favorable* materials purchase price variance indicates that the price paid for materials is less than the standard price. The following summary of variances and their meanings and calculations are given to help you see the overall picture:

Materials

The *purchase price variance* is caused by paying more or less than the standard price when materials are purchased.

(actual quantity x actual price) - (actual quantity x standard price)

OR

(actual price - standard price) x actual quantity

The *quantity variance* is caused by using more or less than the standard quantity for the equivalent units of product produced.

(actual quantity x standard price) - (standard quantity x standard price)

OR

(actual quantity - standard quantity) x standard price

Labor

The *wage rate variance* is caused by paying a higher or lower pay rate for labor than the standard wage rate.

(actual hours x actual rate) - (actual hours x standard rate)

OR

(actual rate - standard rate) x actual hours

The *labor efficiency variance* is caused by using more or less than the standard number of direct labor hours for the equivalent units of product produced.

(actual hours x standard rate) - (standard hours x standard rate)

OR

(actual hours - standard hours) x standard rate

Manufacturing Overhead

The *controllable variance* is caused by incurring actual manufacturing over-head costs greater or less than costs that would be allowed by a budget adjusted to the equivalent units produced (remember the flexible budget adjustment that was presented in Chapter 26).

> Budget adjusted to standard hours for
> production attained:
>   Fixed costs (per budget)
>   Variable costs (standard hours x
>   standard rate)
> Less: Actual overhead costs incurred

The *volume variance* is caused by applying more or less than the actual fixed overhead costs by working at a level below or above the planned level of operations that was used in establishing the standard overhead application rate.

> Applied overhead (standard hours x
>   standard rate)
> Less: Budget adjusted to standard
>   hours for production attained

Recording the Variances

Only standard costs are recorded in the Materials Inventory, Work-in-Process Inventory, and Finished Goods Inventory accounts. To record the variances, we establish six variance accounts--one for each type of variance. An unfavor-able variance is a debit to the variance account; a favorable variance is a credit. By looking at the balances in variance accounts, management can tell at a glance which costs are different from standard, in which direction, and by how much. *This is the primary purpose of standard cost accounting.* The variance account balances are closed at the end of an accounting period--usually into Cost of Goods Sold.

GUIDED STUDY OF THIS CHAPTER

A. *Let's concentrate on the Megware Specialty Company illustration to begin our study.*

1. This company makes a product that passes through several departments. The first department is _____.

A1. Casting

2. In each department, there will be labor and overhead costs; in most, there will be some materials costs. In the Casting Department, the material used is _____.

A2.   clay

A3.   2 ounces (or 1/8 pound)

A4.   0.40

A5.   240 ounces or (15 pounds)

A6.   2, 1/30

A7.   12

A8.   240 minutes (or 4 hours)

A9.   3.60

A10. 14.40 (4 hours at $3.60)

A11. 0.57

A12. 68.40 = ($0.57 x 120)

A13. 6.00

A14. 12.00, 48.00

A15. 3.60, 14.40

A16. 6.00, 48.00, 14.40, 68.40

---

3.   The standard quantity for one mug is _____ _____ of clay.

4.   The standard price of clay is $_____ per pound.

5.   If 120 mugs are cast, the department ought to use _____ of clay.

6.   The standard quantity of direct labor is _____ minutes or _____ hours.

7.   The standard rate of pay per direct labor hour is $_____ per hour.

8.   If 120 mugs are cast, the amount of direct labor used ought to be _____.

9.   The standard overhead rate for the Casting Department is $_____ per direct labor hour.

10. If 120 mugs are cast, the amount of overhead applied ought to be $_____.

11. Note that Figure 27-1 translates these standards into a standard cost of $_____ per mug in Casting.

12. If 120 mugs are cast, their total cost ought to be $_____.

13. This amount can be divided into various cost elements. The materials cost for 120 mugs ought to be $_____.

14. The labor cost to cast 120 mugs should be 4 hours x $_____ = $_____.

15. The overhead applied should be 4 hours x $_____ = $_____.

16. So the total cost is $_____ + $_____ + $_____ = $_____.

17. Is this the same answer as we had in A12? _____

A17.   Yes.

18.   Deviations from the quantities that ought to be used or the prices that ought to be paid are called _____.

A18.   variances

19.   In the next section, we will compute some variances.

A19.   No answer required.

B.   *Variances*

1.   Figure 27-2 contains information on Megware Specialty Company's actual performance for the month of _____ 1985.

B1.   May

2.   In addition to the information in Figure 27-2, we know that the Purchasing Department bought _____ pounds of clay at $_____ per pound.

B2.   80,000, 0.39

3.   As indicated in footnote 2, there are two ways to recognize a materials price variance. When it is recognized at the time of purchase (as it is in the textbook), it is called a materials purchase price variance. This method causes materials to be carried in the Materials Inventory account at standard price.

B3.   No answer required.

4.   Megware purchased _____ pounds of clay at $_____ per pound = $_____.

B4.   80,000, 0.39, 31,200

5.   The standard cost of 80,000 pounds of clay ought to be the standard price of $_____ per pound x 80,000 = $_____.

B5.   0.40, 32,000

6.   The variance is $32,000 - $31,200 = $800, and it is _____ (favorable/unfavorable).

B6.   favorable

7.   The purchase of clay at $0.39 instead of the standard price of $0.40 = a saving of $_____ per pound.

B7.   0.01

8.   Another way to compute this variance is 80,000 pounds x $_____ = $_____.

B8.   0.01, 800

9.   Production (per Figure 27-2) was _____ mugs in May.

B9.   612,000

10. At a standard quantity of 1/8 pound per mug, the Casting Department should use 1/8 x 612,000 = _____ pounds of clay.

B10.   76,500

11. At standard cost, the cost of clay used should be 76,500 pounds x $0.40 = $_____ .

B11.   30,600

12. Actual usage was _____ pounds at $0.40 = $_____ .

B12.   76,800, 30,720

13. Actual usage at standard of $30,720 – standard cost of $30,600 = $_____ which is a(n) _____ (favorable/unfavorable) variance.

B13.   120, unfavorable

14. The materials quantity variance is unfavorable because the department used an excess of _____ pounds of clay at $0.40 = $_____ .

B14.   300, 120

15. Megware actually used _____ hours of direct labor and paid $_____ per direct labor hour for a total direct labor cost of $_____ .

B15.   20,350, 12.10, 246,235

16. The standard cost of actual direct labor hours used should have been 20,350 x $_____ = $_____ .

B16.   12.00, 244,200

17. Thus, they paid $_____ too much for labor or had an _____ wage rate variance.

B17.   2,035, unfavorable

18. To produce 612,000 mugs, Megware should have used _____ direct labor hours.

B18.   20,400

19. The standard hours allowed should have cost them $_____ .

B19.   244,800 = (20,400 x $12)

20. At the standard rate, the actual hours of direct labor used would have cost $_____ .

B20.   244,200 = (20,350 x $12)

21. The difference of $_____ is called the labor _____ variance.

B21.   600, efficiency

22. The labor efficiency variance was _____ because they used _____ direct labor hours less than they should have used.

B22.   favorable, 50

23. The Casting Department's manufacturing overhead rate is $_____ per direct labor hour.

B23. 3.60

24. This rate is applied to _____ (actual/standard) hours.

B24. standard

25. This is a crucial point. In a standard cost system, manufacturing overhead is applied on *standard* hours; not on actual. The standard hours for 612,000 mugs is a total of _____ hours.

B25. 20,400

26. Manufacturing overhead applied is 20,400 standard hours x $3.60 = $_____.

B26. 73,440

27. Actual overhead costs (Figure 27-2) were $_____.

B27. 73,100

28. The difference is the standard overhead cost of $_____ – the actual cost of $_____ = $_____.

B28. 73,440, 73,100, 340

29. Because the standard cost is greater than actual, the overhead is _____ (overapplied/underapplied).

B29. overapplied

30. To determine the reason for this total favorable variance, we must analyze it. This means to break it down into smaller elements and study them. There are several ways to do this; this textbook uses a two-variance analysis.

B30. No answer required.

31. The two elements we will use are called the _____ variance and the _____ variance.

B31. controllable, volume

32. The first step is to adjust the budget just as we have done in flexible budgeting. However, we will adjust it to _____ (standard/actual) hours.

B32. standard

33. *Go through this step carefully*. The variable costs in the manufacturing overhead budget for May were $_____.

B33. 54,000

34. The total of direct labor hours planned for May (and used to establish the $3.60 rate) was _____ hours.

B34. 20,000

35. Variable budgeted costs of $54,000 ÷ 20,000 hours = $_____, which is the *variable* element of the total overhead rate.

B 35. 2.70

36. Standard hours for the production attained (612,000 mugs) were _____ hours.

B 36. 20,400

37. 20,400 standard hours x the $2.70 variable element of the rate means that variable costs ought to have been $_____.

B 37. 55,080

38. Fixed costs are not expected to change, so they should be $_____.

B 38. 18,000

39. $55,080 + $18,000 = the overhead budget adjusted to standard = $_____.

B 39. 73,080

40. Actual total overhead costs (Figure 27-2) were $_____.

B 40. 73,100

41. Actual costs were greater than the budget adjusted to standard by $_____, a(n) _____ (favorable/ unfavorable) variance.

B 41. 20, unfavorable

42. Compare the same adjusted budget of $_____ to $_____ of applied overhead. The difference is $_____.

B 42. 73,080, 73,440, 360

43. This variance is _____ (favorable/ unfavorable) because the amount applied was greater than the adjusted budget.

B 43. favorable

44. An unfavorable _____ variance of $20 resulted from overspending.

B 44. controllable

45. A favorable _____ variance of $360 resulted from applying fixed costs for a standard of 20,400 hours instead of the budgeted 20,000 hours.

B 45. volume

46. The fixed element of the total overhead rate was fixed costs of $18,000 ÷ 20,000 budgeted hours = $_____ per direct labor hour.

B 46. 0.90

47. The 400 excess hours (20,400 standard – 20,000 budgeted) x $0.90 = $_____ applied in excess of the budget.

B 47. 360

48. The total overhead variance was $340 _____ (favorable/unfavorable), designated by (F).

B48. favorable

49. The controllable variance of $20(U) + the volume variance of $360(F) explains the total of $_____(F).

B49. 340

C. *Journal Entries. The journal entries are made at the end of the month. They are separated in textbook Figures 27-5, -6, -7, -8, -9, -10, and -11 so you can match them with their underlying reasons.*

1. In each case, Work-in-Process Inventory is debited with _____ (standard/actual) costs.

C1. standard

2. All variances are journalized to the _____ accounts.

C2. variance

3. Each unfavorable variance is a _____ (debit/credit).

C3. debit

4. Each favorable variance is a _____ (debit/credit).

C4. credit

5. In Figure 27-5 when 80,000 pounds of materials are purchased, they are debited to the Materials Inventory account at their standard price per unit of $_____ or a total of $_____.

C5. 0.40, 32,000

6. The actual cost of $_____ was credited to _____.

C6. 31,200, Accounts Payable

7. The difference or variance is _____ to the _____ account since it was favorable.

C7. credited, Materials Purchase Price Variance

8. When the materials are issued, the standard cost of the quantity of materials that should have been used is _____ to _____.

C8. debited, Work-in-Process Inventory-- Casting

9. And the standard cost of the actual quantity of materials used is _____ to _____.

C9.   credited, Materials
      Inventory

10.   Trace through the remaining journal entries in
      Figures 27-7, -8, -9, and -10. Note that in
      each one the debit to Work-in-Process Inven-
      tory--Casting is for the _____ cost
      of standard usage allowed for actual produc-
      tion.

C10. standard

11.   The mugs completed in Casting are debited to
      the next process at _____ cost
      (Figure 27-11).

C11. standard

12.   Test this: _____ mugs completed at
      $_____ standard cost per mug =
      $_____.

C12. 612,000, 0.57,
      348,840

13.   In Figure 27-11 the next process is the
      _____ process.

C13. First Kiln

14.   And the debit to Work-in-Process--First Kiln
      was $_____.

C14. 348,840

D.   *Marketing Costs. Marketing costs illustrates
      the use of variance analysis in departments
      other than production departments.*

1.   Instead of computing a manufacturing overhead
      rate, we compute a _____ rate.

D1.   charging

2.   Does the Delivery Department at Megware
      Specialty Company have both fixed and
      variable costs? _____

D2.   Yes.

3.   The Delivery Department budget is $_____
      for May, and its supervisor plans to use
      _____ labor hours.

D3.   13,000, 800

4. $13,000 ÷ 800 hours = $_____ per labor
      hour = the _____ rate.

D4.   16.25, charging

5.   To evaluate the department's performance, we
      can make a _____-variance analysis in the
      same manner as we did for manufacturing
      overhead.

D5.   two

6.   During May, the Delivery Department actually
      delivered _____ mugs and used
      _____ labor hours.

D6. 481,250, 780

7. The standard hours for delivering 481,250 mugs would be _____ .

D7. 770 = (481,250 ÷ 625)

8. The standard cost for 770 hours would be $_____ .

D8. 12,512.50

9. Since the actual cost for May was $_____ , they have spent $_____ more than they should have.

D9. 12,770.00, 257.50

10. This variance can be broken down into a controllable and a volume variance. The controllable variance would be found by subtracting the budget adjusted to _____ _____ for production attained.

D10. standard hours

11. The budget adjusted to standard hours for production attained would be fixed expenses of $_____ plus variable expenses of _____ labor hours times $_____ charging rate, for a total of $_____ .

D11. 3,000, 770,
     12.50, 12,625

12. Thus, the controllable variance would be $_____ minus $_____ or $_____ unfavorable.

D12. 12,770, 12,625, 145

13. The volume variance would be the budget adjusted to standard hours, $_____ minus the standard amount charged _____ labor hours times $_____ charging rate or $_____ .

D13. 12,625, 770,
     16.50, 12,512.50

14. Thus, the volume variance would be $_____ _____ (favorable/unfavorable).

D14. 112.50, unfavorable

15. Could this type of variance analysis be done with other costs--say, for the Billing Department? _____

D15. Yes.

16. To do so, we would need to know the total planned (budgeted) costs for the Billing Department and a standard that could be expressed in terms of _____ hours per invoice typed.

D16. direct labor

17. We would also need to know the total _____ planned for the month.

D17. invoices (or
workload)

18. We would then develop a _____
rate and use it to evaluate the Billing Department's performance.

D18. charging

19. Note how important to these analyses the flexible budget becomes. Understanding that concept is the key to many analyses made to
evaluate performance.

D19. No answer required.

SELF TEST OF LEARNING GOAL ACHIEVEMENT

1. The following apply to standards and standard costs in general:

   a. A standard is _____.
   b. Standard usage for labor and materials is usually developed by
      _____.
   c. Standard prices for materials are usually dependent on _____
      _____.
   d. Standard labor rates are developed by _____
      _____.
   e. The overhead standard rate can be developed from a predetermined
      _____.
   f. Manufacturing overhead costs are composed of fixed costs and
      _____ costs.
   g. Flexible budgeting requires the ability to adjust _____
      costs to an actual or a standard level of activity.
   h. In the two-variance analysis of overhead, the budgeted variable costs
      are adjusted to _____ (actual/standard).
   i. The fixed costs are adjusted to _____.

2. Following are data for the Treetop Birdhouse Company for July 1985:

   Standard cost specification for one birdhouse:
   Materials: 2 feet at $0.30 . . . . $0.60
   Labor: 1/4 hour at $10.00 . . . .   2.50
   Overhead (1/2 fixed, 1/2 variable) at $4 per
   direct labor hour 1.00
   Actual performance in July (budget was to
   produce 100,000 birdhouses):
   Birdhouses produced   100,000
   Materials purchased (220,000 feet at $0.31) . . . . $ 68,200
   Materials used (199,600 feet at $0.30)   59,880
   Labor used (25,150 hours at $9.90)   248,985
   Overhead costs:
   Fixed   50,000
   Variable   50,300

Required: Compute the following variances:

        a. Materials purchase price.
        b. Materials quantity.
        c. Wage rate.
        d. Labor efficiency.
        e. Overhead controllable.
        f. Overhead volume.

3.   Check your answers to Question 2, then make general journal entries for:

    a.   Purchase of materials.
    b.   Issuance of materials to production.
    c.   Payment of direct labor (ignore all taxes).
    d.   Charging direct labor to production.
    e.   Recording overhead costs (credit "Various Accounts").
    f.   Applying overhead to production.
    g.   Transfer of completed birdhouses to finished goods storeroom.

GENERAL JOURNAL

Date	Account Titles and Explanation	F	Debit	Credit

ANSWERS TO LEARNING GOAL ACHIEVEMENT TEST

1. a. what something ought to be
    b. engineering studies
    c. the market price
    d. negotiations or the union rate
    e. budget
    f. variable
    g. variable
    h. standard
    i. They do not change.

2. a. 220,000 feet x $0.30 (standard) . . . . $ 66,000
        220,000 feet x $0.31 (actual)   68,200
        Materials purchase price variance . . . . . $ (2,200)(U)

    b. 100,000 x 2 x $0.30 (standard) . . . . $ 60,000
        199,600 x $0.30 (actual).   59,880
        Materials quantity variance . . . . $ 120(F)

    c. 25,150 x $10 (at standard rate) $251,500
        25,150 x $9.90 (at actual rate)   248,985
        Wage rate variance . . . . $ 2,515(F)

    d. 100,000 x 1/4 x $10 . . . . $250,000
        25,150 x $10 (actual)   251,500
        Labor efficiency variance . . . . $ 1,500(U)

    e. Actual overhead costs. $100,300
        Adjusted budget:
          Fixed costs $50,000
          Variable costs (25,000 x $2).   50,000   100,000
            Overhead controllable variance . . . . . $ 300(U)

    f. Adjusted budget $100,000
        Applied overhead (25,000 x $4)   100,000
        Overhead volume variance . . . . $ 0

3.

GENERAL JOURNAL

Date		Account Titles and Explanation	F	Debit	Credit
1985		(a)			
Jul.	31	Materials Inventory		66,000	
		Materials Purchase Price Variance		2,200	
		Accounts Payable			68,200
		(b)			
	31	Work-in-Process Inventory		60,000	
		Materials Inventory			59,880
		Materials Quantity Variance			120
		(c)			
	31	Factory Payroll		248,985	
		Cash			248,985
		(d)			
	31	Work-in-Process Inventory		250,000	
		Labor Efficiency Variance		1,500	
		Wage Rate Variance			2,515
		Factory Payroll			248,985
		(e)			
	31	Manufacturing Overhead Control		100,300	
		"Various Accounts"			100,300
		(f)			
	31	Work-in-Process Inventory		100,000	
		Overhead Controllable Variance		300	
		Manufacturing Overhead Control			100,300
		(g)			
	31	Finished Goods Inventory		410,000	
		Work-in-Process Inventory			410,000

Chapter 28
Using Cost Information for Management Decisions

■■■

EXPLANATION OF MAJOR CONCEPTS

Cost Concepts

Seven basic cost concepts were used in the chapter. A summary review of each follows:

Fixed cost--a cost which is constant in total as volume changes. Thus, the per unit amount will change as volume changes.

Variable cost--a cost which is constant on a per unit basis and whose total changes proportionally to changes in volume.

Semivariable cost--a cost that includes both fixed and variable components.

Differential cost--a cost that is different between two alternative courses of action.

Opportunity cost--the benefit given up by not following a course of action.

Out-of-pocket cost--a cost that requires an expenditure.

Sunk cost--a cost that has already been incurred and which cannot be avoided by some future action.

Managerial Decisions Based on Cost Analysis

Some decisions related to production and sales are:

- ▶ Pricing of special orders.
- ▶ Make or buy situations.
- ▶ Discontinuance or abandonment of products, territories, or departments.

In the pricing of special orders, the revenue to be generated by the special order should be compared to the differential (or incremental) cost of the special order. If the company is currently operating below capacity, differential cost may be equal to variable cost, although some fixed costs may even be different under the special order. If a fixed cost were to change, it would have to be added to the differential cost. As was shown in the text example, it is often safest to compare the total added revenue with the total differential cost. In that way, there will be less of a tendency to use irrelevant cost data.

When a manager is faced with the decision of making a part or buying it, differential cost is again the relevant cost to the decision. The differential cost of making the part should be compared to the cost of buying. Another type of cost may come up in this type of decision, what will we do with the productive facilities that are idled if we buy the part. If these facilities will just set idle, they do not come into the decision. But, if they can be rented out or otherwise used, the revenues given up by using them to make the part would be an opportunity cost.

In the decision on the abandonment of a segment of the business, the contribution margin given up by abandoning the segment is the relevant amount to be considered. If the lost contribution margin is greater than zero, the segment should not be abandoned as the companies total profit will decrease by dropping the segment. This basic "rule of thumb" assumes that nothing else can be done with the facilities used by the segment. If alternatives exist, the opportunity costs of these alternatives would have to be considered. Also, if the segment producing a loss is related closely to a profitable segment, we may continue to operate a losing segment even when the calculation indicates otherwise.

Most decisions about such situations hinge on differential costs. Although it is not always the case, it is usually variable (and not fixed) costs that hold the key to a decision. Accordingly, it is important to a business to determine as accurately as possible what its variable costs are.

Each decision presents a special situation, of course. When the added revenues of an action are greater than its differential cost, it is profitable. If there is a change in fixed cost, that change must carefully be considered. The important point is to recognize that choices must be made based upon costs that *will be changed* by the choice and not based upon historical profit and cost data.

Capital Budgeting

Each firm has a limited amount of funds to spend on capital projects. *Capital budgeting decisions,* therefore, involve choices of the most profitable projects in which to invest. Three methods were illustrated in the chapter.

Payback--a measure of the time required for the cash inflows from the project to accumulate to an amount equal to the cost of the investment.

Accounting Rate of Return--the rate of profitability which an investment project will have.

Excess Present Value--a method that compares the present value of the cash outflows from the project with the present value of the cash inflows.

You should recognize that all of them involve estimates. Even the *payback* method, with its simplicity, requires an estimate of the additional cash inflows that a project will generate. In theory, the best method of comparing capital expenditure products is the *present value method,* but it has several weaknesses. We must estimate three elements: the cash flows, how many years those flows will continue, and the proper rate of return (or interest). To the degree that such estimates are correct, the present value method is best. However, you should note carefully that these pieces of information are estimates of future possibilities-- not past facts.

GUIDED STUDY OF THIS CHAPTER

A. *Cost Concepts. Several of the cost behavior patterns which were studied in earlier chapters are important to managerial decision making. These were reviewed in this chapter.*

1. A cost which remains constant on a per unit basis as volume changes is a _____ cost.

A1. variable

2. A cost whose total changes proportionally to changes in volume is a _____ cost.

A2. variable

3. A cost which remains constant in total as volume changes is a _____ cost.

A3. fixed

4. If a cost remains constant in total as volume changes, the per unit cost must _____ as volume changes.

A4. change

5. A cost which is different under two alternative courses of action or at two different levels of output is termed a _____ cost.

A5. differential

6. The benefit given up by foregoing an alternative is termed an _____ cost.

A6. opportunity

7. A cost which has already been incurred and cannot be avoided by a future course of action is known as a _____ cost.

A7. sunk

8. Costs which will require a direct expenditure are called _____ costs.

A8. out-of-pocket

9. When a manager is faced with a decision, the costs that will be relevant to making the decision are those that will be _____ between the alternatives available.

A9.   different

B1.   75

B2.   20,000

B3.   9

B4.   6.

B5.   are not

B6.   6.00, 0.05, 5.95

B7.   2.55

B8.   51,000.

B9.   No answer required.

B.   Production Decisions

1.   An example of the role of variable costs is the pricing of special orders. The Lane Company is producing at _____ percent of capacity.

2.   It could produce _____ more units of product at 100 percent of capacity.

3.   Since Lane's present unit cost of production is $_____, it would appear unwise to accept an order to produce an additional 20,000 units at $8.50.

4.   How much of the $9 unit cost is variable cost? $_____

5.   Since their plant can move to 100 percent production without an increase in fixed costs, the fixed costs _____ (are/are not) relevant to the decision.

6.   The costs that are relevant are those that will change as a result of accepting the special order. In this case, the relevant costs are the variable costs of $_____ per unit less the $_____ cost of the label that will not be required, or $_____.

7.   This special order will generate additional profits of $_____ per unit.

8.   Therefore, it should be accepted. Suppose, however, that additional fixed costs would be required. What is the level of additional fixed costs at which Lane would have to reject the offer? $_____

9.   So, fixed costs are part of the decision *if they will change* upon acceptance of a special order.

10.   Make or buy decisions include fixed costs if they are *sunk costs*. Sunk costs are costs that _____

_____

_____

_____.

B 10. can be recovered
only by using the
object of cost for
its intended purpose

11. In the Nivals Company illustration, an opportunity arises to purchase a part for $_____
less than it is costing the company to make it.

B 11. 2.25

12. But $_____ of Nivals Company's unit cost
to make the part is fixed overhead that might
continue if the company stops making the part.

B 12. 4.80

13. In other words, $4.80 might be a _____
cost.

B 13. sunk

14. If the overhead is a sunk cost, the real cost to
buy the part would be $18.15 + $4.80 =
$_____.

B 14. 22.95

15. In this case, the better decision would be to

_____.

B 15. continue to make the
part

16. If the Nivals Company could make alternative
use of the facilities idled by buying the part,
an _____ cost would be
involved in the decision.

B 16. opportunity

17. It is costing Nivals $20.40 to make 10,000 parts
and it would cost $22.95 to buy the part. If
they could earn more than $22.95 minus $20.40
times 10,000, or $_____, by some alter-
native use of the facilities, they should _____
the part and use the idled facilities for the
alternative.

B 17. 25,500, buy

18. In the chapter illustration when Lani Pau
agreed to pay $_____ to rent the facili-
ties, it was more profitable to buy the part and
rent to Lani Pau.

B 18. 40,000

19. But, when Lani Pau only agreed to pay $20,000,
it _____ (was/was not) more prof-
itable to buy.

B 19. was not

20. This is because the $20,000 was less than the
$25,500 which we calculated in B 17.

B 20. No answer required.

21. Discontinuance of a product, department, or
territory also depends upon the types of cost
involved. In Figure 28-1, the Children's
Department of Muskegon Clothing Company
had a loss of $_____ in December 1985.

B21. 202

22. From the regular income statement (Figure 28-1), it appears that the Children's Department should be _____ (retained/discontinued).

B22. discontinued

23. By using a contribution margin format income statement (Figure 28-2), it can be seen that the Children's Department is producing a contribution margin of $_____.

B23. 1,658

24. If the Children's Department were eliminated, the $_____ would be lost by Muskegon Clothing.

B24. 1,658

25. Assuming no alternative use of the space now occupied by the children's department, the _____ costs would continue to be incurred.

B25. fixed

26. Therefore, in making the decision, the relevant cost would be the contribution margin that would be lost by dropping the department.

B26. No answer required.

27. Since the contribution margin that would be lost is greater than $_____, the department should be continued, because it is covering some of the fixed costs that will continue.

B27. 0 (zero)

28. If they did drop the Children's Department, the net income of the whole company would drop from $7,772.50 to $_____.

B28. 6,114.50

29. As in other decisions, this illustration assumes that a more profitable use cannot be made of the space now being used by the Children's Department. This assumption may not be correct and should be carefully investigated.

B29. No answer required.

C. *Capital Budgeting*

1. Capital budgeting refers to commitment of funds to _____ investment projects.

C1. long-term

2. All capital budgeting decisions require certain estimates. Probably the estimate that can be made most accurately is the _____

_____.

C2. cost of the project

3. A more difficult estimate to make that is required in all capital budgeting decisions is the amount of _____ that projects will bring.

C3. cash inflows

4. Cash inflows may be in the form of increases in cash coming in or in the form of _____

_____ .

C4. decreases in costs

5. The payback method requires only those two estimates. By dividing annual inflows into _____ , we can determine the number of years it will take to pay back the project cost.

C5. investment cost

6. The payback method is popular because it is simple. But it ignores _____

_____

_____ .

C6. the value of cash flows after the payback period

7. The accounting rate of return does consider the cash flows after the payback period, but it requires an additional estimate to be made. What is it? _____

_____

C7. The estimated useful life of the project.

8. When the accounting rate of return is computed for several projects, one would normally choose the one offering the _____

_____ .

C8. greatest return rate

9. A factor not included in the accounting rate of return is the _____ of money.

C9. time value

10. The time value of money and compound interest techniques are covered thoroughly in the Appendix to Part Three. An understanding of those concepts is essential to an understanding of the present value method (discounted cash flows).

C10. No answer required.

11. An annual cash inflow from a capital investment is, in effect, an annuity. The cash inflows are like annuity withdrawals. The investment required to produce those cash inflows is the _____ .

C11. present value

12. To compute the present value, we must use an annual interest rate. This is another estimate. Each firm must decide the proper rate of interest its investments should earn. In the textbook illustration, the East Company feels that _____ percent compounded semiannually is the amount it should earn.

C12. 14

13. A capital investment is desirable if *the present value of the cash inflows* it will bring is greater that the _____ of the investment.

C13. cost

14. East Company is contemplating the purchase of a new press. The net investment in the new press would be equal to the _____ _____ of the new press plus _____ _____ minus the _____ from the sale of the old press.

C14. purchase price, freight and installa- tion, proceeds

15. In the illustration, the net investment was $_____ .

C15. 22,500

16. If the present value of the cash _____ is _____ than $22,500, the new press would be a desirable investment.

C16. inflows, greater

17. It is estimated that costs will decrease by $_____ from use of the new press, but that power will increase by $_____ , for a net annual savings of $_____ .

C17. 5,500, 1,000, 4,500

18. East Company has a cost of money equal to _____ percent.

C18. 14

19. The cost of money to the company should be used as the _____ rate to calcu- late the present value of the cash inflows.

C19. discount

20. Since the $4,500 savings will occur each year for 10 years, the present value of an _____ table should be used.

C20. ordinary annuity

21. The present value of the cash inflows was $_____ .

C21. 24,551.50

22. Since this is _____ than the net investment, the new press _____ (is/is not) a desirable alternative.

C22. greater, is

23. If East Company has more than one capital project that shows an excess present value (making all desirable), it can rank them in order of desirability by computing a _____ _____ for each.

C23. profitability index

24. A profitability index is the ratio of the _____ of the cash inflows to the _____ of the investment.

C24. present value, present value

25. Since the numerator of the fraction is the present value of the inflows, an index of less than 1 indicates that cost is _____ (greater/less) than present value.

C25. greater

26. Therefore, the investment is _____ (desirable/undesirable).

C26. undesirable

27. Any index greater than _____ would be a desirable investment.

C27. 1

28. A higher index indicates a _____ (more/less) desirable investment.

C28. more

29. Remember that the present value method depends on an estimate of the proper interest rate. Other estimates also required are _____ _____.

C29. net cash inflows and useful life

30. Several of the formulas used for decision making are summarized at the end of this chapter. It is important that you follow each one through carefully and understand it. Trying to memorize them is not as useful to you when you are trying to apply them to problems.

C30. No answer required.

SELF TEST OF LEARNING GOAL ACHIEVEMENT

1. What type of cost is being described in each of the following?

    a. The cost of imprinting the company name on office forms. _____

    _____

    b. The lost rental value of an apartment that the owner of the building uses as an office instead of renting it. _____

    c. A monthly salary paid to the production supervisor that does not change if the level of production changes. _____

    d. Wages paid to the production workers based on the number of units that they produce. _____

    e. The cost of a monthly maintenance contract to keep a computer system in operation; the contract can be cancelled at any time. _____

    _____

2. Steinberg Company's product has a unit sales price of $60.   The company computes costs and profit per unit as follows:

Fixed costs	$14
Variable costs	36
Profit	10
Selling price	$60

    The company has received an offer from a foreign firm to purchase 100,000 units at a price of $50. Although the company has the capacity to produce these additional units without changing fixed costs and current sales would not be affected, the sales manager proposes to reject the offer because a $50 selling price leaves no profit. Is rejection a good decision? _____ Show computations.

3. Capital Company has a proposal to invest $36,000 in a machine that would return $2,000 quarterly for the next ten years. At the end of ten years, the machine would have no salvage value. The company considers that it should earn 16 percent compounded quarterly.

    Required:

    a. Compute the payback period.

    b. Compute the accounting rate of return on original investment, assuming use of straight line depreciation.

    c. Compute the net present value and a profitability index.

ANSWERS TO LEARNING GOAL ACHIEVEMENT TEST

1. a. Variable cost. Sunk cost if forms are on hand.
    b. Opportunity cost.
    c. Fixed cost
    d. Variable cost.
    e. Out-of-pocket cost.

2. No, rejection is not a good decision.

    Additional sales (100,000 times $50) $5,000,000
    Additional costs (100,000 times $36)   3,600,000
       Additional profit $1,400,000

3. a.

$$\text{Payback period} = \frac{\text{Investment}}{\text{Annual return}} = \frac{\$36,000}{\$8,000} = 4.5 \text{ years.}$$

   b.

$$\text{Accounting rate of return} = \frac{\text{Annual return} - \text{Depreciation}}{\text{Investment}} =$$

$$\frac{\$8,000 - \$3,600}{\$36,000} = 0.1222222 = 12.2\%.$$

   c. Present value of cash inflows (19.792774 times $2,000) . . $39,585.55
       Present value of investment 36,000.00
         Net present value . . . . $ 3,585.55

$$\text{Profitability index} = \frac{\$39,585.55}{\$36,000.00} = 1.0996.$$

Appendix A
Federal Income Taxes

■■■

EXPLANATION OF MAJOR CONCEPTS

The Federal Income Tax System

Our federal income tax system is one under which each taxpayer makes an annual
report to the Internal Revenue Service (IRS). This report, made on prescribed
forms provided by the IRS, is called an *income tax return*. Each individual taxpayer must "file" (mail a report of) his or her return with the IRS by April 15
of the following year. Married couples may combine their information to be
reported into one return called a *joint return,* or they may elect to file separate
returns. In addition to individuals, there are three classes of taxpayers--the
most important of these is corporations.

Federal income tax is partially paid month by month during the tax year. The
most used method to do this is withholding. In this method, an employer is required by law to withhold a portion of each employee's pay check and remit it to
the IRS. Individuals who have income other than salary (and thus have income
not subject to withholding) must file a declaration of estimated tax on such amounts
and make quarterly payments of those estimates. Corporations must also make prepayments based on estimated income. Amounts withheld and amounts prepaid with
estimates are credited by the IRS to the taxpayer's account during the year. Then,
when the return is filed with the actual tax due computed, the taxpayer may take
credit for these amounts against the total tax due. Actually, millions of taxpayers
each year find that their prepayments are greater than the tax due and receive a
refund check from the IRS.

Computing the Tax Due

Figure A-1 shows in complete detail the steps that an individual (or joint return)
taxpayer takes to compute the amount of tax due. You should refer to this Figure
constantly as you study Appendix A. Figure A-1 should be read from top down.
Note that it splits into two paths just below the determination of adjusted gross
income. Each taxpayer takes only one of these two paths. The path chosen by
the taxpayer will depend upon whether or not they have itemized deductions in
excess of the zero bracket amount. If they do not, they will follow the nonitemizer path in which they are permitted to deduct a portion of their charitable
contributions. If they follow the itemizer path, they will list all of their quali-
fying deductions. Both the itemizer and nonitemizer then deduct their exemptions
to arrive at their taxable income.

At this point, there is again a choice. Which path to take is not a matter of choice with the taxpayer; it is set forth by law and IRS regulations. Usually, it depends on the taxpayer's income level. Some taxpayers find their amount of tax due simply by looking in a tax table which automatically shows amount of tax for the taxpayer's amount of income, number of dependents, and filing status. Other taxpayers--usually with higher incomes--must compute their tax from tax rate schedules. Tax tables are illustrated in Figure A-5. The tax rate schedules are illustrated in Figure A-9.

To determine the amount of tax due, a taxpayer reports the gross amount of income for the year--usually on a cash basis. Only a few specified items (listed in the textbook) may be excluded from reporting (see Figure A-2). Although it may appear that taxpayers are on an "honor system" to report all income items, the IRS has many ways to check the accuracy of reporting. Every employer reports to IRS the amount of wages and salaries paid to each person; banks and other interest-paying institutions report on interest paid; corporations report dividends and interest paid; and so on. With an enormous computer network, the IRS can match this information with a taxpayer's return to ensure that items of gross income are reported.

Most taxpayers have reason to adjust their gross incomes downward. They are allowed to deduct business and trade expenses, employee moving expenses (to take another job), and other like items to determine *adjusted gross income*. Adjusted gross income (AGI) is a key amount in most tax returns. For example, it is used to compute limitations on amounts of deductions for medical expenses and for contributions. The AGI computation is illustrated in Figure A-3.

A taxpayer is allowed to deduct certain items (excess itemized deductions) from AGI to determine the amount of taxable income. These items are discussed in the textbook; they fall into five major categories.

▶ Contributions to religious, educational, or charitable institutions.
▶ Excess medical and dental expenses.
▶ State and local taxes.
▶ Personal interest paid.
▶ Miscellaneous deductions such as union dues, special work clothes, or dues to professional societies.

The law provides a *zero bracket amount* that is the maximum adjusted gross income a taxpayer may have and pay no income tax. If the deductible items listed above are less than the zero bracket amount, the zero bracket amount is, in effect, a standard deduction. If, however, the taxpayer has itemized deductions greater than the zero bracket amount, he or she should list them and then should deduct the excess. This applies both to taxpayers who use tax tables and tax rate schedules.

The final step is computation of the amount of tax due and the application of certain credits against that tax. The taxpayer then files the return with a check for the amount due or an indication on the return form that a refund is due.

Tax Planning

It is illegal to fail to report income or, in some other manner, to evade the payment of income taxes that are legally due. It is perfectly proper, however, to make business decisions in a way that will have the most favorable income tax effect. Suppose an individual (a cash basis taxpayer) incurs a medical expense in late December but has not yet been billed for it. If that person has already accumulated enough medical expenses to qualify for a deduction, he or she would want to pay before receipt of the bill to ensure that this expense is included in a year that has excess medical expenses. On the other hand, if the taxpayer will not have enough medical expenses to qualify, he or she will want to wait until January to pay (even if billed by the end of December) because there is a chance that medical expenses may qualify as excess in the following year. Business managers, while not on a cash basis, do a similar type of tax planning. The use of LIFO to place a valuation on inventory usually produces a lower reported net income to the stockholders, but it also provides a lower taxable income to be reported to IRS. The use of accelerated depreciation methods for tax purposes is another way to produce a lower tax. The important point is that a manager should consider the effect that a decision will have on income taxes before making decisions to purchase more equipment, hire additional people, or other actions that could affect the taxes of the business.

Interperiod Tax Allocation

The income tax expense of a business based on income computed with generally accepted accounting principles and the income tax actually paid by a company may differ for several reasons. Sometimes, these differences are only a matter of *timing* and will cancel each other in a few years. The Accounting Principles Board has ruled (APB *Opinion No. 11*) that a proportionate amount of tax expense should be allocated to each year that has a timing difference even though the tax may be paid in an earlier or later year. The textbook has two examples of this; they will be taken up later in the *Guided Study* section.

GUIDED STUDY OF THIS APPENDIX

A. *The Federal Income Tax System*

1. The overall rules and regulations for federal income tax are set forth in the U.S. _____ _____ and in IRS _____.

A1. Internal Revenue Code, regulations

2. The basic tax law _____ (is/is not) frequently amended by passage of additional tax acts.

A2.　is

3.　Individuals in the United States are subject to payment of tax on their income. Are proprietorships also required to pay income tax?

_____ Explain. _____

_____

_____

A3.　No. The individual proprietor (owner) includes business earnings in personal income tax.

4.　Is a partnership a taxpaying entity? _____

Explain. _____

_____

_____

_____

A4.　No. The individual tax items are allocated to partners who report them in their individual returns.

5.　Is a corporation a taxpaying entity? _____

Explain. _____

_____

_____

_____

A5.　Yes. A corporation is a *legal* entity (as well as an accounting entity) and pays income taxes in its own name.

6.　An income tax return is filed by each taxpayer once per _____.

A6.　year

7.　Taxpayers are not allowed to wait until the end of a tax year to make tax payments. Persons whose income comes from salaries pay a part of their income tax each payday through the _____ system.

A7.　withholding

8.　Persons with income amounts not subject to withholding must also pay taxes during the year by _____

_____

_____.

A8.　filing an estimate of such taxes and making quarterly payments

9.　At the end of the year, a taxpayer whose total of withholdings and other payments is less than actual tax due will _____

_____.

A9. send a check to the IRS for the difference

A10. receive a refund

A11. cash

A12. accrual

B1. specifically excluded by the tax law

B2. Yes.

B3. All of these items are nontaxable.

B4. 10, 30,000

B5. gross margin on sales, 20,000

B6. No answer required.

10. Conversely, a taxpayer who has overpaid may _____.

11. Individuals compute their personal tax liabilities on a(n) _____ (cash/accrual) basis.

12. Business income--especially that of corporations--is determined on a(n) _____ (cash/accrual) basis.

B. *Tax Items. Figure A-2 shows the flow of work done in computing the amount of an individual's gross income.*

1. All items of income are considered to be taxable unless they are _____ _____.

2. Some people are not aware of the status of tips. Are tips considered to be taxable income? _____

3. What is the status (taxable/nontaxable) of gifts? _____ GI bill educational benefits? _____ Amounts your parents pay for tuition, board, and room in your behalf? _____

4. Two earner married couples may exclude _____ percent of the first $_____ earned by the lower income spouse.

5. Gross income includes wages and salaries, certain other items, and for a business proprietorship _____, and one-half of social security receipts for taxpayers over $_____.

6. Form 1040 is the individual federal tax return. Gross income on this form is the total taxable items such as those in Figure A-3.

7. Next, in Figure A-3, follow deductions to arrive at _____.

B7.   adjusted gross income (AGI)

8.   Deductions to arrive at adjusted gross income are generally those _____ required to earn the gross income.

B8.   expenses

9.   For example, travel expenses of employees _____ (are/are not) deductible to arrive at AGI.

B9.   are

10.   But travel reimbursement by employers is included in gross income. This means that an employee who travels is taxed on travel reimbursements if they _____

_____.

B10.   are greater than actual expenses

11.   On the other hand, if expenses are greater than reimbursement, the employee will end up with a _____ (lower/higher) adjusted gross income.

B11.   lower

12.   Certain deductions may be taken from AGI by *itemizer taxpayers*. Figure A-4 shows one under the general heading of _____

_____.

B12.   charitable contributions

13.   Contributions, to be deductible, must be to a *religious, educational,* or *charitable* organization. Does a contribution to a college fraternity qualify? _____

B13.   No.

14.   Suppose a fraternity or sorority holds a walkathon with all proceeds going to the Heart Fund. May sponsors of individual walkers deduct as contributions the amounts they donate? _____

B14.   Yes.

15.   These types of deductions are known as itemized deductions. Another category is

_____.

B15.   excess medical expenses

16.   In 1983, what is the limitation on inclusion of the costs of medicines and drugs in gross medical expenses? _____

_____

_____

B16. Only costs in excess of 1 percent of AGI are deductible.

17. For this reason, the illustrated taxpayer with an AGI of $20,000 can deduct only $_____ for medicines and drugs.

B17. 110

18. Note also another limitation on the medical expense deduction. This taxpayer with an AGI of $20,000 must reduce the deduction by _____ percent of AGI or $_____.

B18. 5, 1,000

19. Some state and local taxes may be deducted. Do you see state taxes on alcohol or tobacco among them? _____

B19. No.

20. What is the tax-deductible status of the cost of automobile license tags and the state tax on gasoline? _____

B21. They are not deductible.

21. Another category of deductions is personal interest. One of the most common of these is interest on a home mortgage. Interest paid on most other personal indebtedness is deductible. The fifth category of deductions, called miscellaneous, includes many unrelated items.

B21. No answer required.

22. A taxpayer who lists and reports deductions in these categories is called an _____ taxpayer.

B22. itemizer

23. A taxpayer whose itemized deductions are less than zero bracket income would not claim itemized deductions and would be called a _____ taxpayer.

B23. nonitemizer

C. *Tax Terms. Let's study the meaning of some specific tax terms.*

1. Adjusted gross income is _____.

C1. gross income with certain earnings-related deductions subtracted

2. Business travel to and from one's job is not deductible. Is the cost of business travel (say, from your place of work to attend a meeting and back to the place of work) deductible to determine AGI? _____

C2.   Yes.

C3.   Yes. Yes.
(See Figure A-3.)

C4.   They may be claimed
by either an itemizer
or nonitemizer tax-
payer to determine
AGI.

C5.   When personal
deductions are
greater than the
zero bracket amount.

C6.   of the maximum
taxable income a
person can have
and still pay no tax

C7.   No.

C8.   contributions,
allowable medical
expenses, personal
interest, state and
local taxes, and
some miscellaneous
items

3.   Suppose part of your gross income is from
rent of a building you own. Can you deduct
repairs expense on that building? _____
Depreciation expense on that building? _____

4.   How are these deductions from gross income
different from itemized deductions? _____

_____

_____

_____

5.   When should an individual decide to be an
itemizer taxpayer? _____

_____

_____

6.   The zero bracket amount is the amount _____

_____

_____

_____.

7.   Are personal deductions and personal exemptions the same thing? _____

8.   Personal deductions from AGI cover such
things as _____

_____

_____

_____

_____.

9.   May total itemized deductions be deducted?
_____ Explain. _____

_____

_____

C9. No. Only those in excess of the zero bracket amount.

10. What is a personal exemption? _____

_____

_____

_____

_____

_____

_____

C10. An amount, $1,000, which is deducted in calculating taxable income for each person who qualifies as a dependent. Additional exemptions allowed for blind and over 65.

11. In general, what are tax credits? _____

_____

_____

_____

C11. Deductions against the amount of computed income tax.

12. Do tax-table and tax-rate-schedule taxpayers both have credits? _____

C12. Yes.

13. The tax credits common to all taxpayers are credits for _____

_____.

C13. taxes withheld or already paid on declarations (or both

D. *Tax Allocation. Timing differences arise when a company has income on its books that is different from taxable income for a reason that will "wash out" over a period of time.*

1. In the Calgary Corporation example, the total tax to be paid over the 5-year period is $_____.

D1. 1,100,000 = ($2,200,000 x .50)

2. One-fifth (or what would appear to be income tax for each year) is $_____.

D2. 220,000

3. However, in Year 1, Calgary actually paid income tax of $_____.

D3.   200,000

4. This resulted in deferring until a later date
    $20,000 of tax. Why? _____

    _____

    _____

    _____

    _____

D4.   Calgary's deprecia-
       tion, computed by an
       accelerated method
       for tax purposes,
       made the taxable
       income less than
       the book income.

5. For accounting records, the depreciation
    (straight line) was $_____ in Year 1,
    but on the tax return, the depreciation (SYD)
    was $_____.

D5.   60,000, 100,000

6. This $40,000 difference in depreciation made a
    difference between tax expense in the books
    and on the tax return (at a 50 percent rate)
    of $_____.

D6.   20,000

7. The actual effect is that $20,000 of taxes for
    Year 1 was deferred until later years. As in
    all accelerated depreciation methods, however,
    there is a crossover point where the straight
    line depreciation for a year is greater than
    accelerated. At that point, tax expense on
    the books is _____ (more/less) than
    the tax actually paid.

D7.   less

8. Note the example of Calgary Corporation in
    Year 4. The book tax expense was
    $_____.

D8.   220,000

9. The tax paid was $_____.

D9.   230,000

10. Thus, $10,000 of _____
    _____ was paid in Year 4
    rather than in prior years.

D10.   deferred tax
       liability

11. In the five-year period, the account, Deferred
    Income Tax Liability, received total credits of
    $_____ and total debits of $_____.

D11.   30,000, 30,000

12.   Thus, in the five-year period, the debits and credits cancelled each other. Study the Guelph Company for an opposite example, that of prepaid income taxes. The principle is the same. Note that *FASB Statement No. 37* prescribes certain rules to determine when a deferred income tax liability or a prepaid income tax item is a current or long-term item on the balance sheet.

D12.   No answer required.

SELF TEST OF LEARNING GOAL ACHIEVEMENT

1.   Indicate whether the following are true or false?

____ a.   The types of entities subject to federal income tax are (1) individuals, (2) corporations, (3) income-producing estates, and (4) income-producing trusts.

____ b.   Employee business expenses are deductible from gross income to determine adjusted gross income (AGI).

____ c.   Gross income for tax purposes includes every dollar that an individual receives in a tax year.

____ d.   After AGI has been determined, there are additional amounts that may be deducted to determine taxable income if a person is an itemizer taxpayer.

____ e.   Both itemizer and nonitemizer taxpayers who earn $50,000 or less per year must use the tax tables.

____ f.   Persons who use the tax tables deduct one or more personal exemptions of $1,000 to determine tax-table income because these personal exemptions are not built into the tax tables.

____ g.   Single taxpayers who earn more than $50,000 per year and married taxpayers filing joint returns who earn more than $50,000 per year cannot use the tax tables, but must compute the tax due using tax rate schedules.

____ h.   Taxpayers using the tax rate schedules do deduct the $1,000 personal exemptions because these exemptions are not built into the tax rate schedules.

____ i.   Partnerships are taxable entities and pay income taxes on total partnerships net income before it is divided among partners.

____ j.   Corporations are taxable entities and pay income taxes on total corporate income before it is passed out to the stockholders as dividends.

____ k.   The law does not allow a corporation to use an accelerated depreciation method for income tax purposes even though the company may use such a method to determine its annual net income.

____ l.   The fact that the law does allow a corporation to report greater depreciation on its tax return than on its income statement can cause the income tax expense to be greater than the tax actually paid.

____ m.   Any difference between income tax expense on the income statement and the tax actually paid caused by using different methods of depreciation for the two purposes is a permanent gain or loss and will never be repaid or recovered.

____n. Because the difference described in *m* on the preceding page are self-reversing, they are called *timing differences*.

____o. The fact that a timing difference exists is a signal that the corporation should practice interperiod tax allocation in the accounting records.

ANSWERS TO LEARNING GOAL ACHIEVEMENT TEST

1. a. T   f. T   k. F
    b. T   g. T   l. T
    c. F   h. T   m. F
    d. T   i. F   n. T
    e. T   j. T   o. T